FANTASTIC FOUR

By Aguirre-Sacasa & McNiven

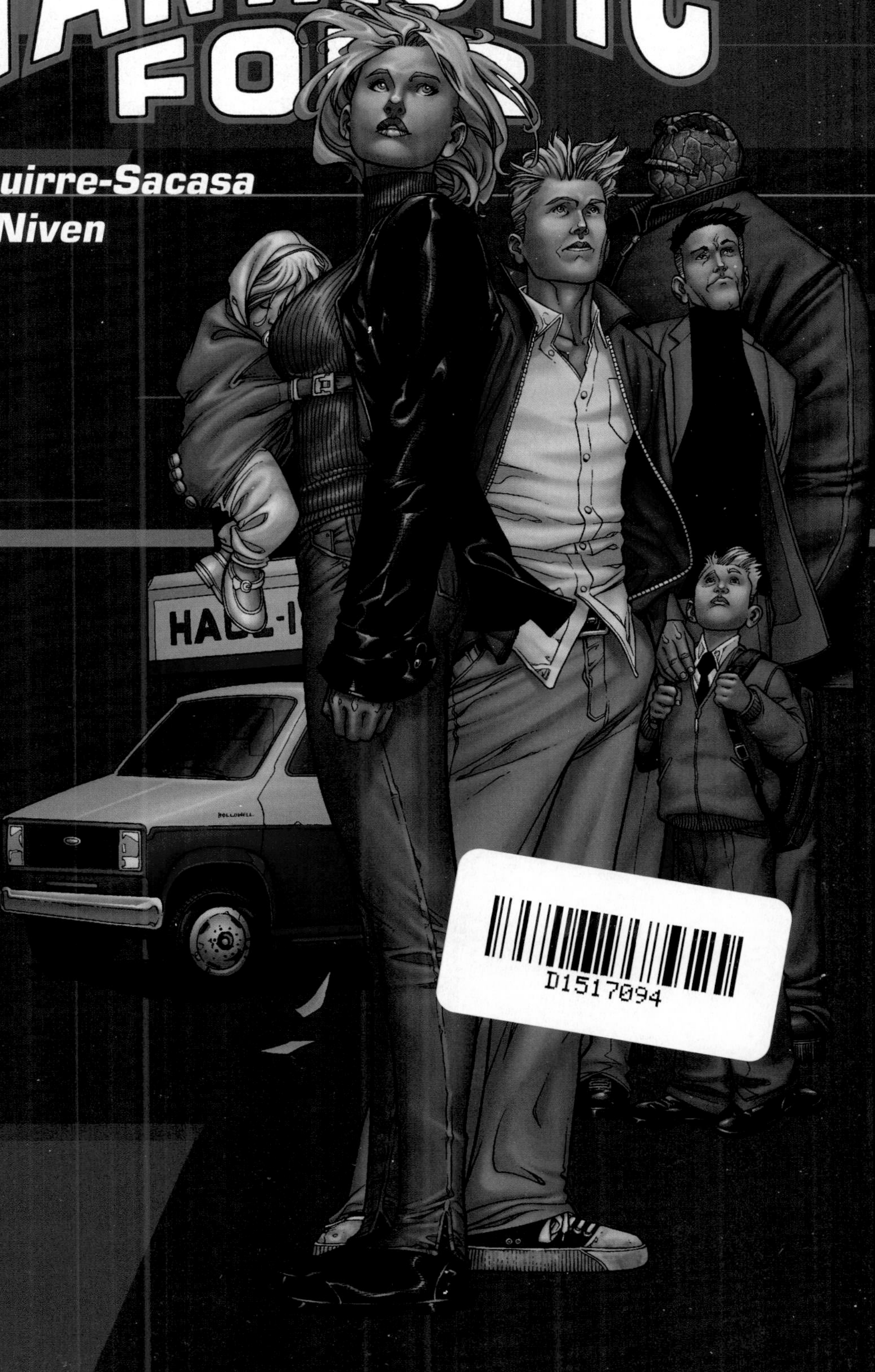

COLLECTION EDITOR **Jennifer Grünwald** ASSISTANT EDITOR **Sarah Brunstad**
ASSOCIATE MANAGING EDITOR **Alex Starbuck** EDITOR, SPECIAL PROJECTS **Mark D. Beazley**
SENIOR EDITOR, SPECIAL PROJECTS **Jeff Youngquist**
SVP PRINT, SALES & MARKETING **David Gabriel** BOOK DESIGNER **Jay Bowen**

EDITOR IN CHIEF **Axel Alonso** CHIEF CREATIVE OFFICER **Joe Quesada**
PUBLISHER **Dan Buckley** EXECUTIVE PRODUCER **Alan Fine**

FANTASTIC FOUR BY AGUIRRE-SACASA & MCNIVEN. Contains material originally published in magazine form as MARVEL KNIGHTS 4 #1-7. First printing 2015. ISBN# 978-0-7851-9743-0. Published b
MARVEL WORLDWIDE, INC., a subsidiary of MARVEL ENTERTAINMENT, LLC. OFFICE OF PUBLICATION: 135 West 50th Street, New York, NY 10020. Copyright © 2015 MARVEL No similarity between any of th
names, characters, persons, and/or institutions in this magazine with those of any living or dead person or institution is intended, and any such similarity which may exist is purely coincidental. Printed i
Canada. ALAN FINE, President, Marvel Entertainment; DAN BUCKLEY, President, TV, Publishing and Brand Management; JOE QUESADA, Chief Creative Officer; TOM BREVOORT, SVP of Publishing; DAVID BOGAR
SVP of Operations & Procurement, Publishing; C.B. CEBULSKI, VP of International Development & Brand Management; DAVID GABRIEL, SVP Print, Sales & Marketing; JIM O'KEEFE, VP of Operations & Logistic
DAN CARR, Executive Director of Publishing Technology; SUSAN CRESPI, Editorial Operations Manager; ALEX MORALES, Publishing Operations Manager; STAN LEE, Chairman Emeritus. For information regardi
advertising in Marvel Comics or on Marvel.com, please contact Jonathan Rheingold, VP of Custom Solutions & Ad Sales, at jrheingold@marvel.com. For Marvel subscription inquiries, please call 800-217-915

WRITER: **Roberto Aguirre-Sacasa**
PENCILER: **Steve McNiven**

INKER: **Mark Morales**
COLORIST: **Morry Hollowell**
LETTERER: **VC's Randy Gentile**
EDITOR: **Warren Simons**
SUPERVISING EDITOR: **Axel Alonso**

Special thanks to Teresa Focarile & Nicole Wiley

FANTASTIC FOUR CREATED BY **STAN LEE** & **JACK KIRBY**

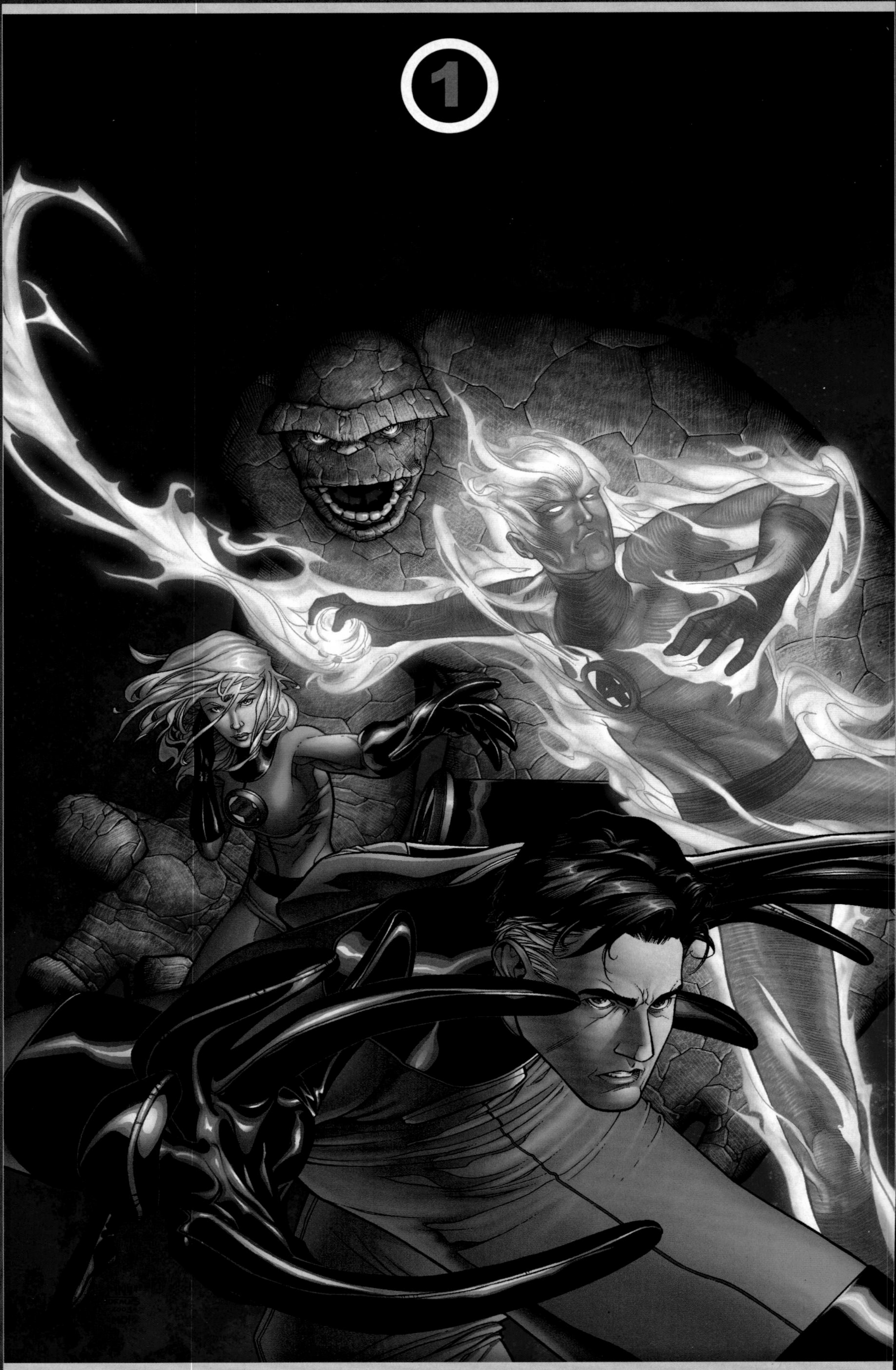
1

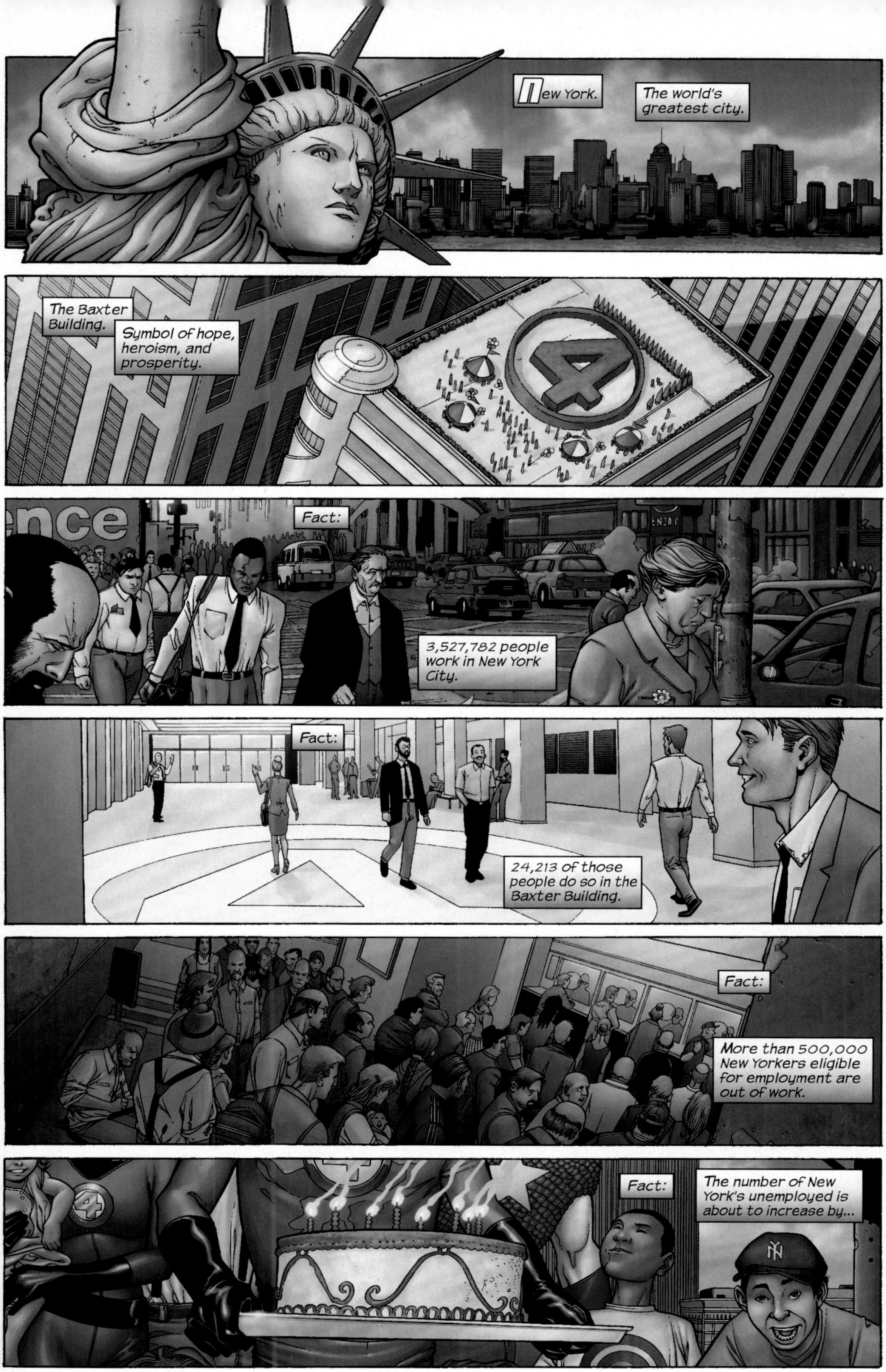
New York.
The world's greatest city.
The Baxter Building.
Symbol of hope, heroism, and prosperity.
Fact:
3,527,782 people work in New York City.
Fact:
24,213 of those people do so in the Baxter Building.
Fact:
More than 500,000 New Yorkers eligible for employment are out of work.
Fact:
The number of New York's unemployed is about to increase by...

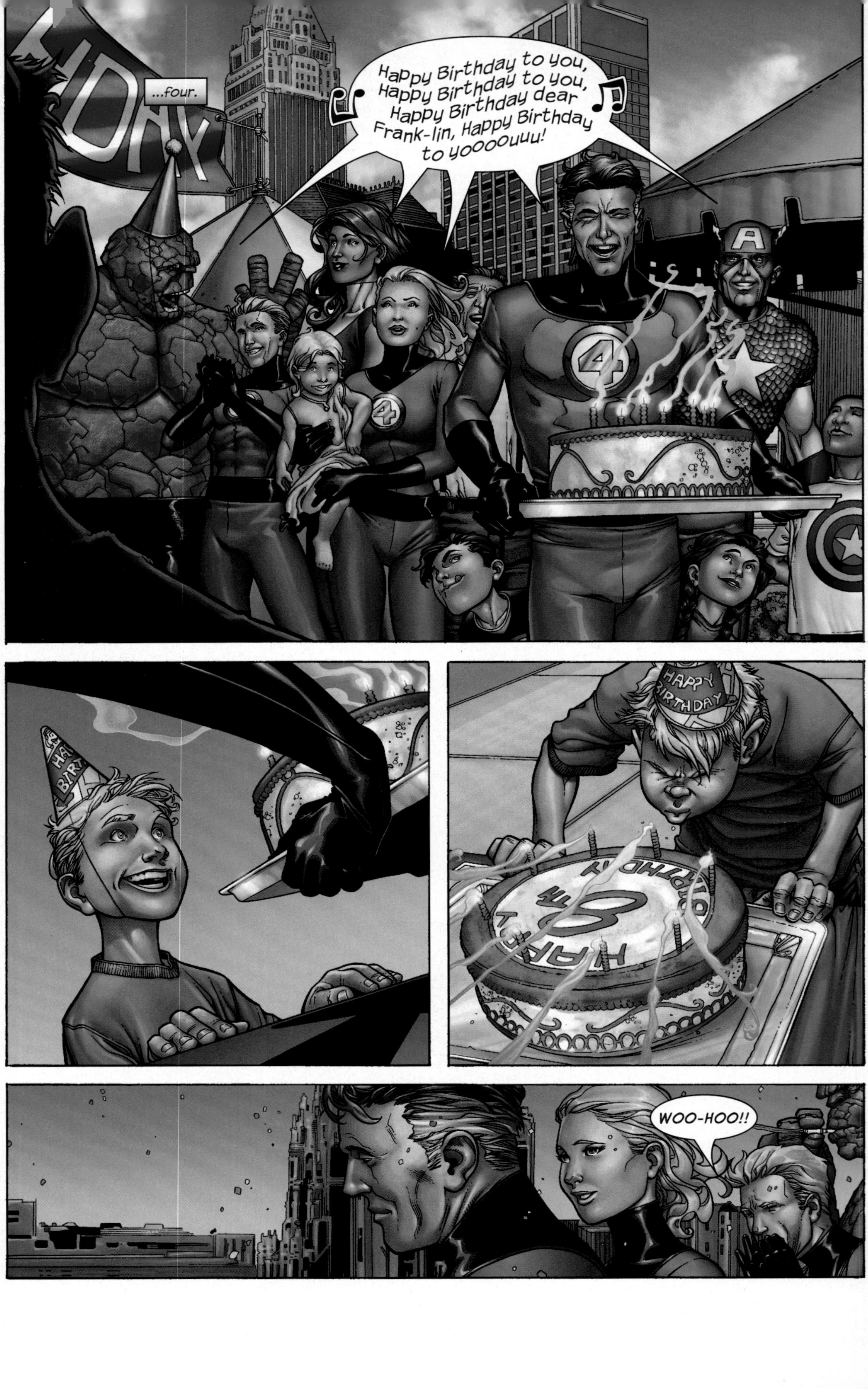

HDAY
...four.
Happy Birthday to you, Happy Birthday to you, Happy Birthday dear Frank-lin, Happy Birthday to yooooouuu!
HAPPY BIRTHDAY
HAPPY BIRTHDAY
WOO-HOO!!

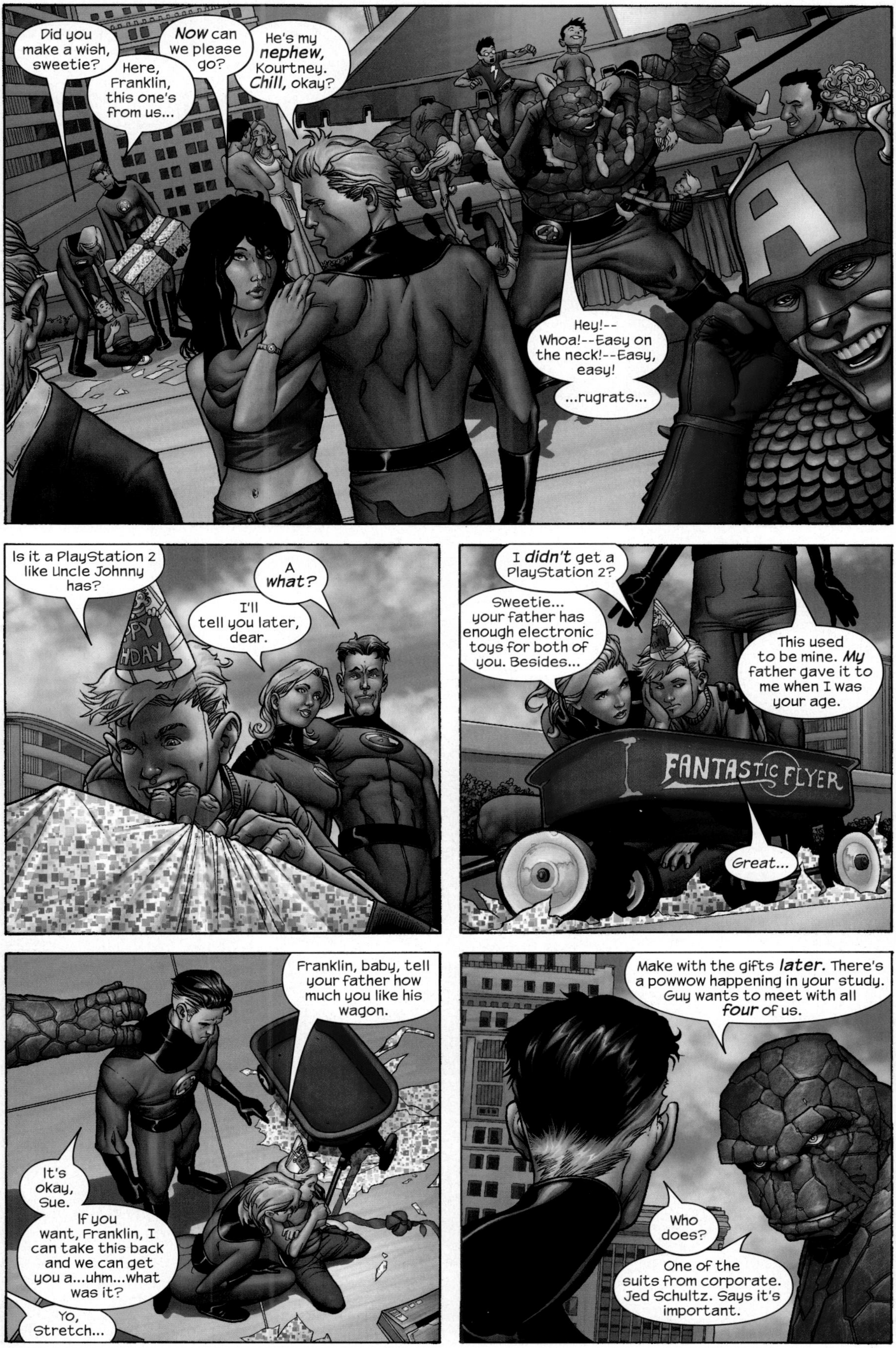

Did you make a wish, sweetie?
Here, Franklin, this one's from us...
Now can we please go?
He's my nephew, Kourtney. Chill, okay?
Hey!--Whoa!--Easy on the neck!--Easy, easy!
...rugrats...
Is it a PlayStation 2 like Uncle Johnny has?
A what?
I'll tell you later, dear.
I didn't get a PlayStation 2?
Sweetie... your father has enough electronic toys for both of you. Besides...
This used to be mine. My father gave it to me when I was your age.
FANTASTIC FLYER
Great...
Franklin, baby, tell your father how much you like his wagon.
It's okay, Sue.
If you want, Franklin, I can take this back and we can get you a...uhm...what was it?
Yo, Stretch...
Make with the gifts later. There's a powwow happening in your study. Guy wants to meet with all four of us.
Who does?
One of the suits from corporate. Jed Schultz. Says it's important.

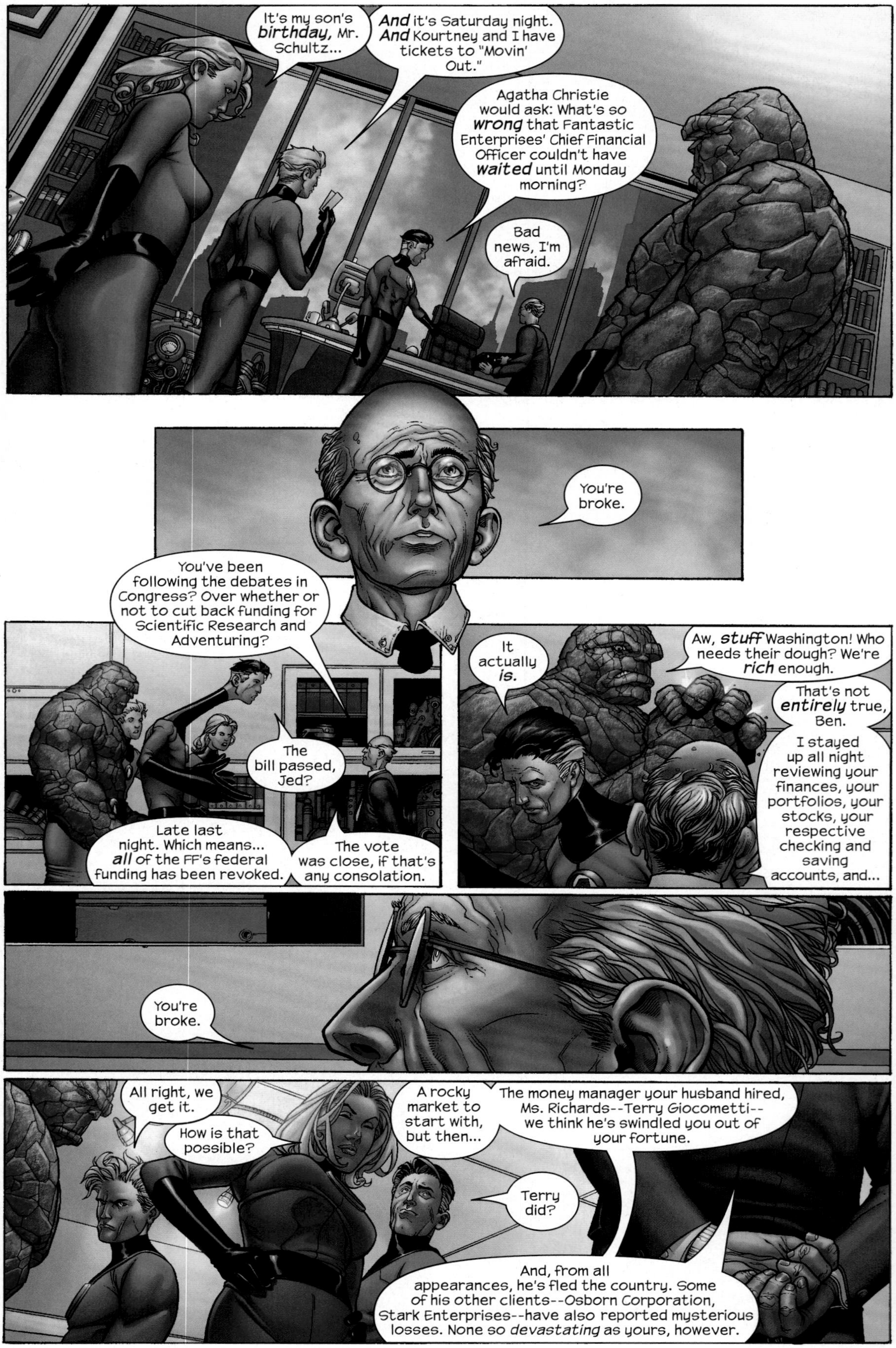
It's my son's *birthday,* Mr. Schultz...
And it's Saturday night. *And* Kourtney and I have tickets to "Movin' Out."
Agatha Christie would ask: What's so *wrong* that Fantastic Enterprises' Chief Financial Officer couldn't have *waited* until Monday morning?
Bad news, I'm afraid.
You're broke.
You've been following the debates in Congress? Over whether or not to cut back funding for Scientific Research and Adventuring?
The bill passed, Jed?
Late last night. Which means... *all* of the FF's federal funding has been revoked.
The vote was close, if that's any consolation.
It actually *is.*
Aw, *stuff* Washington! Who needs their dough? We're *rich* enough.
That's not *entirely* true, Ben.
I stayed up all night reviewing your finances, your portfolios, your stocks, your respective checking and saving accounts, and...
You're broke.
All right, we get it.
How is that possible?
A rocky market to start with, but then...
The money manager your husband hired, Ms. Richards--Terry Giocometti--we think he's swindled you out of your fortune.
Terry did?
And, from all appearances, he's fled the country. Some of his other clients--Osborn Corporation, Stark Enterprises--have also reported mysterious losses. None so *devastating* as yours, however.

I always *knew* that Terry guy was rotten...

How bad?

I have the exact *figure* here...

Your total net worth.

But that's--

--*chump* change!

As your friend and advisor, I recommend you declare bankruptcy immediately-- lay off your employees and start liquidating your assets.

But surely we have *recourse.*

I've been crunching numbers for the last seventeen hours and...I can't think of any.

Then you're not thinking *hard* enough.

Johnny...

You see this "4"? It means something, okay? That we're *celebrities. Super heroes.* And *super heroes* do not declare *bankruptcy.*

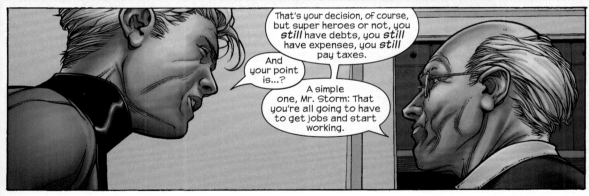

That's your decision, of course, but super heroes or not, you *still* have debts, you *still* have expenses, you *still* pay taxes.

And your point is...?

A simple one, Mr. Storm: That you're all going to have to get jobs and start working.

...goodnight, Squirt.

Uncle Ben...?

What, Big Guy?

How come Mommy and Daddy looked so sad when everyone was leaving my party?

Well, Li'l Buddy, that's 'cause...

"...your mom and pop have a lot on their minds."

Valeria's already asleep, and Ben's putting Franklin to bed.

Underneath all that rock, he really *is* a softie.

At least *nowadays*. You remember?

Right after we were transformed, we could barely talk to Ben he was so full of rage.

Susan--!

When I *think* of what Terry Giocometti did! That he's out there--*somewhere*--spending our money!

We're too *young* to have everything taken from us. We're just *starting out*.

I know. And I'm already *implementing contingencies*.

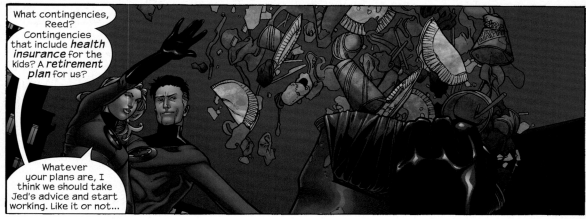

What contingencies, Reed? Contingencies that include *health insurance* for the kids? A *retirement plan* for us?

Whatever your plans are, I think we should take Jed's advice and start working. Like it or not...

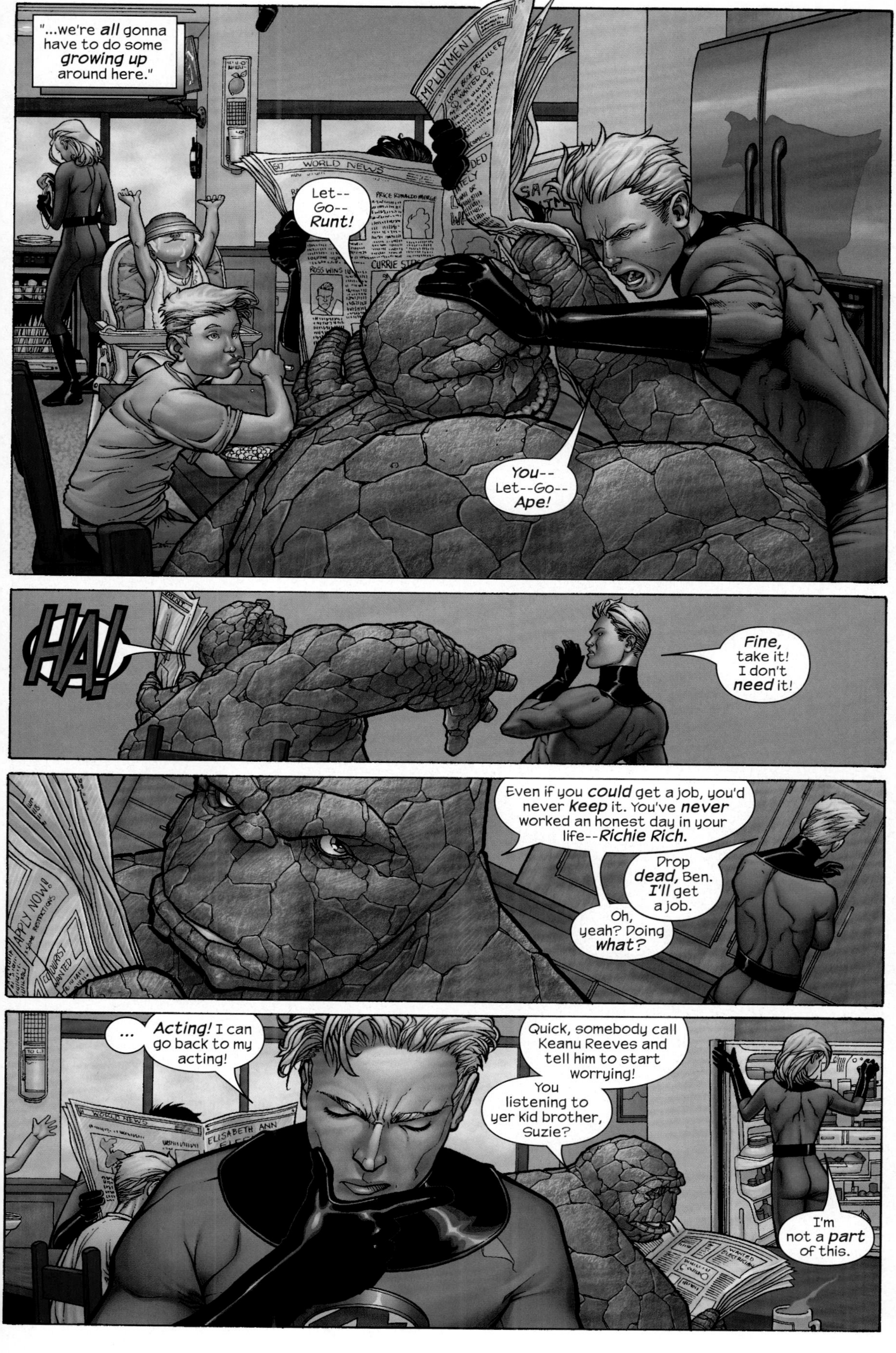
"...we're *all* gonna have to do some *growing up* around here."
Let-- Go-- *Runt!*
You-- Let--Go-- *Ape!*
HA!
Fine, take it! I don't *need* it!
Even if you *could* get a job, you'd never *keep* it. You've *never* worked an honest day in your life--*Richie Rich.*
Drop *dead,* Ben. *I'll* get a job.
Oh, yeah? Doing *what?*
... *Acting!* I can go back to my acting!
Quick, somebody call Keanu Reeves and tell him to start worrying!
You listening to yer kid brother, Suzie?
I'm not a *part* of this.

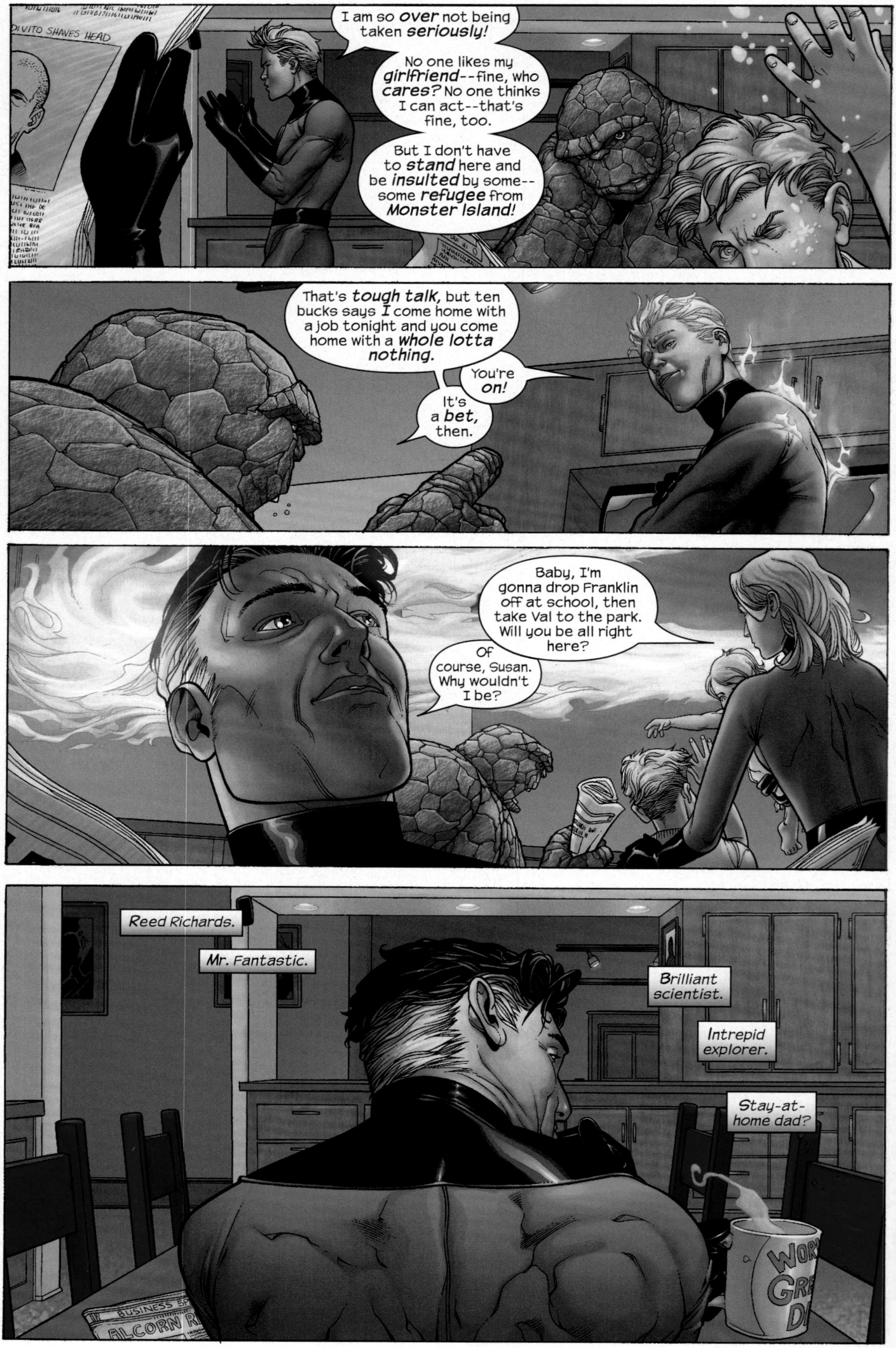
DIVITO SHAVES HEAD
I am so over not being taken seriously!
No one likes my girlfriend--fine, who cares? No one thinks I can act--that's fine, too.
But I don't have to stand here and be insulted by some--some refugee from Monster Island!
That's tough talk, but ten bucks says I come home with a job tonight and you come home with a whole lotta nothing.
You're on!
It's a bet, then.
Baby, I'm gonna drop Franklin off at school, then take Val to the park. Will you be all right here?
Of course, Susan. Why wouldn't I be?
Reed Richards.
Mr. Fantastic.
Brilliant scientist.
Intrepid explorer.
Stay-at-home dad?

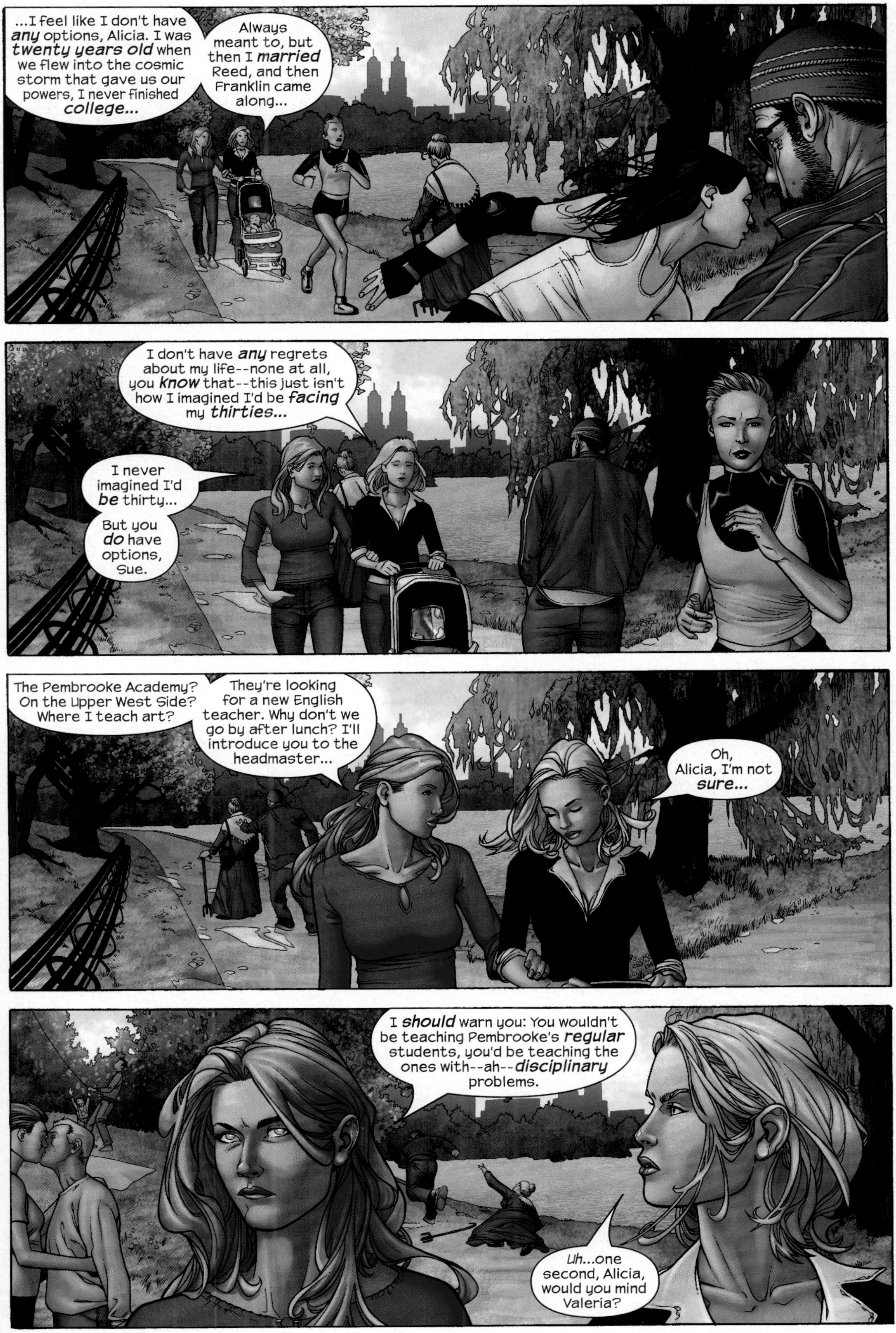
...I feel like I don't have *any* options, Alicia. I was *twenty years old* when we flew into the cosmic storm that gave us our powers, I never finished *college...*
Always meant to, but then I *married* Reed, and then Franklin came along...
I don't have *any* regrets about my life--none at all, you *know* that--this just isn't how I imagined I'd be *facing* my *thirties...*
I never imagined I'd *be* thirty...
But you *do* have options, Sue.
The Pembrooke Academy? On the Upper West Side? Where I teach art?
They're looking for a new English teacher. Why don't we go by after lunch? I'll introduce you to the headmaster...
Oh, Alicia, I'm not *sure...*
I *should* warn you: You wouldn't be teaching Pembrooke's *regular* students, you'd be teaching the ones with--ah--*disciplinary* problems.
Uh...one second, Alicia, would you mind Valeria?

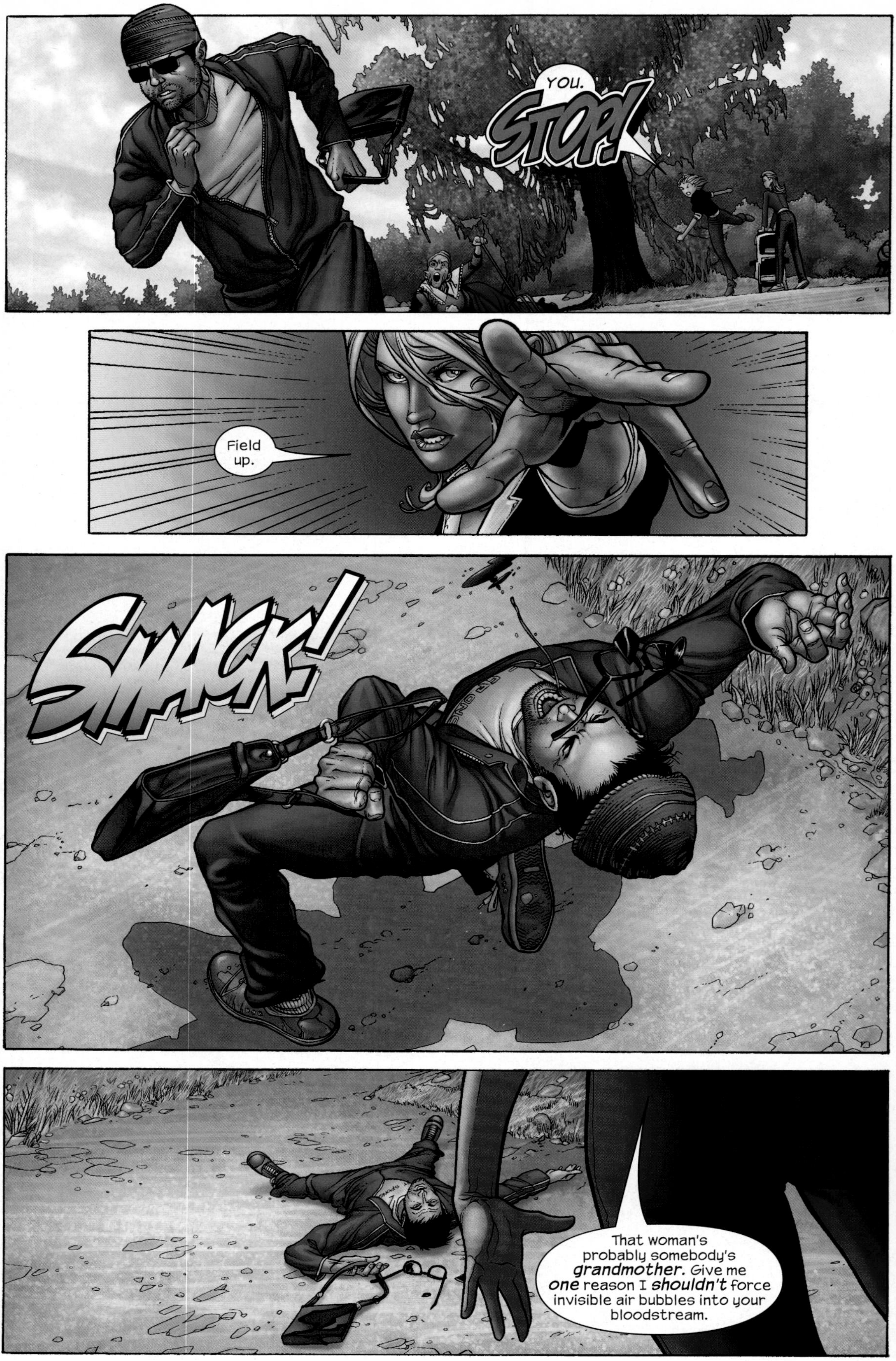

YOU.
STOP!
Field up.
SMACK!
That woman's probably somebody's grandmother. Give me one reason I shouldn't force invisible air bubbles into your bloodstream.

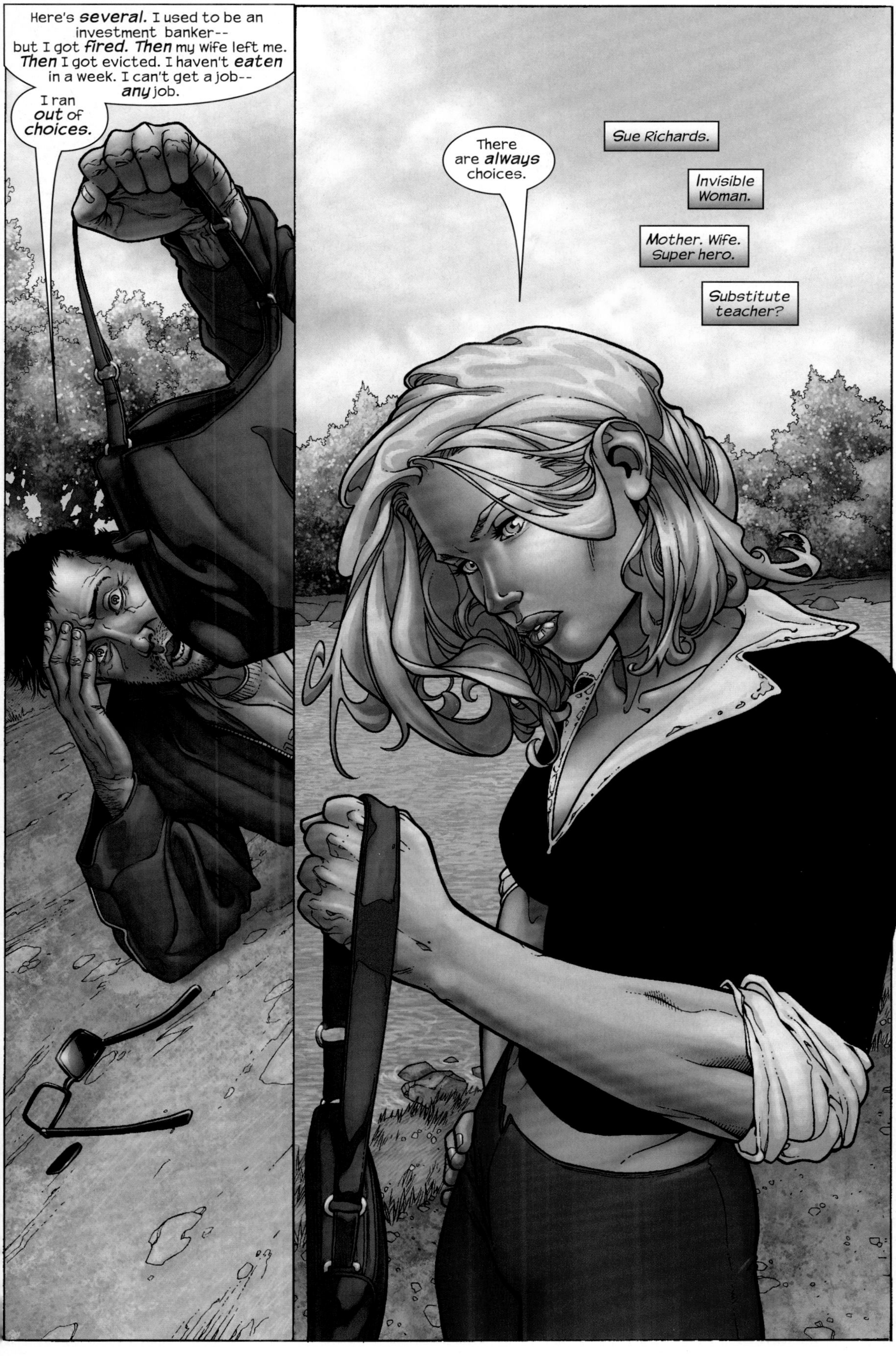
Here's several. I used to be an investment banker-- but I got fired. Then my wife left me. Then I got evicted. I haven't eaten in a week. I can't get a job-- any job.
I ran out of choices.
There are always choices.
Sue Richards.
Invisible Woman.
Mother. Wife. Super hero.
Substitute teacher?

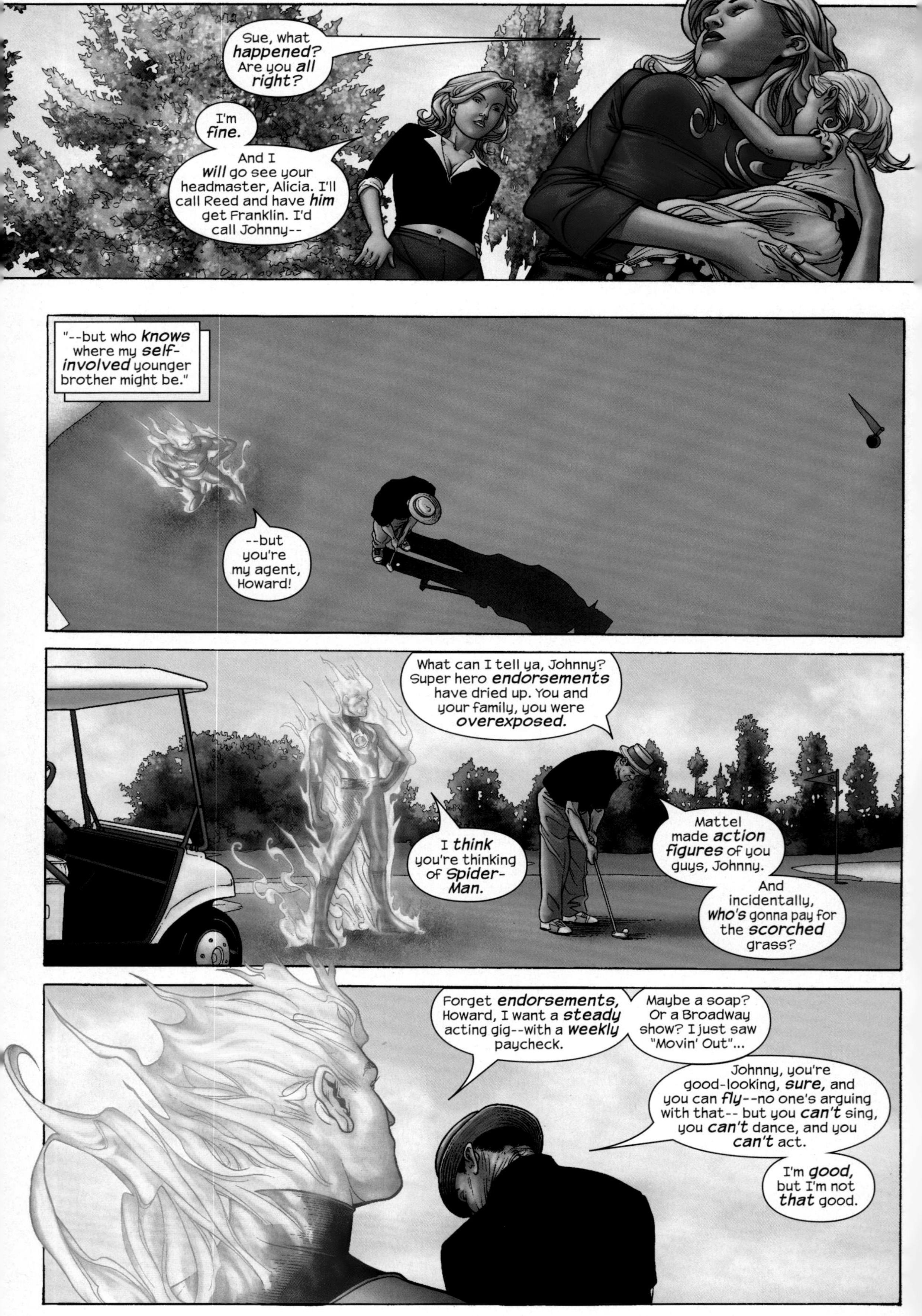

Sue, what happened? Are you all right?
I'm fine.
And I will go see your headmaster, Alicia. I'll call Reed and have him get Franklin. I'd call Johnny--
"--but who knows where my self-involved younger brother might be."
--but you're my agent, Howard!
What can I tell ya, Johnny? Super hero endorsements have dried up. You and your family, you were overexposed.
I think you're thinking of Spider-Man.
Mattel made action figures of you guys, Johnny.
And incidentally, who's gonna pay for the scorched grass?
Forget endorsements, Howard, I want a steady acting gig--with a weekly paycheck.
Maybe a soap? Or a Broadway show? I just saw "Movin' Out"...
Johnny, you're good-looking, sure, and you can fly--no one's arguing with that-- but you can't sing, you can't dance, and you can't act.
I'm good, but I'm not that good.

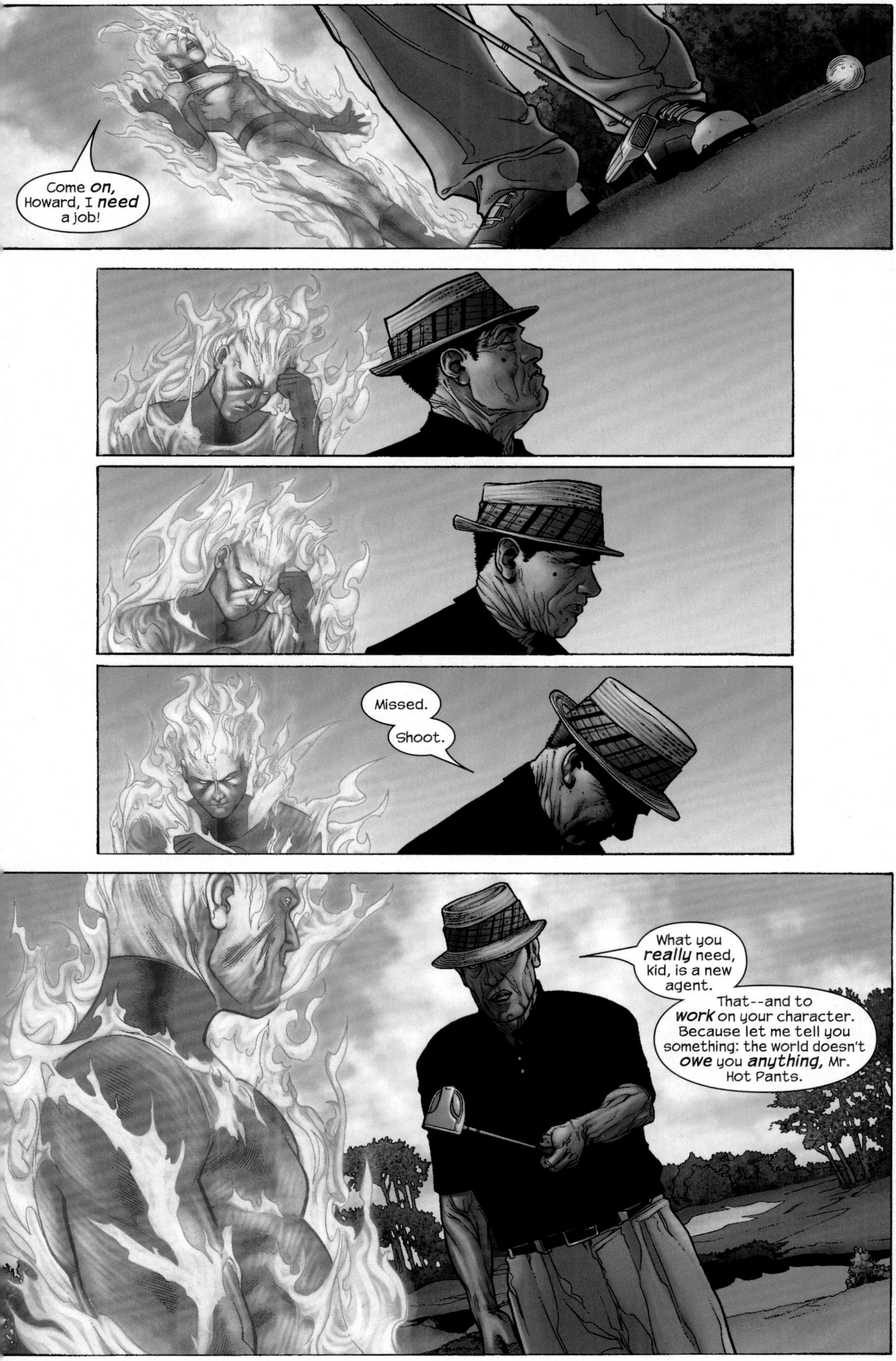
Come on, Howard, I need a job!
Missed.
Shoot.
What you really need, kid, is a new agent.
That--and to work on your character. Because let me tell you something: the world doesn't owe you anything, Mr. Hot Pants.

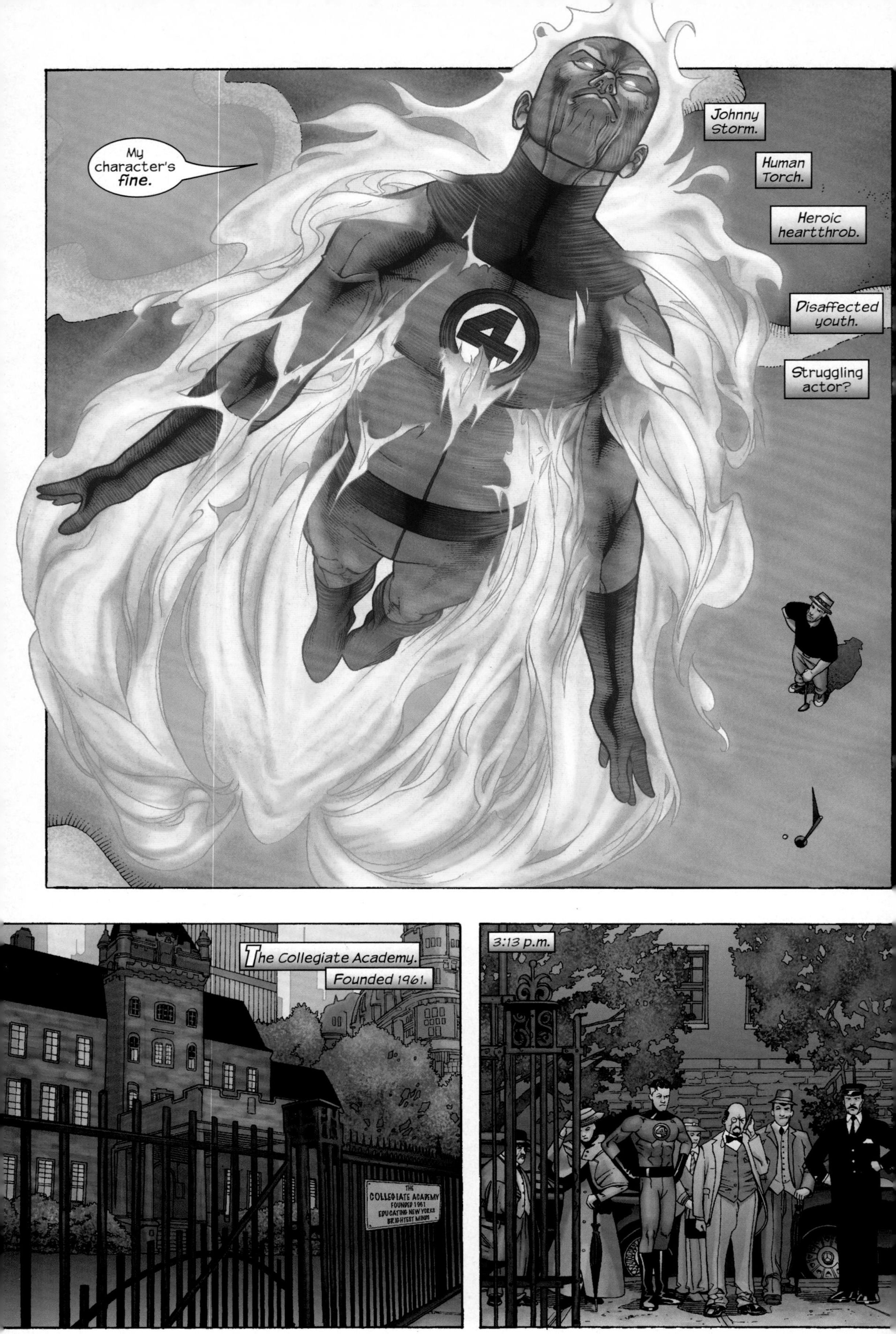

My character's fine.
Johnny Storm.
Human Torch.
Heroic heartthrob.
Disaffected youth.
Struggling actor?
The Collegiate Academy.
Founded 1961.
THE COLLEGIATE ACADEMY FOUNDED 1961 EDUCATING NEW YORK'S BRIGHTEST MINDS
3:13 p.m.

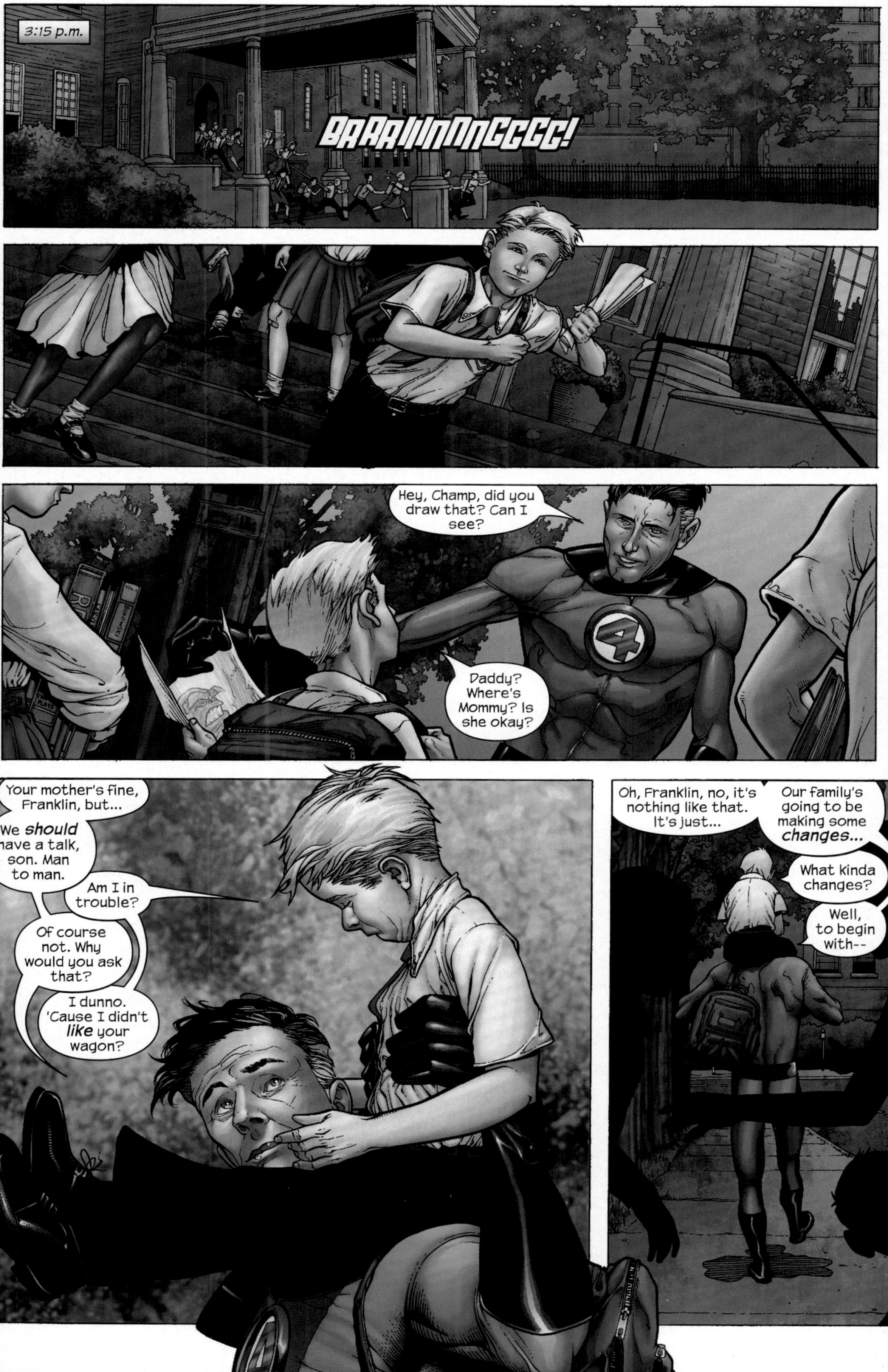
3:15 p.m.
BRRRIIINNNGGGG!
Hey, Champ, did you draw that? Can I see?
Daddy? Where's Mommy? Is she okay?
Your mother's fine, Franklin, but...
We *should* have a talk, son. Man to man.
Am I in trouble?
Of course not. Why would you ask that?
I dunno. 'Cause I didn't *like* your wagon?
Oh, Franklin, no, it's nothing like that. It's just...
Our family's going to be making some *changes...*
What kinda changes?
Well, to begin with--

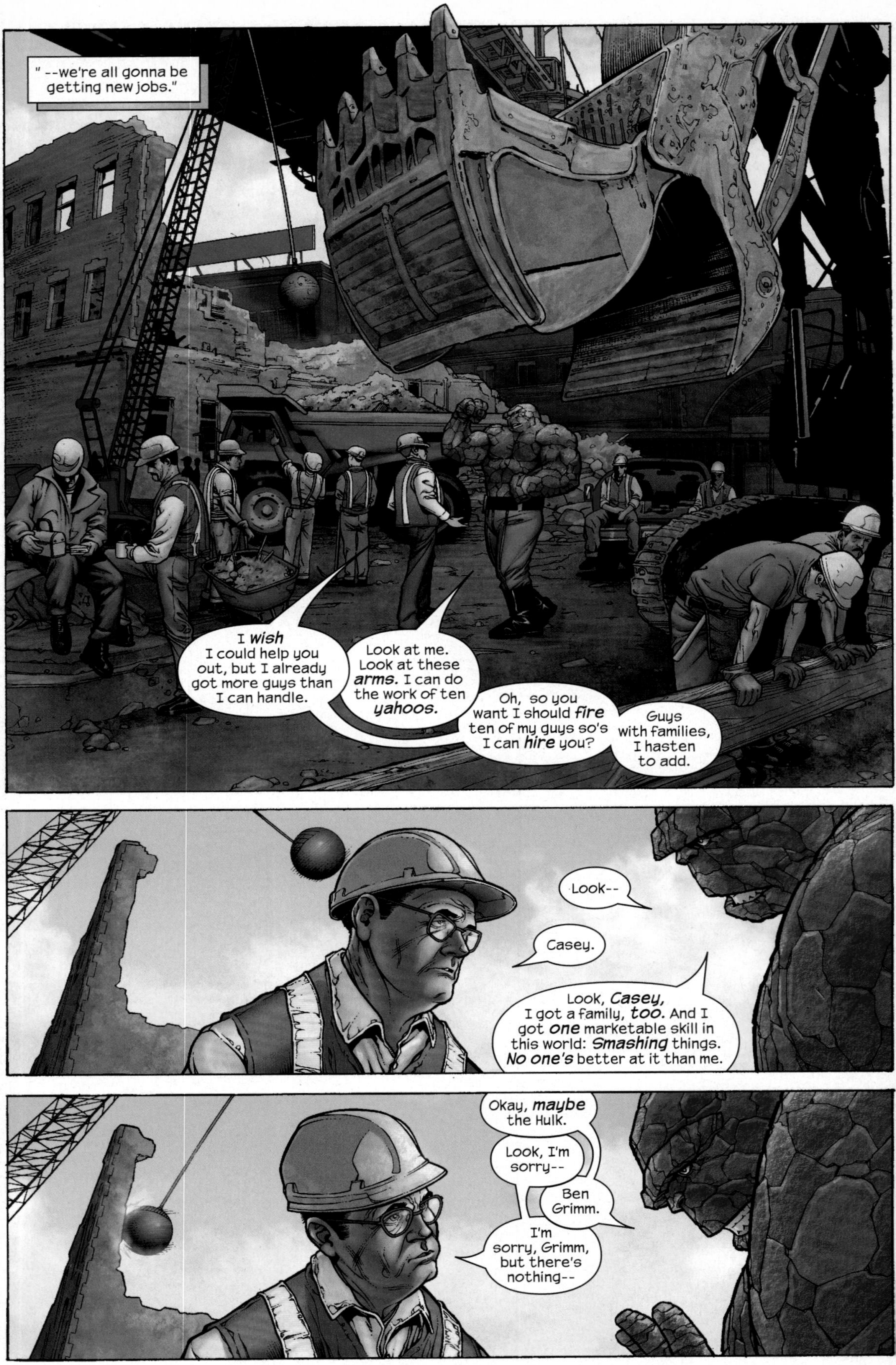
" --we're all gonna be getting new jobs."
I wish I could help you out, but I already got more guys than I can handle.
Look at me. Look at these arms. I can do the work of ten yahoos.
Oh, so you want I should fire ten of my guys so's I can hire you?
Guys with families, I hasten to add.
Look--
Casey.
Look, Casey, I got a family, too. And I got one marketable skill in this world: Smashing things. No one's better at it than me.
Okay, maybe the Hulk.
Look, I'm sorry--
Ben Grimm.
I'm sorry, Grimm, but there's nothing--

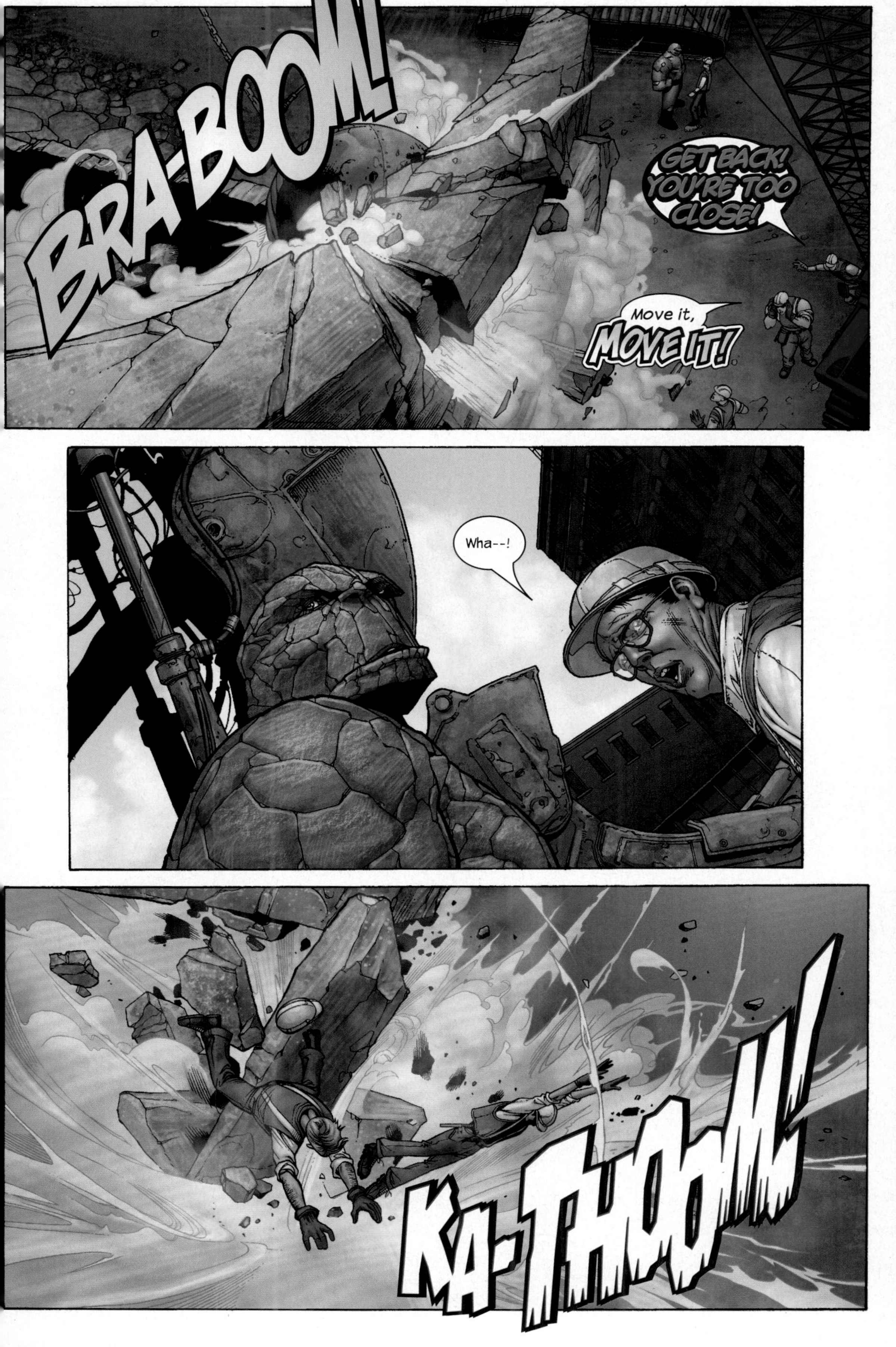
BRA-BOOM!
GET BACK! YOU'RE TOO CLOSE!
Move it, MOVE IT!
Wha--!
KA-THOOM!

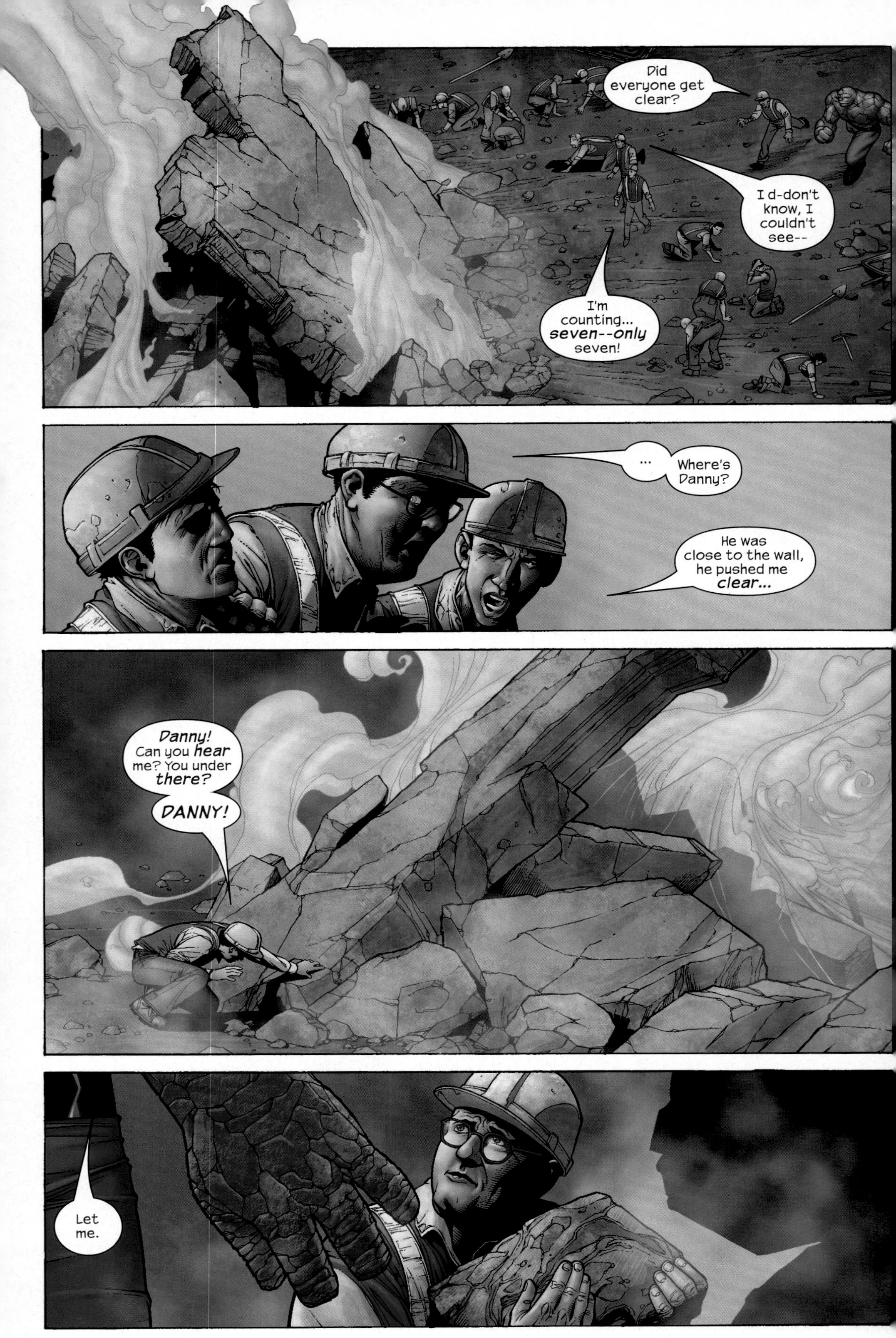
Did everyone get clear?
I d-don't know, I couldn't see--
I'm counting... seven--only seven!
...
Where's Danny?
He was close to the wall, he pushed me clear...
Danny! Can you hear me? You under there?
DANNY!
Let me.

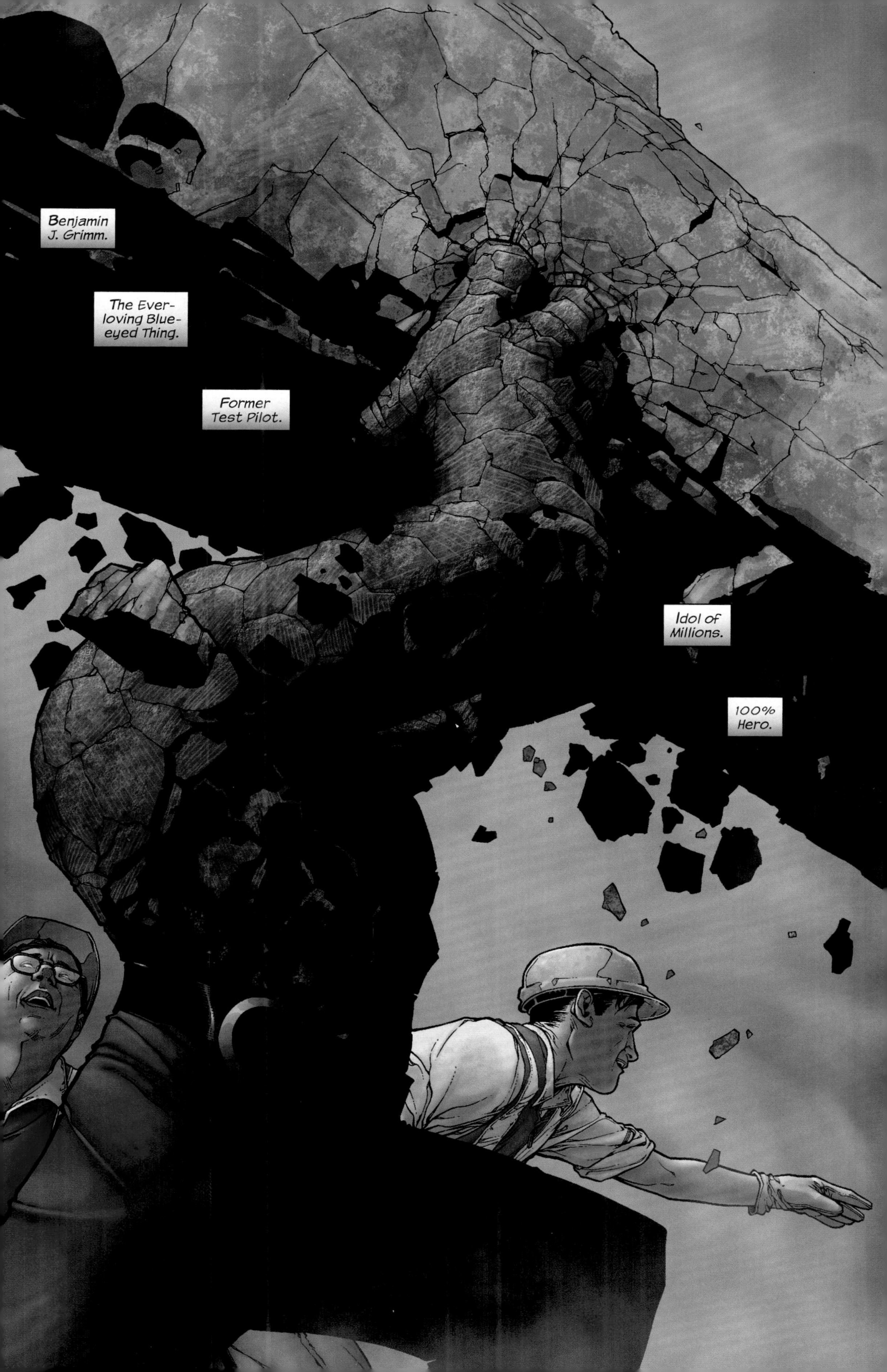
Benjamin J. Grimm.
The Ever-loving Blue-eyed Thing.
Former Test Pilot.
Idol of Millions.
100% Hero.

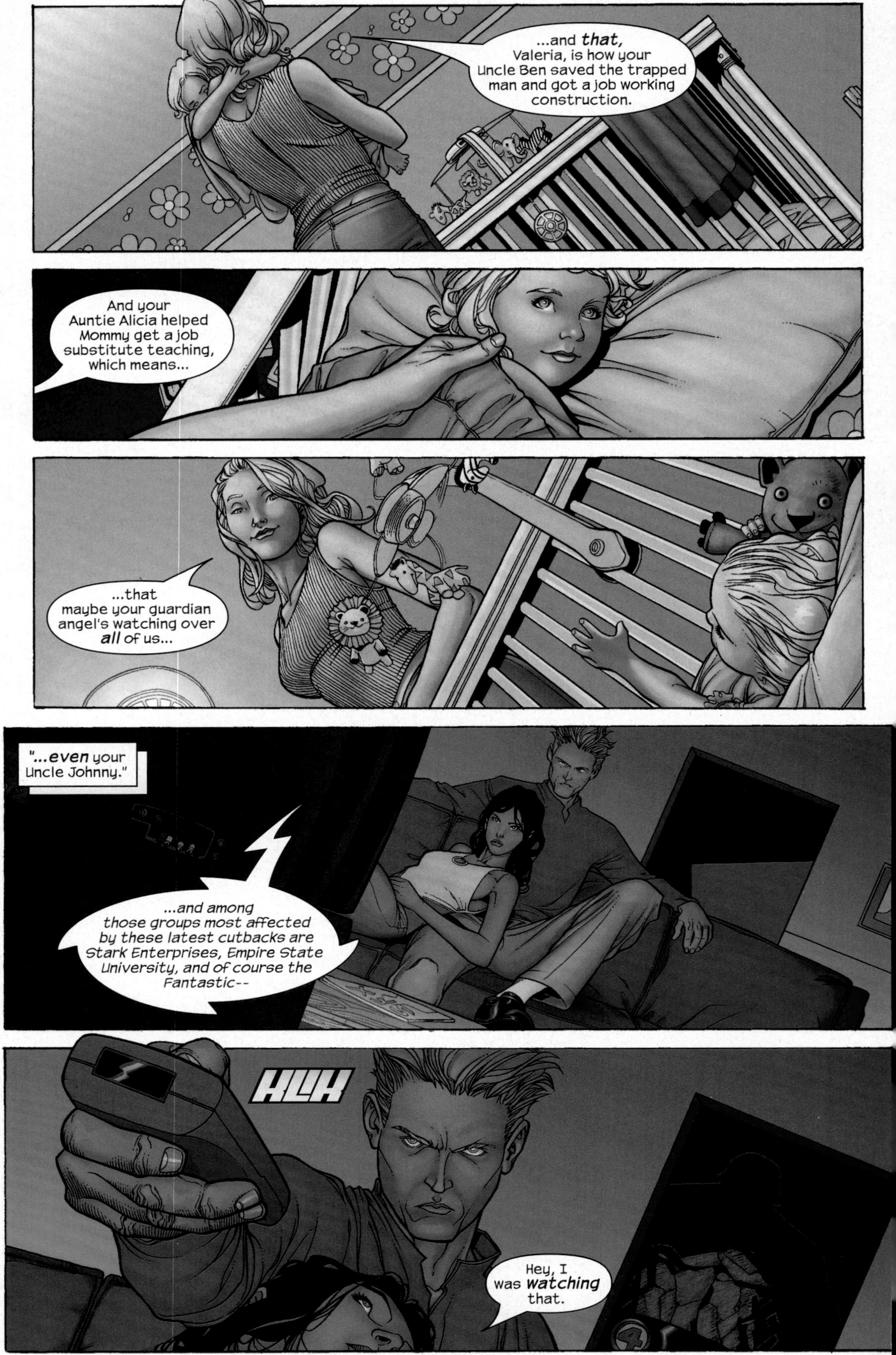

...and *that,* Valeria, is how your Uncle Ben saved the trapped man and got a job working construction.
And your Auntie Alicia helped Mommy get a job substitute teaching, which means...
...that maybe your guardian angel's watching over *all* of us...
"...*even* your Uncle Johnny."
...and among those groups most affected by these latest cutbacks are Stark Enterprises, Empire State University, and of course the Fantastic--
KLIK
Hey, I was *watching* that.

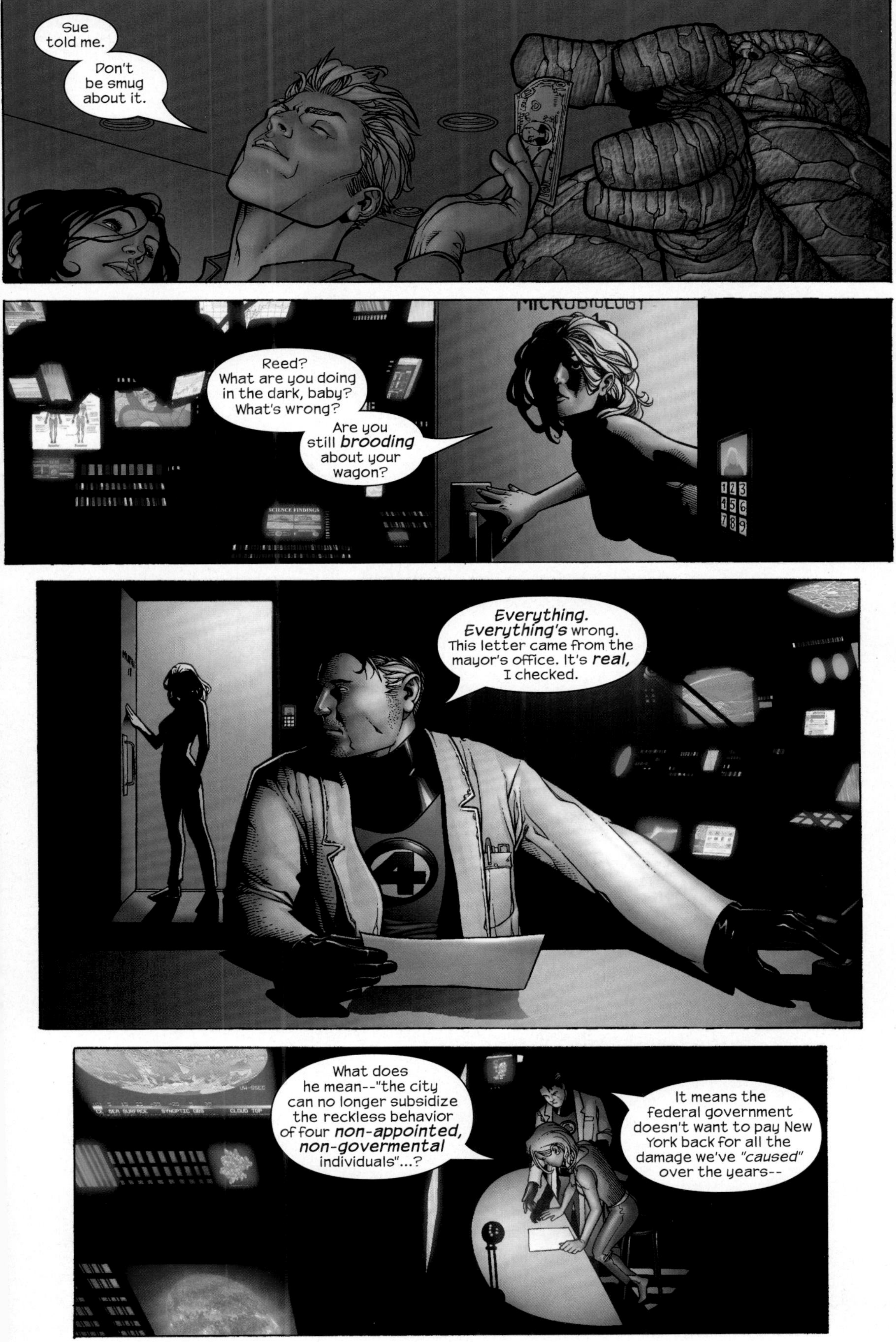
Sue told me.
Don't be smug about it.
Reed? What are you doing in the dark, baby? What's wrong?
Are you still brooding about your wagon?
MICROBIOLOGY
SCIENCE FINDINGS
Everything. Everything's wrong. This letter came from the mayor's office. It's real, I checked.
What does he mean--"the city can no longer subsidize the reckless behavior of four non-appointed, non-govermental individuals"...?
It means the federal government doesn't want to pay New York back for all the damage we've "caused" over the years--

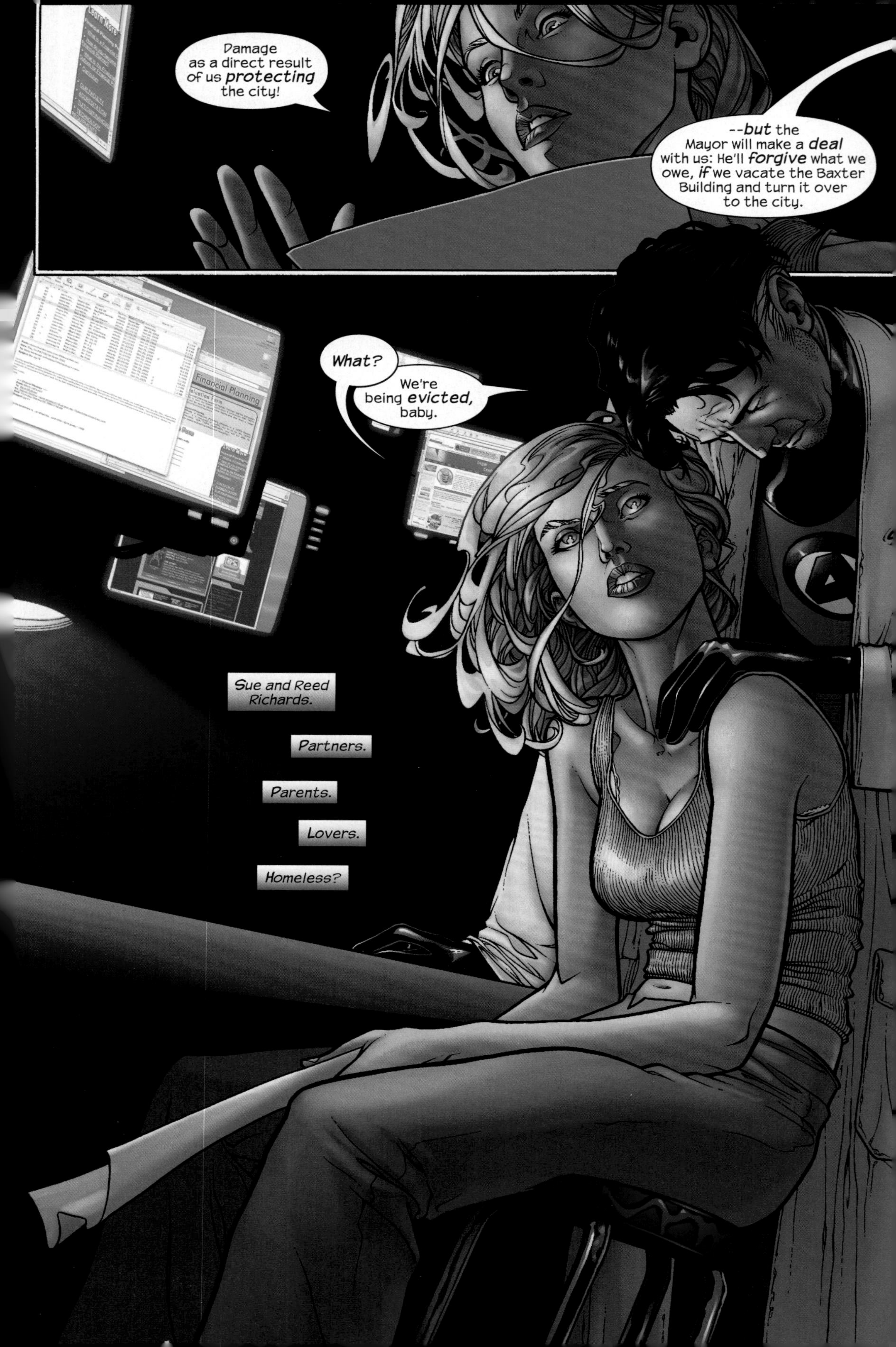
Damage as a direct result of us protecting the city!
--but the Mayor will make a deal with us: He'll forgive what we owe, if we vacate the Baxter Building and turn it over to the city.
What?
We're being evicted, baby.
Sue and Reed Richards.
Partners.
Parents.
Lovers.
Homeless?

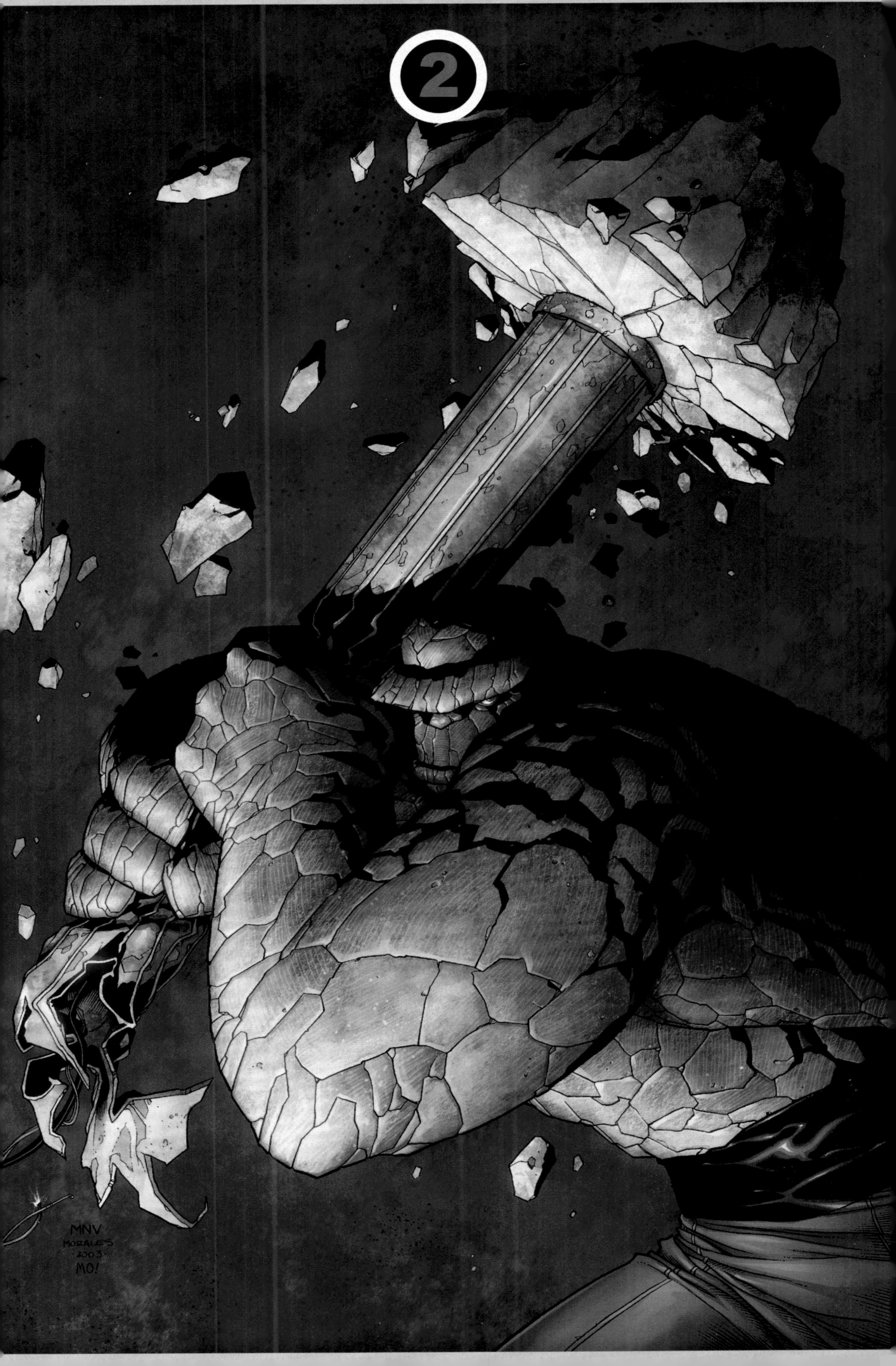
2
MNV
MORALES
2003
MO!

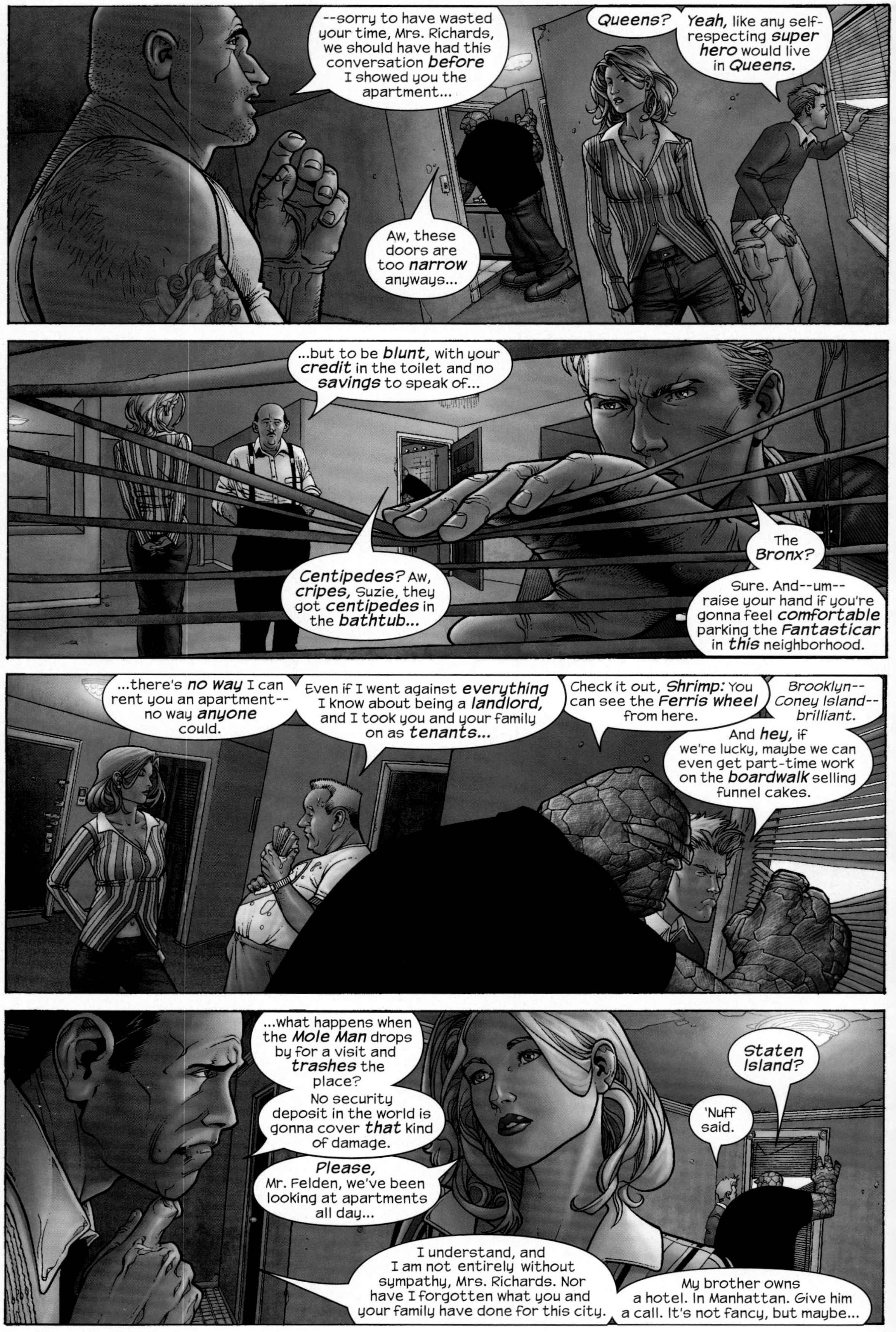

--sorry to have wasted your time, Mrs. Richards, we should have had this conversation before I showed you the apartment...
Aw, these doors are too narrow anyways...
Queens?
Yeah, like any self-respecting super hero would live in Queens.
...but to be blunt, with your credit in the toilet and no savings to speak of...
Centipedes? Aw, cripes, Suzie, they got centipedes in the bathtub...
The Bronx?
Sure. And--um--raise your hand if you're gonna feel comfortable parking the Fantasticar in this neighborhood.
...there's no way I can rent you an apartment--no way anyone could.
Even if I went against everything I know about being a landlord, and I took you and your family on as tenants...
Check it out, Shrimp: You can see the Ferris wheel from here.
Brooklyn--Coney Island--brilliant.
And hey, if we're lucky, maybe we can even get part-time work on the boardwalk selling funnel cakes.
...what happens when the Mole Man drops by for a visit and trashes the place?
No security deposit in the world is gonna cover that kind of damage.
Please, Mr. Felden, we've been looking at apartments all day...
Staten Island?
'Nuff said.
I understand, and I am not entirely without sympathy, Mrs. Richards. Nor have I forgotten what you and your family have done for this city.
My brother owns a hotel. In Manhattan. Give him a call. It's not fancy, but maybe...

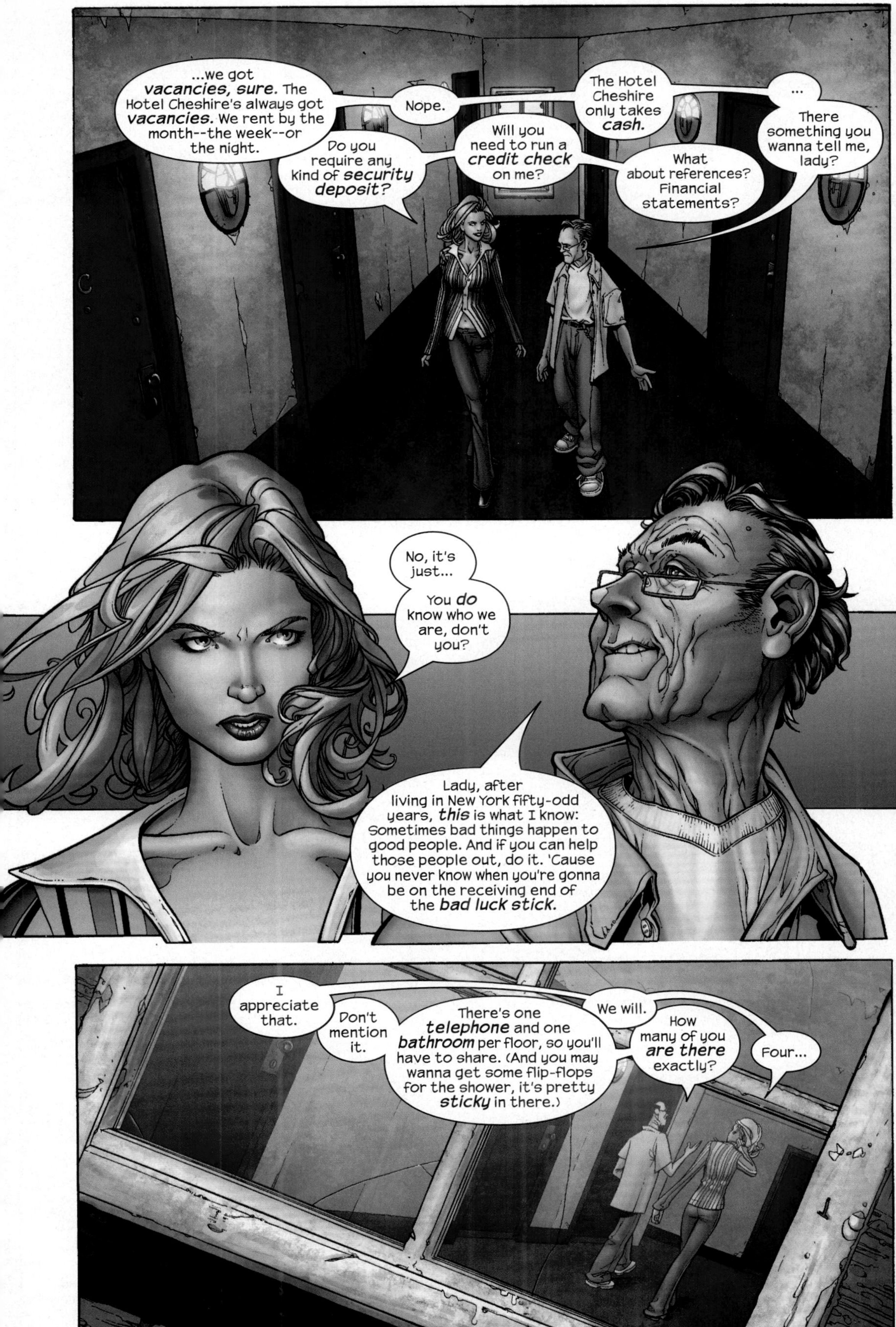

...we got **vacancies, sure.** The Hotel Cheshire's always got **vacancies.** We rent by the month--the week--or the night.
Do you require any kind of **security deposit?**
Nope.
Will you need to run a **credit check** on me?
The Hotel Cheshire only takes **cash.**
What about references? Financial statements?
...
There something you wanna tell me, lady?
No, it's just...
You **do** know who we are, don't you?
Lady, after living in New York fifty-odd years, **this** is what I know: Sometimes bad things happen to good people. And if you can help those people out, do it. 'Cause you never know when you're gonna be on the receiving end of the **bad luck stick.**
I appreciate that.
Don't mention it.
There's one **telephone** and one **bathroom** per floor, so you'll have to share. (And you may wanna get some flip-flops for the shower, it's pretty **sticky** in there.)
We will.
How many of you **are there** exactly?
Four...

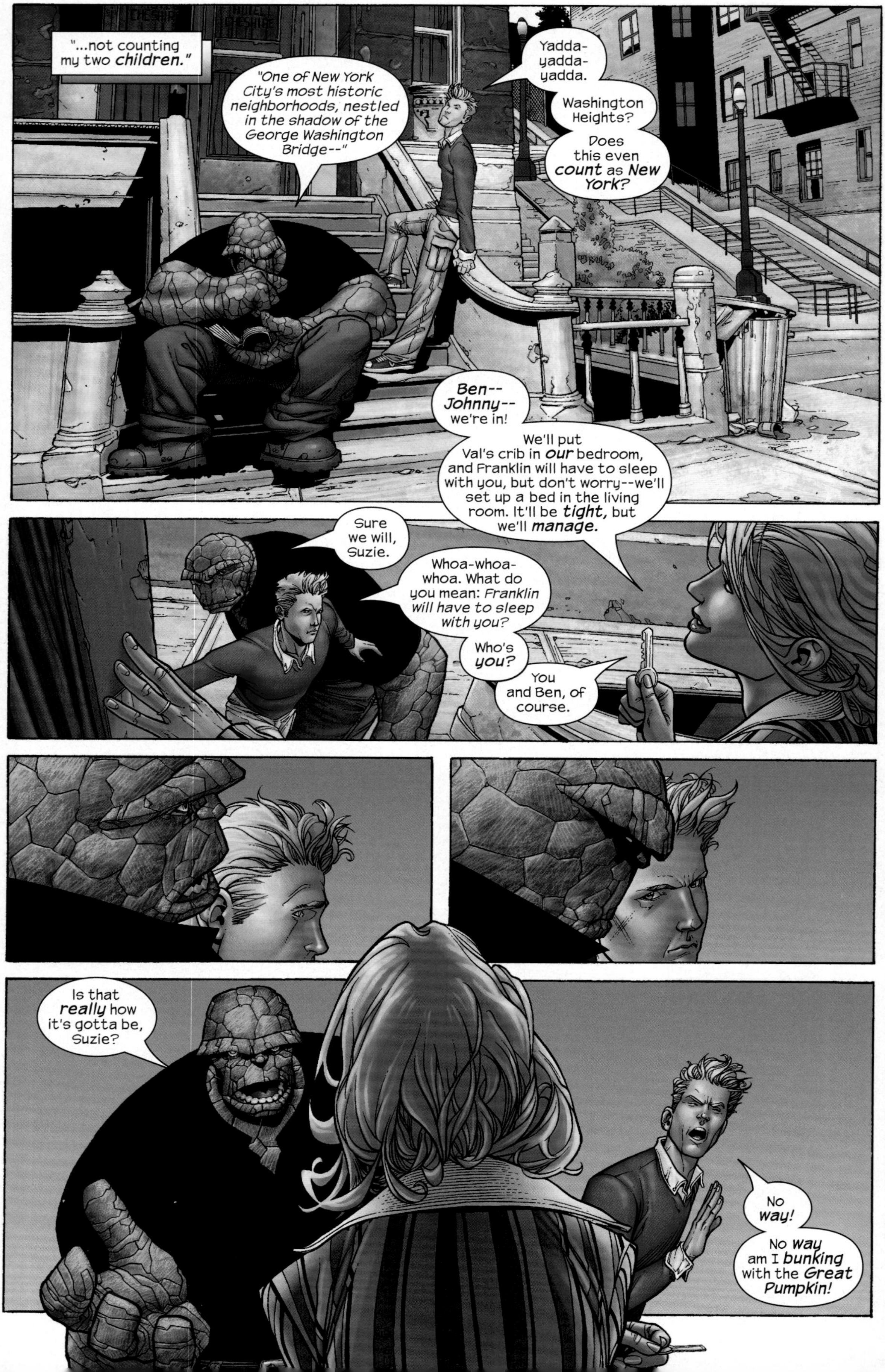

"...not counting my two children."
"One of New York City's most historic neighborhoods, nestled in the shadow of the George Washington Bridge--"
Yadda-yadda-yadda.
Washington Heights?
Does this even count as New York?
Ben--Johnny--we're in!
We'll put Val's crib in our bedroom, and Franklin will have to sleep with you, but don't worry--we'll set up a bed in the living room. It'll be tight, but we'll manage.
Sure we will, Suzie.
Whoa-whoa-whoa. What do you mean: Franklin will have to sleep with you?
Who's you?
You and Ben, of course.
Is that really how it's gotta be, Suzie?
No way!
No way am I bunking with the Great Pumpkin!

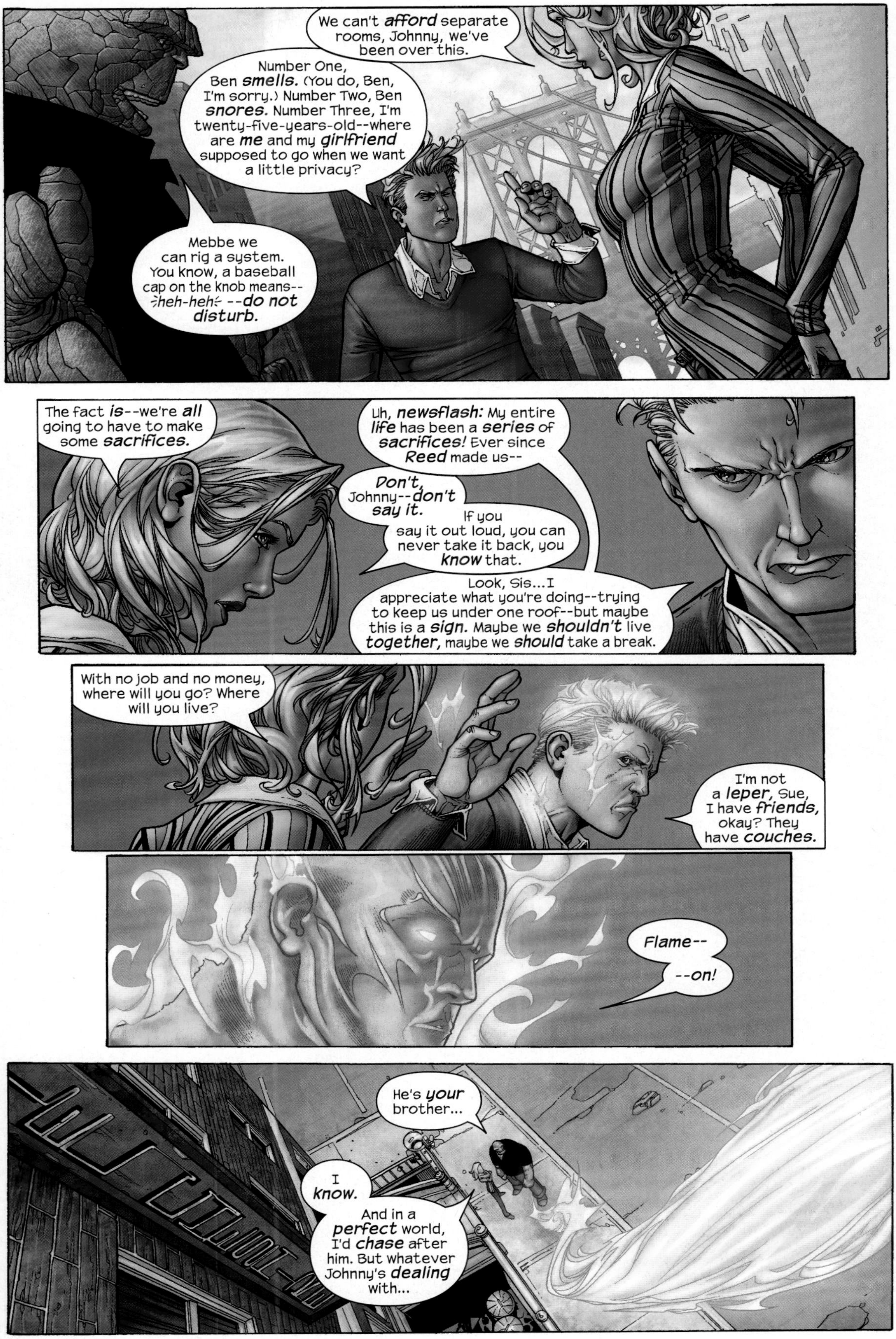

We can't afford separate rooms, Johnny, we've been over this.
Number One, Ben smells. (You do, Ben, I'm sorry.) Number Two, Ben snores. Number Three, I'm twenty-five-years-old--where are me and my girlfriend supposed to go when we want a little privacy?
Mebbe we can rig a system. You know, a baseball cap on the knob means-- heh-heh --do not disturb.
The fact is--we're all going to have to make some sacrifices.
Uh, newsflash: My entire life has been a series of sacrifices! Ever since Reed made us--
Don't, Johnny--don't say it.
If you say it out loud, you can never take it back, you know that.
Look, Sis...I appreciate what you're doing--trying to keep us under one roof--but maybe this is a sign. Maybe we shouldn't live together, maybe we should take a break.
With no job and no money, where will you go? Where will you live?
I'm not a leper, Sue, I have friends, okay? They have couches.
Flame--
--on!
He's your brother...
I know.
And in a perfect world, I'd chase after him. But whatever Johnny's dealing with...

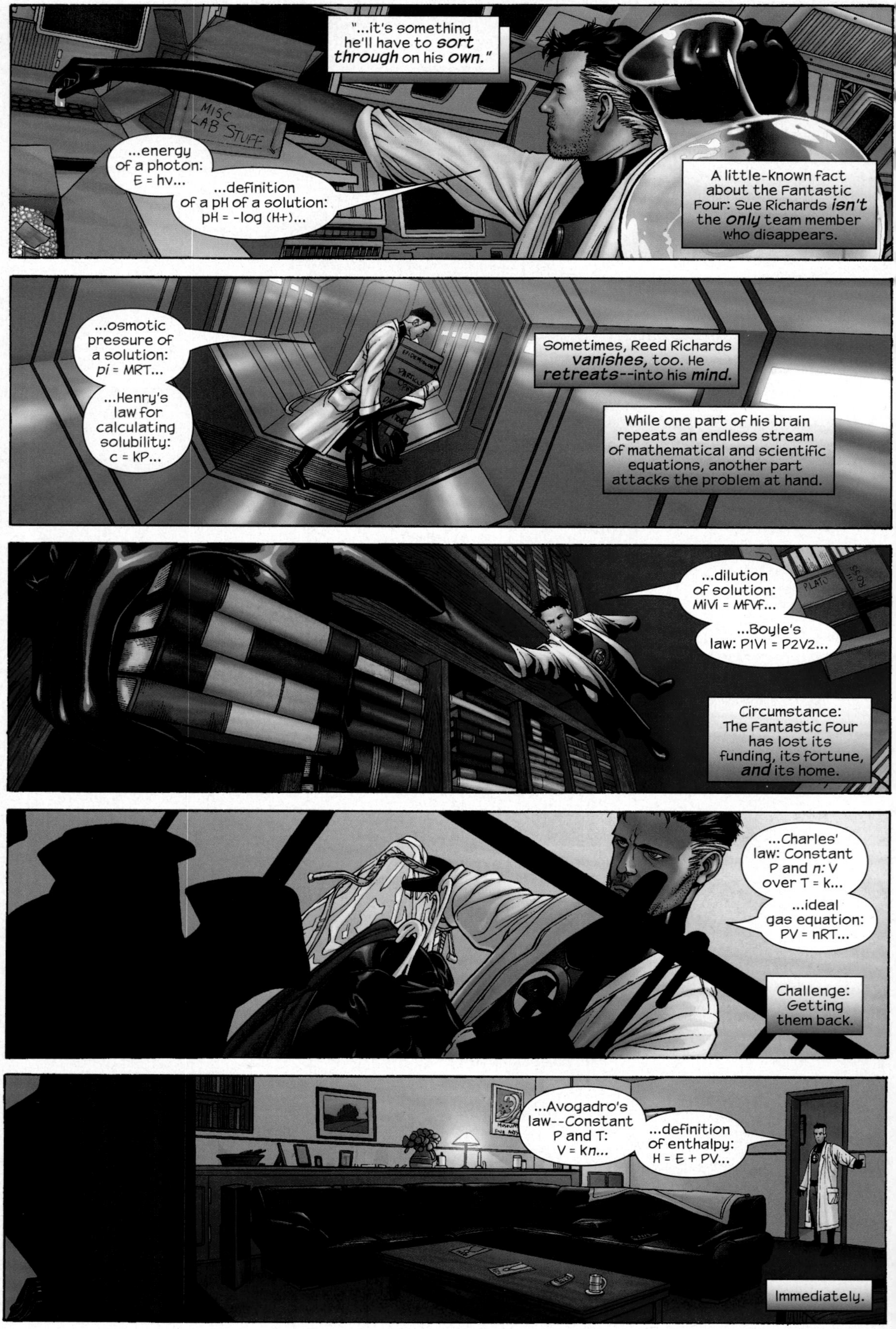
"...it's something he'll have to sort through on his own."
MISC LAB STUFF
...energy of a photon: E = hv...
...definition of a pH of a solution: pH = -log (H+)...
A little-known fact about the Fantastic Four: Sue Richards isn't the only team member who disappears.
...osmotic pressure of a solution: pi = MRT...
...Henry's law for calculating solubility: c = KP...
Sometimes, Reed Richards vanishes, too. He retreats--into his mind.
While one part of his brain repeats an endless stream of mathematical and scientific equations, another part attacks the problem at hand.
...dilution of solution: MiVi = MfVf...
...Boyle's law: P1V1 = P2V2...
PLATO
Circumstance: The Fantastic Four has lost its funding, its fortune, and its home.
...Charles' law: Constant P and n: V over T = k...
...ideal gas equation: PV = nRT...
Challenge: Getting them back.
...Avogadro's law--Constant P and T: V = kn...
...definition of enthalpy: H = E + PV...
Immediately.

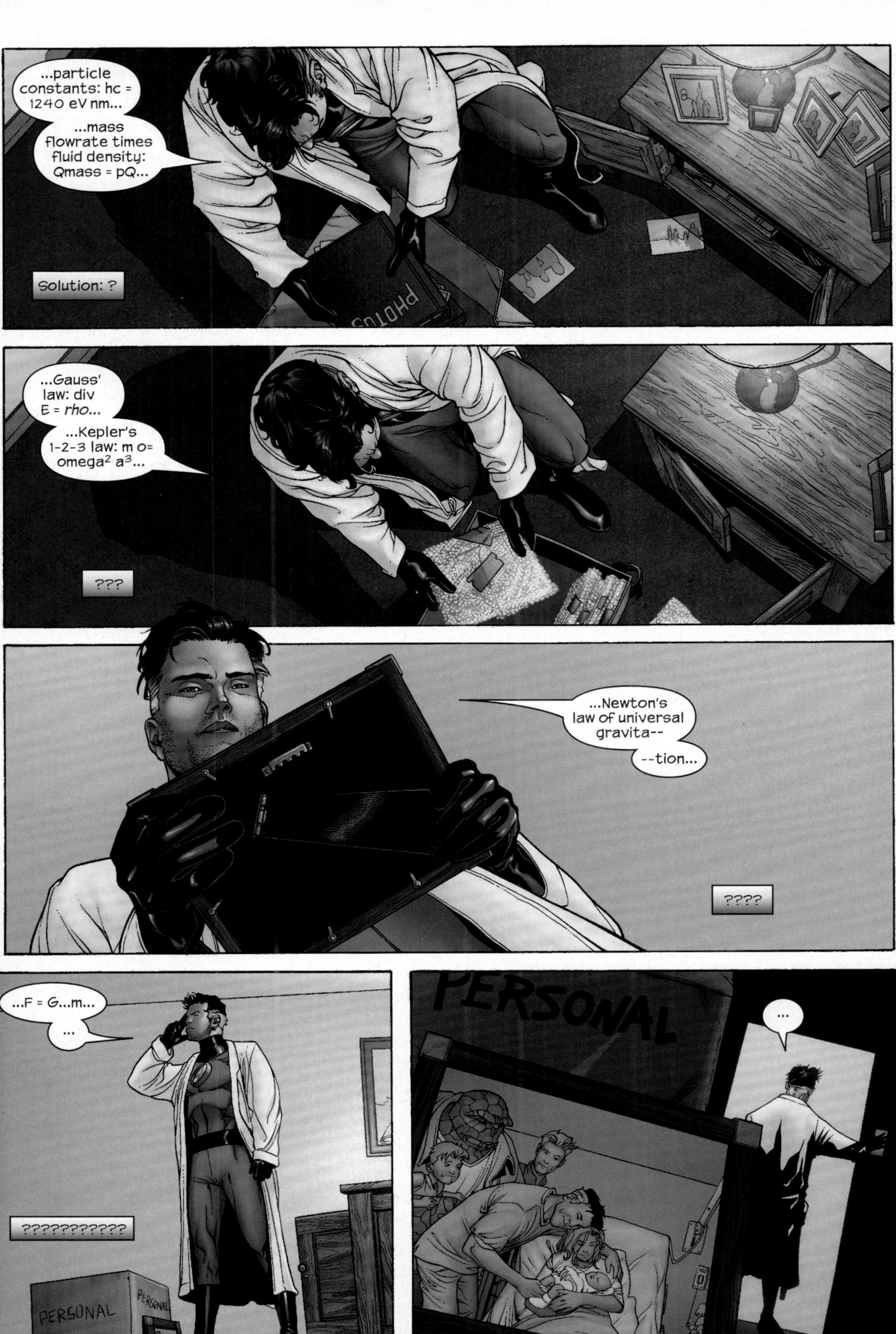
...particle constants: hc = 1240 eV nm...
...mass flowrate times fluid density: Qmass = pQ...
Solution: ?
PHOTOS
...Gauss' law: div E = *rho*...
...Kepler's 1-2-3 law: m o= omega² a³...
???
...Newton's law of universal gravita--
--tion...
????
...F = G...m...
...
???????????
PERSONAL
PERSONAL
PERSONAL
...

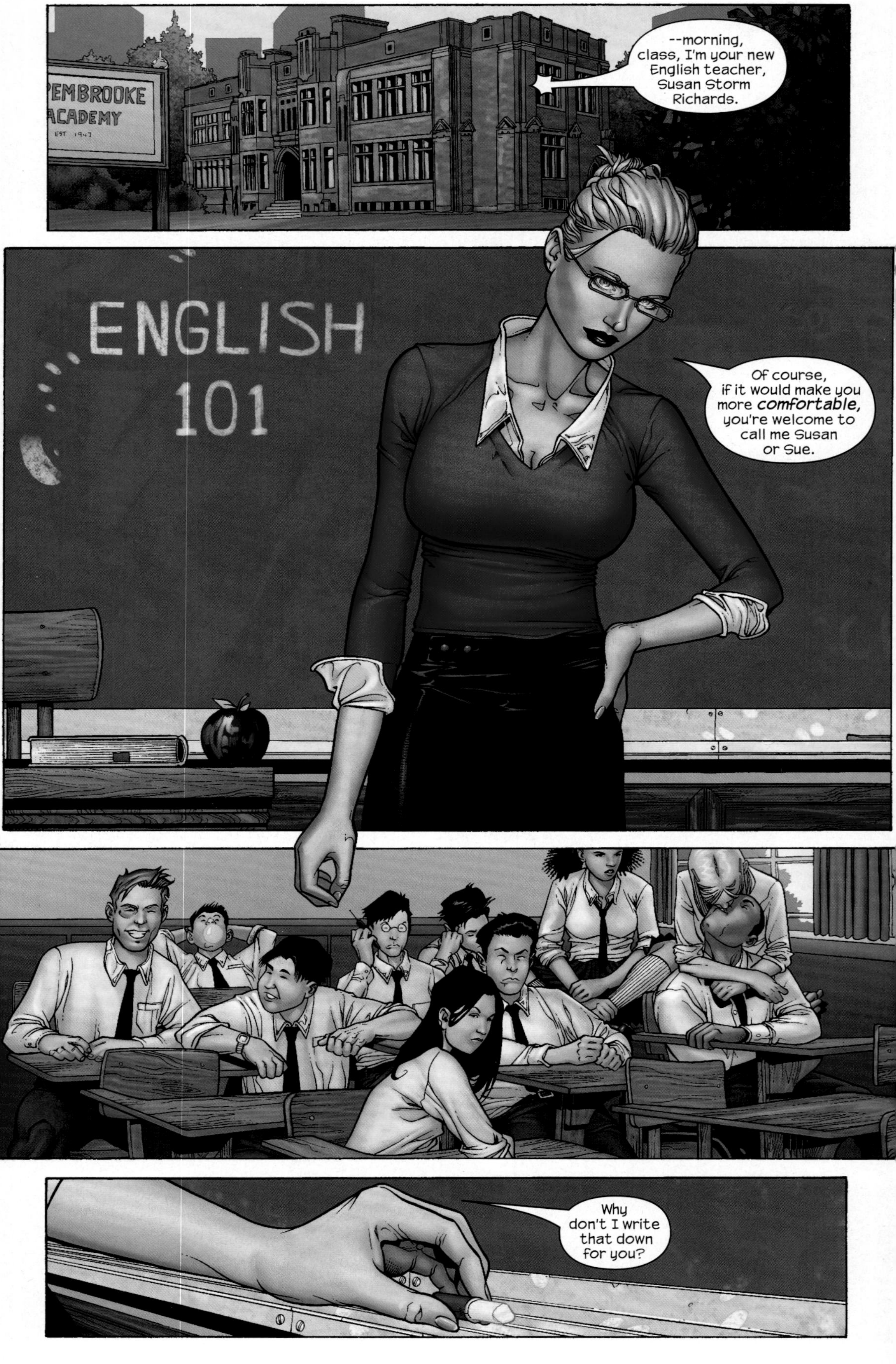
PEMBROOKE ACADEMY
EST 1947
--morning, class, I'm your new English teacher, Susan Storm Richards.
ENGLISH 101
Of course, if it would make you more *comfortable,* you're welcome to call me Susan or Sue.
Why don't I write that down for you?

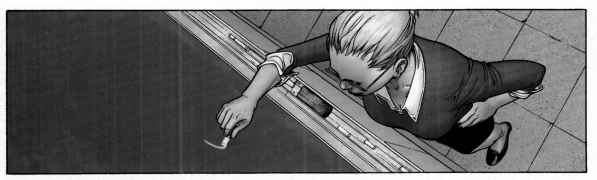

THWAPP!

I *realize* that getting used to a new teacher can be difficult, but let's not start off on the wrong foot, all right?

As I was saying, you can call me either--

THWUMP!

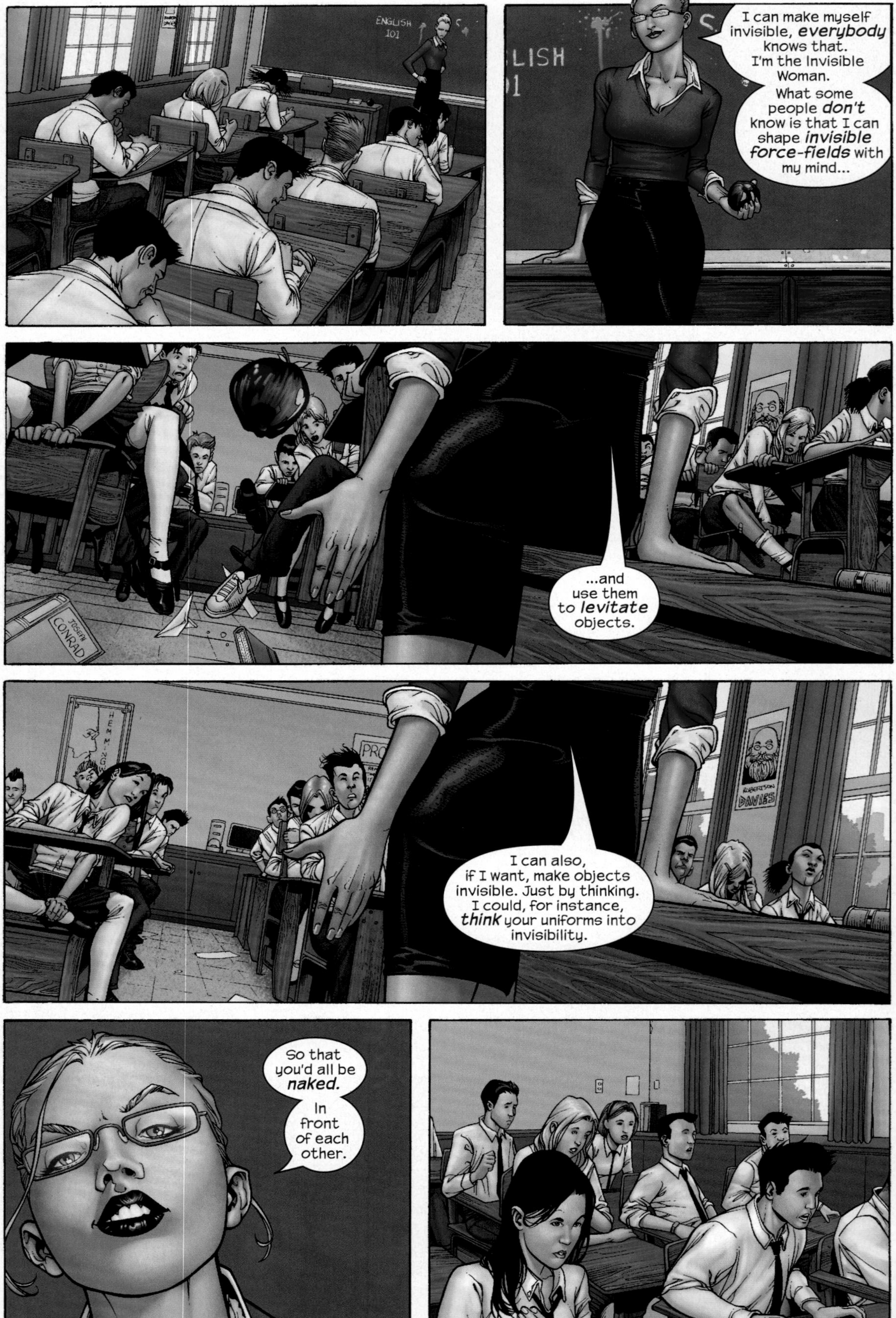
ENGLISH 101
I can make myself invisible, everybody knows that. I'm the Invisible Woman.
What some people don't know is that I can shape invisible force-fields with my mind...
JOSEPH CONRAD
...and use them to levitate objects.
HEMMINGWAY
ROBERTSON DAVIES
I can also, if I want, make objects invisible. Just by thinking. I could, for instance, think your uniforms into invisibility.
So that you'd all be naked.
In front of each other.

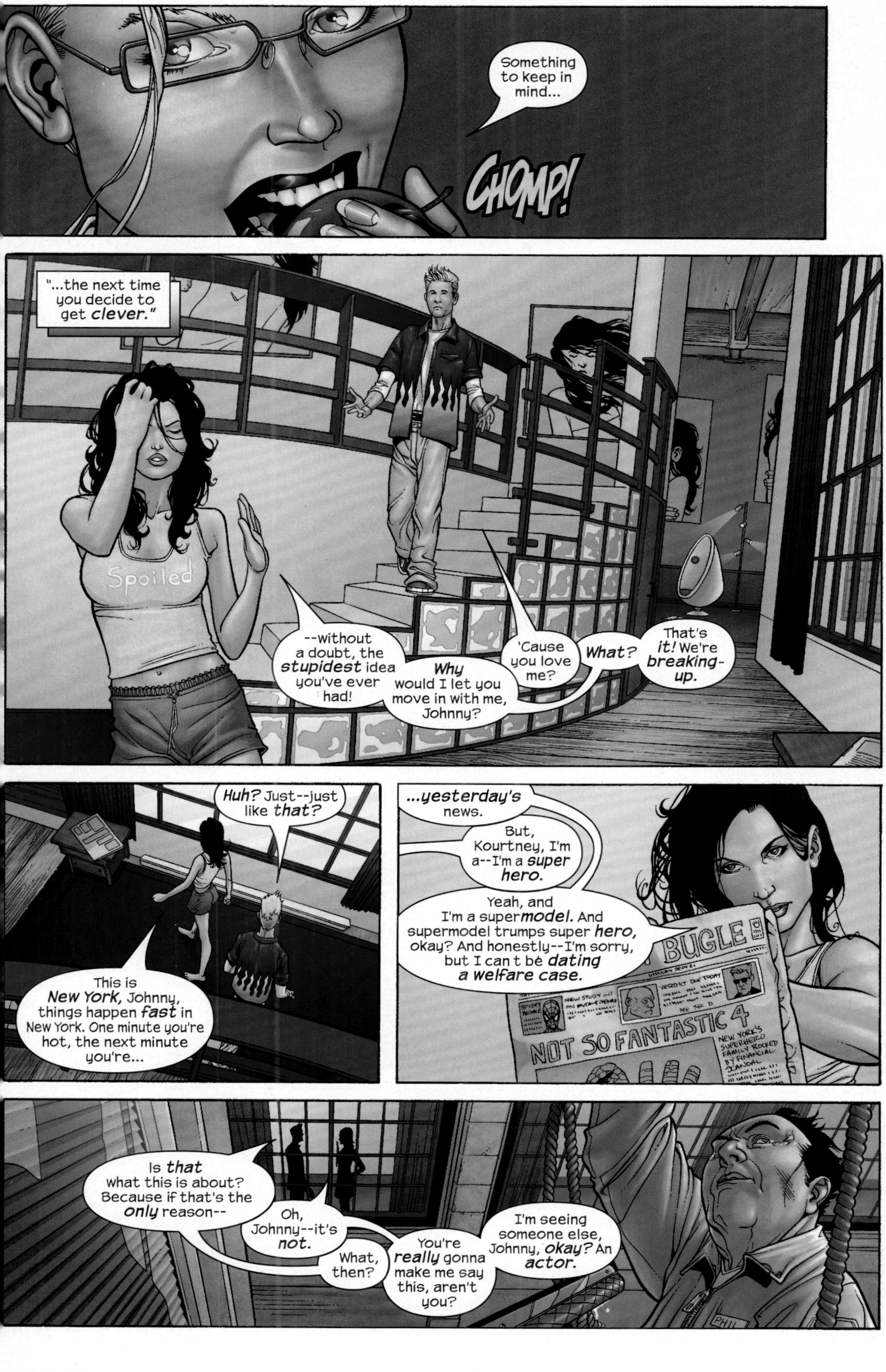
Something to keep in mind...
CHOMP!
"...the next time you decide to get clever."
--without a doubt, the stupidest idea you've ever had!
Why would I let you move in with me, Johnny?
'Cause you love me?
What?
That's it! We're breaking-up.
Huh? Just--just like that?
This is New York, Johnny, things happen fast in New York. One minute you're hot, the next minute you're...
...yesterday's news.
But, Kourtney, I'm a--I'm a super hero.
Yeah, and I'm a supermodel. And supermodel trumps super hero, okay? And honestly--I'm sorry, but I can't be dating a welfare case.
BUGLE
NOT SO FANTASTIC 4
NEW YORK'S SUPERHERO FAMILY ROCKED BY FINANCIAL SCANDAL
Is that what this is about? Because if that's the only reason--
Oh, Johnny--it's not.
What, then?
You're really gonna make me say this, aren't you?
I'm seeing someone else, Johnny, okay? An actor.
PHIL

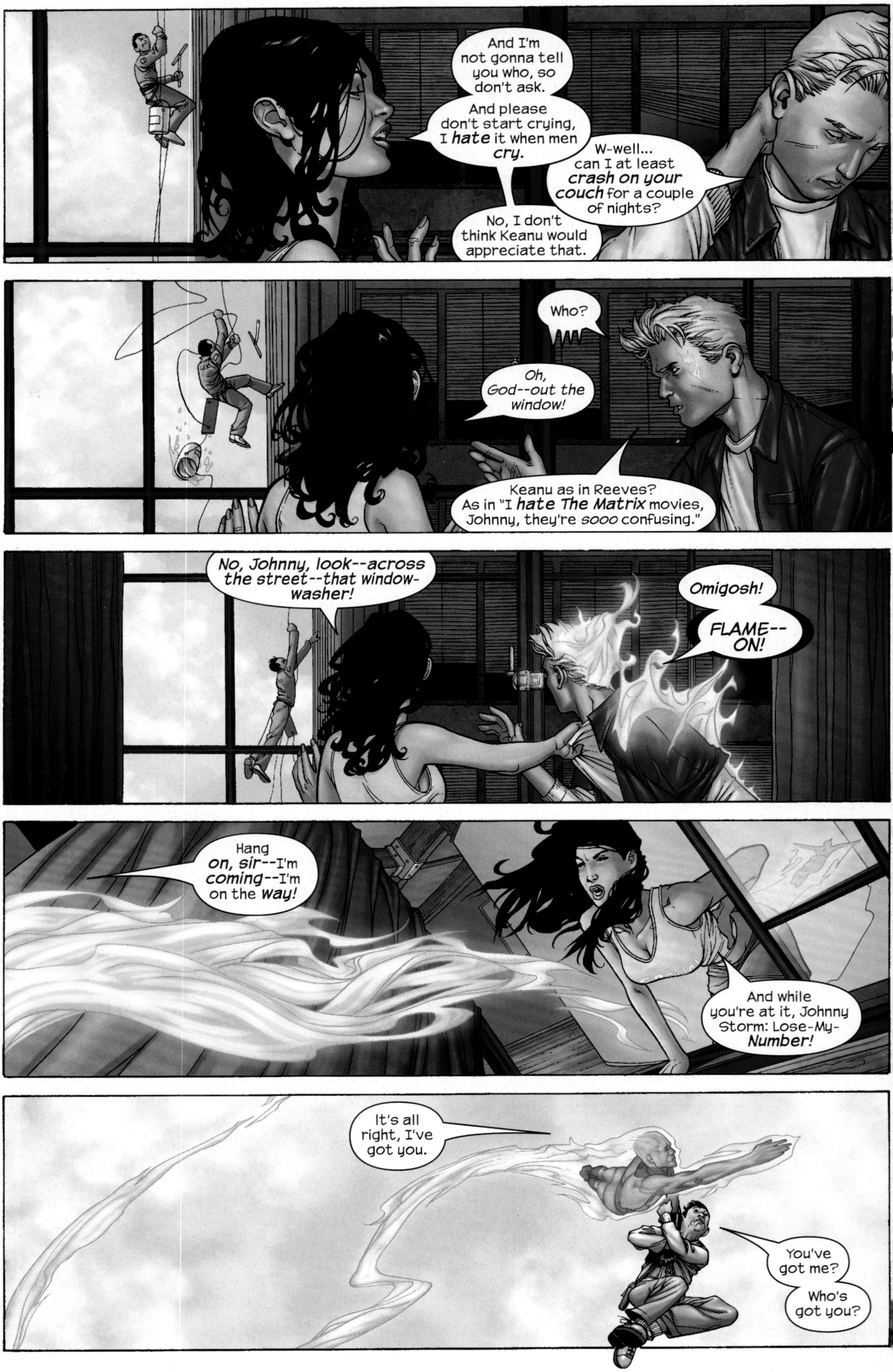

And I'm not gonna tell you who, so don't ask.
And please don't start crying, I *hate* it when men *cry.*
W-well... can I at least **crash on your couch** for a couple of nights?
No, I don't think Keanu would appreciate that.
Who?
Oh, God--out the window!
Keanu as in Reeves? As in "I *hate The Matrix* movies, Johnny, they're *sooo* confusing."
No, Johnny, look--across the street--that window-washer!
Omigosh!
FLAME--ON!
Hang *on, sir*--I'm *coming*--I'm on the *way!*
And while you're at it, Johnny Storm: Lose-My-*Number!*
It's all right, I've got you.
You've got me?
Who's got you?

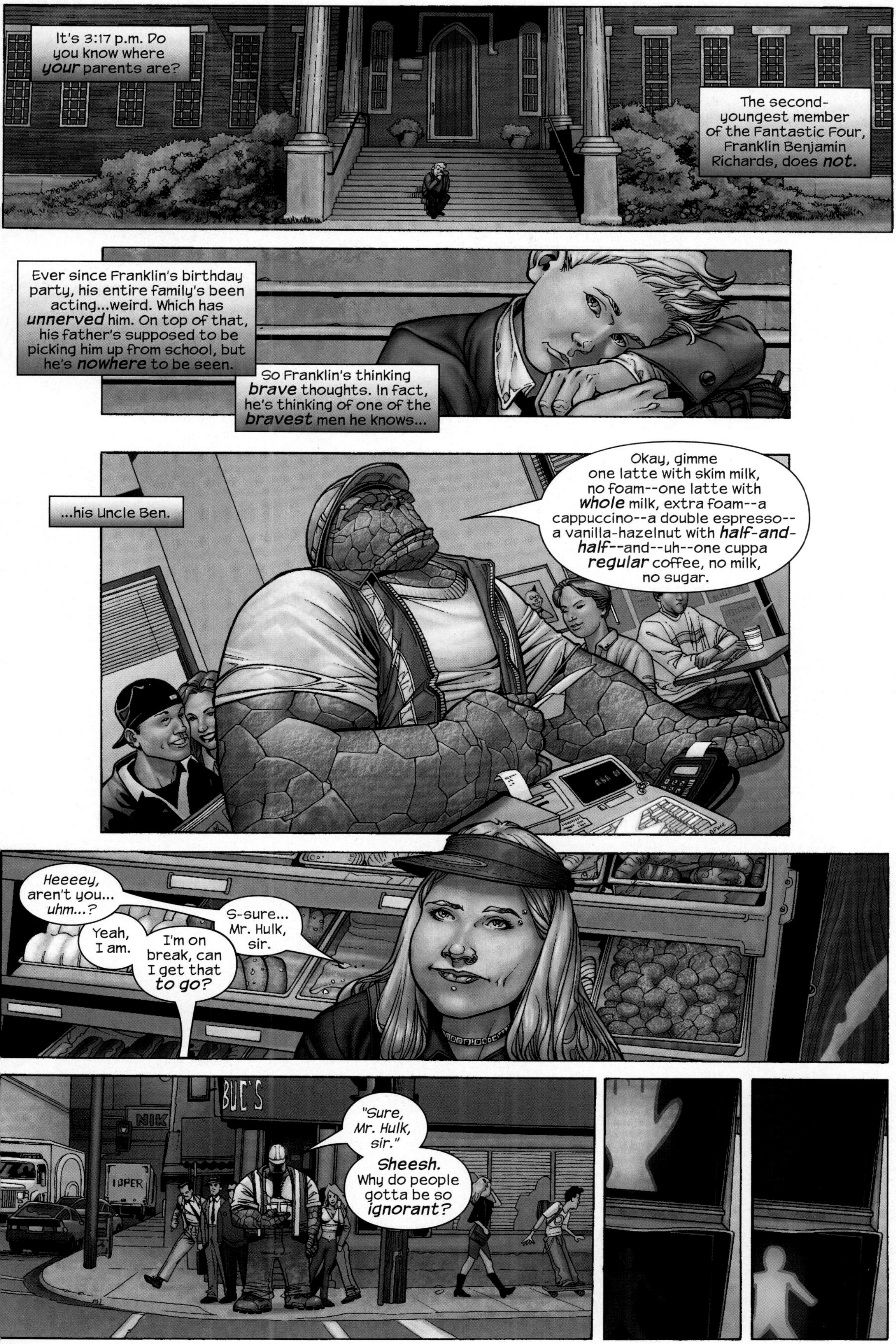
It's 3:17 p.m. Do you know where your parents are?
The second-youngest member of the Fantastic Four, Franklin Benjamin Richards, does not.
Ever since Franklin's birthday party, his entire family's been acting...weird. Which has unnerved him. On top of that, his father's supposed to be picking him up from school, but he's nowhere to be seen.
So Franklin's thinking brave thoughts. In fact, he's thinking of one of the bravest men he knows...
...his Uncle Ben.
Okay, gimme one latte with skim milk, no foam--one latte with whole milk, extra foam--a cappuccino--a double espresso--a vanilla-hazelnut with half-and-half--and--uh--one cuppa regular coffee, no milk, no sugar.
Heeeey, aren't you... uhm...?
Yeah, I am.
I'm on break, can I get that to go?
S-sure... Mr. Hulk, sir.
BUC'S
"Sure, Mr. Hulk, sir."
Sheesh. Why do people gotta be so ignorant?

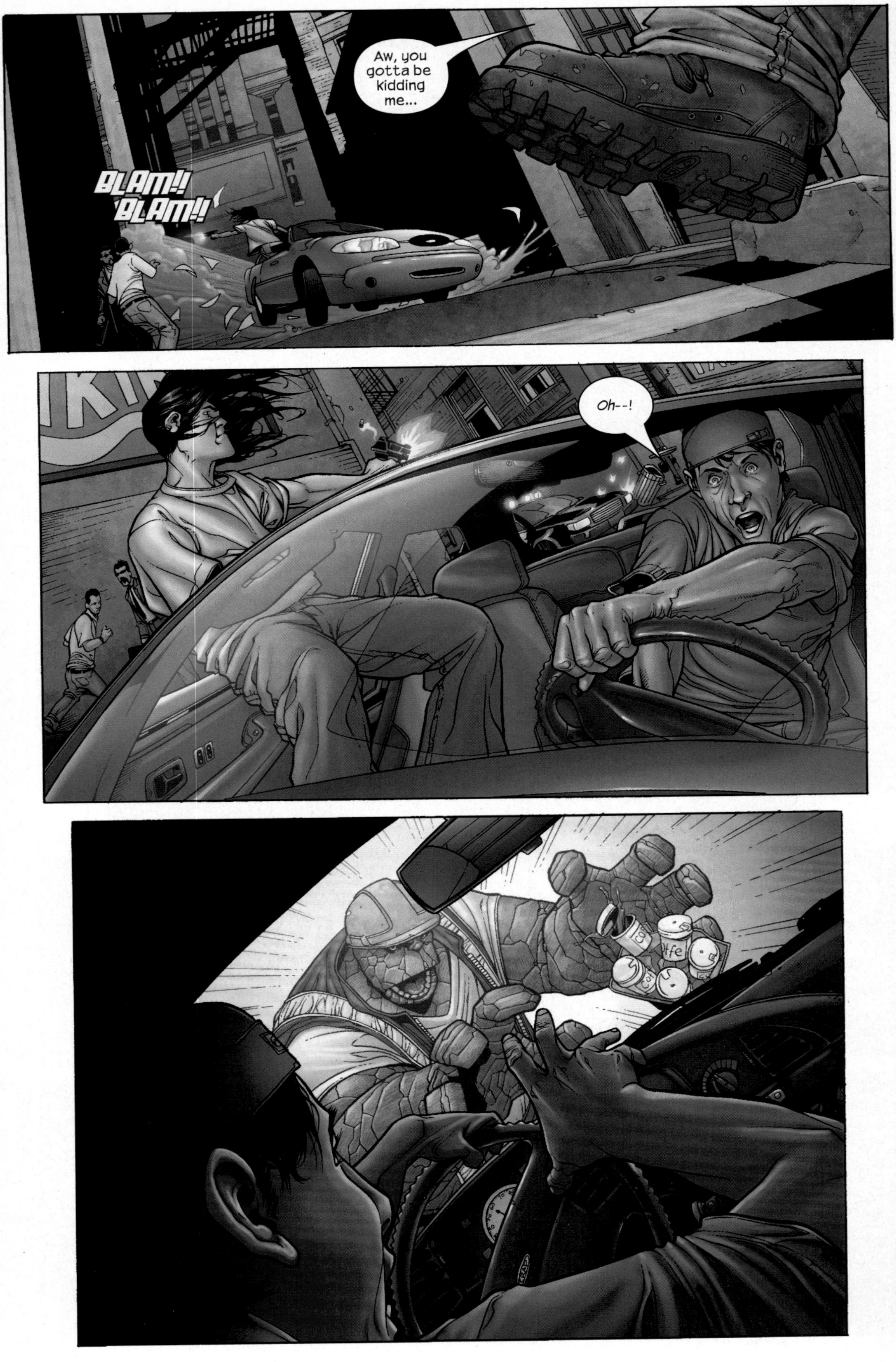
Aw, you gotta be kidding me...
BLAM!! BLAM!!
Oh--!

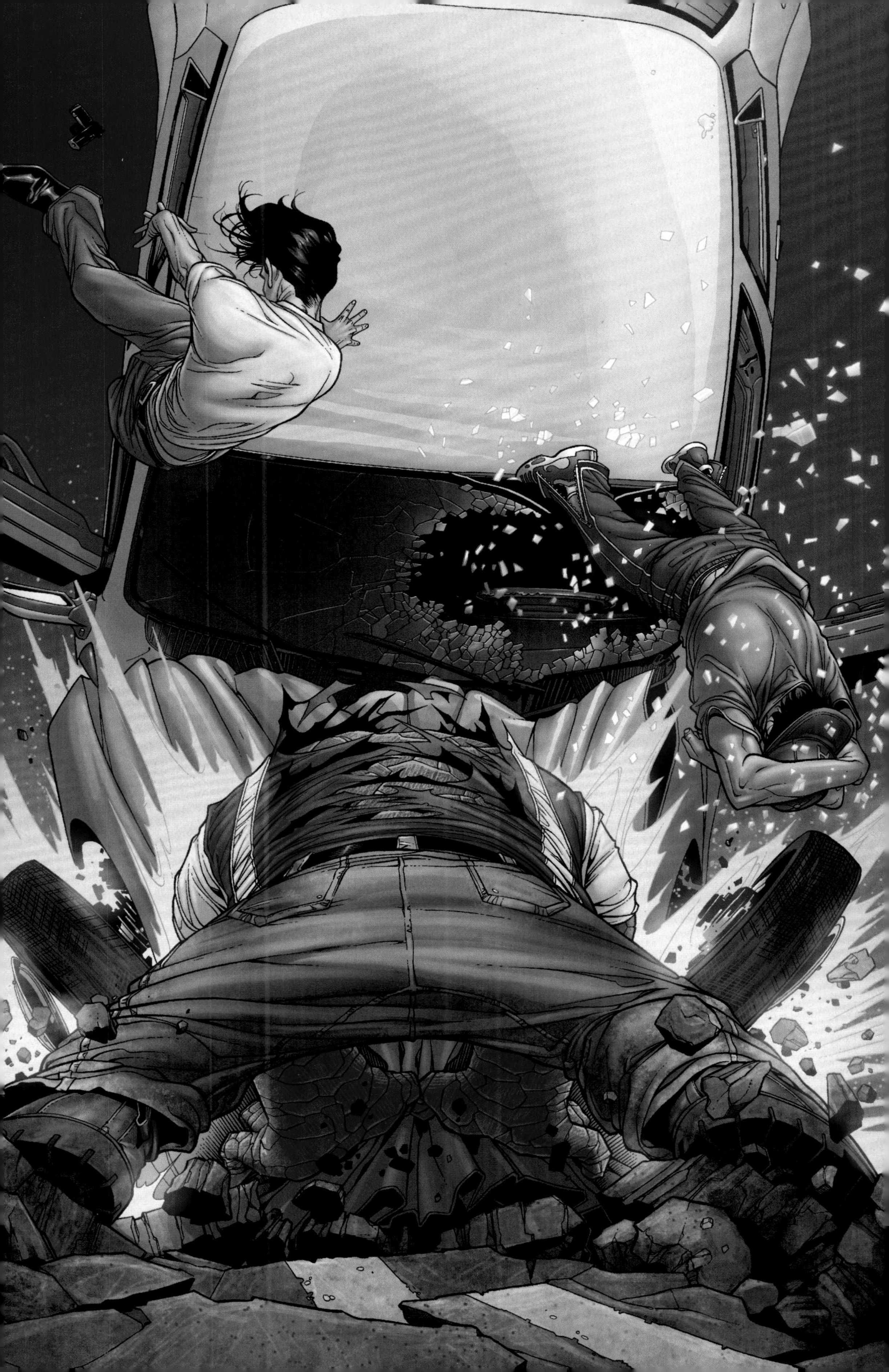

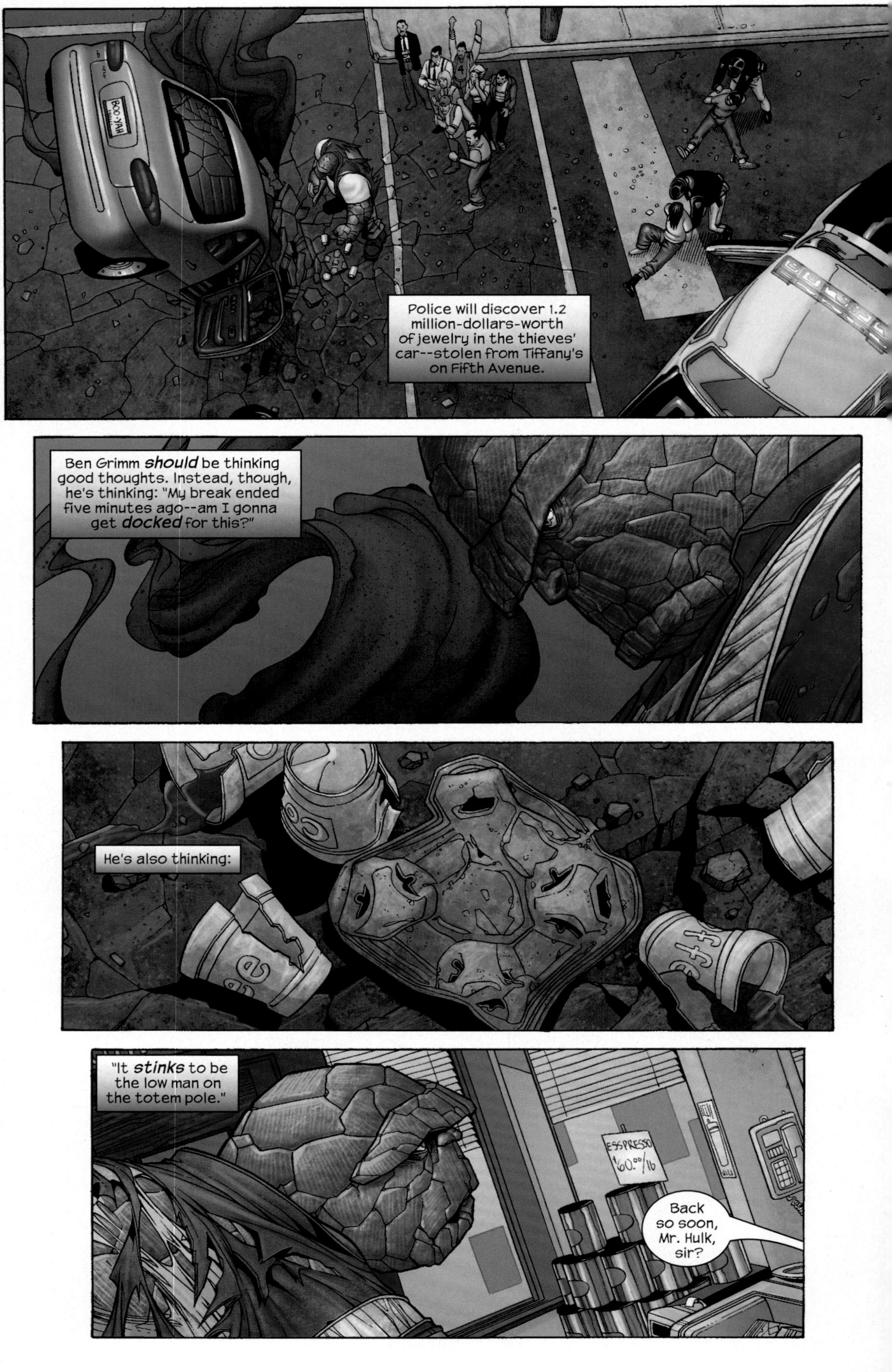
BOO-YAH
Police will discover 1.2 million-dollars-worth of jewelry in the thieves' car--stolen from Tiffany's on Fifth Avenue.
Ben Grimm *should* be thinking good thoughts. Instead, though, he's thinking: "My break ended five minutes ago--am I gonna get *docked* for this?"
He's also thinking:
"It *stinks* to be the low man on the totem pole."
ESPRESSO $60.00/lb
Back so soon, Mr. Hulk, sir?

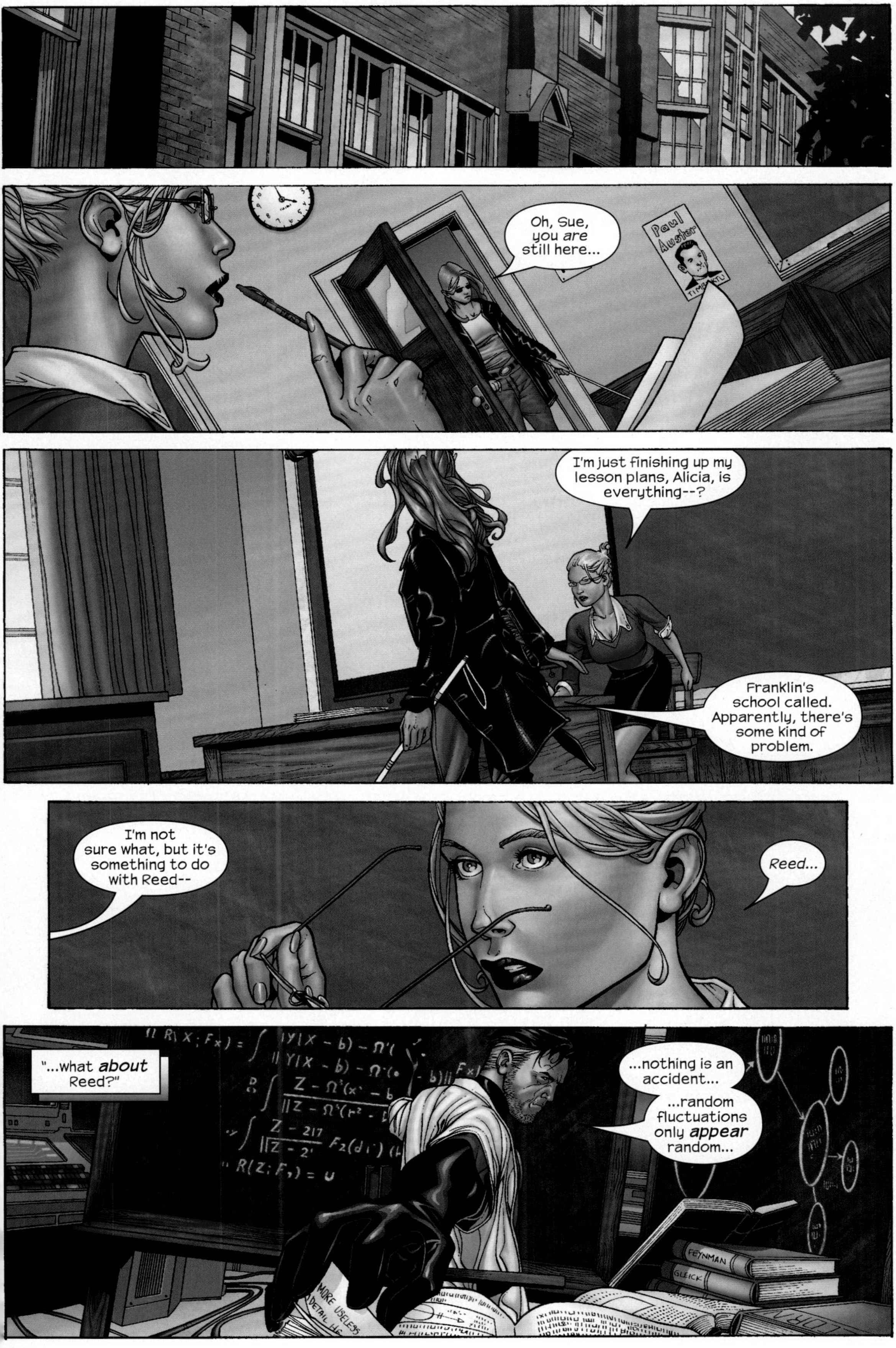

Oh, Sue, you *are* still here...
Paul Auster
I'm just finishing up my lesson plans, Alicia, is everything--?
Franklin's school called. Apparently, there's some kind of problem.
I'm not sure what, but it's something to do with Reed--
Reed...
"...what **about** Reed?"
...nothing is an accident...
...random fluctuations only **appear** random...
FEYNMAN
GLEICK

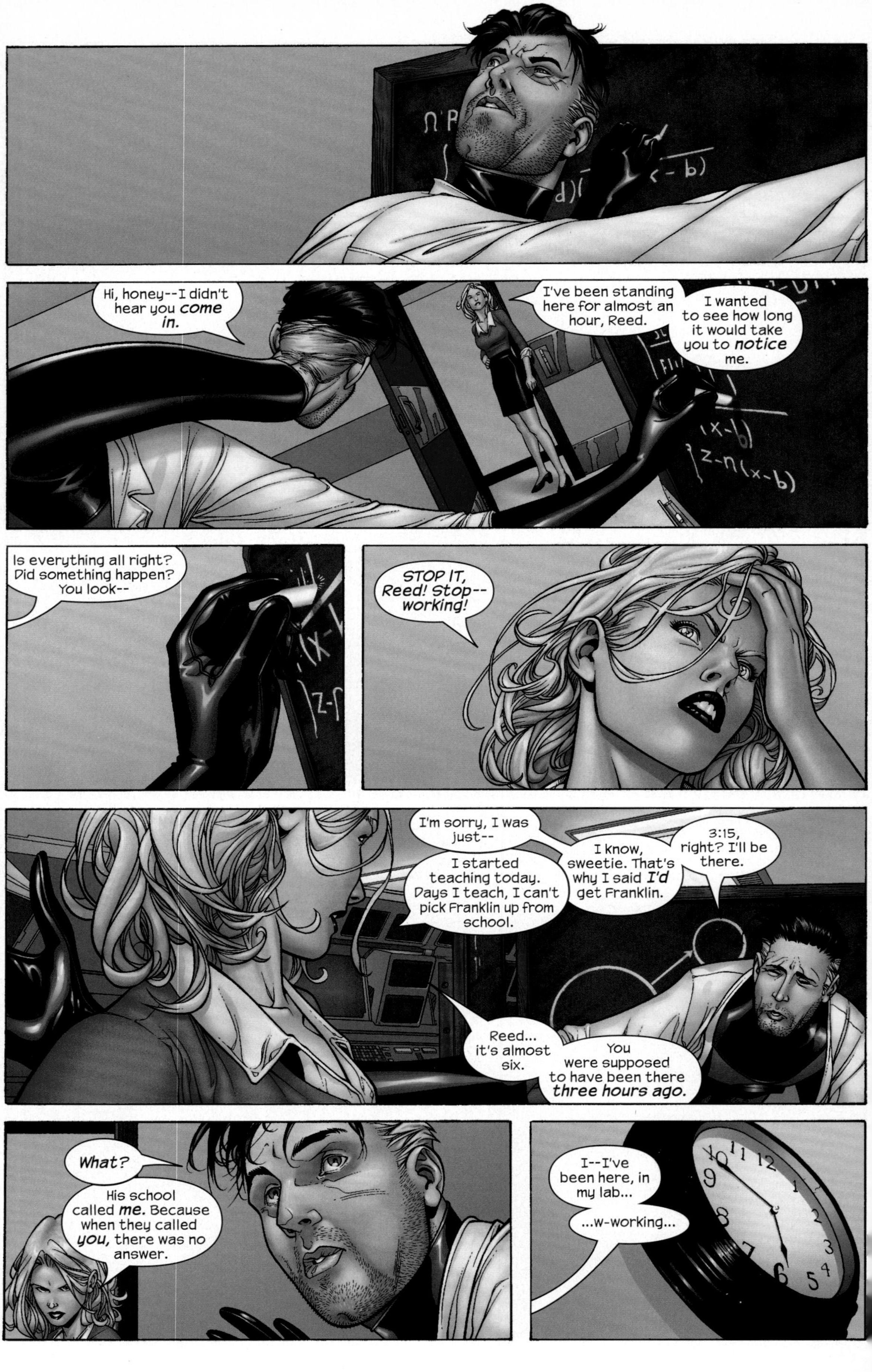
Hi, honey--I didn't hear you *come in.*
I've been standing here for almost an hour, Reed.
I wanted to see how long it would take you to *notice* me.
Is everything all right? Did something happen? You look--
STOP IT, Reed! Stop-- working!
I'm sorry, I was just--
I started teaching today. Days I teach, I can't pick Franklin up from school.
I know, sweetie. That's why I said *I'd* get Franklin.
3:15, right? I'll be there.
Reed... it's almost six.
You were supposed to have been there *three hours ago.*
What?
His school called *me.* Because when they called *you,* there was no answer.
I--I've been here, in my lab...
...w-working...

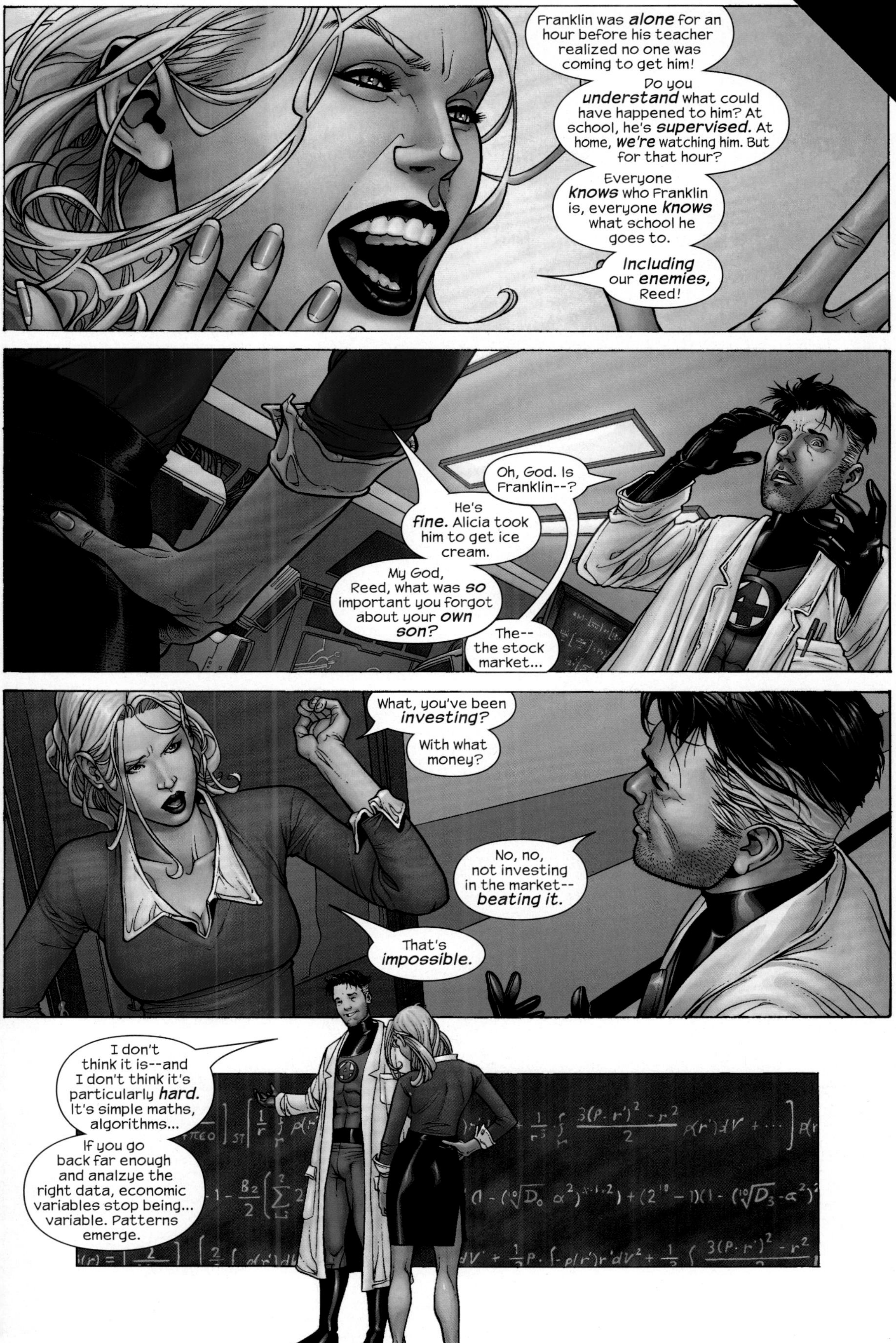
Franklin was alone for an hour before his teacher realized no one was coming to get him!
Do you understand what could have happened to him? At school, he's supervised. At home, we're watching him. But for that hour?
Everyone knows who Franklin is, everyone knows what school he goes to.
Including our enemies, Reed!
Oh, God. Is Franklin--?
He's fine. Alicia took him to get ice cream.
My God, Reed, what was so important you forgot about your own son?
The-- the stock market...
What, you've been investing?
With what money?
No, no, not investing in the market-- beating it.
That's impossible.
I don't think it is--and I don't think it's particularly hard. It's simple maths, algorithms...
If you go back far enough and analzye the right data, economic variables stop being... variable. Patterns emerge.

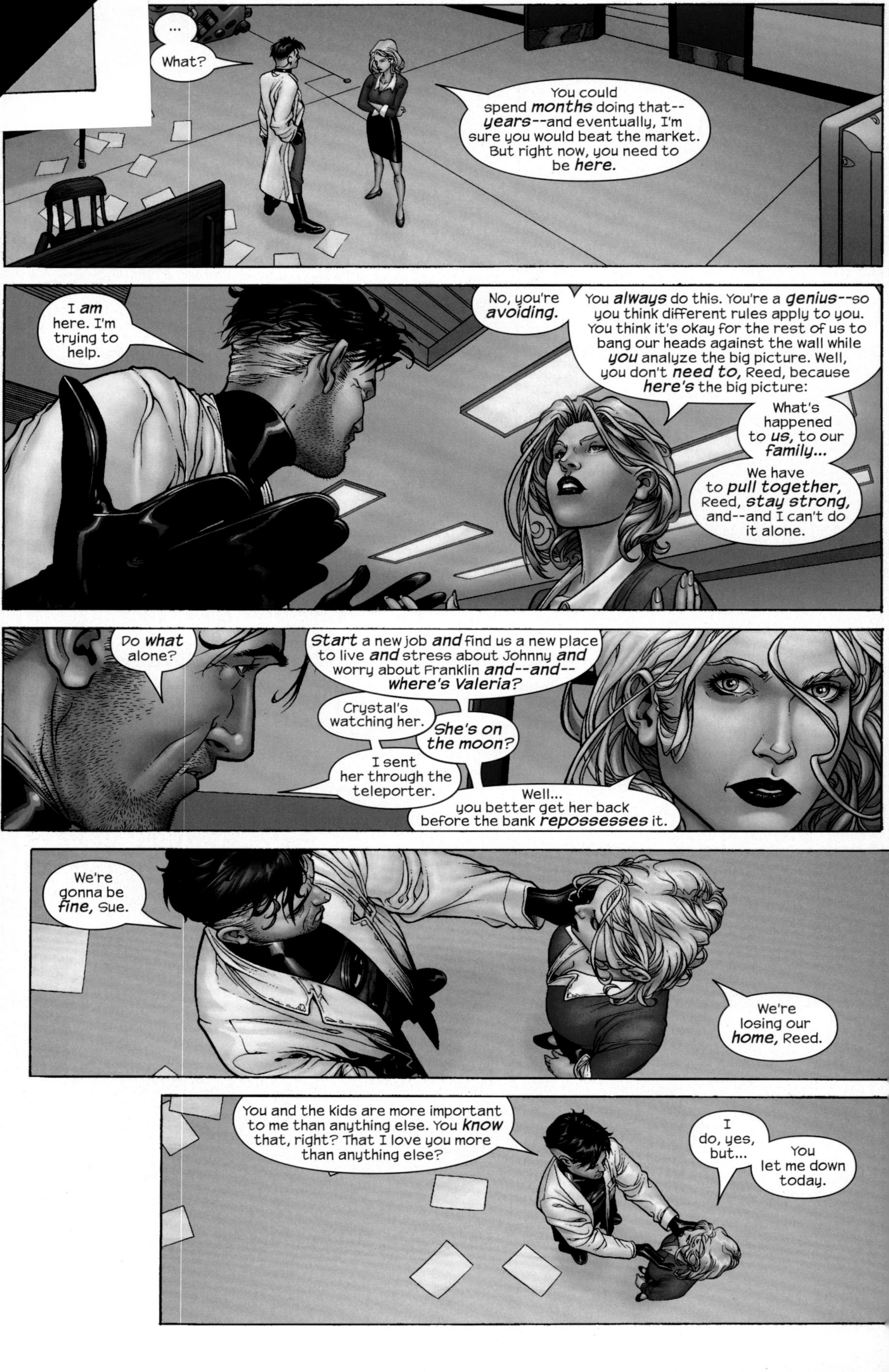
...
What?
You could spend months doing that--years--and eventually, I'm sure you would beat the market. But right now, you need to be here.
I am here. I'm trying to help.
No, you're avoiding.
You always do this. You're a genius--so you think different rules apply to you. You think it's okay for the rest of us to bang our heads against the wall while you analyze the big picture. Well, you don't need to, Reed, because here's the big picture:
What's happened to us, to our family...
We have to pull together, Reed, stay strong, and--and I can't do it alone.
Do what alone?
Start a new job and find us a new place to live and stress about Johnny and worry about Franklin and--and--where's Valeria?
Crystal's watching her.
She's on the moon?
I sent her through the teleporter.
Well... you better get her back before the bank repossesses it.
We're gonna be fine, Sue.
We're losing our home, Reed.
You and the kids are more important to me than anything else. You know that, right? That I love you more than anything else?
I do, yes, but...
You let me down today.

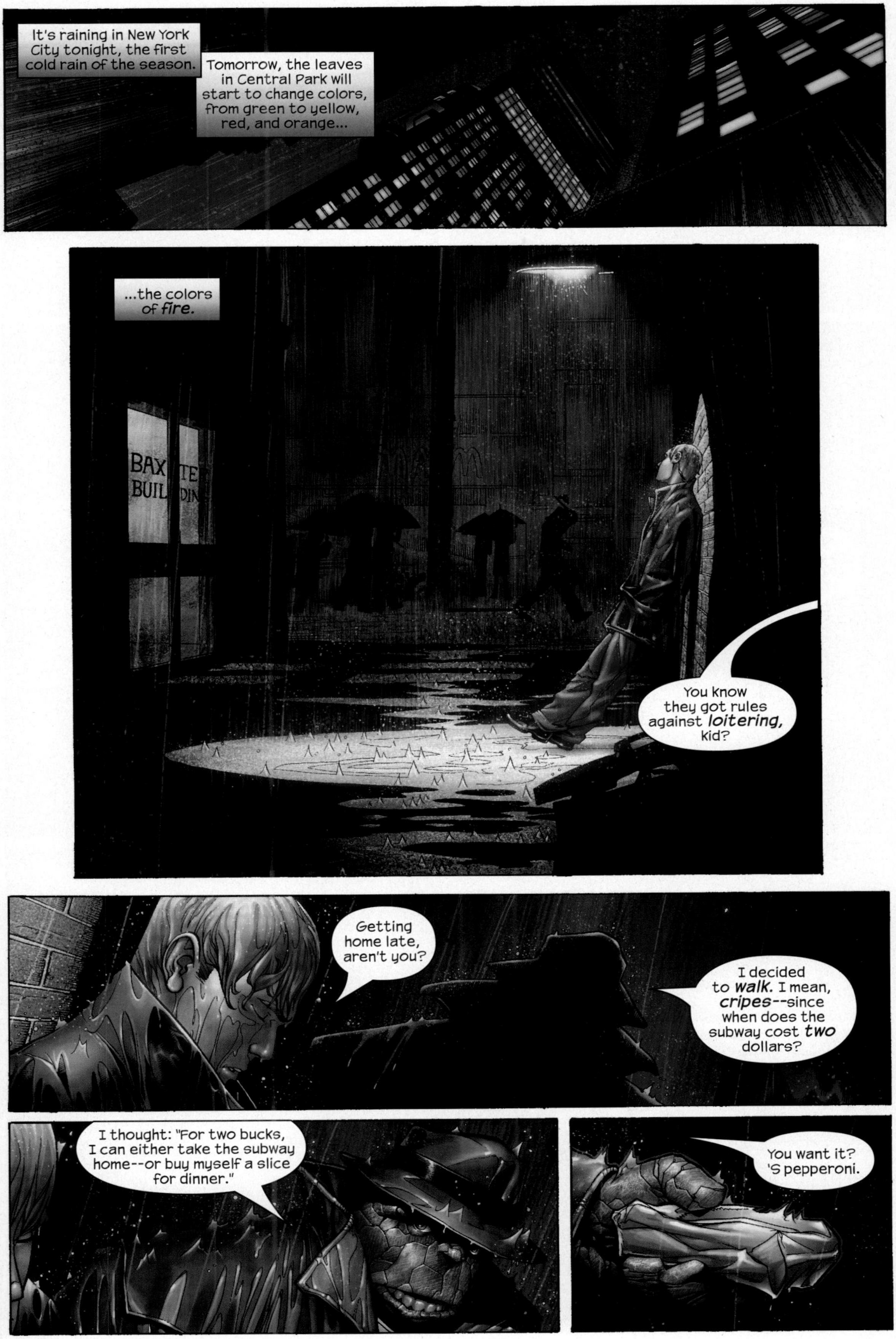
It's raining in New York City tonight, the first cold rain of the season.
Tomorrow, the leaves in Central Park will start to change colors, from green to yellow, red, and orange...
...the colors of *fire.*
BAX TE BUIL DIN
You know they got rules against *loitering,* kid?
Getting home late, aren't you?
I decided to *walk.* I mean, *cripes*--since when does the subway cost *two* dollars?
I thought: "For two bucks, I can either take the subway home--or buy myself a slice for dinner."
You want it? 'S pepperoni.

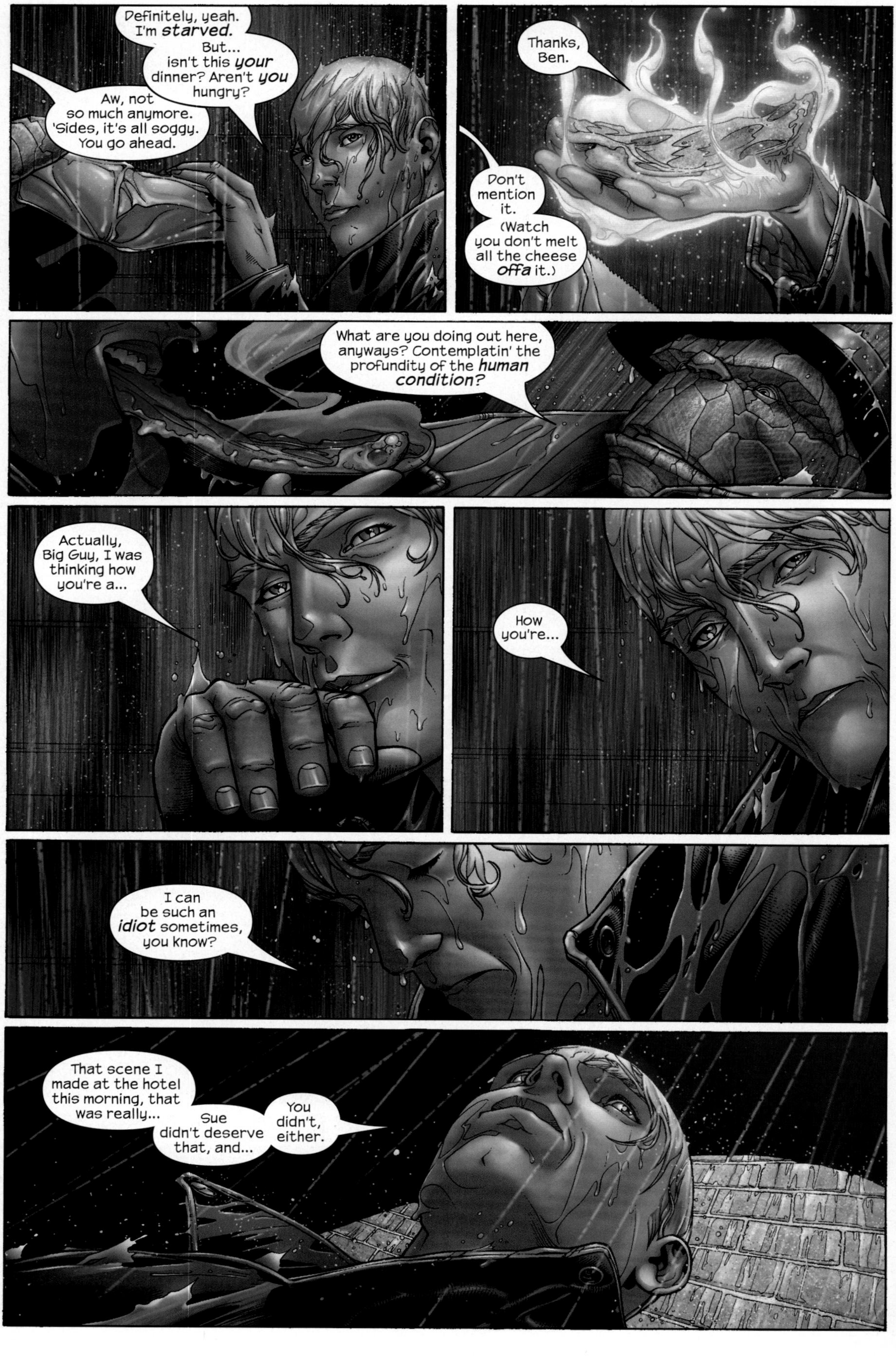

Definitely, yeah. I'm *starved.*
But... isn't this *your* dinner? Aren't *you* hungry?
Aw, not so much anymore. 'Sides, it's all soggy. You go ahead.
Thanks, Ben.
Don't mention it.
(Watch you don't melt all the cheese *offa* it.)
What are you doing out here, anyways? Contemplatin' the profundity of the *human condition?*
Actually, Big Guy, I was thinking how you're a...
How you're...
I can be such an *idiot* sometimes, you know?
That scene I made at the hotel this morning, that was really...
Sue didn't deserve that, and...
You didn't, either.

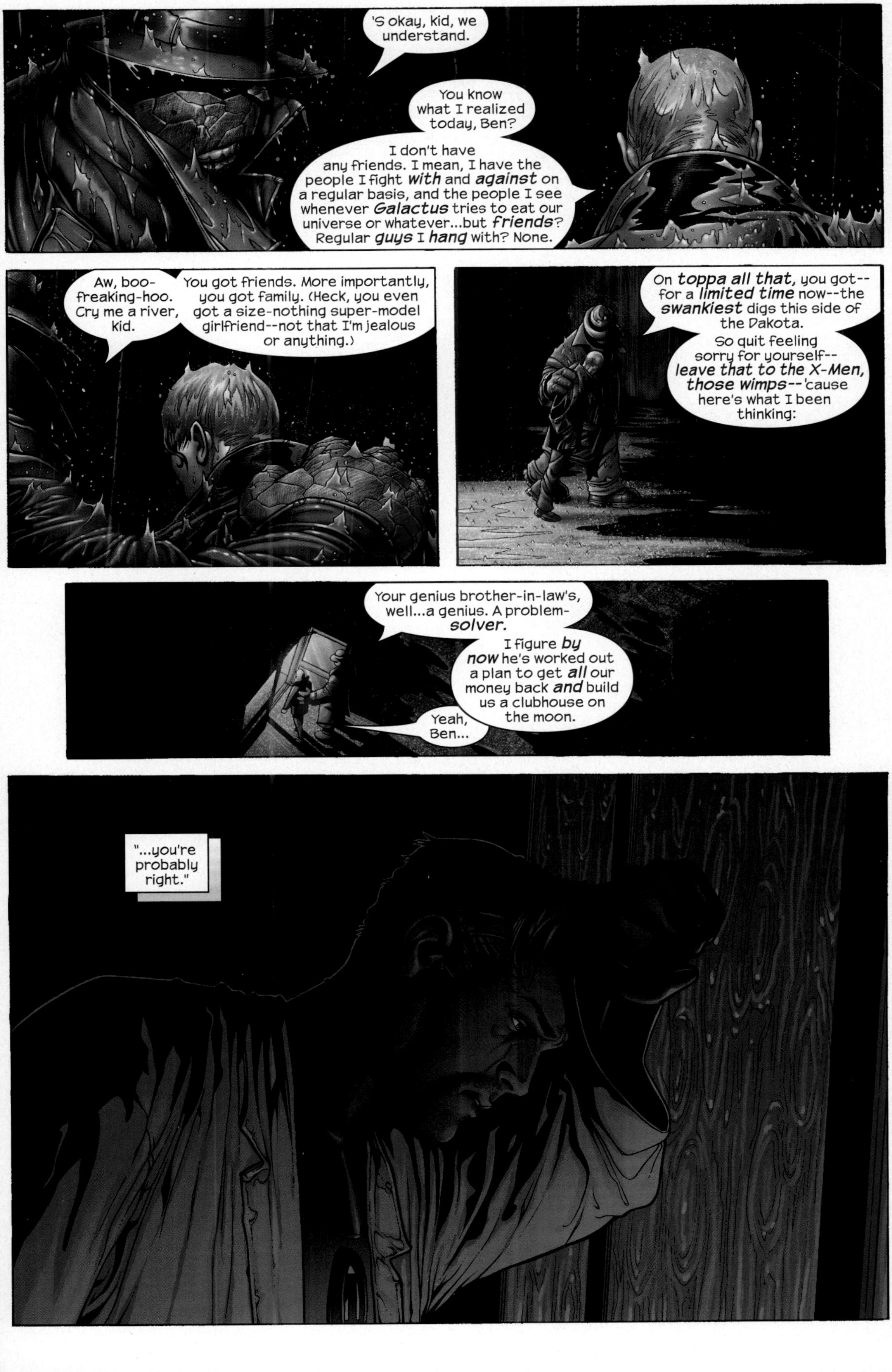
'S okay, kid, we understand.
You know what I realized today, Ben?
I don't have any friends. I mean, I have the people I fight with and against on a regular basis, and the people I see whenever Galactus tries to eat our universe or whatever...but friends? Regular guys I hang with? None.
Aw, boo-freaking-hoo. Cry me a river, kid.
You got friends. More importantly, you got family. (Heck, you even got a size-nothing super-model girlfriend--not that I'm jealous or anything.)
On toppa all that, you got--for a limited time now--the swankiest digs this side of the Dakota.
So quit feeling sorry for yourself--leave that to the X-Men, those wimps--'cause here's what I been thinking:
Your genius brother-in-law's, well...a genius. A problem-solver.
I figure by now he's worked out a plan to get all our money back and build us a clubhouse on the moon.
Yeah, Ben...
"...you're probably right."

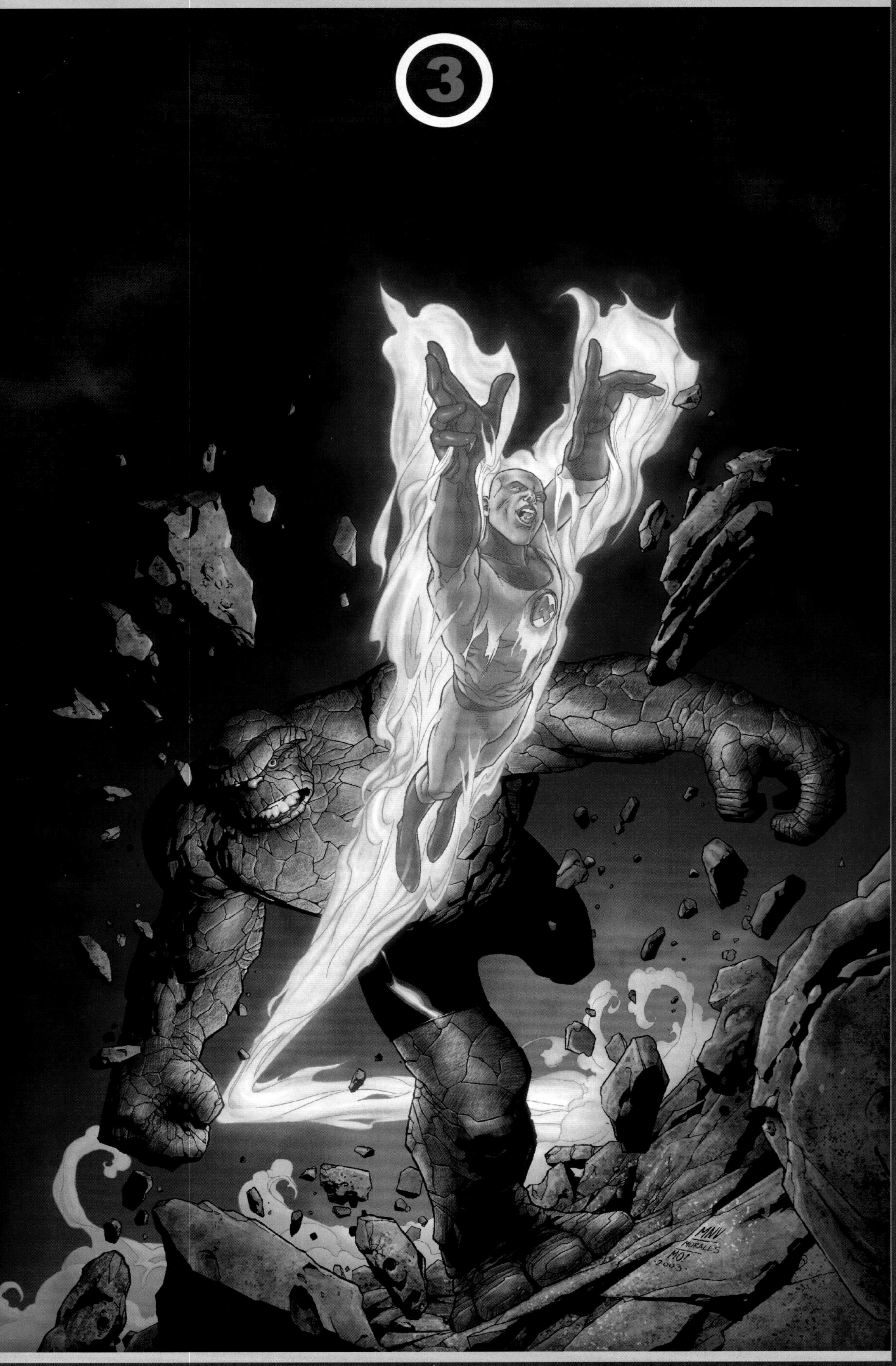
3

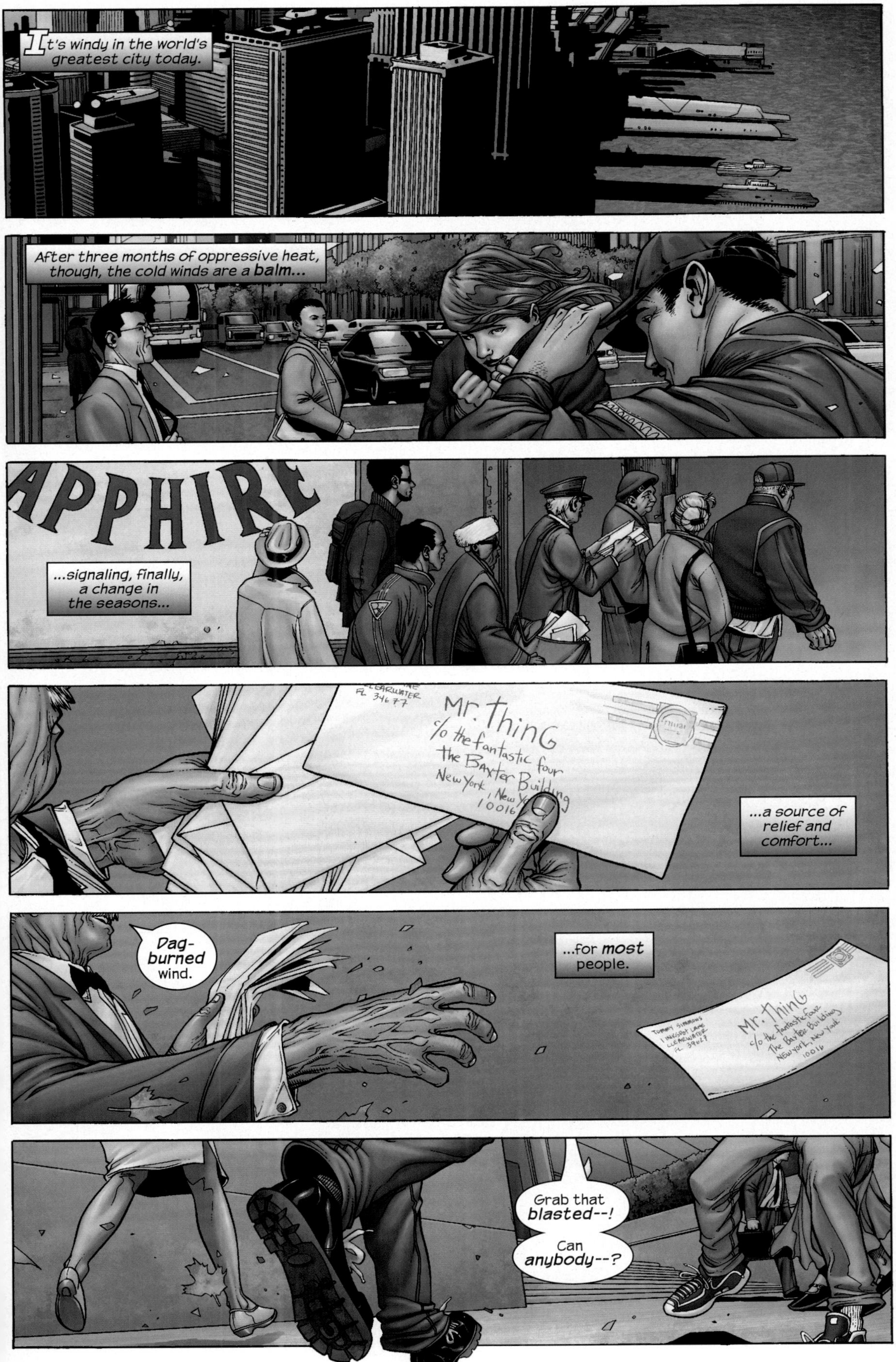
It's windy in the world's greatest city today.
After three months of oppressive heat, though, the cold winds are a balm...
APPHIRE
...signaling, finally, a change in the seasons...
Mr. Thing
c/o the fantastic four
the Baxter Building
New York, New York
10016
...a source of relief and comfort...
Dag-burned wind.
...for most people.
Mr. Thing
c/o the fantastic four
The Baxter Building
New York, New York
10016
Grab that blasted--!
Can anybody--?

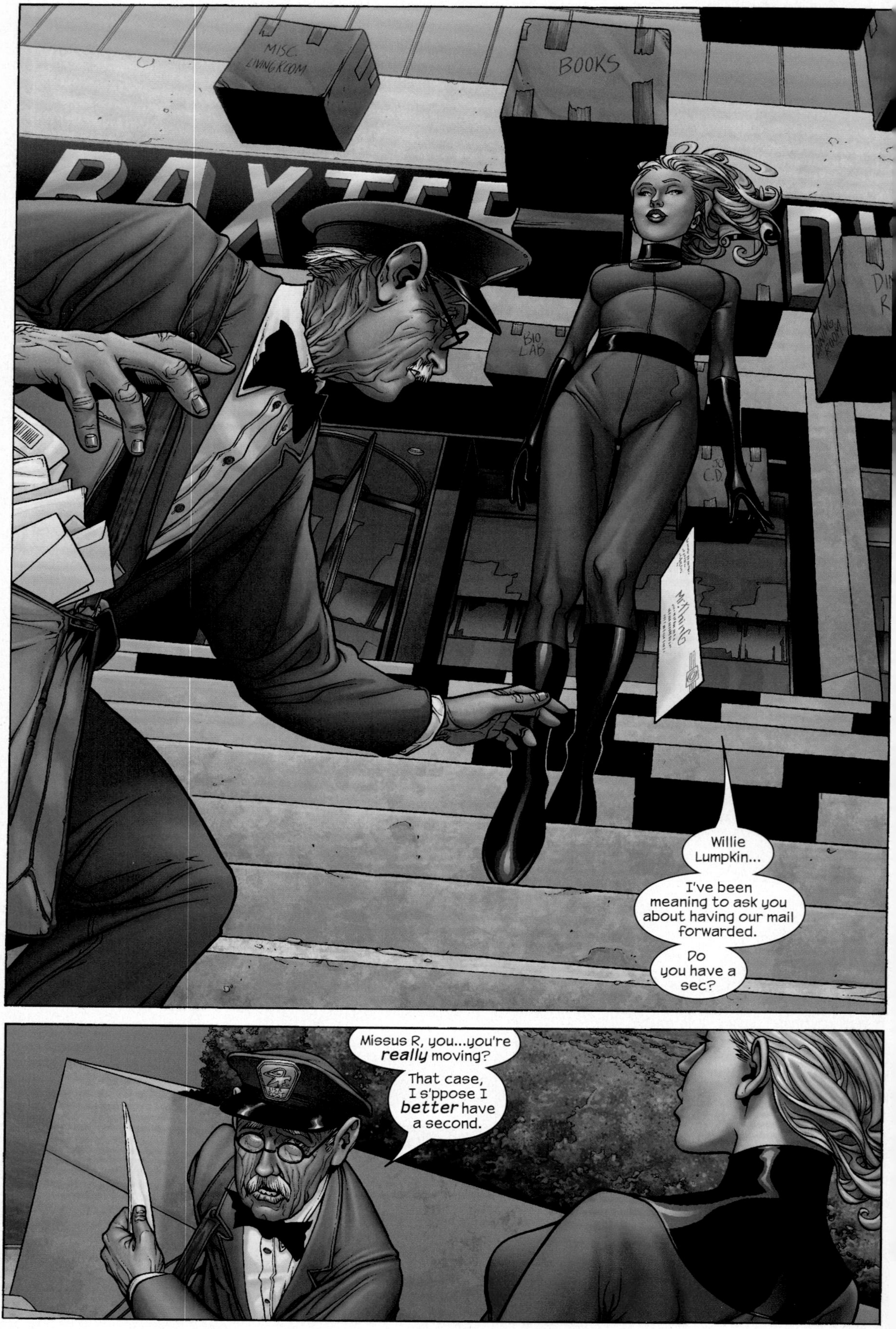

MISC. LIVINGROOM
BOOKS
BIO LAB
Willie Lumpkin...
I've been meaning to ask you about having our mail forwarded.
Do you have a sec?
Missus R, you...you're *really* moving?
That case, I s'ppose I *better* have a second.

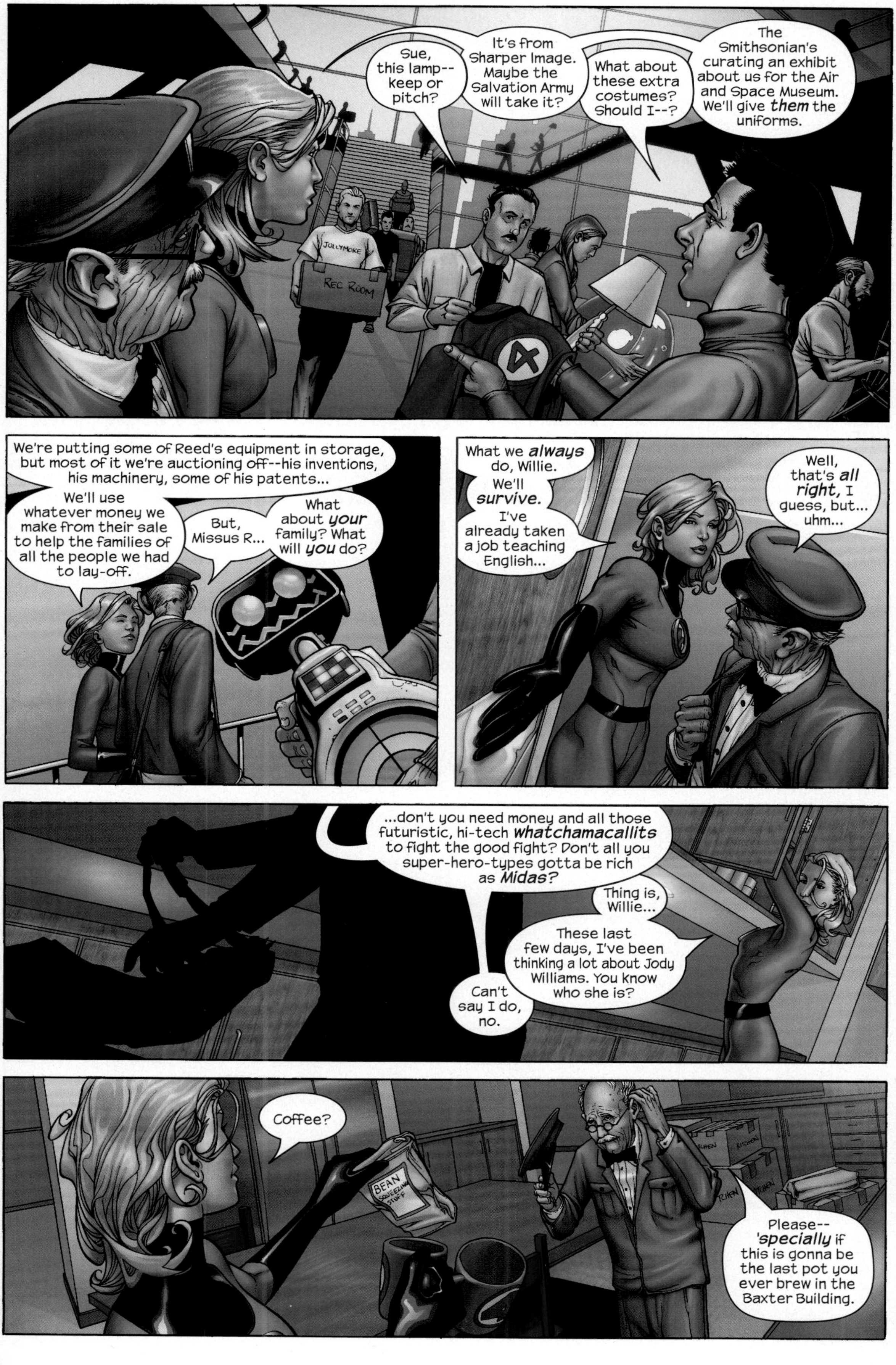
Sue, this lamp--keep or pitch?
It's from Sharper Image. Maybe the Salvation Army will take it?
What about these extra costumes? Should I--?
The Smithsonian's curating an exhibit about us for the Air and Space Museum. We'll give *them* the uniforms.
JOLLYMOKE
REC ROOM
We're putting some of Reed's equipment in storage, but most of it we're auctioning off--his inventions, his machinery, some of his patents...
We'll use whatever money we make from their sale to help the families of all the people we had to lay-off.
But, Missus R...
What about *your* family? What will *you* do?
What we *always* do, Willie.
We'll *survive.*
I've already taken a job teaching English...
Well, that's *all right,* I guess, but... uhm...
...don't you need money and all those futuristic, hi-tech *whatchamacallits* to fight the good fight? Don't all you super-hero-types gotta be rich as *Midas?*
Thing is, Willie...
These last few days, I've been thinking a lot about Jody Williams. You know who she is?
Can't say I do, no.
Coffee?
BEAN SQUEEZING STUFF
Please--*'specially* if this is gonna be the last pot you ever brew in the Baxter Building.

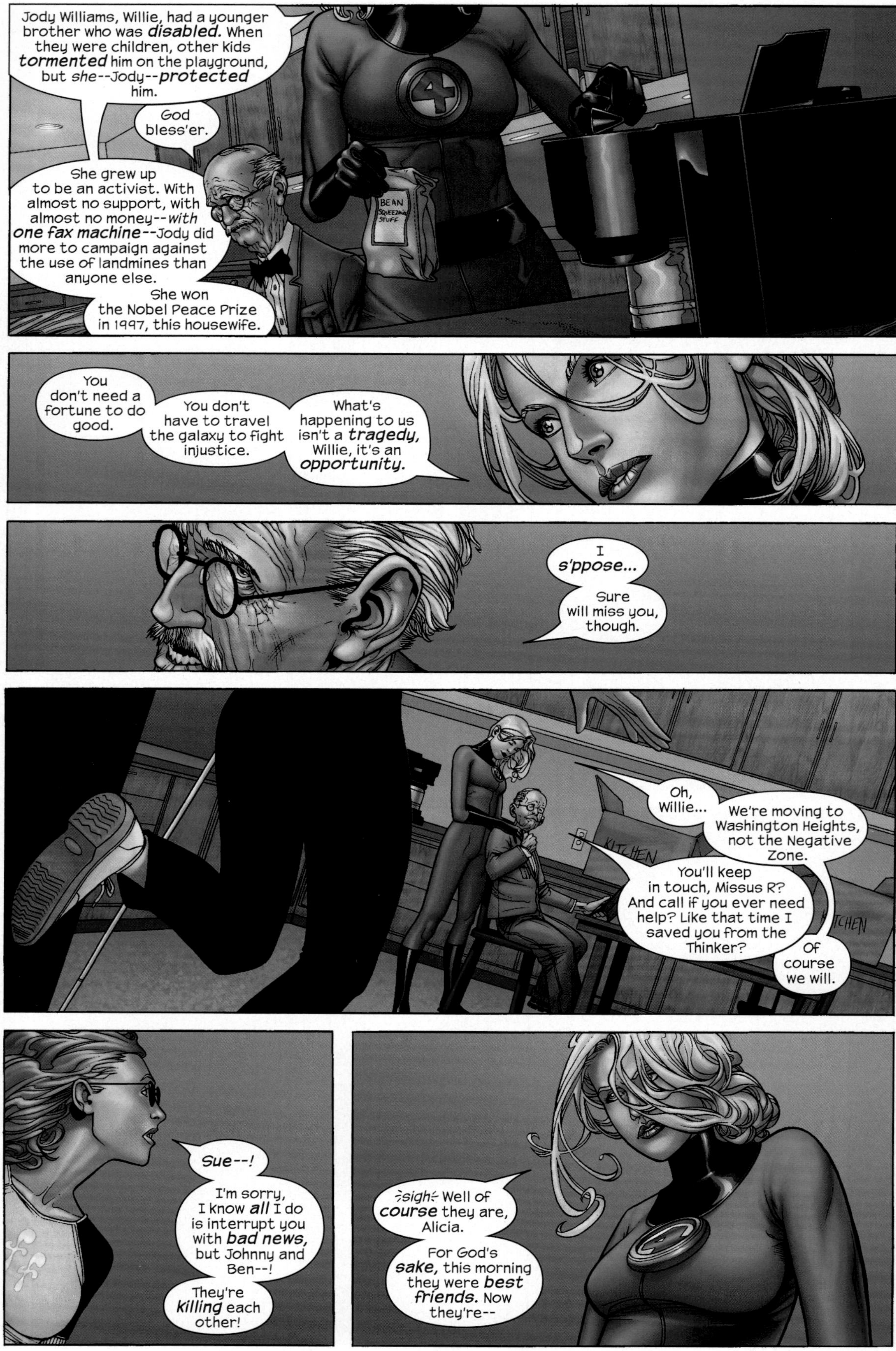

Jody Williams, Willie, had a younger brother who was disabled. When they were children, other kids tormented him on the playground, but she--Jody--protected him.
God bless'er.
She grew up to be an activist. With almost no support, with almost no money--with one fax machine--Jody did more to campaign against the use of landmines than anyone else.
She won the Nobel Peace Prize in 1997, this housewife.
BEAN SQUEEZING STUFF
You don't need a fortune to do good.
You don't have to travel the galaxy to fight injustice.
What's happening to us isn't a tragedy, Willie, it's an opportunity.
I s'ppose...
Sure will miss you, though.
Oh, Willie...
We're moving to Washington Heights, not the Negative Zone.
You'll keep in touch, Missus R? And call if you ever need help? Like that time I saved you from the Thinker?
Of course we will.
KITCHEN
KITCHEN
Sue--!
I'm sorry, I know all I do is interrupt you with bad news, but Johnny and Ben--!
They're killing each other!
sigh Well of course they are, Alicia.
For God's sake, this morning they were best friends. Now they're--

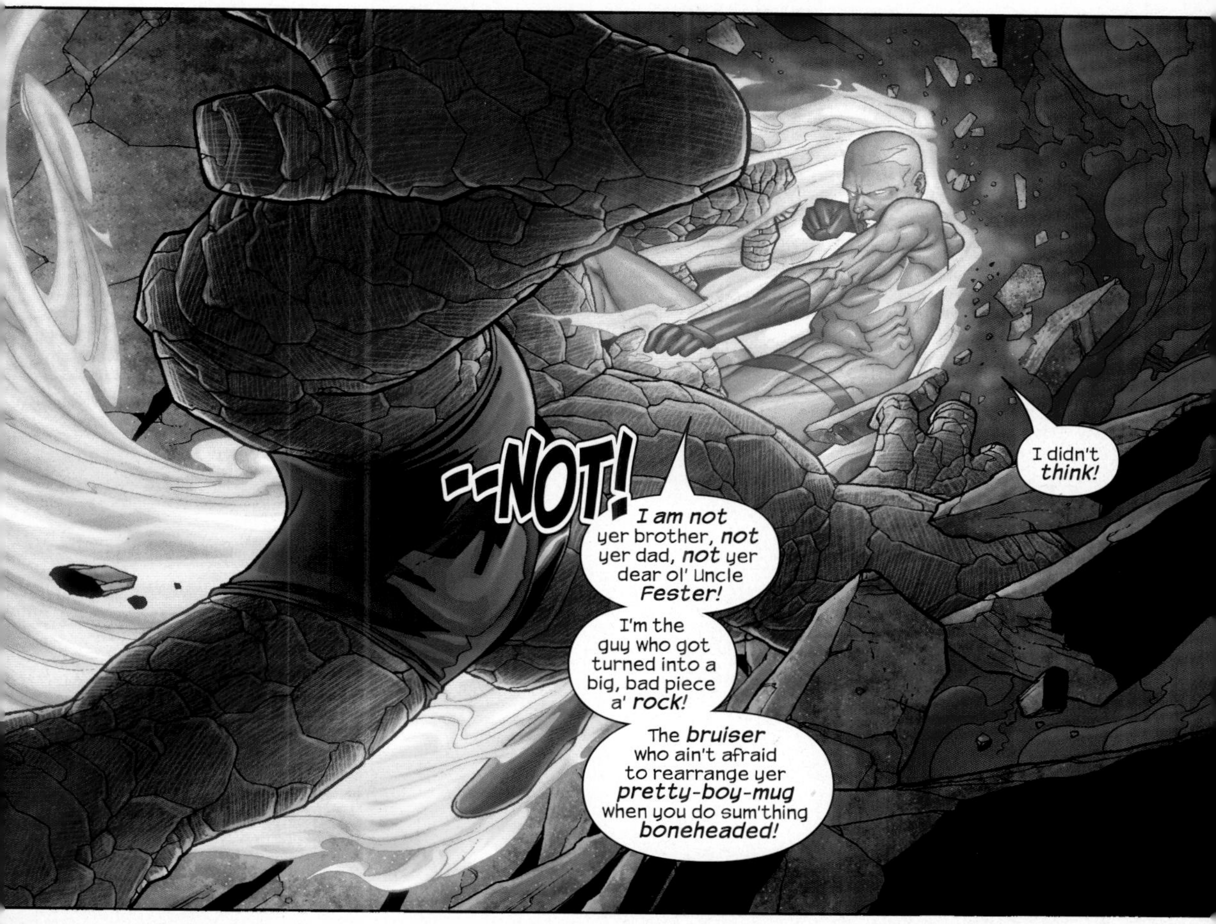
--NOT!
I am not yer brother, not yer dad, not yer dear ol' Uncle Fester!
I'm the guy who got turned into a big, bad piece a' rock!
The bruiser who ain't afraid to rearrange yer pretty-boy-mug when you do sum'thing boneheaded!
I didn't think!

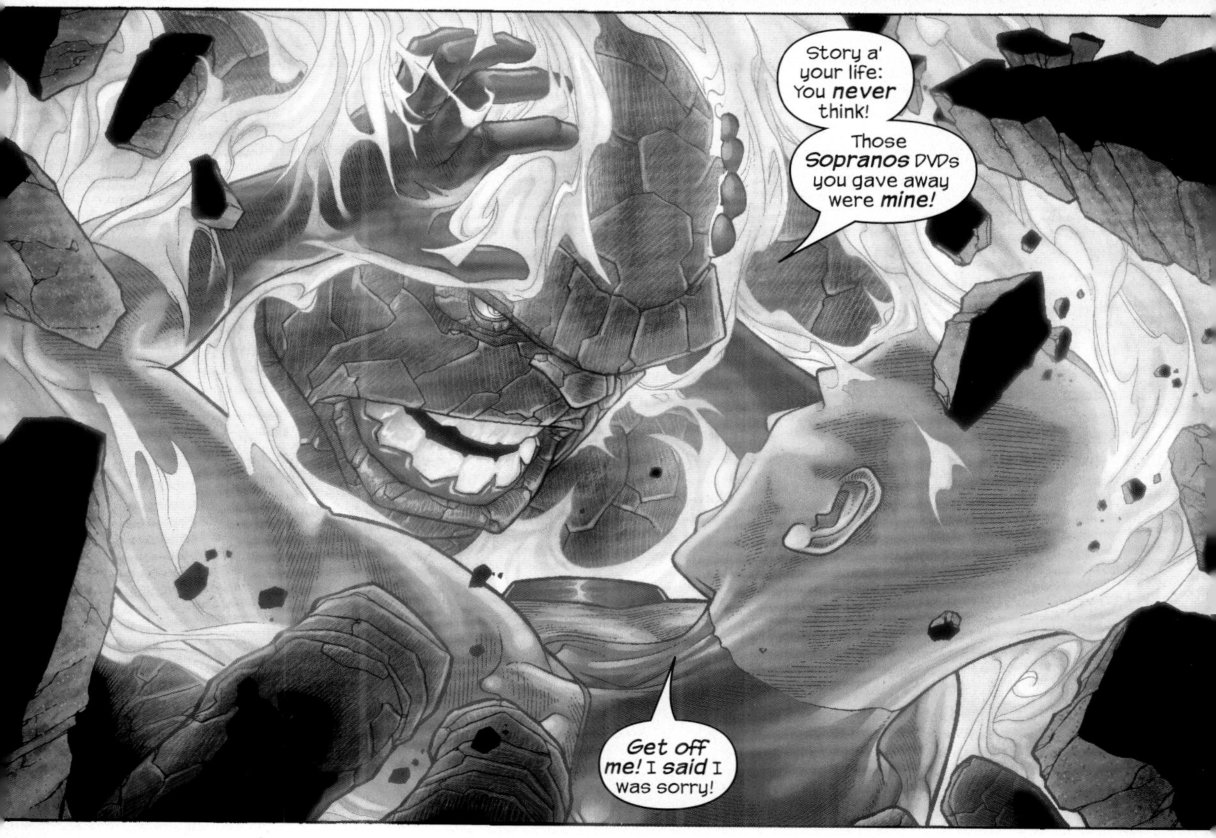
Story a' your life: You never think!
Those Sopranos DVDs you gave away were mine!
Get off me! I said I was sorry!

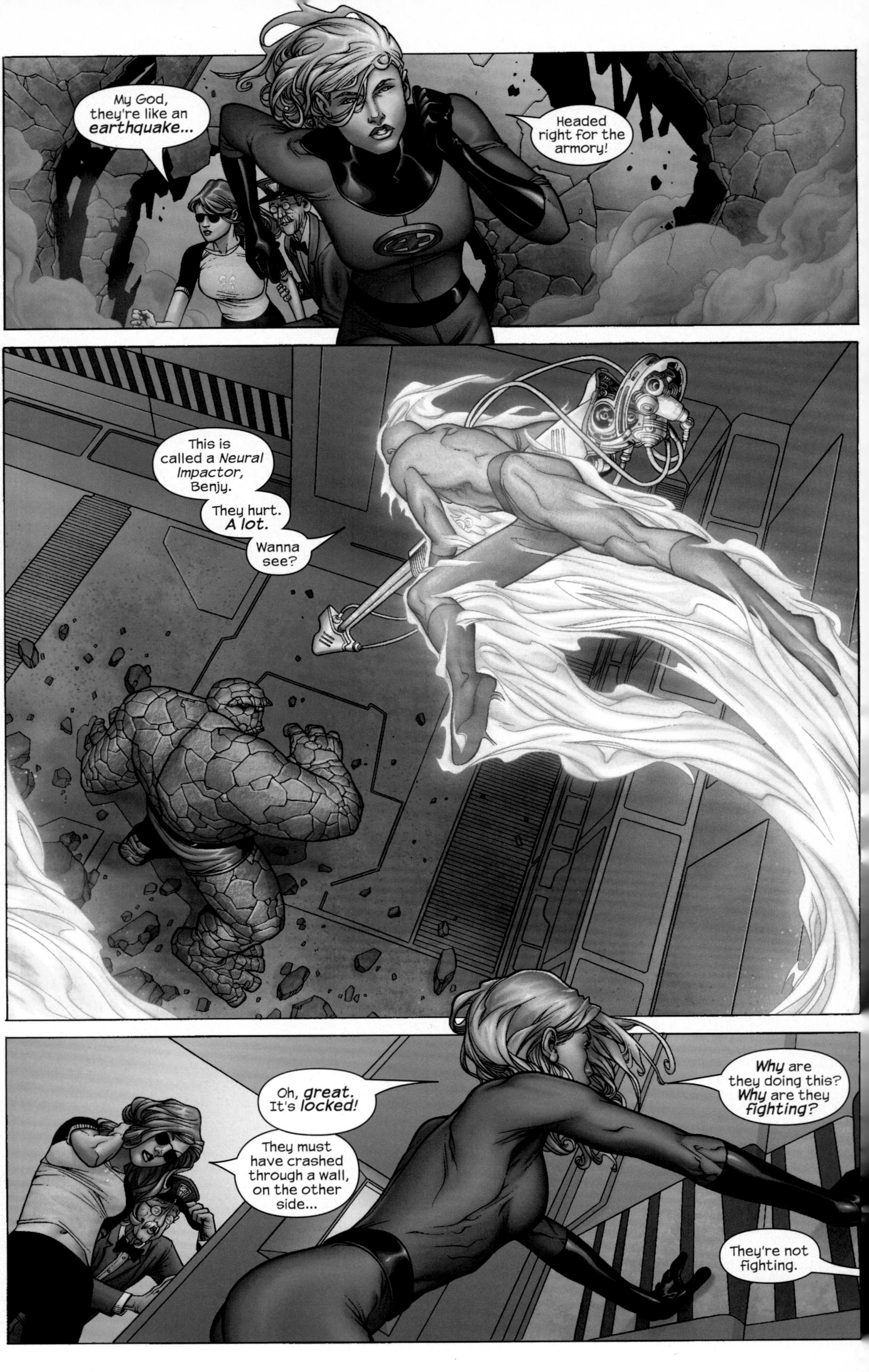
My God, they're like an *earthquake...*
Headed right for the armory!
This is called a *Neural Impactor,* Benjy.
They hurt. ***A lot.***
Wanna see?
Oh, ***great.*** It's ***locked!***
They must have crashed through a wall, on the other side...
Why are they doing this? ***Why*** are they ***fighting?***
They're not fighting.

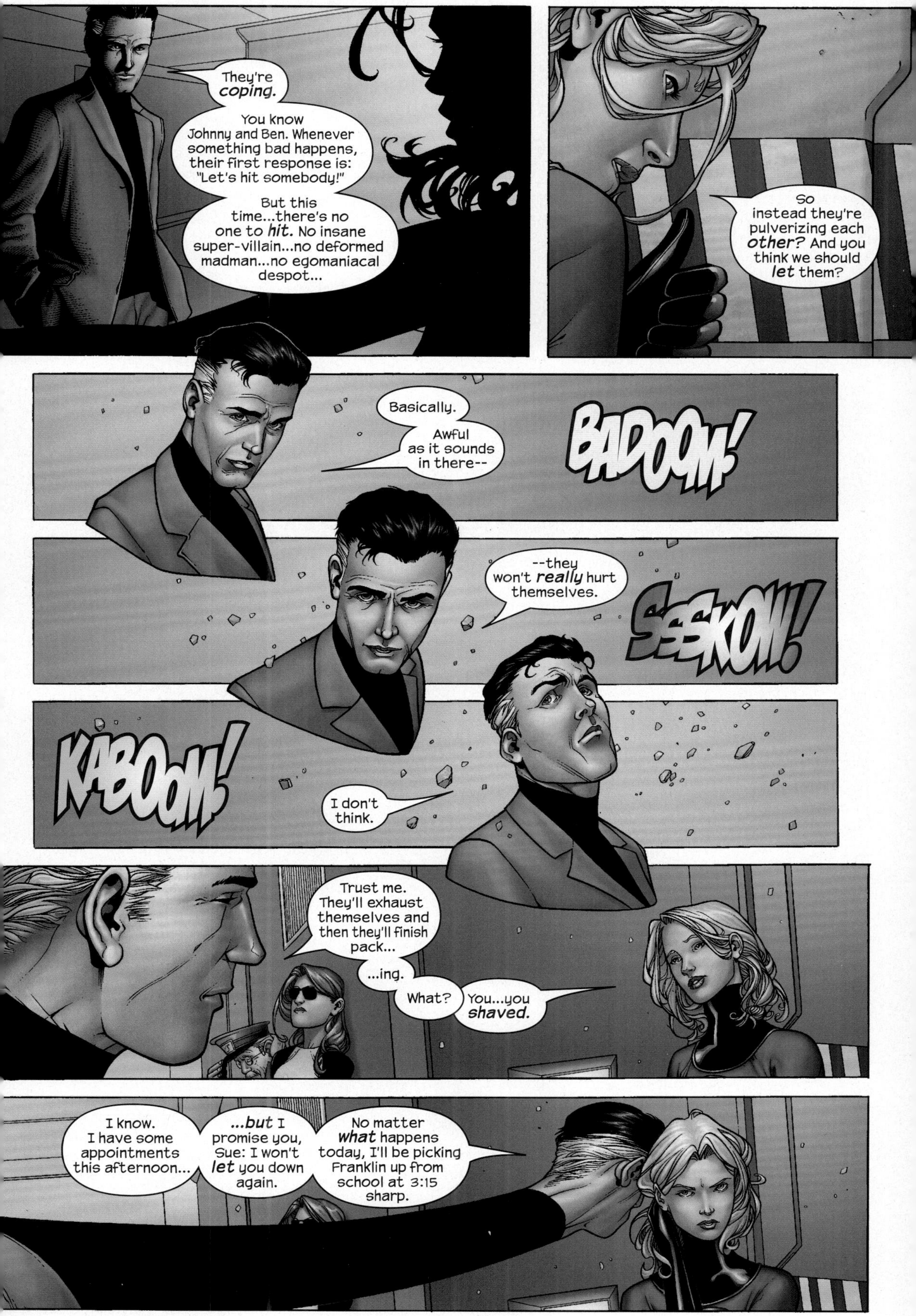
They're coping.
You know Johnny and Ben. Whenever something bad happens, their first response is: "Let's hit somebody!"
But this time...there's no one to hit. No insane super-villain...no deformed madman...no egomaniacal despot...
So instead they're pulverizing each other? And you think we should let them?
Basically.
Awful as it sounds in there--
BADOOM!
--they won't really hurt themselves.
SSSKOW!
KABOOM!
I don't think.
Trust me. They'll exhaust themselves and then they'll finish pack...
...ing.
What?
You...you shaved.
I know. I have some appointments this afternoon...
...but I promise you, Sue: I won't let you down again.
No matter what happens today, I'll be picking Franklin up from school at 3:15 sharp.

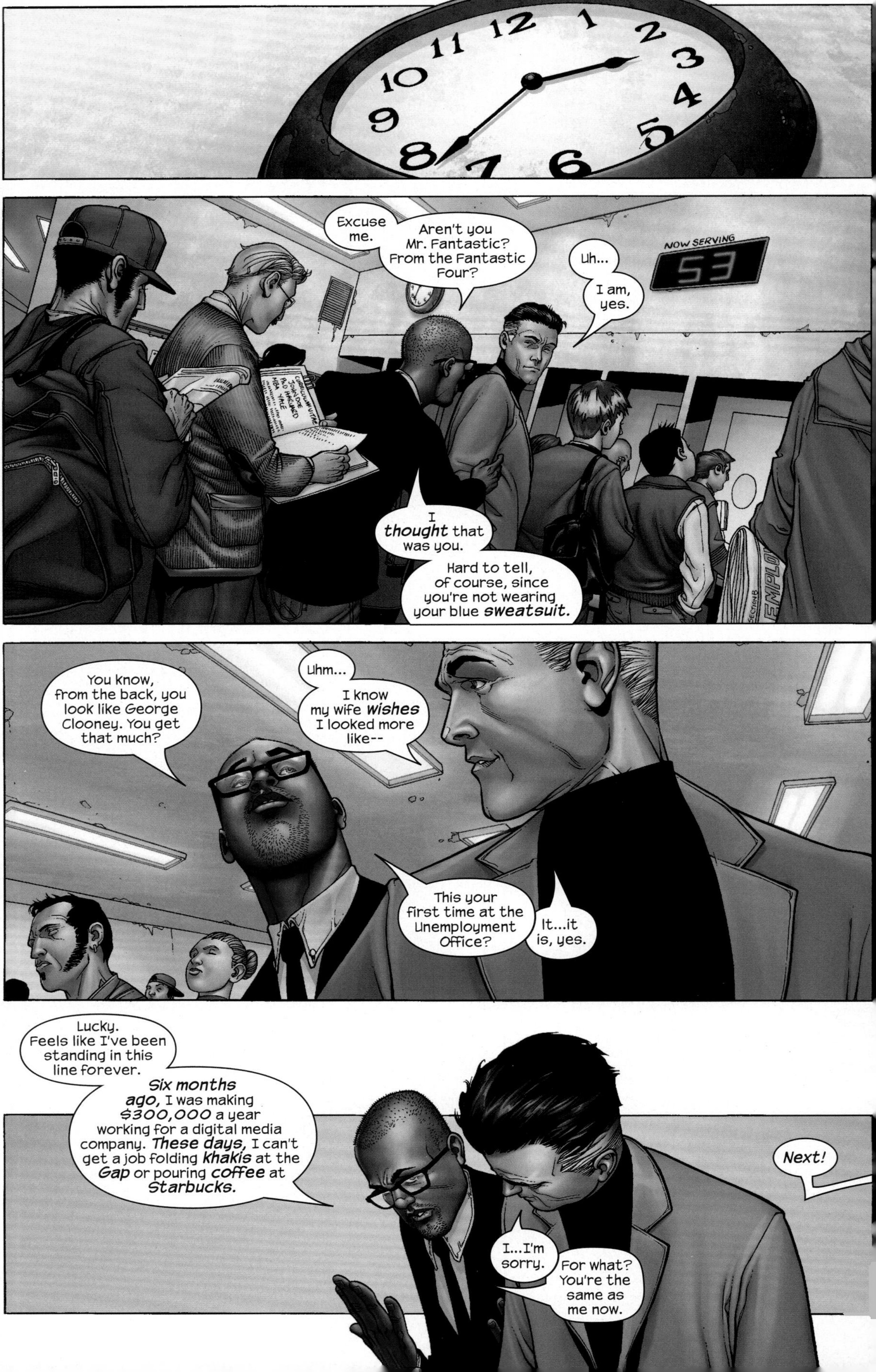

NOW SERVING
53
Excuse me.
Aren't you Mr. Fantastic? From the Fantastic Four?
Uh...
I am, yes.
I *thought* that was you.
Hard to tell, of course, since you're not wearing your blue *sweatsuit.*
You know, from the back, you look like George Clooney. You get that much?
Uhm...
I know my wife *wishes* I looked more like--
This your first time at the Unemployment Office?
It...it is, yes.
Lucky. Feels like I've been standing in this line forever.
Six months ago, I was making *$300,000* a year working for a digital media company. *These days,* I can't get a job folding *khakis* at the *Gap* or pouring *coffee* at *Starbucks.*
Next!
I...I'm sorry.
For what? You're the same as me now.

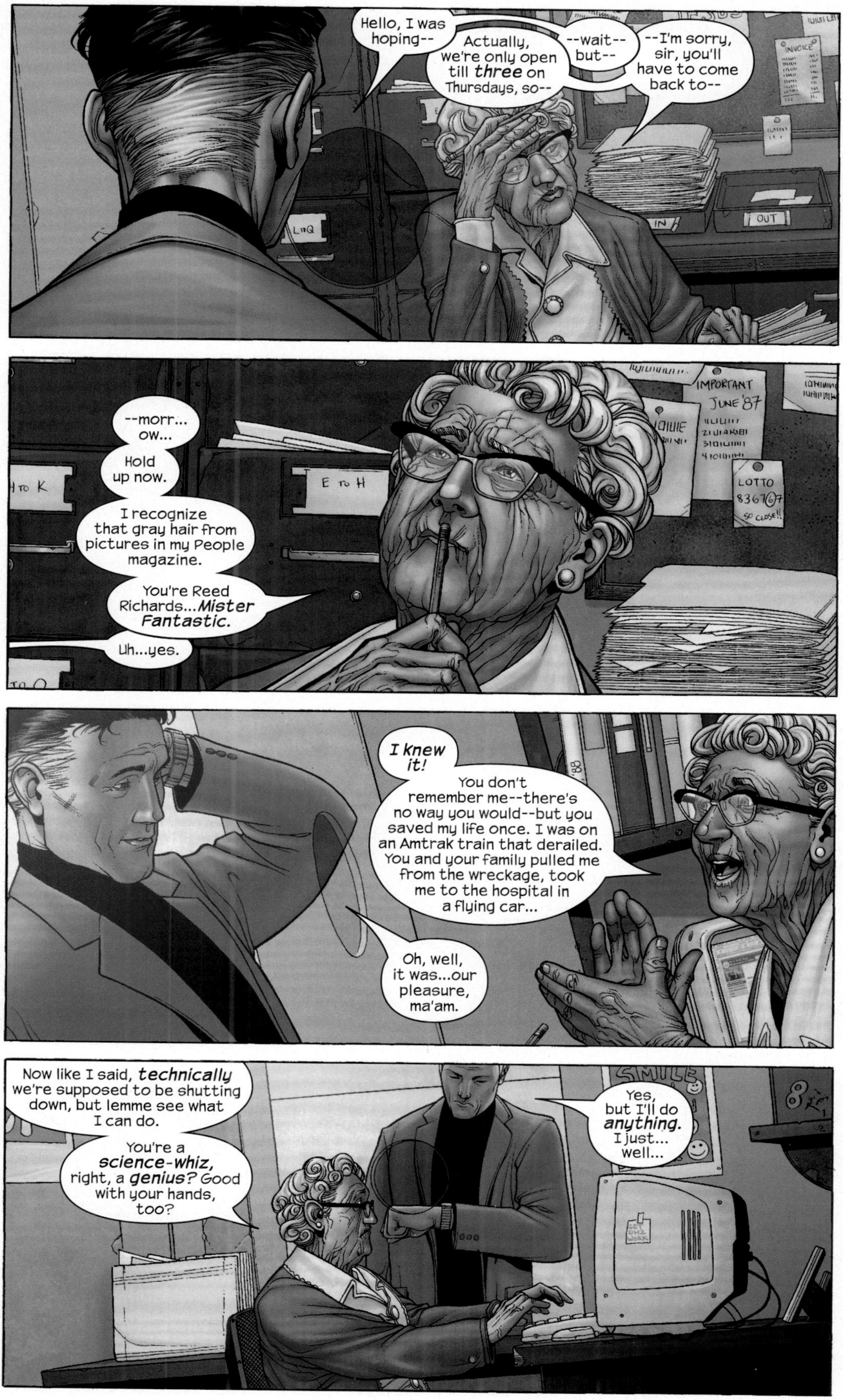

Hello, I was hoping--
Actually, we're only open till *three* on Thursdays, so--
--wait-- but--
--I'm sorry, sir, you'll have to come back to--
INVOICE
IN
OUT
--morr... ow...
Hold up now.
I recognize that gray hair from pictures in my People magazine.
You're Reed Richards...***Mister Fantastic.***
Uh...yes.
H TO K
E TO H
IMPORTANT JUNE '87
LOTTO 8367(6)7 SO CLOSE!!
I knew it!
You don't remember me--there's no way you would--but you saved my life once. I was on an Amtrak train that derailed. You and your family pulled me from the wreckage, took me to the hospital in a flying car...
Oh, well, it was...our pleasure, ma'am.
Now like I said, ***technically*** we're supposed to be shutting down, but lemme see what I can do.
You're a ***science-whiz,*** right, a ***genius?*** Good with your hands, too?
Yes, but I'll do ***anything.*** I just... well...
SMILE

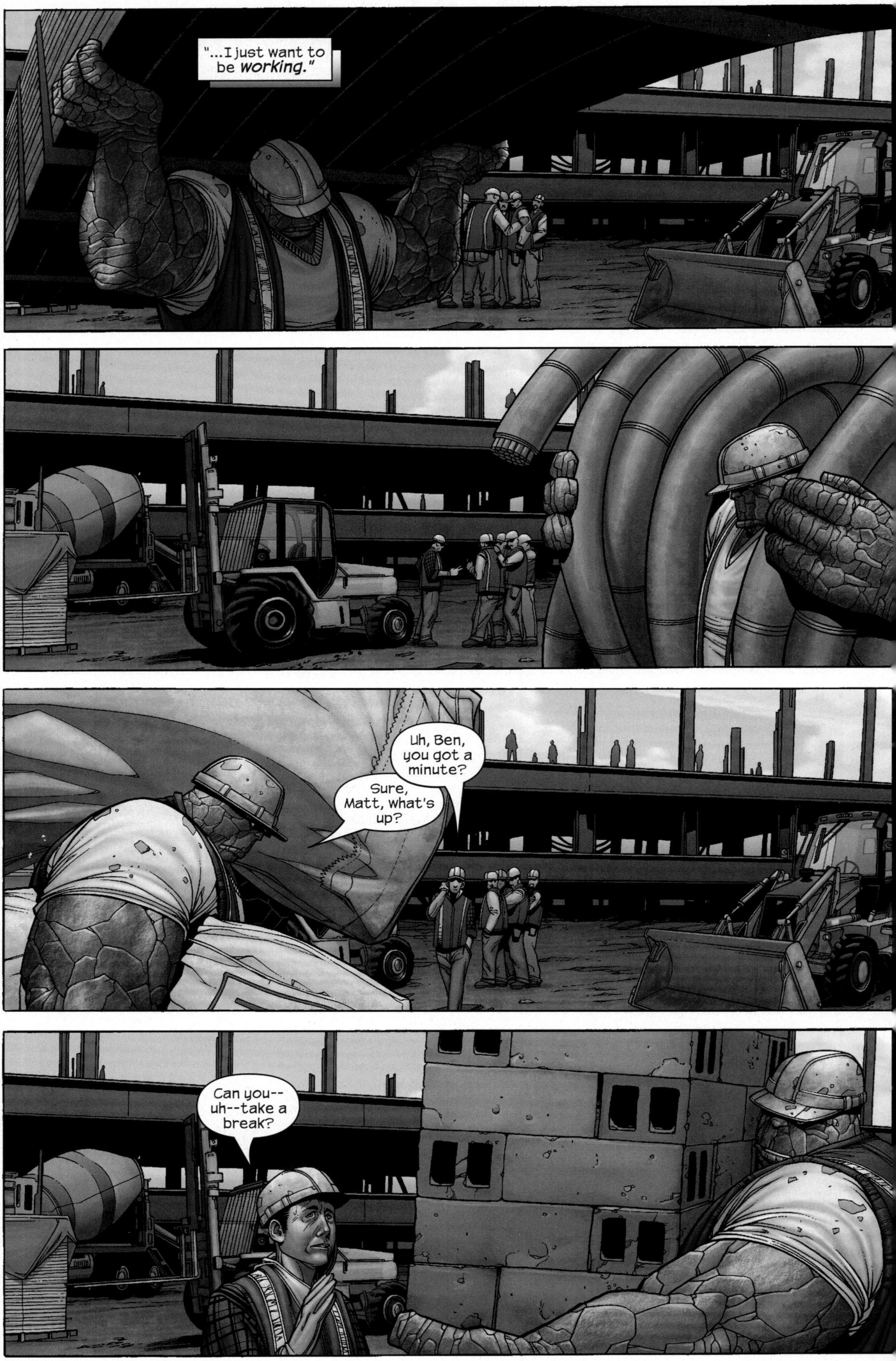
"...I just want to be *working*."
Uh, Ben, you got a minute?
Sure, Matt, what's up?
Can you--uh--take a break?

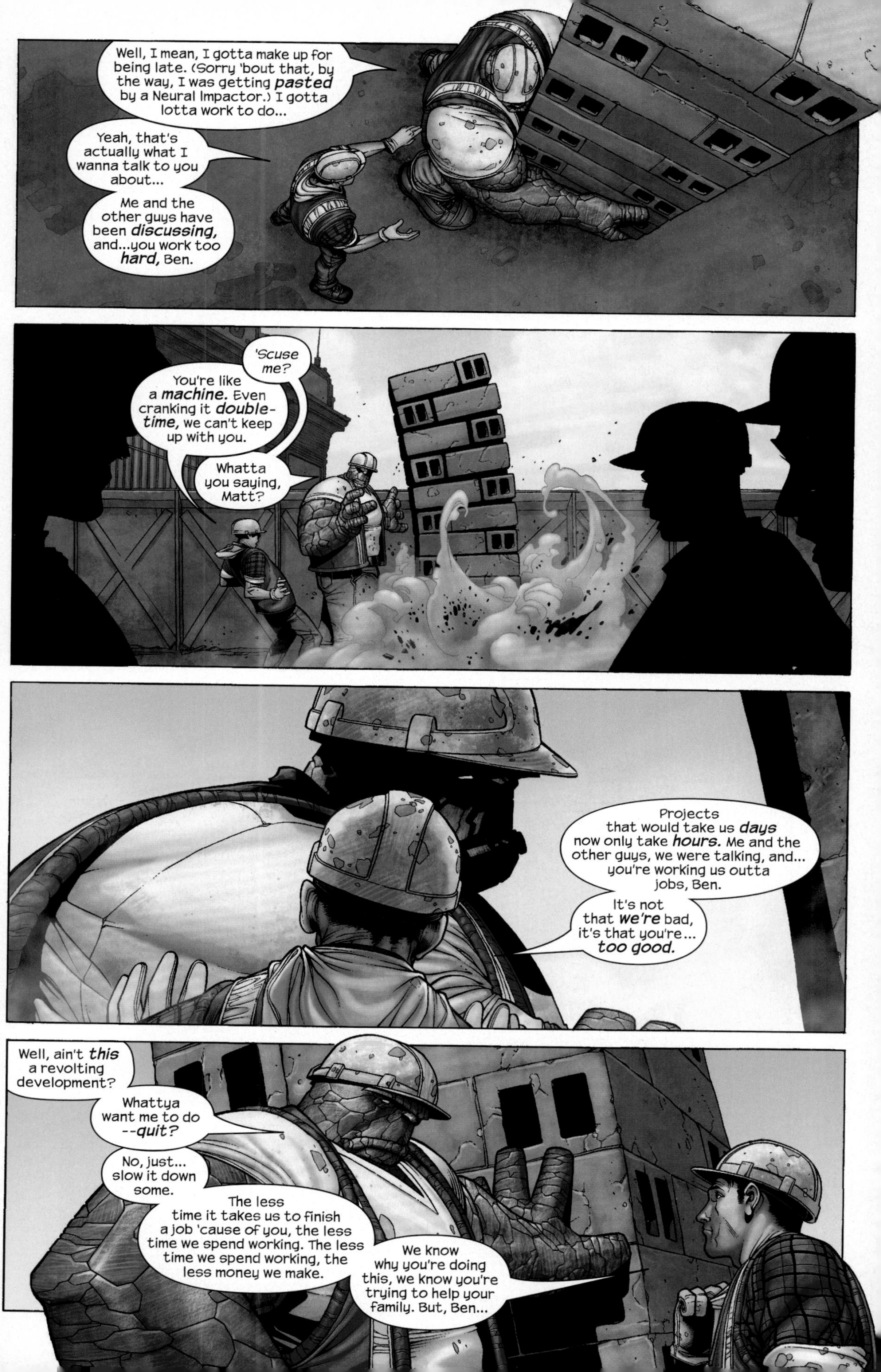
Well, I mean, I gotta make up for being late. (Sorry 'bout that, by the way, I was getting *pasted* by a Neural Impactor.) I gotta lotta work to do...
Yeah, that's actually what I wanna talk to you about...
Me and the other guys have been *discussing,* and...you work too *hard,* Ben.
'Scuse me?
You're like a *machine.* Even cranking it *double-time,* we can't keep up with you.
Whatta you saying, Matt?
Projects that would take us *days* now only take *hours.* Me and the other guys, we were talking, and... you're working us outta jobs, Ben.
It's not that *we're* bad, it's that you're... *too good.*
Well, ain't *this* a revolting development?
Whattya want me to do --*quit?*
No, just... slow it down some.
The less time it takes us to finish a job 'cause of you, the less time we spend working. The less time we spend working, the less money we make.
We know why you're doing this, we know you're trying to help your family. But, Ben...

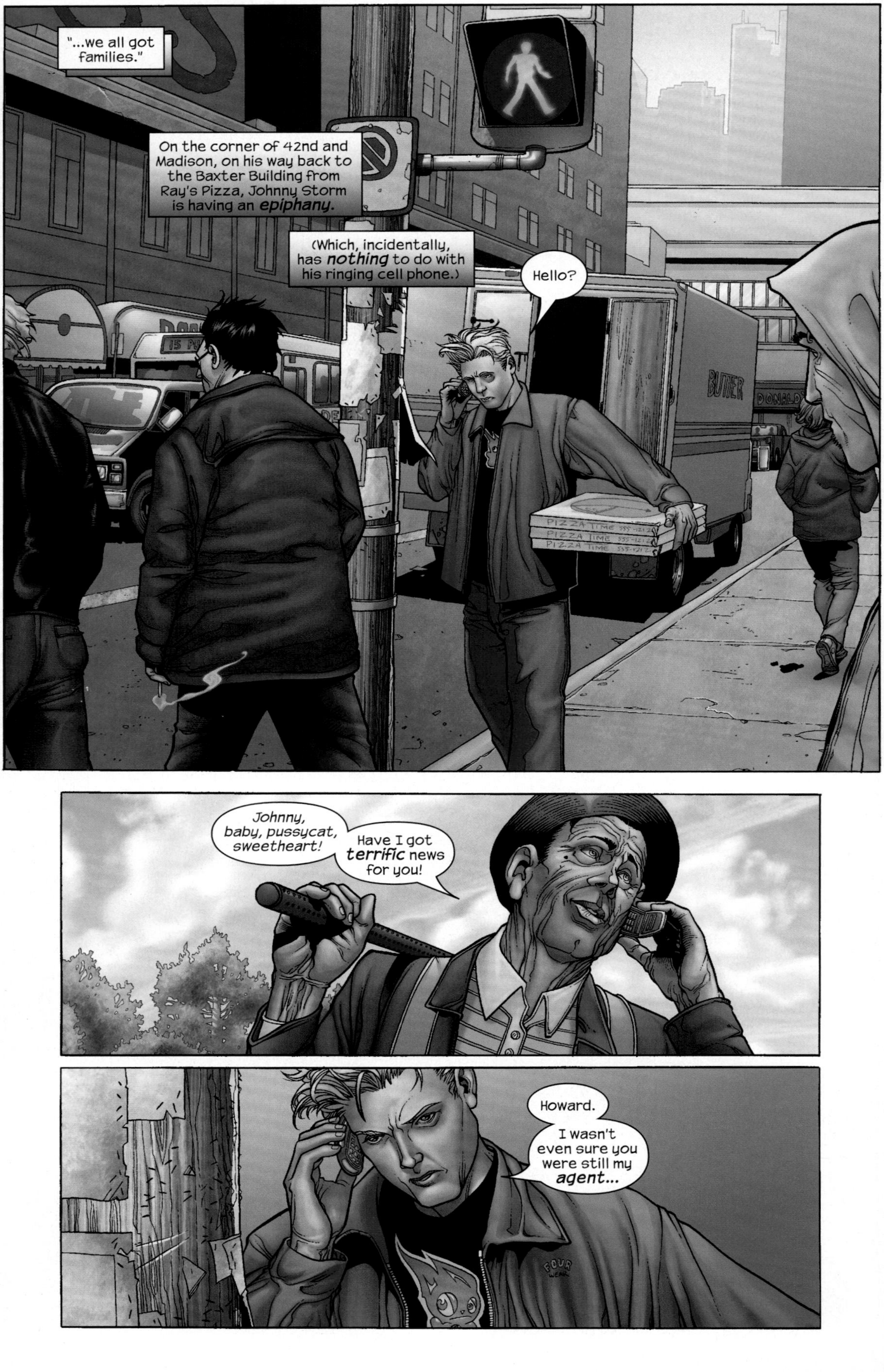
"...we all got families."
On the corner of 42nd and Madison, on his way back to the Baxter Building from Ray's Pizza, Johnny Storm is having an *epiphany.*
(Which, incidentally, has *nothing* to do with his ringing cell phone.)
Hello?
Johnny, baby, pussycat, sweetheart!
Have I got *terrific* news for you!
Howard.
I wasn't even sure you were still my *agent...*

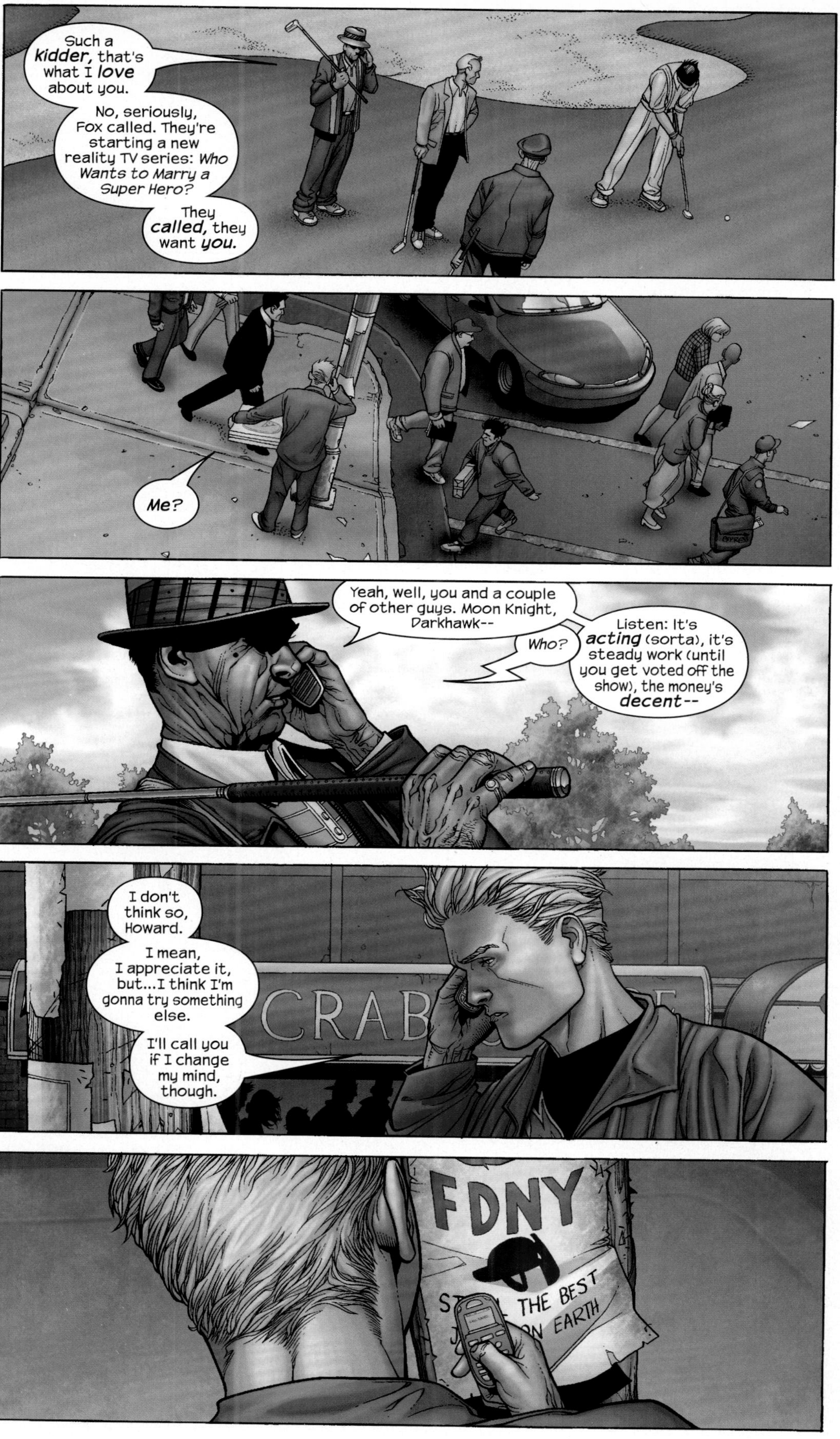

Such a *kidder,* that's what I *love* about you.
No, seriously, Fox called. They're starting a new reality TV series: *Who Wants to Marry a Super Hero?*
They *called,* they want *you.*
Me?
Yeah, well, you and a couple of other guys. Moon Knight, Darkhawk--
Who?
Listen: It's *acting* (sorta), it's steady work (until you get voted off the show), the money's *decent*--
I don't think so, Howard.
I mean, I appreciate it, but...I think I'm gonna try something else.
I'll call you if I change my mind, though.
FDNY

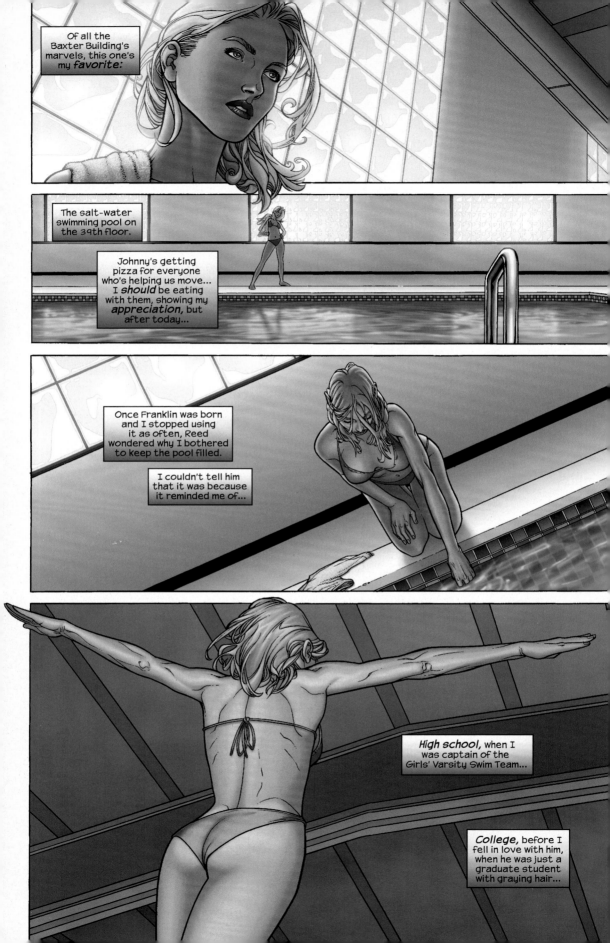

Of all the Baxter Building's marvels, this one's *favorite*:

The salt-water swimming pool on the 39th floor.

Johnny's getting pizza for everyone who's helping us move... I *should* be eating with them, showing my *appreciation*, but after today...

Once Franklin was born and I stopped using it as often, Reed wondered why I bothered to keep the pool filled.

I couldn't tell him that it was because it reminded me of...

High school, when I was captain of the Girls' Varsity Swim Team...

College, before I fell in love with him, when he was just a graduate student with graying hair...

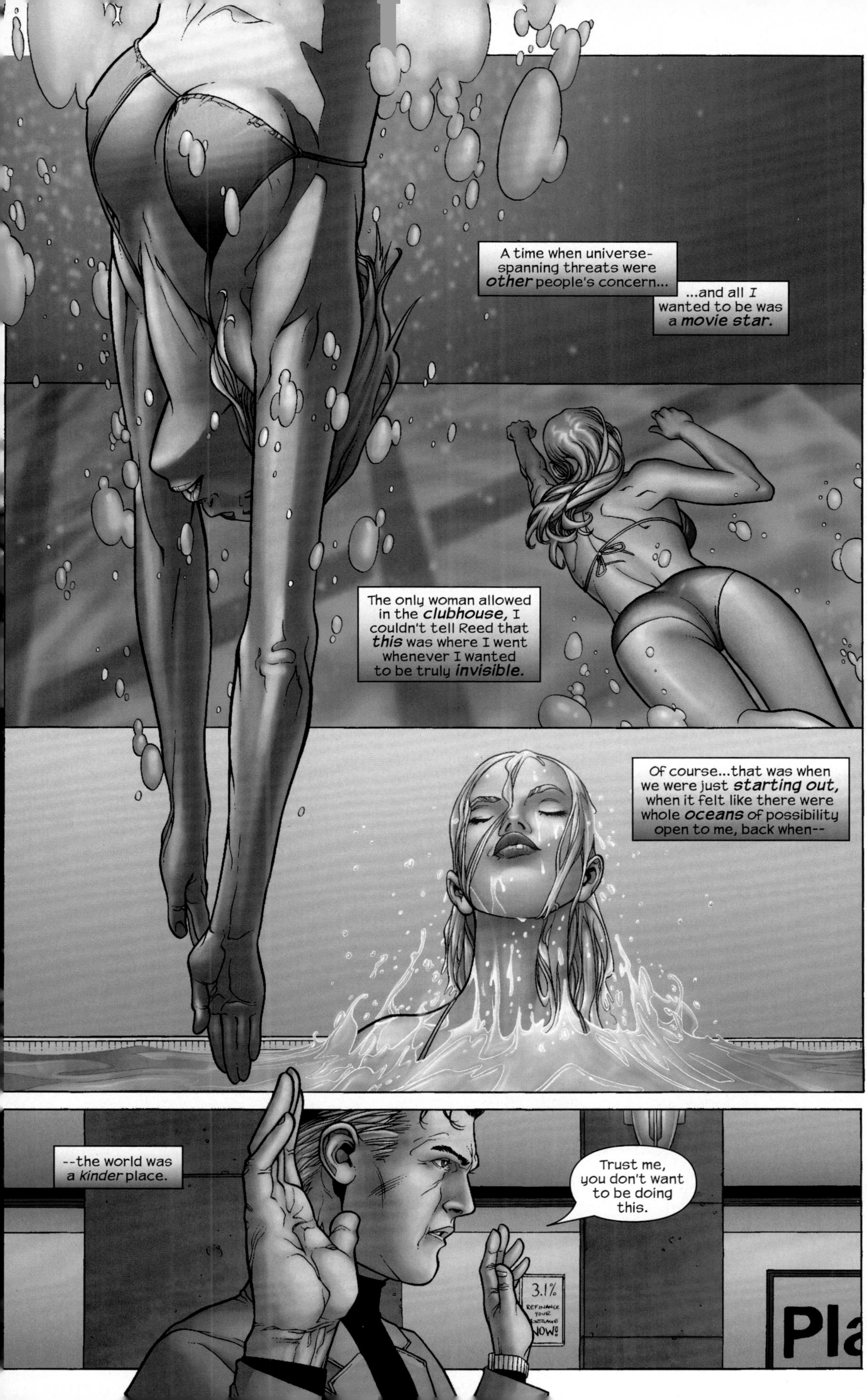
A time when universe-spanning threats were *other* people's concern...
...and all *I* wanted to be was a *movie star.*
The only woman allowed in the *clubhouse,* I couldn't tell Reed that *this* was where I went whenever I wanted to be truly *invisible.*
Of course...that was when we were just *starting out,* when it felt like there were whole *oceans* of possibility open to me, back when--
--the world was a *kinder* place.
Trust me, you don't want to be doing this.
3.1%
NOW!
Pla

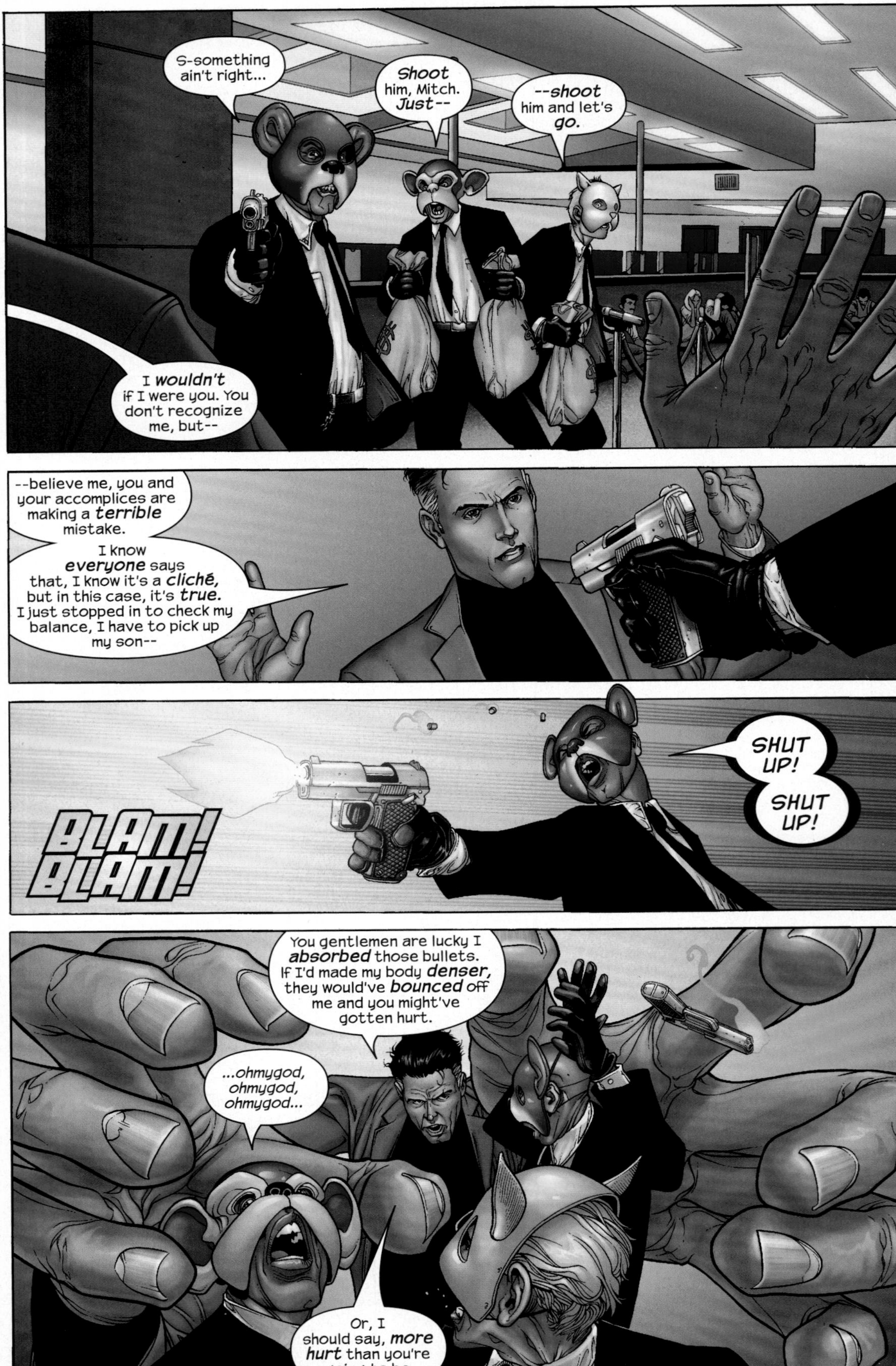
S-something ain't right...
Shoot him, Mitch. Just--
--shoot him and let's go.
I wouldn't if I were you. You don't recognize me, but--
--believe me, you and your accomplices are making a terrible mistake.
I know everyone says that, I know it's a cliché, but in this case, it's true. I just stopped in to check my balance, I have to pick up my son--
BLAM! BLAM!
SHUT UP!
SHUT UP!
You gentlemen are lucky I absorbed those bullets. If I'd made my body denser, they would've bounced off me and you might've gotten hurt.
...ohmygod, ohmygod, ohmygod...
Or, I should say, more hurt than you're going to be.

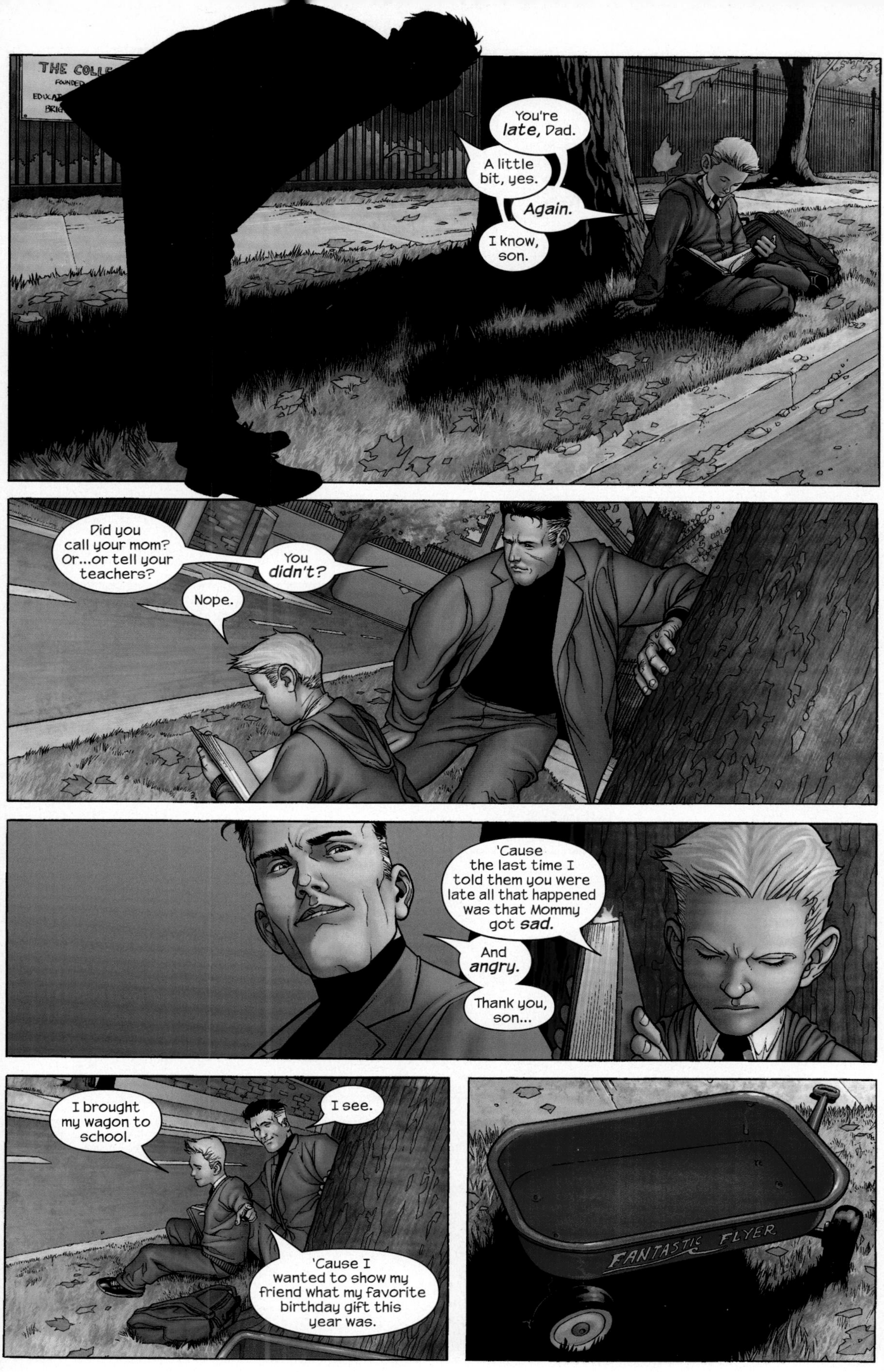

You're *late,* Dad.
A little bit, yes.
Again.
I know, son.
Did you call your mom? Or...or tell your teachers?
Nope.
You *didn't?*
'Cause the last time I told them you were late all that happened was that Mommy got *sad.*
And *angry.*
Thank you, son...
I brought my wagon to school.
I see.
'Cause I wanted to show my friend what my favorite birthday gift this year was.
FANTASTIC FLYER

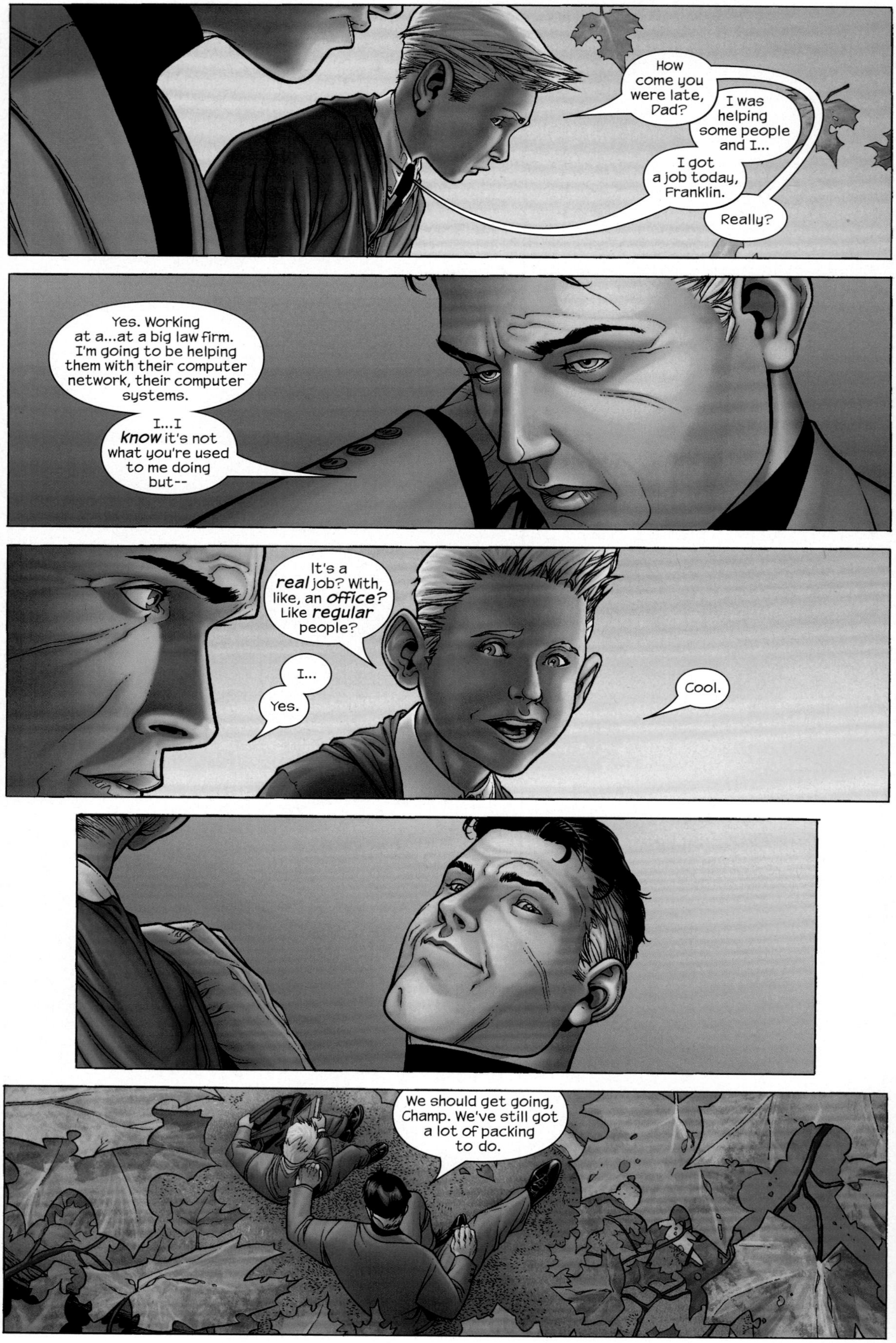
How come you were late, Dad?
I was helping some people and I...
I got a job today, Franklin.
Really?
Yes. Working at a...at a big law firm. I'm going to be helping them with their computer network, their computer systems.
I...I ***know*** it's not what you're used to me doing but--
It's a ***real*** job? With, like, an ***office***? Like ***regular*** people?
I...
Yes.
Cool.
We should get going, Champ. We've still got a lot of packing to do.

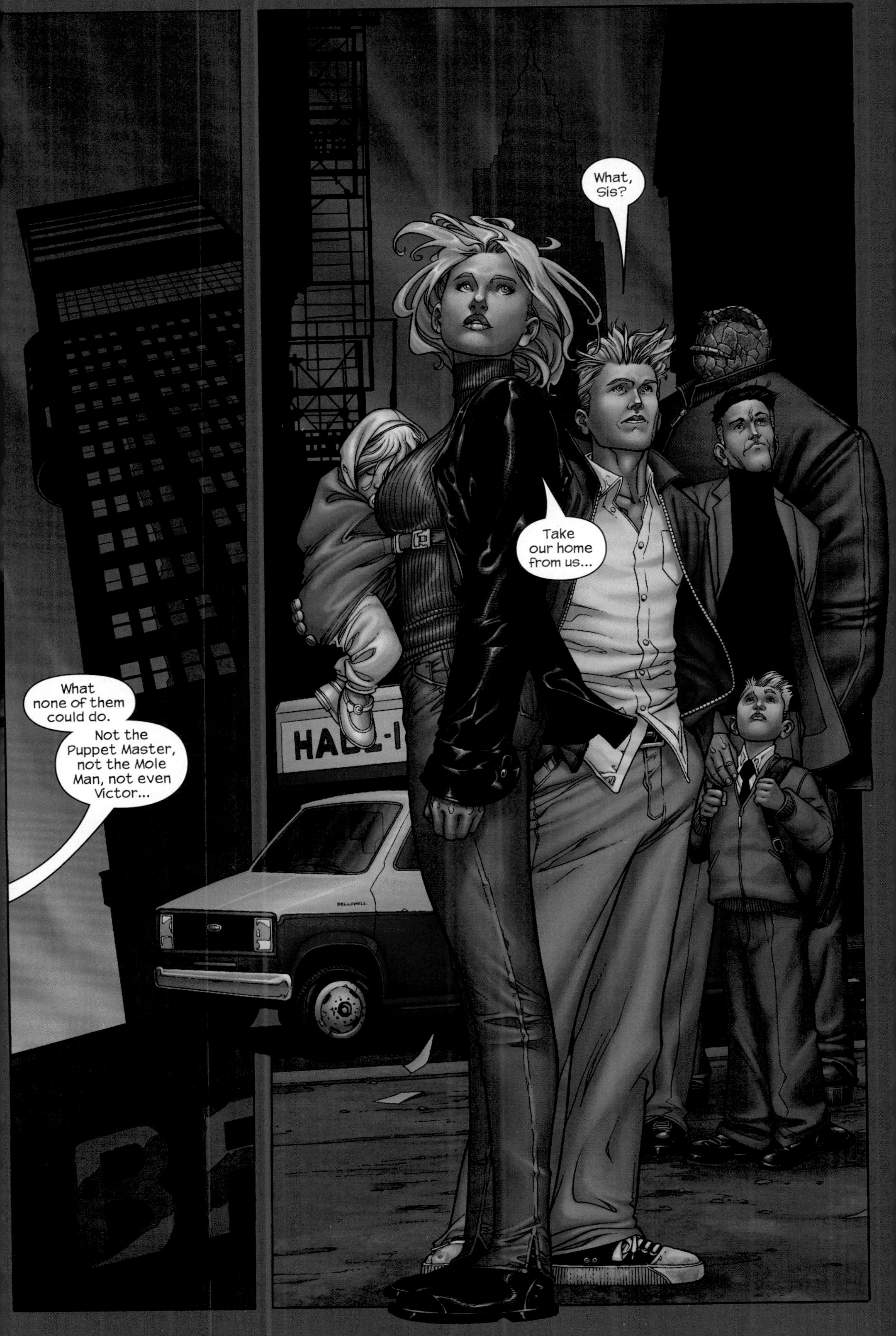
What, Sis?
Take our home from us...
What none of them could do.
Not the Puppet Master, not the Mole Man, not even Victor...
HAUL-I

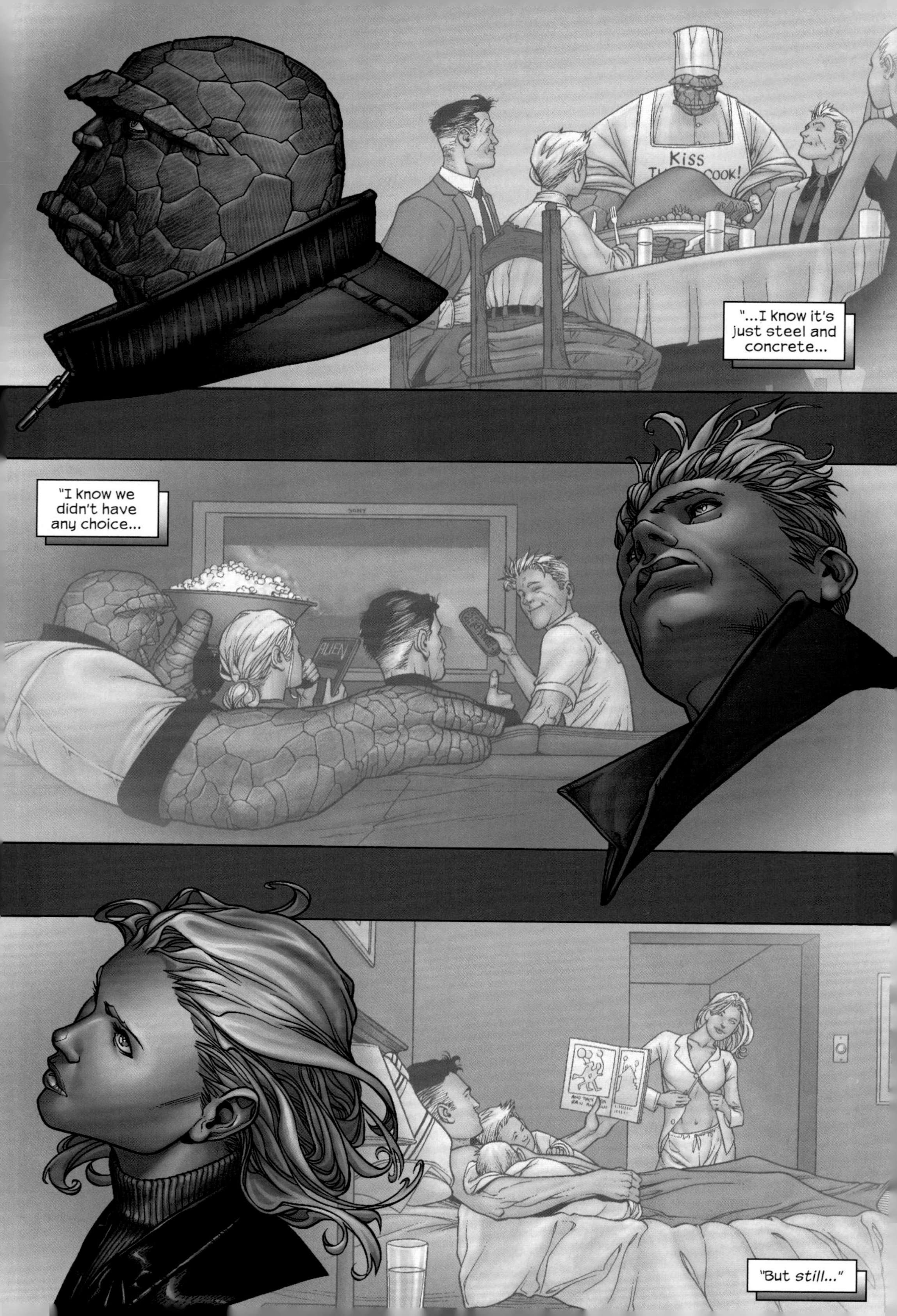

Kiss
"...I know it's just steel and concrete...
"I know we didn't have any choice...
"But still..."

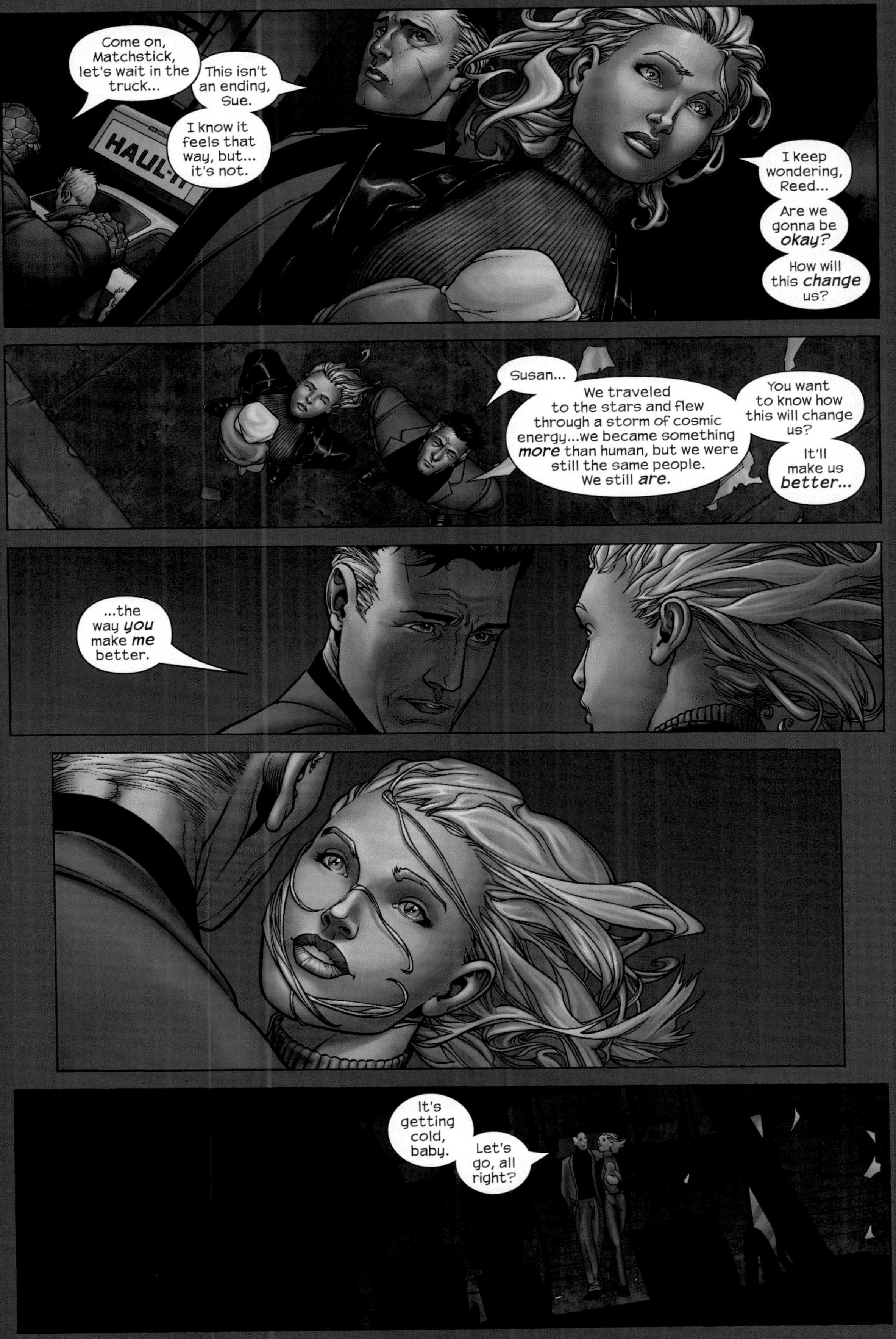
Come on, Matchstick, let's wait in the truck...
This isn't an ending, Sue.
I know it feels that way, but... it's not.
HAUL-IT
I keep wondering, Reed...
Are we gonna be *okay?*
How will this *change* us?
Susan...
We traveled to the stars and flew through a storm of cosmic energy...we became something *more* than human, but we were still the same people. We still *are.*
You want to know how this will change us?
It'll make us *better...*
...the way *you* make *me* better.
It's getting cold, baby.
Let's go, all right?

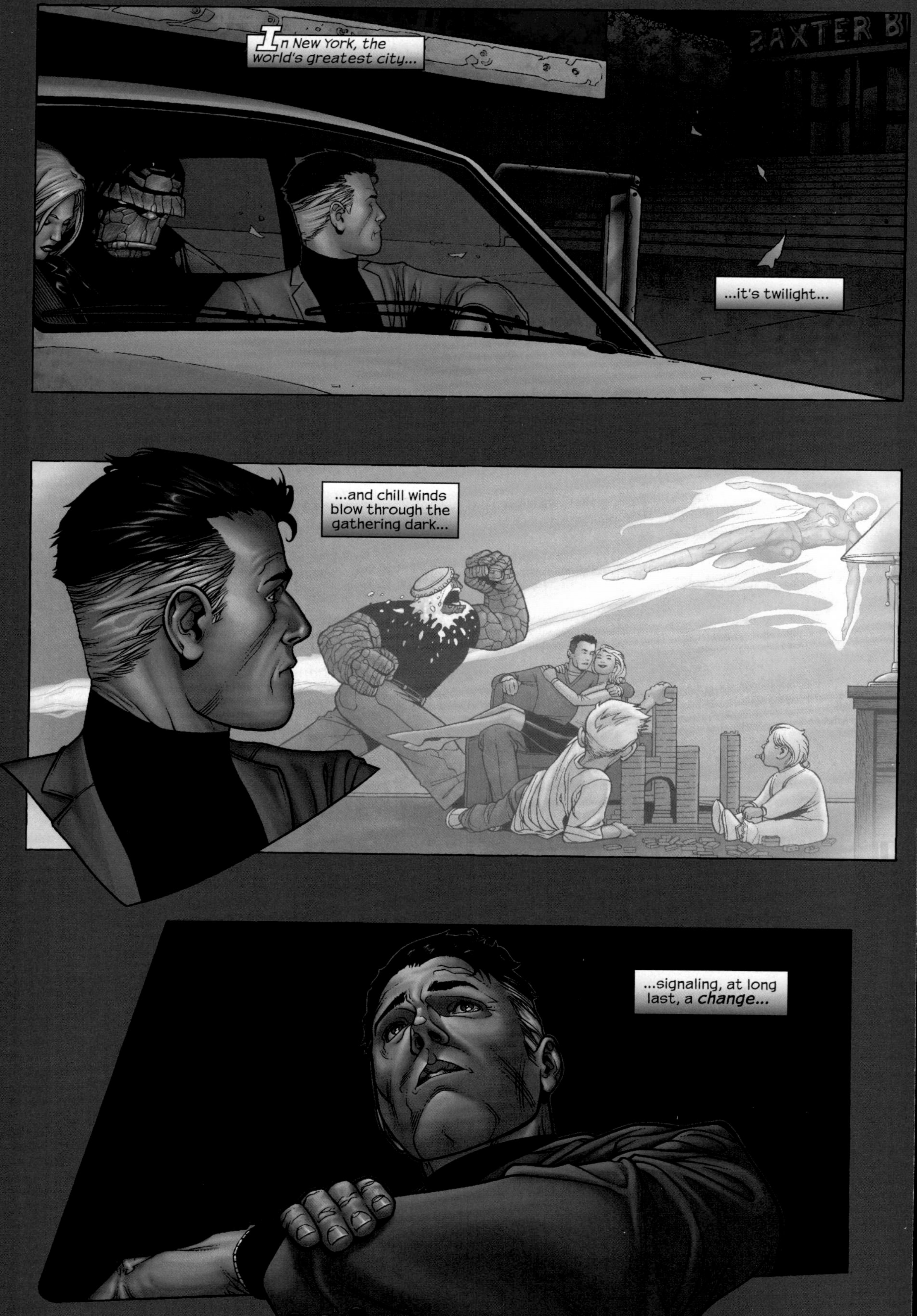

In New York, the world's greatest city...
BAXTER B
...it's twilight...
...and chill winds blow through the gathering dark...
...signaling, at long last, a change...

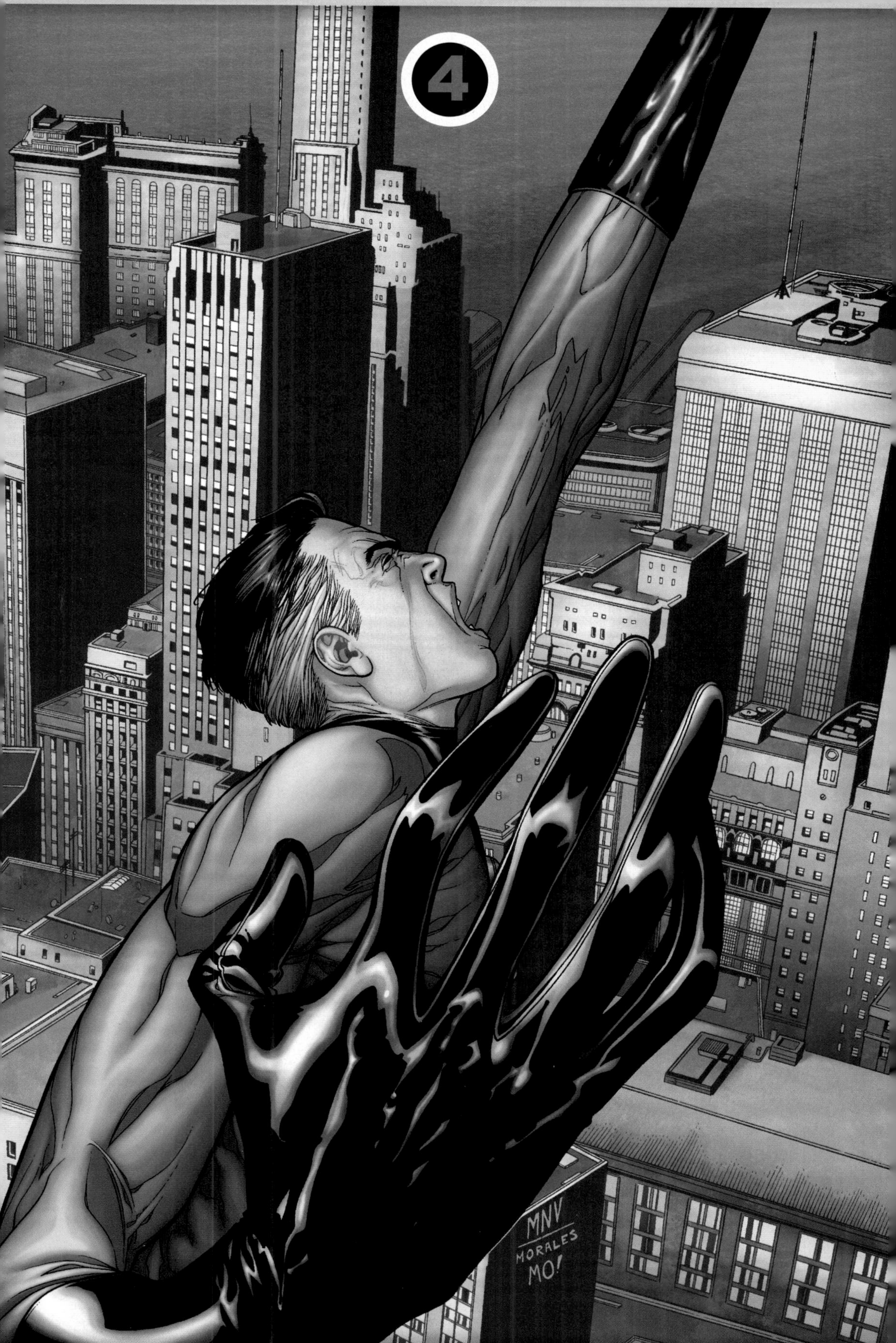
4
MNV
MORALES
MO!

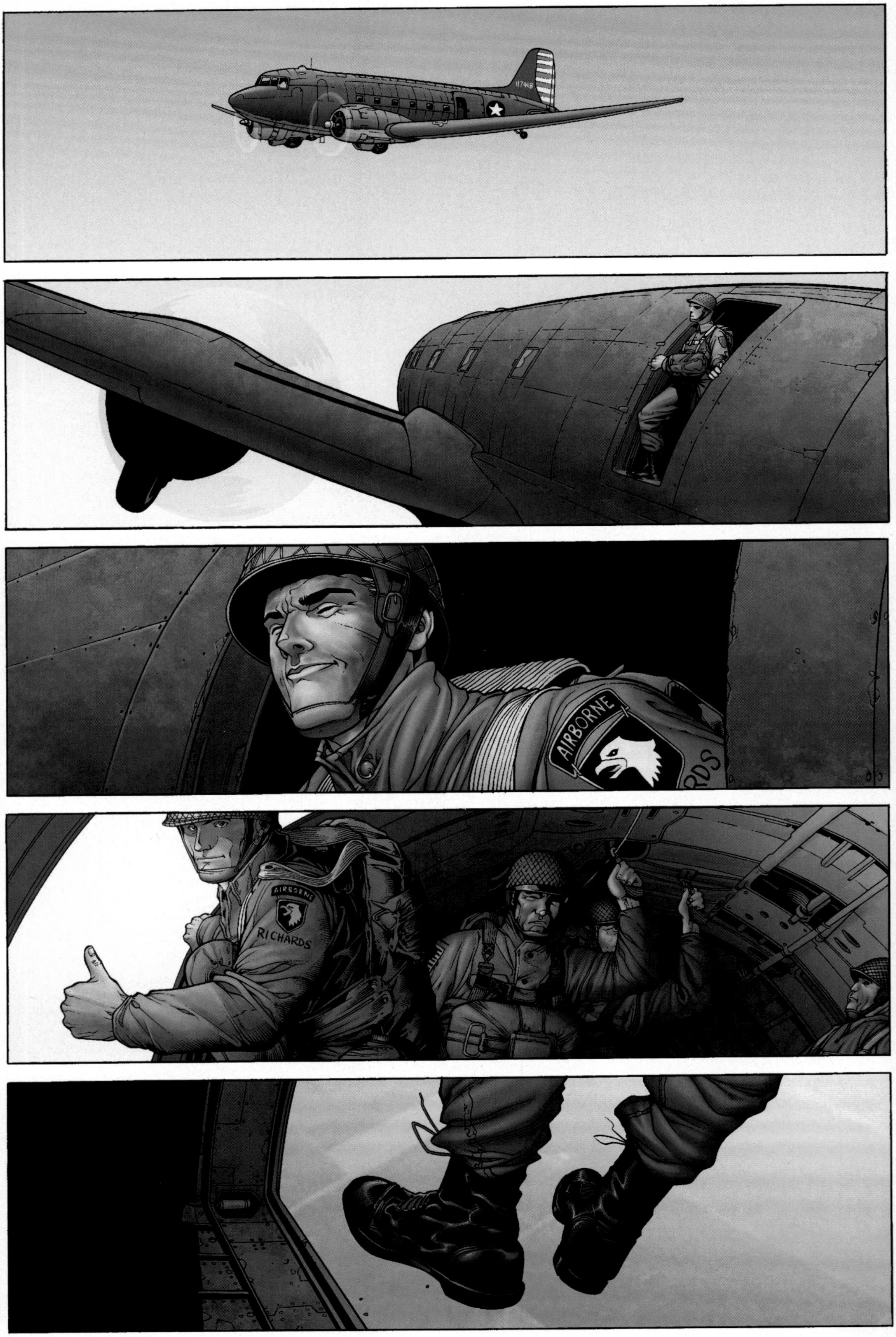
AIRBORNE
RDS
AIRBORNE
RICHARDS

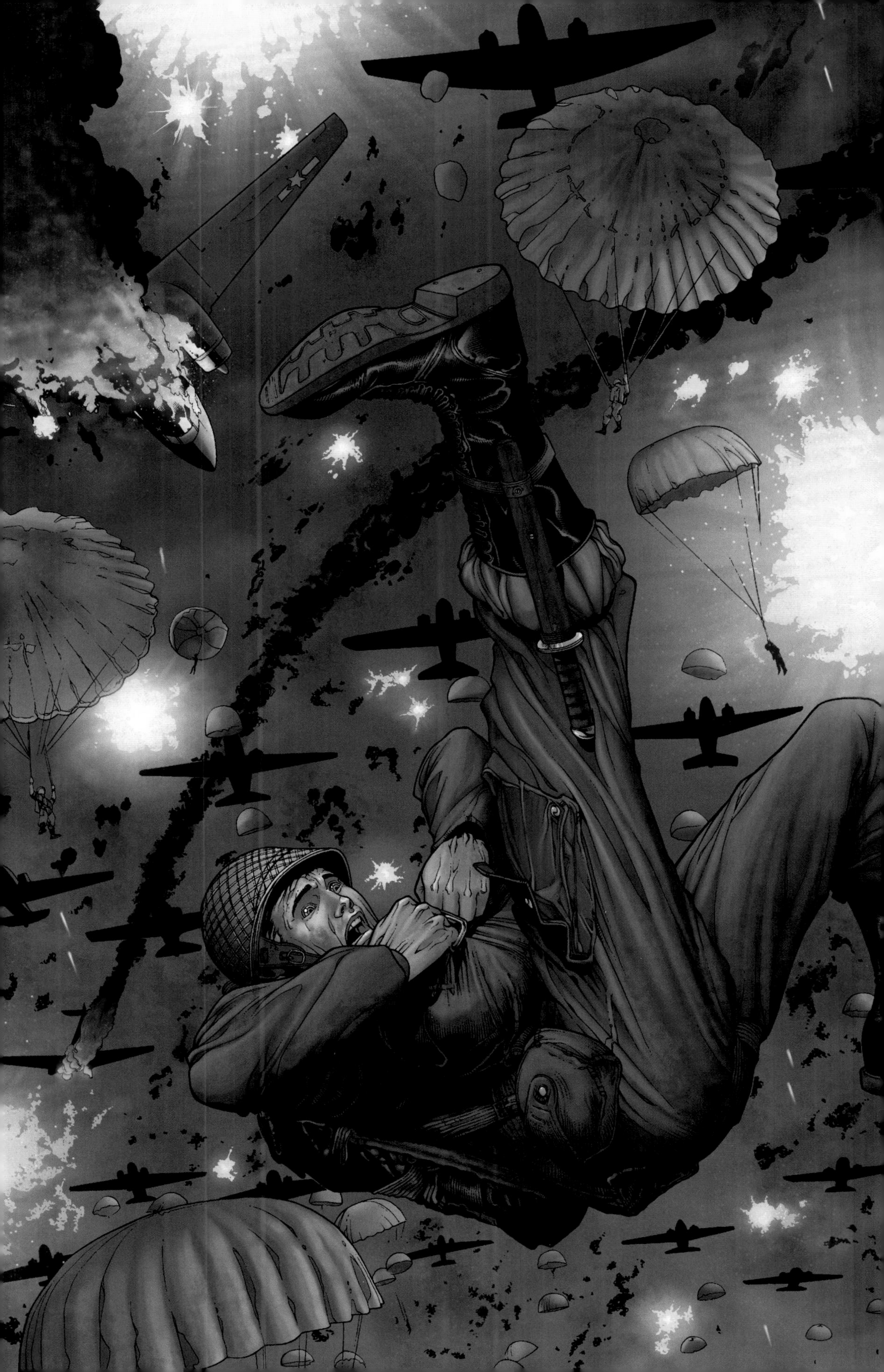

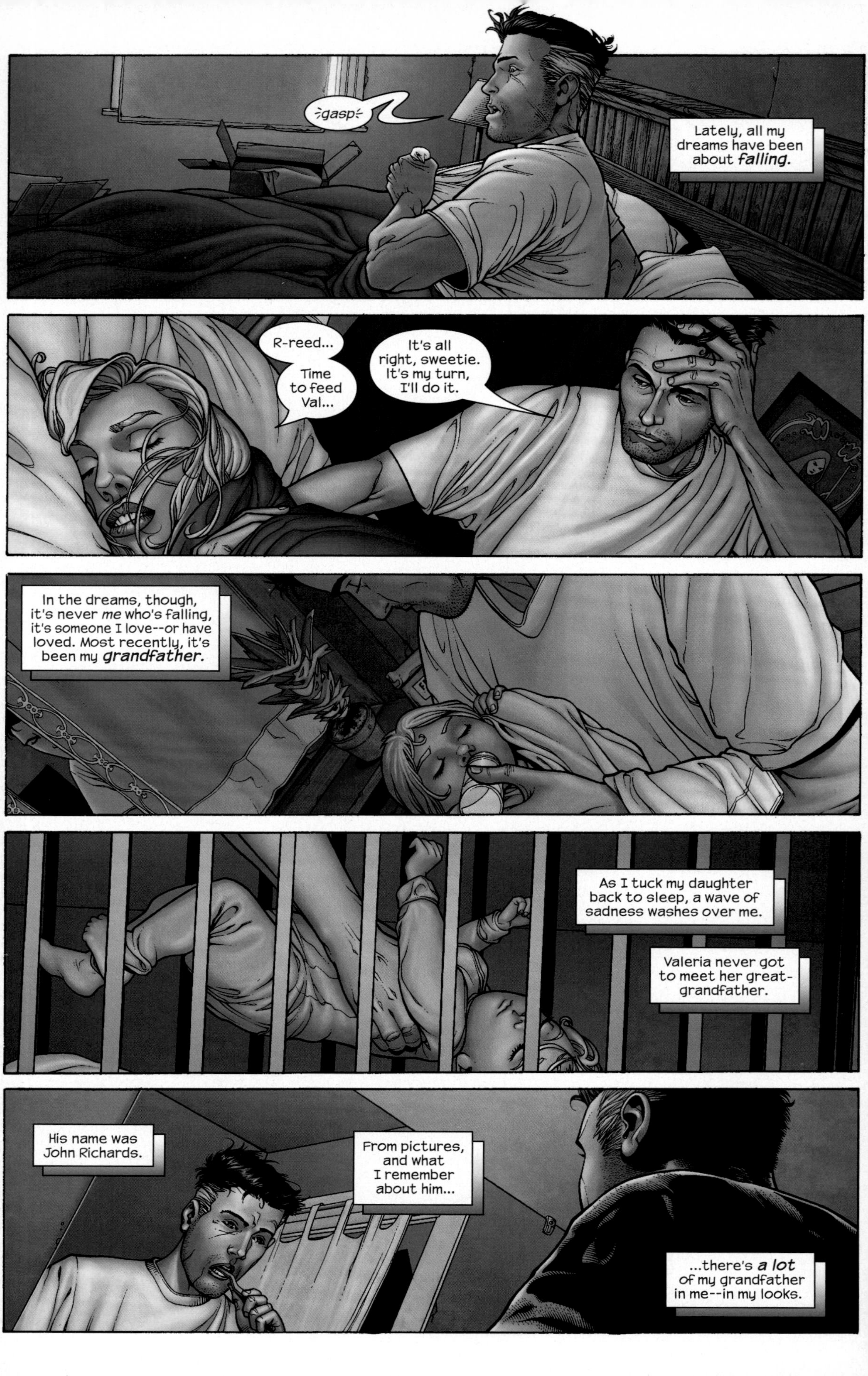

gasp
Lately, all my dreams have been about *falling.*
R-reed... Time to feed Val...
It's all right, sweetie. It's my turn, I'll do it.
In the dreams, though, it's never *me* who's falling, it's someone I love--or have loved. Most recently, it's been my *grandfather.*
As I tuck my daughter back to sleep, a wave of sadness washes over me.
Valeria never got to meet her great-grandfather.
His name was John Richards.
From pictures, and what I remember about him...
...there's *a lot* of my grandfather in me--in my looks.

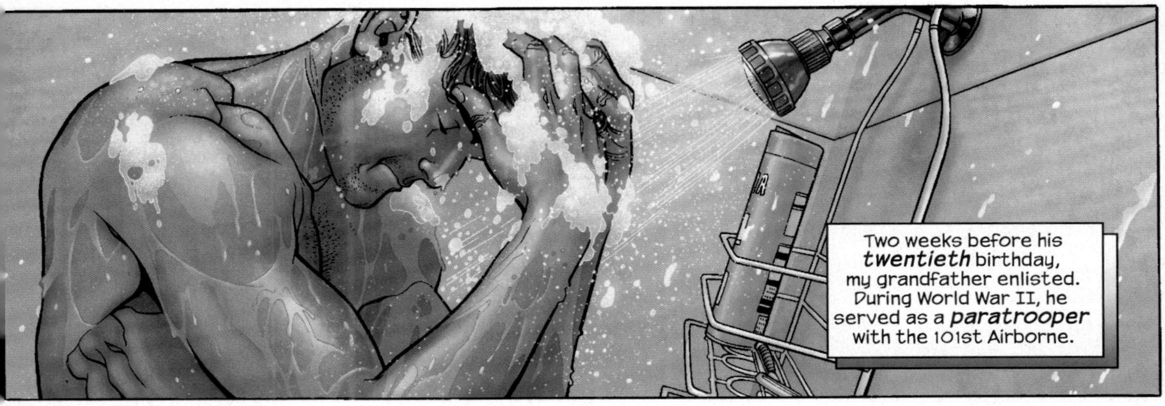
Two weeks before his *twentieth* birthday, my grandfather enlisted. During World War II, he served as a *paratrooper* with the 101st Airborne.

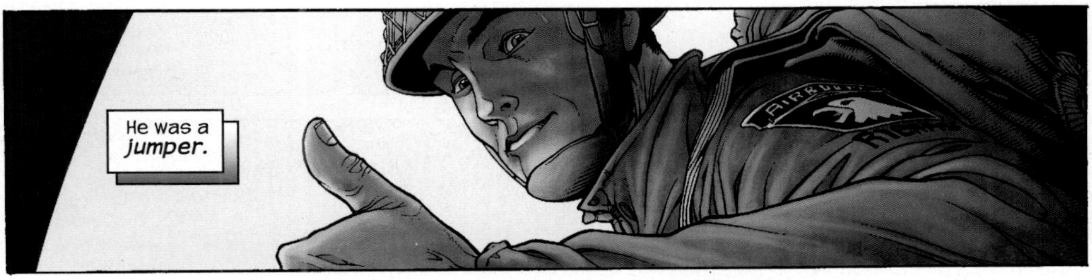
He was a *jumper*.

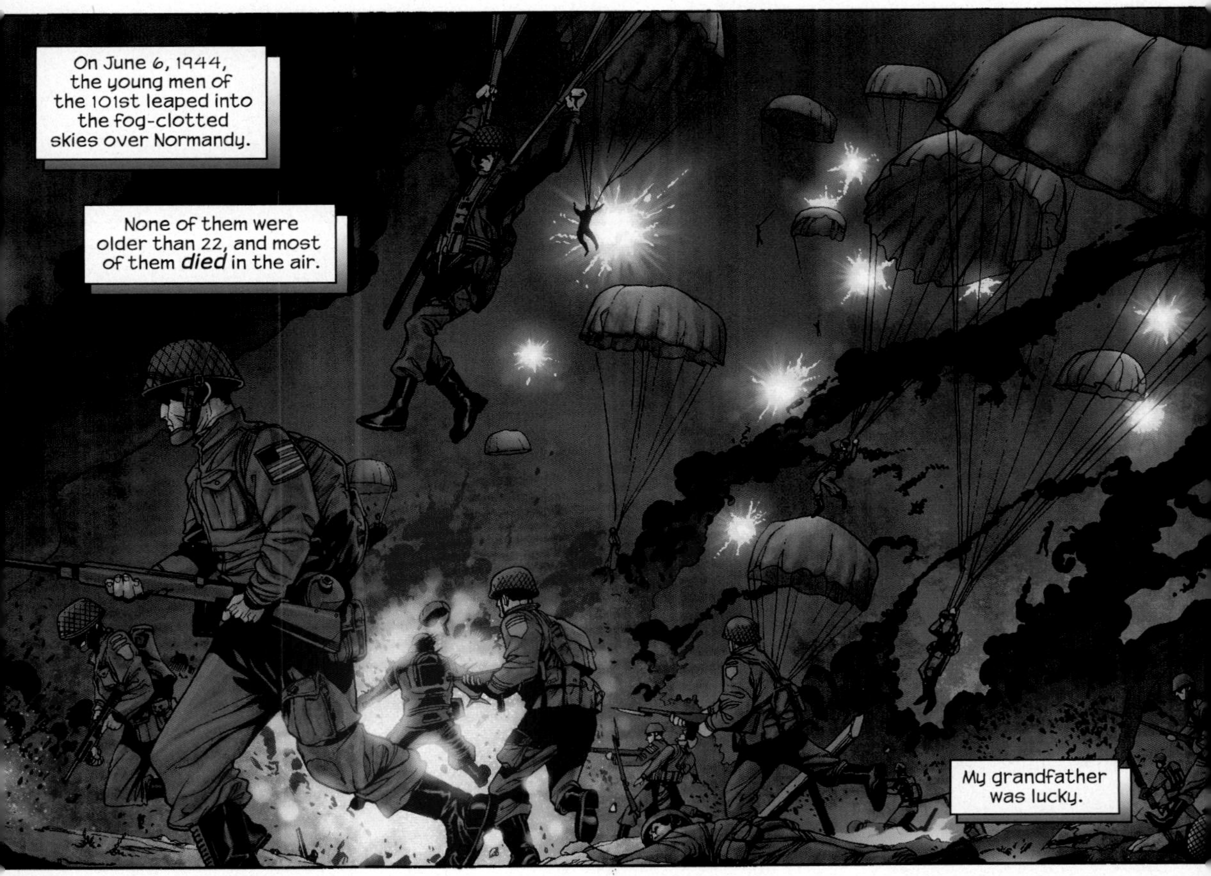
On June 6, 1944, the young men of the 101st leaped into the fog-clotted skies over Normandy.
None of them were older than 22, and most of them *died* in the air.
My grandfather was lucky.

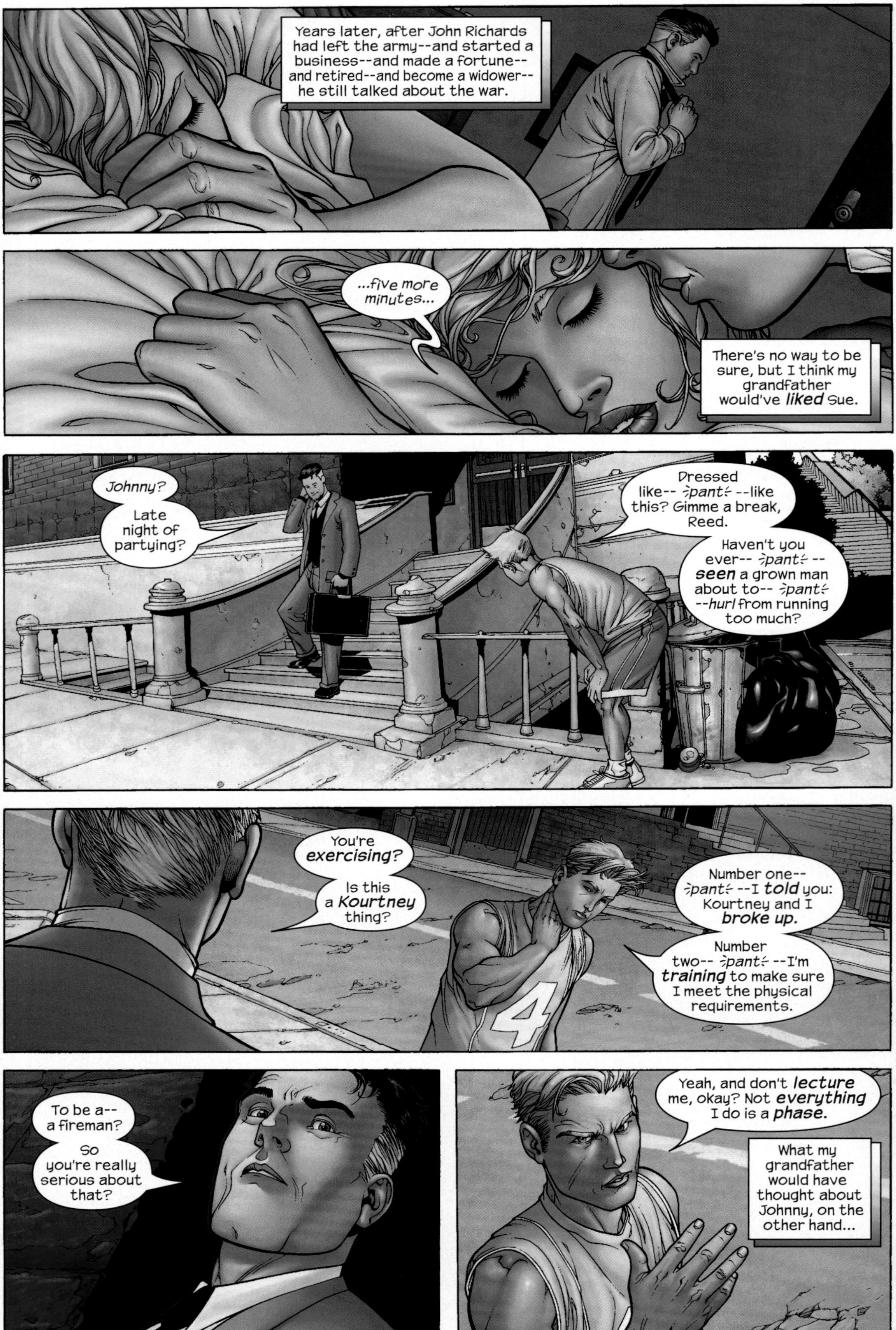
Years later, after John Richards had left the army--and started a business--and made a fortune--and retired--and become a widower--he still talked about the war.
...five more minutes...
There's no way to be sure, but I think my grandfather would've *liked* Sue.
Johnny?
Late night of partying?
Dressed like-- pant --like this? Gimme a break, Reed.
Haven't you ever-- pant -- **seen** a grown man about to-- pant --*hurl* from running too much?
You're ***exercising?***
Is this a ***Kourtney*** thing?
Number one-- pant --I ***told*** you: Kourtney and I ***broke up.***
Number two-- pant --I'm ***training*** to make sure I meet the physical requirements.
To be a--a fireman?
So you're really serious about that?
Yeah, and don't ***lecture*** me, okay? Not ***everything*** I do is a ***phase.***
What my grandfather would have thought about Johnny, on the other hand...

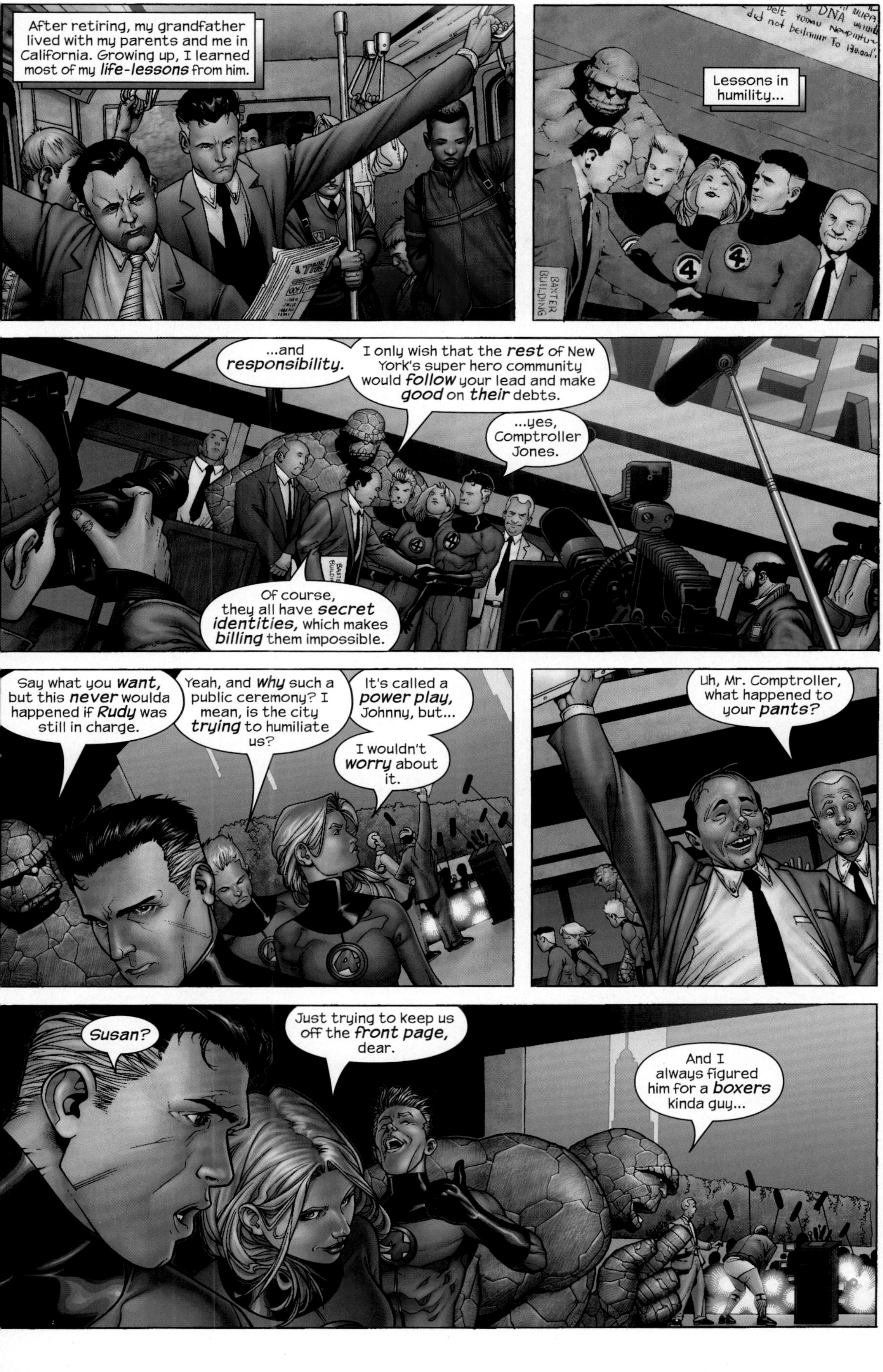
After retiring, my grandfather lived with my parents and me in California. Growing up, I learned most of my life-lessons from him.
Lessons in humility...
BAXTER BUILDING
...and responsibility.
I only wish that the rest of New York's super hero community would follow your lead and make good on their debts.
...yes, Comptroller Jones.
Of course, they all have secret identities, which makes billing them impossible.
Say what you want, but this never woulda happened if Rudy was still in charge.
Yeah, and why such a public ceremony? I mean, is the city trying to humiliate us?
It's called a power play, Johnny, but...
I wouldn't worry about it.
Uh, Mr. Comptroller, what happened to your pants?
Susan?
Just trying to keep us off the front page, dear.
And I always figured him for a boxers kinda guy...

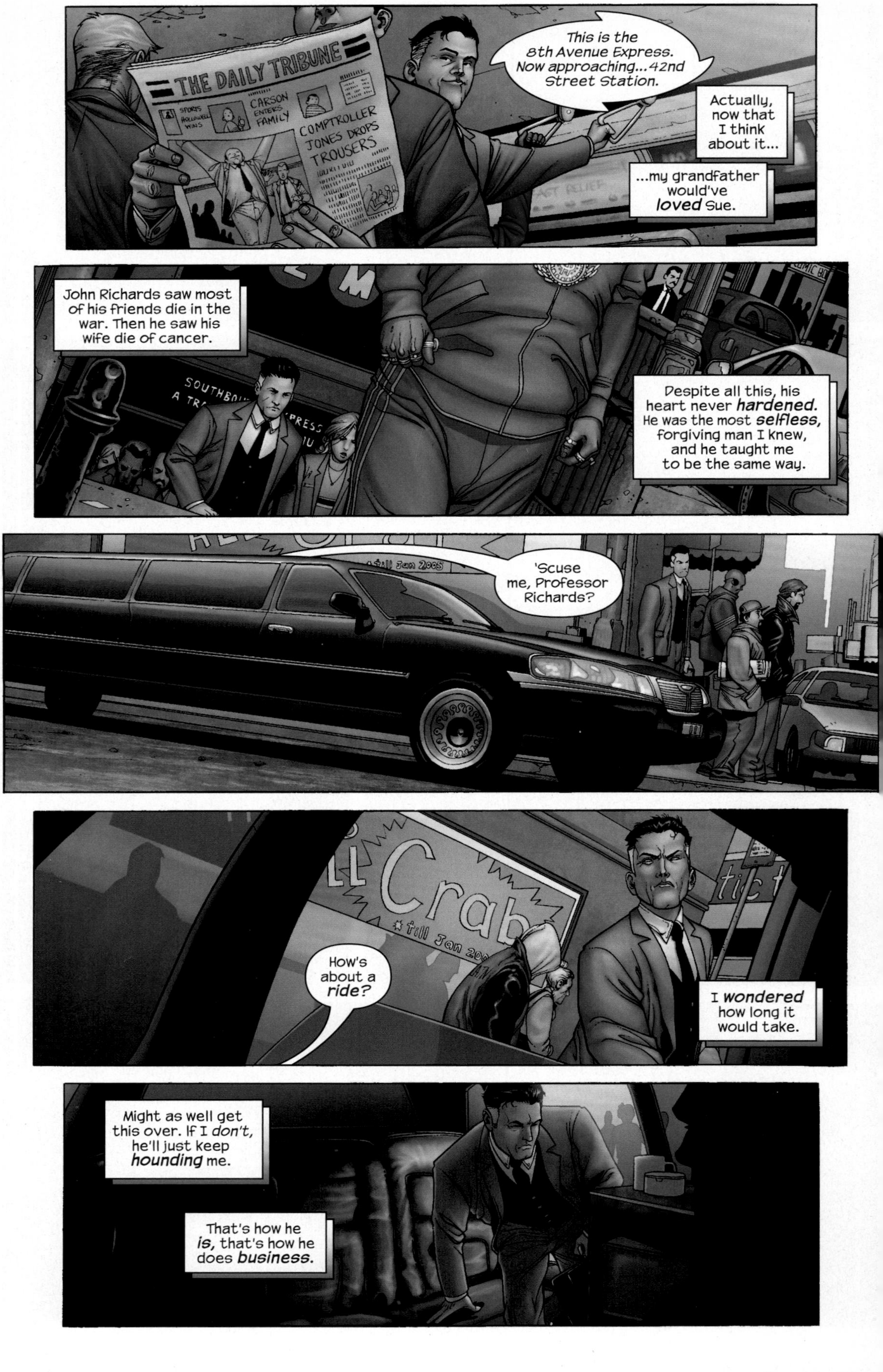

THE DAILY TRIBUNE
CARSON ENTERS FAMILY
COMPTROLLER JONES DROPS TROUSERS
This is the 8th Avenue Express. Now approaching...42nd Street Station.
Actually, now that I think about it...
...my grandfather would've *loved* Sue.
John Richards saw most of his friends die in the war. Then he saw his wife die of cancer.
Despite all this, his heart never *hardened.* He was the most *selfless,* forgiving man I knew, and he taught me to be the same way.
till Jan 2005
'Scuse me, Professor Richards?
How's about a *ride?*
I *wondered* how long it would take.
Might as well get this over. If I *don't,* he'll just keep *hounding* me.
That's how he *is,* that's how he does *business.*

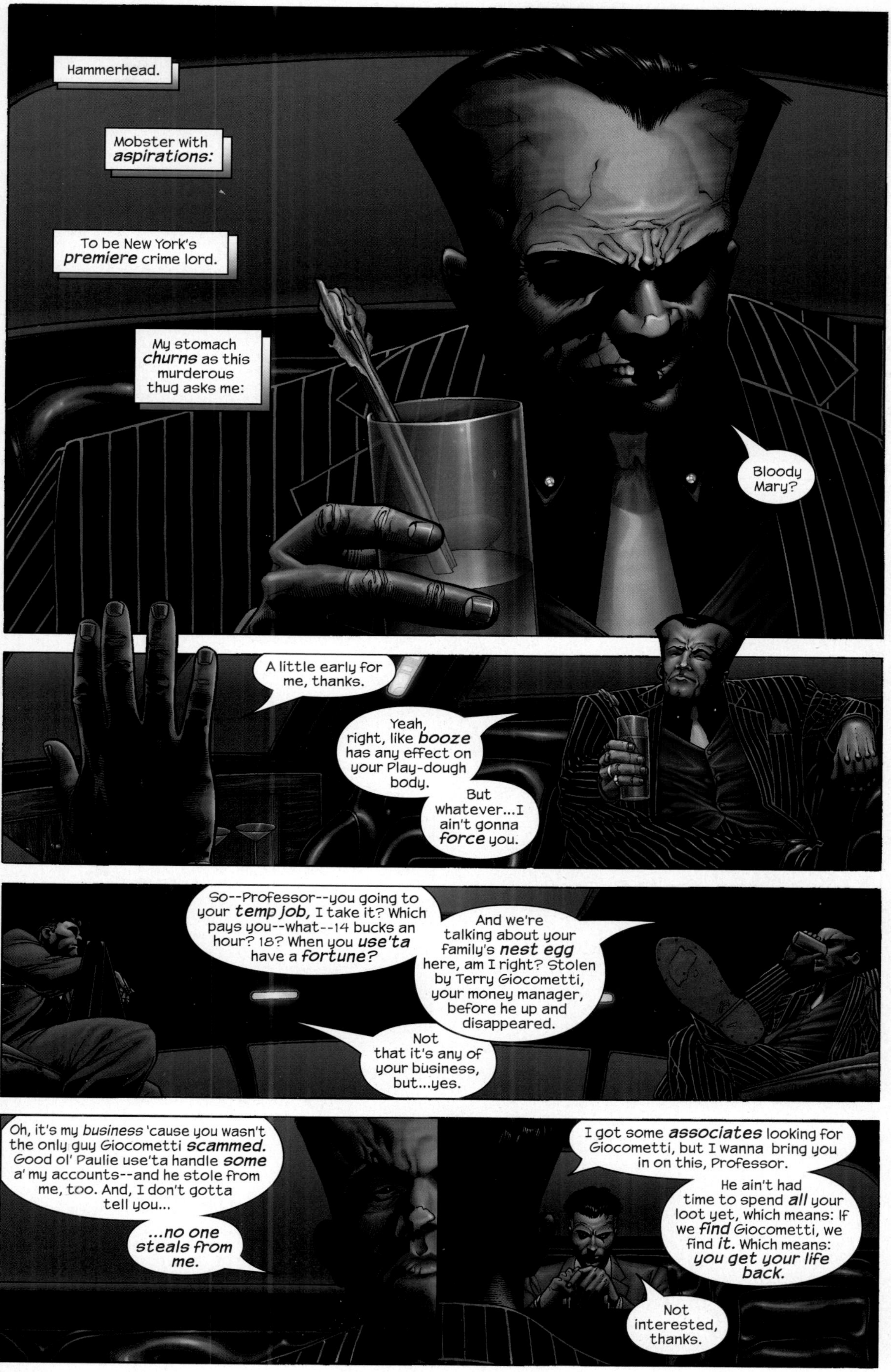

Hammerhead.
Mobster with *aspirations:*
To be New York's *premiere* crime lord.
My stomach *churns* as this murderous thug asks me:
Bloody Mary?
A little early for me, thanks.
Yeah, right, like *booze* has any effect on your Play-dough body.
But whatever...I ain't gonna *force* you.
So--Professor--you going to your *temp job,* I take it? Which pays you--what--14 bucks an hour? 18? When you *use'ta* have a *fortune?*
And we're talking about your family's *nest egg* here, am I right? Stolen by Terry Giocometti, your money manager, before he up and disappeared.
Not that it's any of your business, but...yes.
Oh, it's my *business* 'cause you wasn't the only guy Giocometti *scammed.* Good ol' Paulie use'ta handle *some* a' my accounts--and he stole from me, too. And, I don't gotta tell you...
...no one steals from me.
I got some *associates* looking for Giocometti, but I wanna bring you in on this, Professor.
He ain't had time to spend *all* your loot yet, which means: If we *find* Giocometti, we find *it.* Which means: *you get your life back.*
Not interested, thanks.

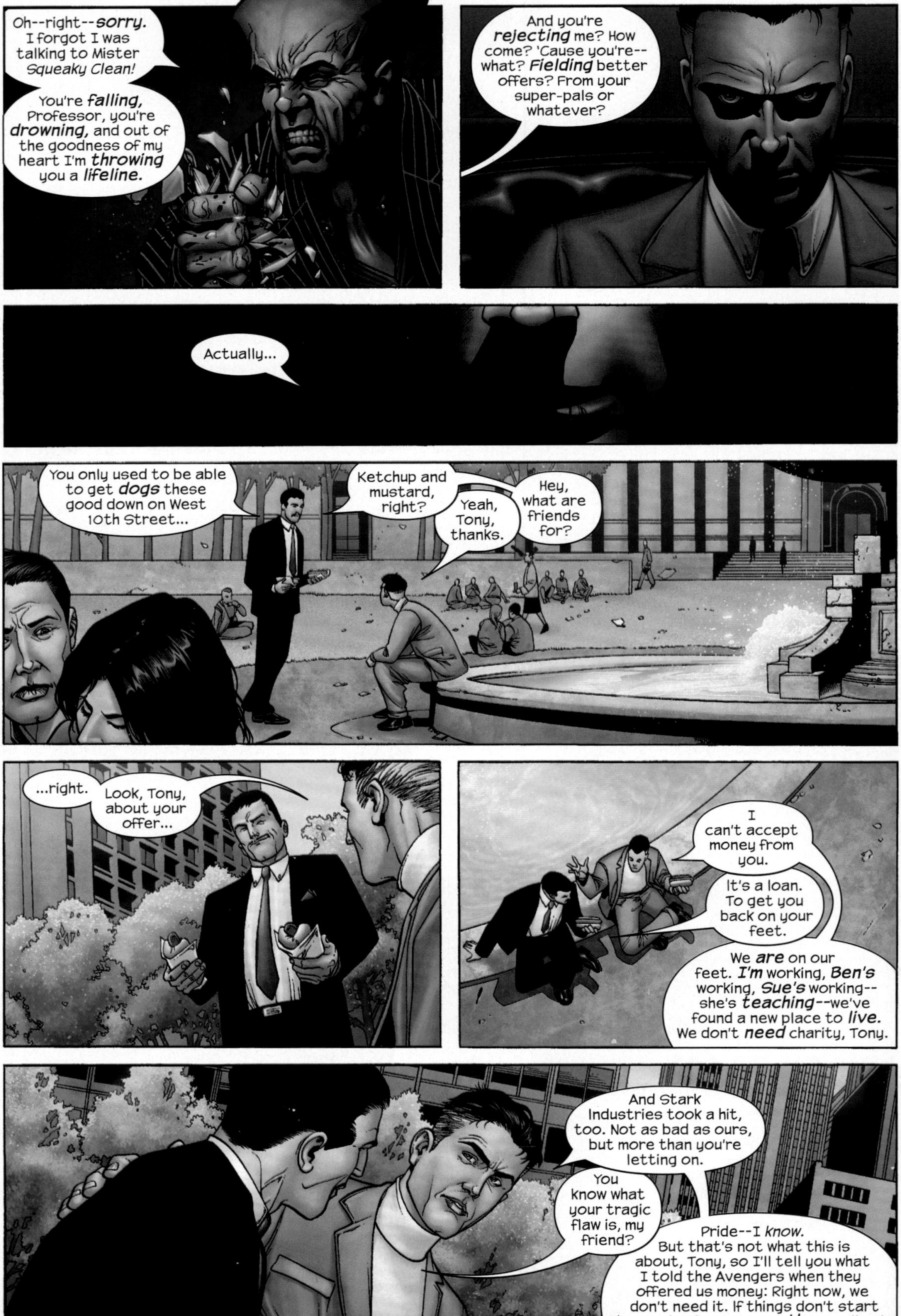

Oh--right--*sorry.* I forgot I was talking to Mister Squeaky Clean!
You're *falling,* Professor, you're *drowning,* and out of the goodness of my heart I'm *throwing* you a *lifeline.*
And you're *rejecting* me? How come? 'Cause you're--what? *Fielding* better offers? From your super-pals or whatever?
Actually...
You only used to be able to get *dogs* these good down on West 10th Street...
Ketchup and mustard, right?
Yeah, Tony, thanks.
Hey, what are friends for?
...right.
Look, Tony, about your offer...
I can't accept money from you.
It's a loan. To get you back on your feet.
We *are* on our feet. *I'm* working, *Ben's* working, *Sue's* working--she's *teaching*--we've found a new place to *live.* We don't *need* charity, Tony.
And Stark Industries took a hit, too. Not as bad as ours, but more than you're letting on.
You know what your tragic flaw is, my friend?
Pride--I *know.* But that's not what this is about, Tony, so I'll tell you what I told the Avengers when they offered us money: Right now, we don't need it. If things don't start happening for us soon, *then* we'll ask for help. But right now...we're okay.

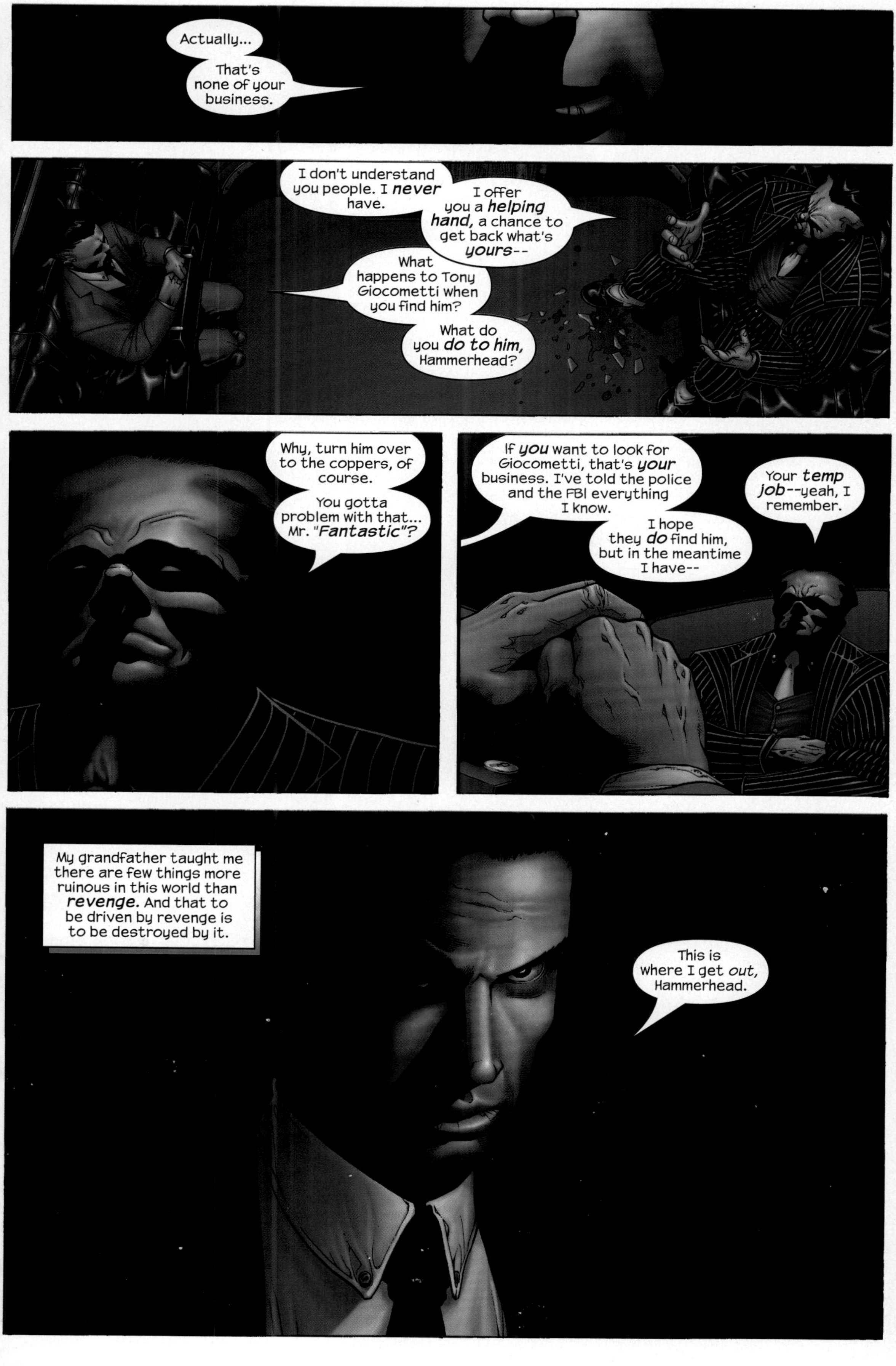

Actually...
That's none of your business.
I don't understand you people. I never have.
I offer you a helping hand, a chance to get back what's yours--
What happens to Tony Giocometti when you find him?
What do you do to him, Hammerhead?
Why, turn him over to the coppers, of course.
You gotta problem with that... Mr. "Fantastic"?
If you want to look for Giocometti, that's your business. I've told the police and the FBI everything I know.
I hope they do find him, but in the meantime I have--
Your temp job--yeah, I remember.
My grandfather taught me there are few things more ruinous in this world than revenge. And that to be driven by revenge is to be destroyed by it.
This is where I get out, Hammerhead.

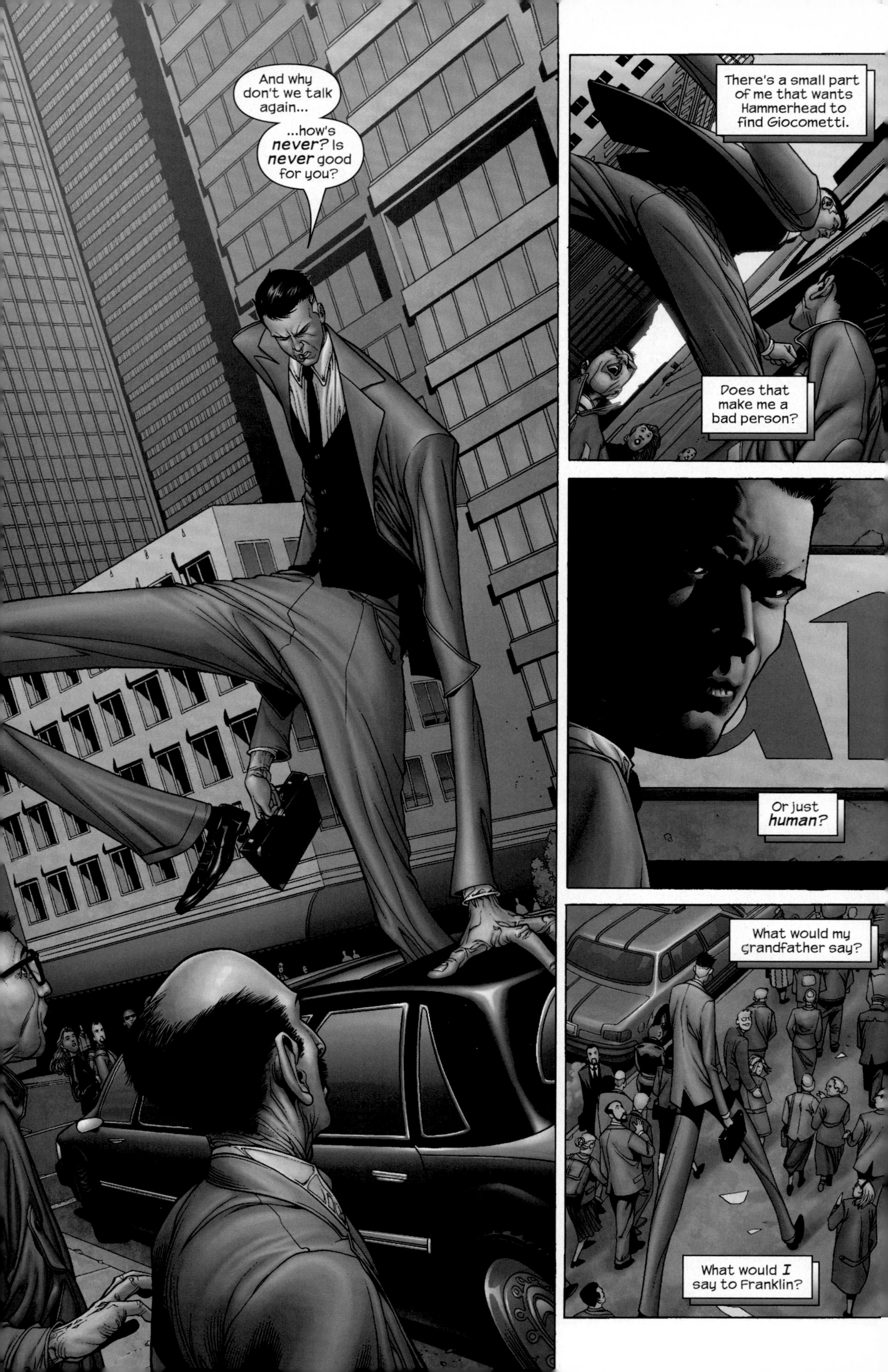

And why don't we talk again...
...how's *never*? Is *never* good for you?
There's a small part of me that wants Hammerhead to find Giocometti.
Does that make me a bad person?
Or just *human*?
What would my grandfather say?
What would *I* say to Franklin?

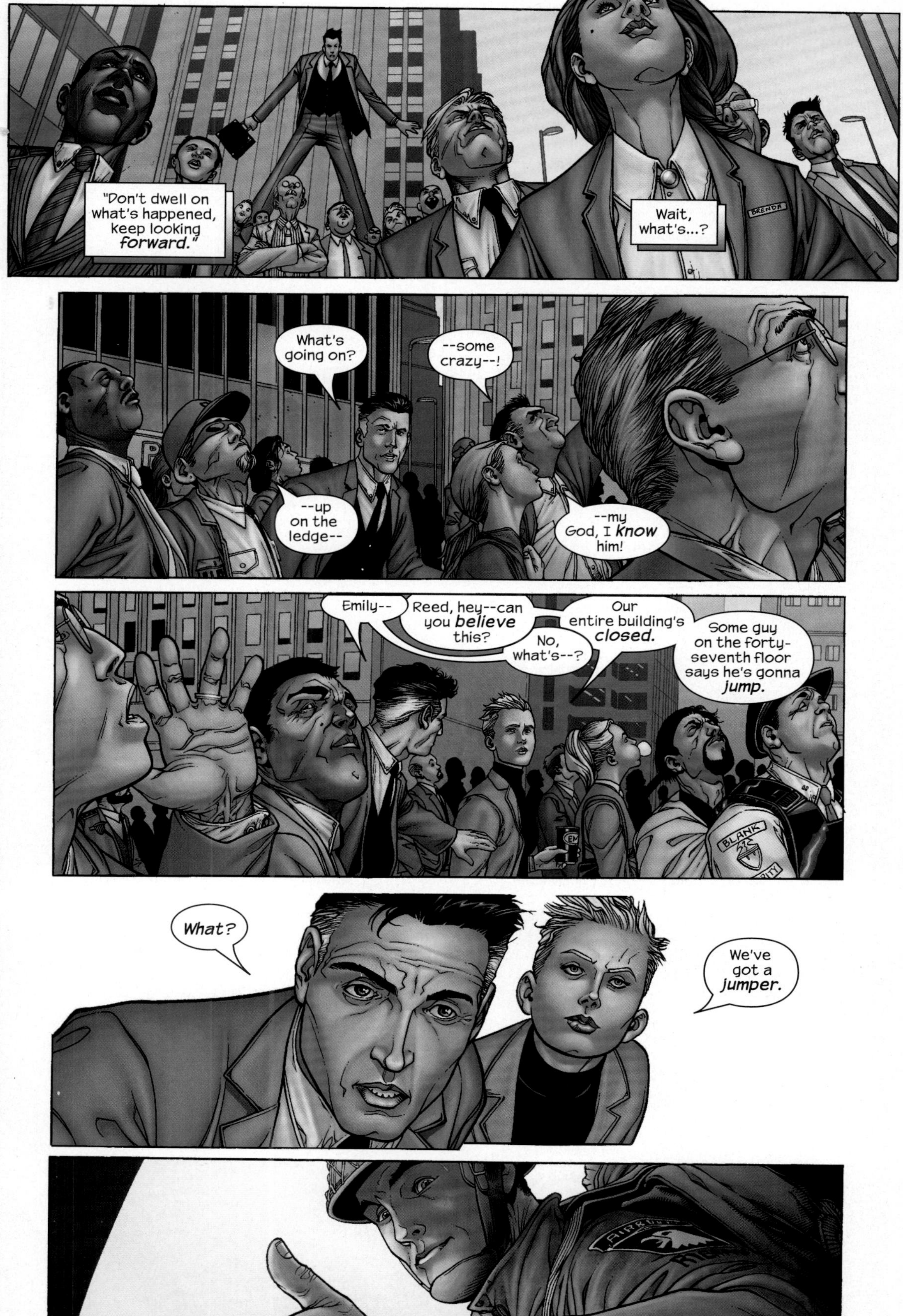
"Don't dwell on what's happened, keep looking forward."
Wait, what's...?
What's going on?
--some crazy--!
--up on the ledge--
--my God, I know him!
Emily--
Reed, hey--can you believe this?
No, what's--?
Our entire building's closed.
Some guy on the forty-seventh floor says he's gonna jump.
What?
We've got a jumper.

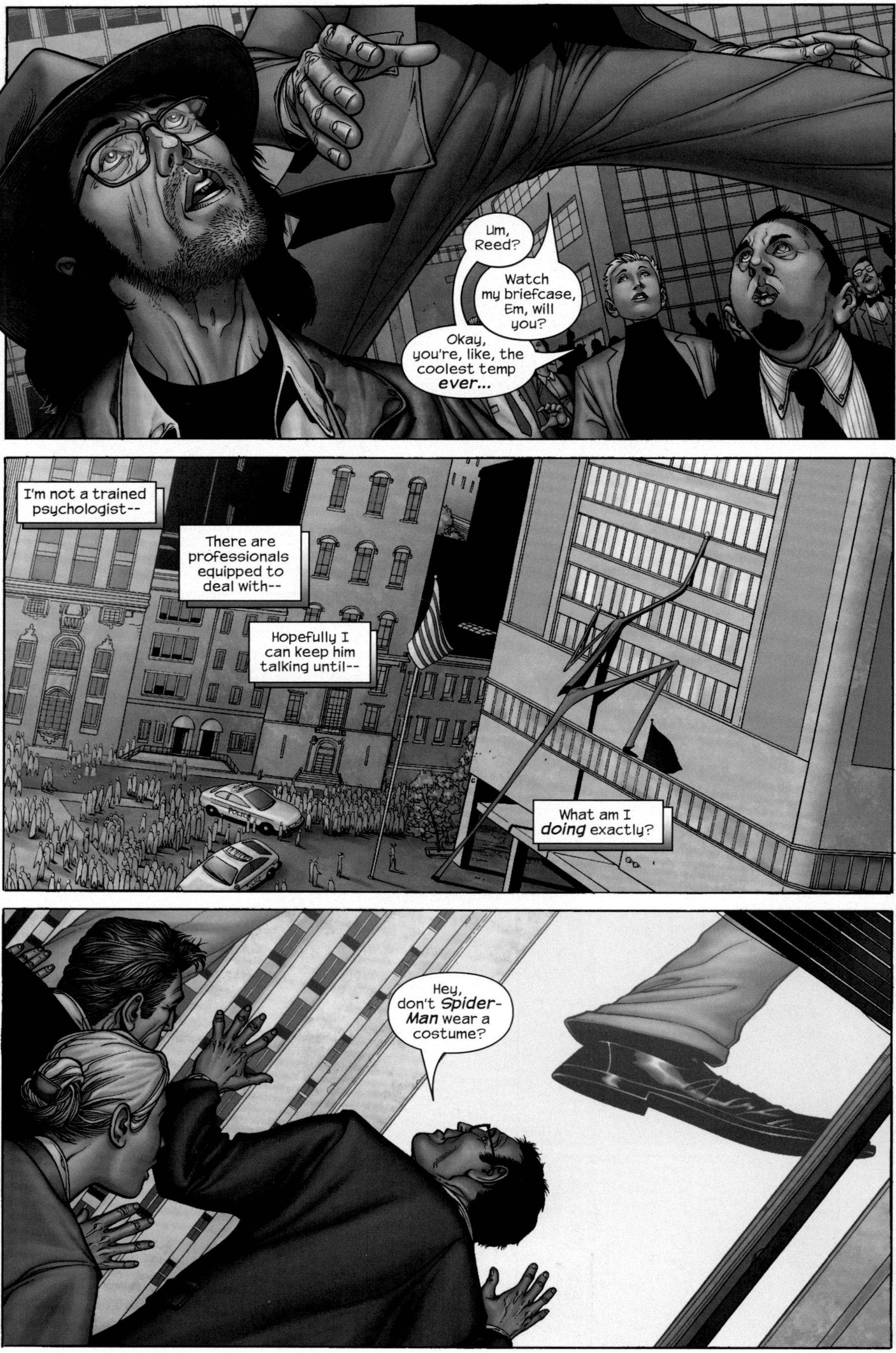
Um, Reed?
Watch my briefcase, Em, will you?
Okay, you're, like, the coolest temp *ever...*
I'm not a trained psychologist--
There are professionals equipped to deal with--
Hopefully I can keep him talking until--
What am I *doing* exactly?
Hey, don't *Spider-Man* wear a costume?

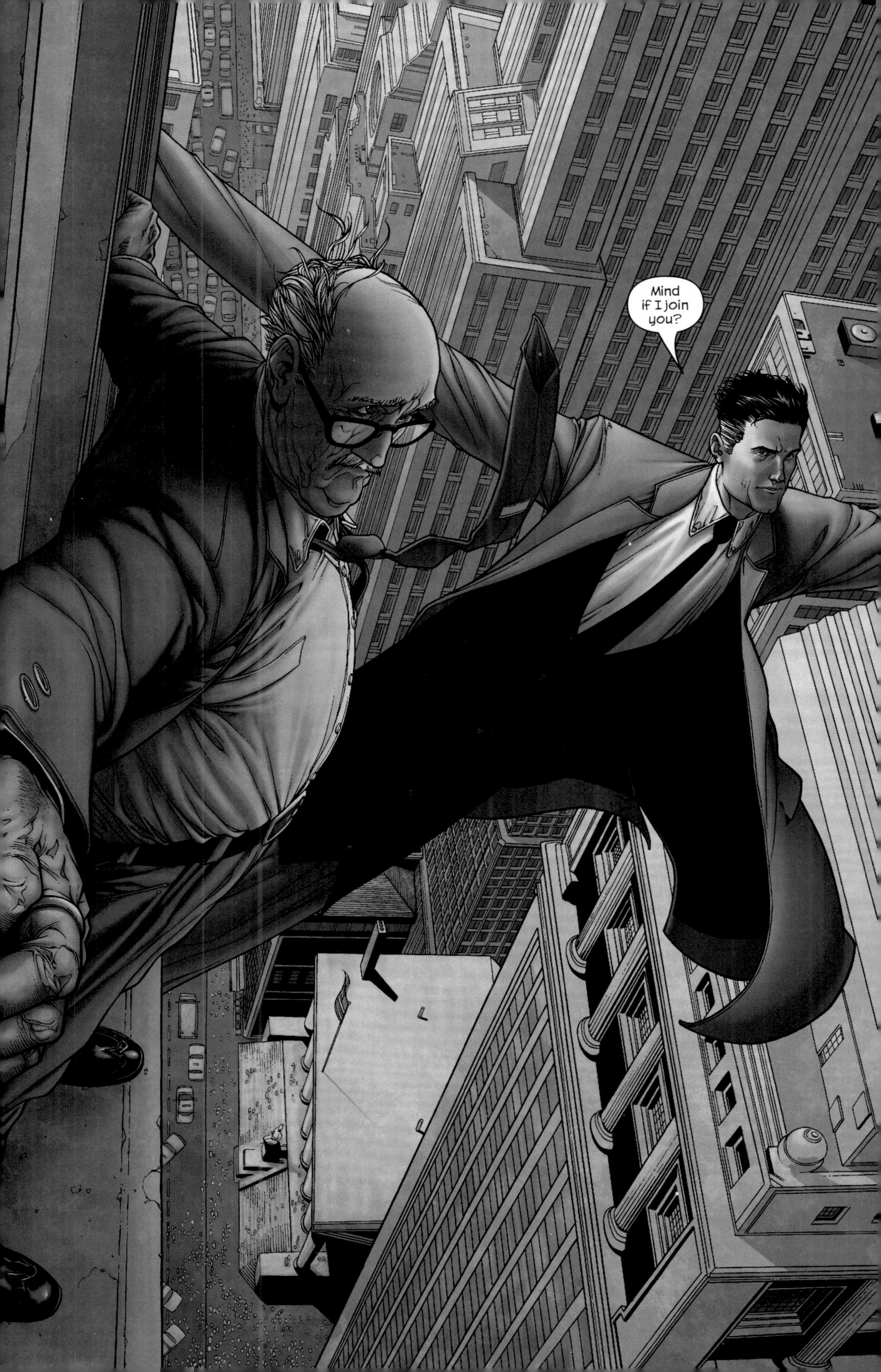
Mind if I join you?

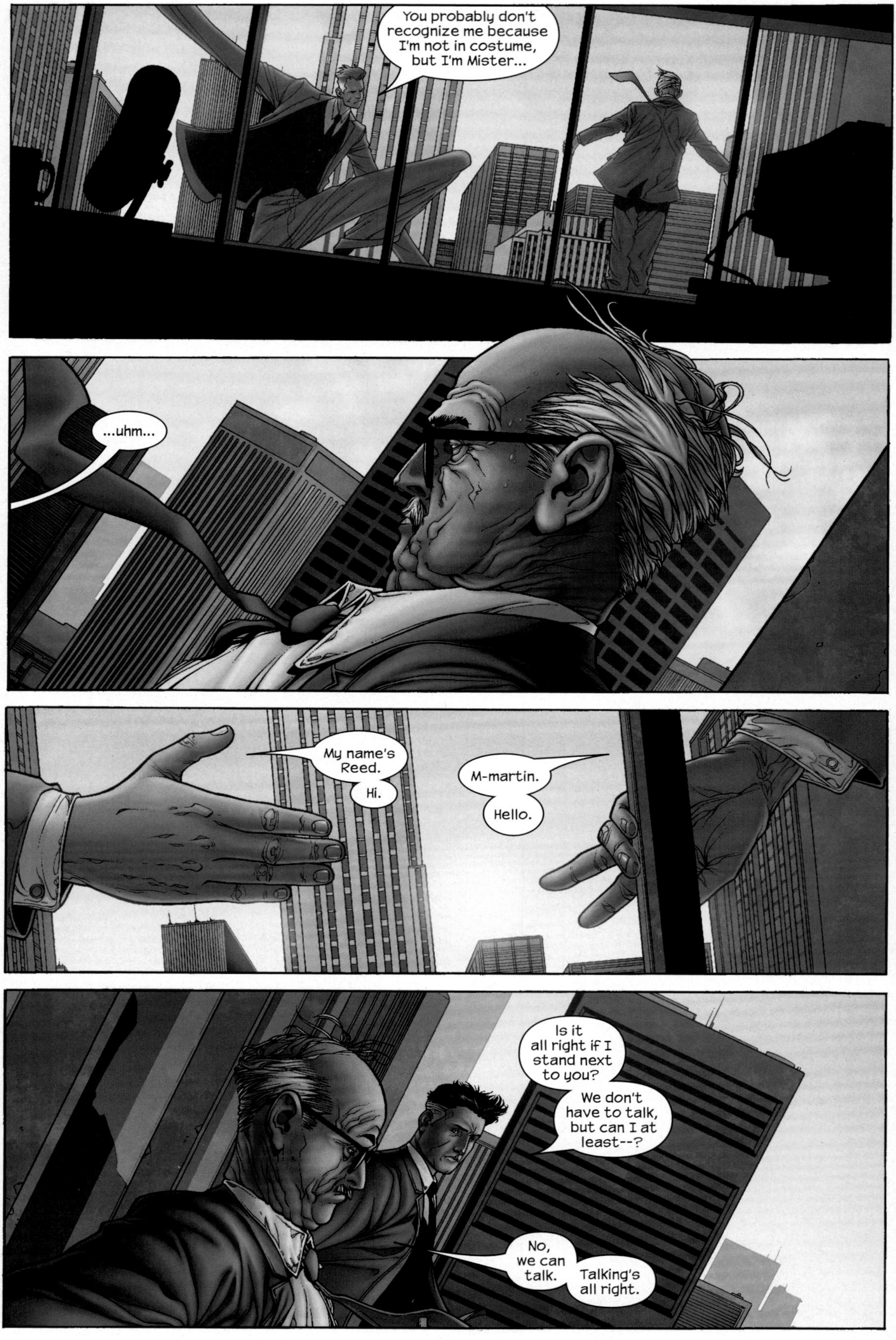
You probably don't recognize me because I'm not in costume, but I'm Mister...
...uhm...
My name's Reed.
Hi.
M-martin.
Hello.
Is it all right if I stand next to you?
We don't have to talk, but can I at least--?
No, we can talk.
Talking's all right.

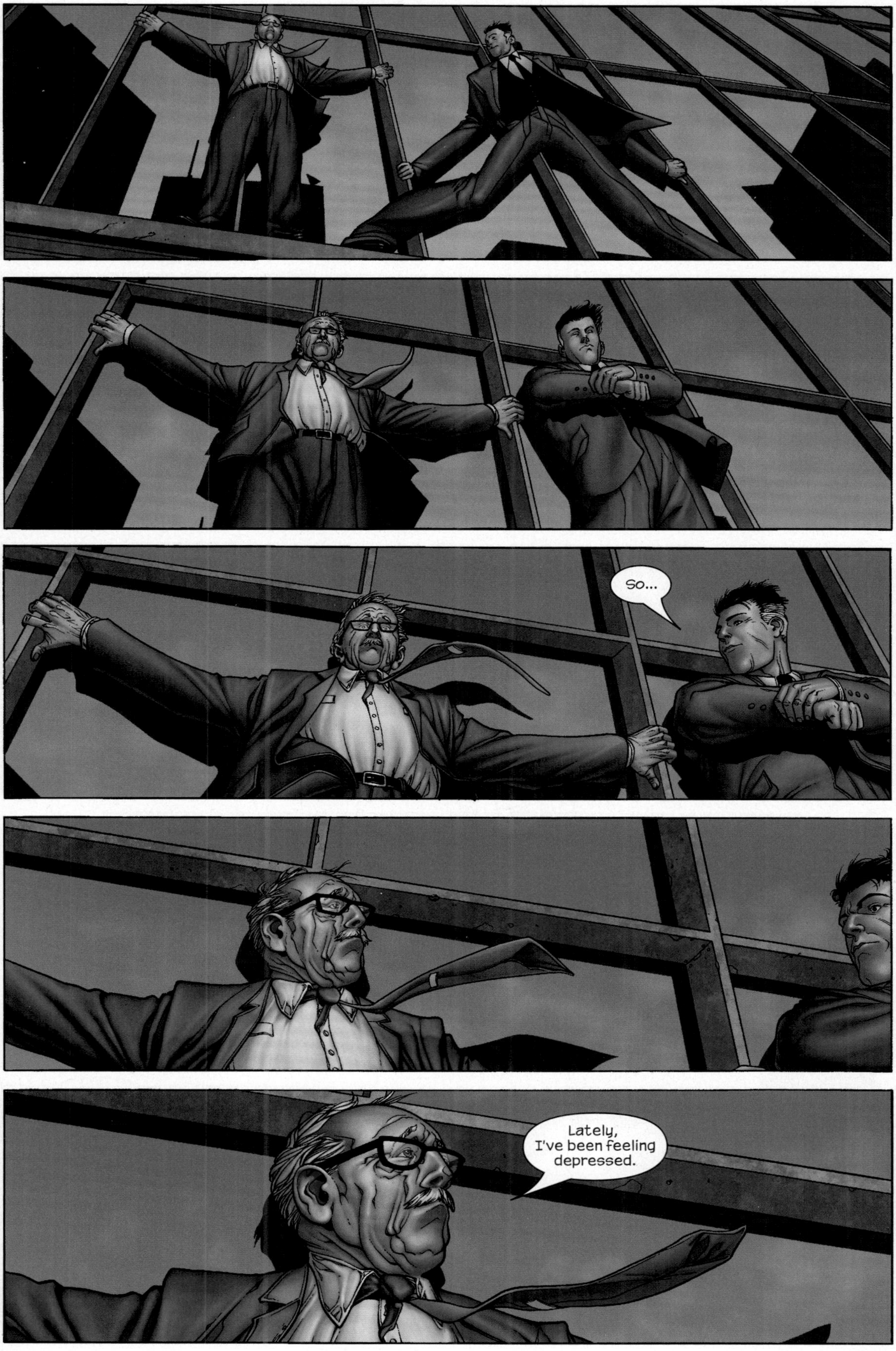
So...
Lately, I've been feeling depressed.

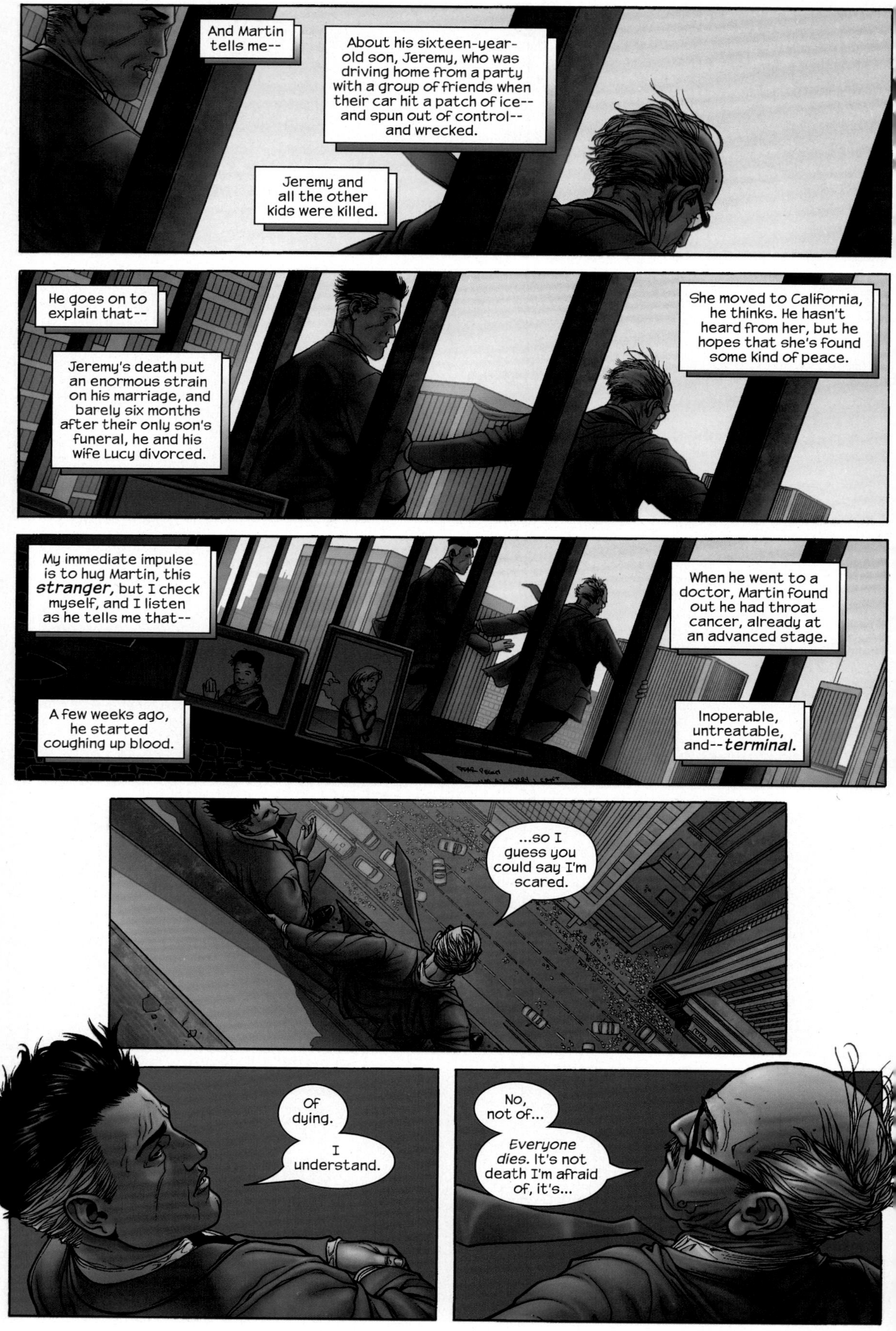

And Martin tells me--
About his sixteen-year-old son, Jeremy, who was driving home from a party with a group of friends when their car hit a patch of ice--and spun out of control--and wrecked.
Jeremy and all the other kids were killed.
He goes on to explain that--
Jeremy's death put an enormous strain on his marriage, and barely six months after their only son's funeral, he and his wife Lucy divorced.
She moved to California, he thinks. He hasn't heard from her, but he hopes that she's found some kind of peace.
My immediate impulse is to hug Martin, this *stranger,* but I check myself, and I listen as he tells me that--
When he went to a doctor, Martin found out he had throat cancer, already at an advanced stage.
A few weeks ago, he started coughing up blood.
Inoperable, untreatable, and--*terminal.*
...so I guess you could say I'm scared.
Of dying.
I understand.
No, not of...
Everyone dies. It's not death I'm afraid of, it's...

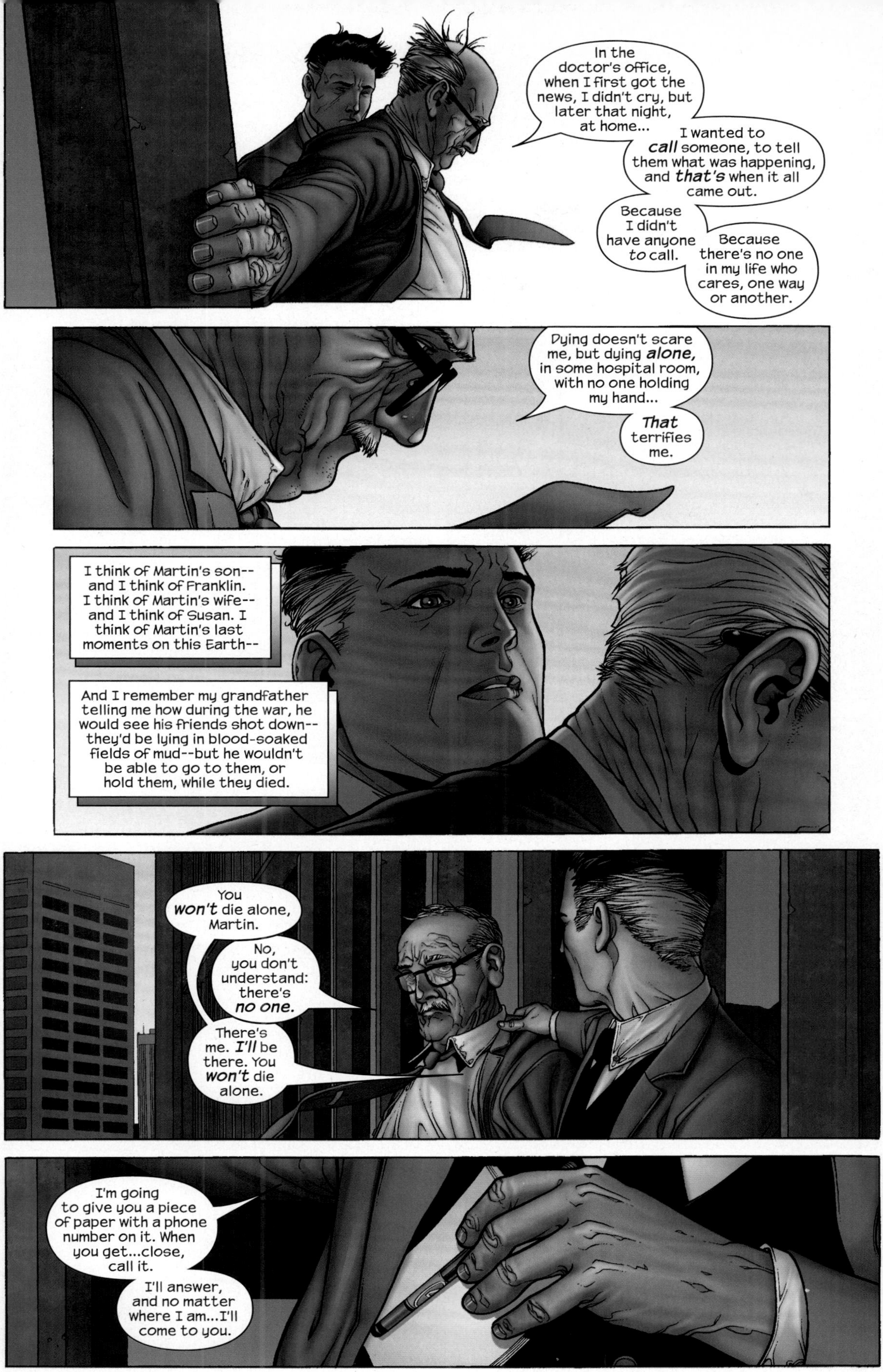
In the doctor's office, when I first got the news, I didn't cry, but later that night, at home...
I wanted to *call* someone, to tell them what was happening, and *that's* when it all came out.
Because I didn't have anyone *to* call.
Because there's no one in my life who cares, one way or another.
Dying doesn't scare me, but dying *alone,* in some hospital room, with no one holding my hand...
That terrifies me.
I think of Martin's son--and I think of Franklin. I think of Martin's wife--and I think of Susan. I think of Martin's last moments on this Earth--
And I remember my grandfather telling me how during the war, he would see his friends shot down--they'd be lying in blood-soaked fields of mud--but he wouldn't be able to go to them, or hold them, while they died.
You *won't* die alone, Martin.
No, you don't understand: there's *no one.*
There's me. *I'll* be there. You *won't* die alone.
I'm going to give you a piece of paper with a phone number on it. When you get...close, call it.
I'll answer, and no matter where I am...I'll come to you.

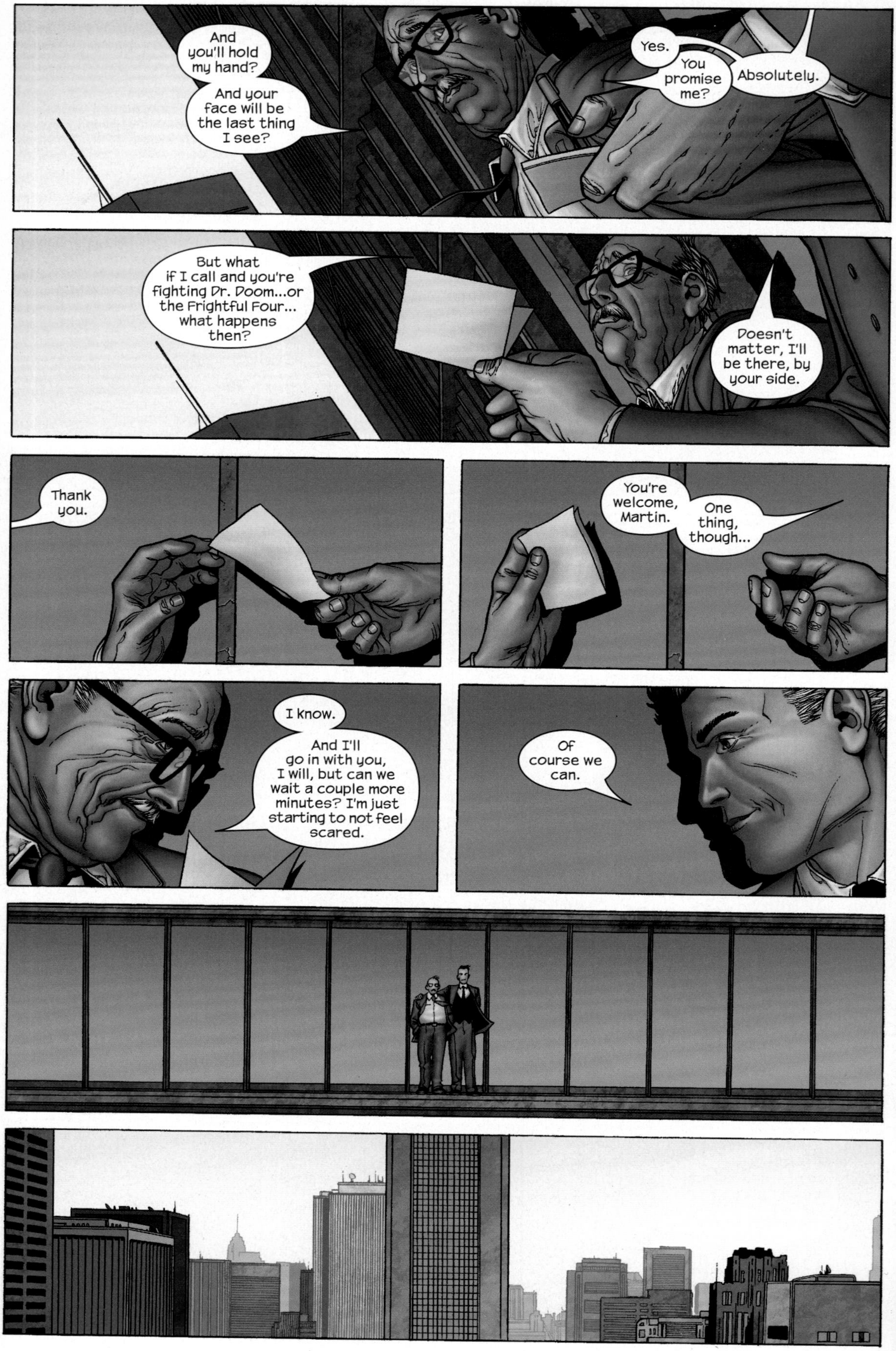
And you'll hold my hand?
And your face will be the last thing I see?
Yes.
You promise me?
Absolutely.
But what if I call and you're fighting Dr. Doom...or the Frightful Four... what happens then?
Doesn't matter, I'll be there, by your side.
Thank you.
You're welcome, Martin.
One thing, though...
I know.
And I'll go in with you, I will, but can we wait a couple more minutes? I'm just starting to not feel scared.
Of course we can.

Comparatively speaking, the rest of my day's fairly uneventful.

When I finally get to my desk, I have 49 e-mails waiting for me. All from law firm people needing technical support.

It takes me most of the morning to go through them.

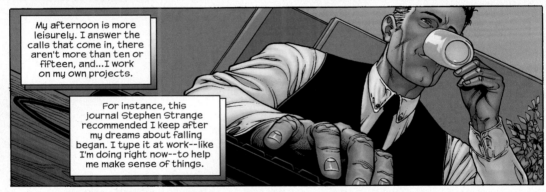

My afternoon is more leisurely. I answer the calls that come in, there aren't more than ten or fifteen, and...I work on my own projects.

For instance, this journal Stephen Strange recommended I keep after my dreams about falling began. I type it at work--like I'm doing right now--to help me make sense of things.

I write about my dreams...and how I spend my days...and my memories.

It's *odd* what comes back to you. How you remember things you didn't even know you'd *forgotten*.

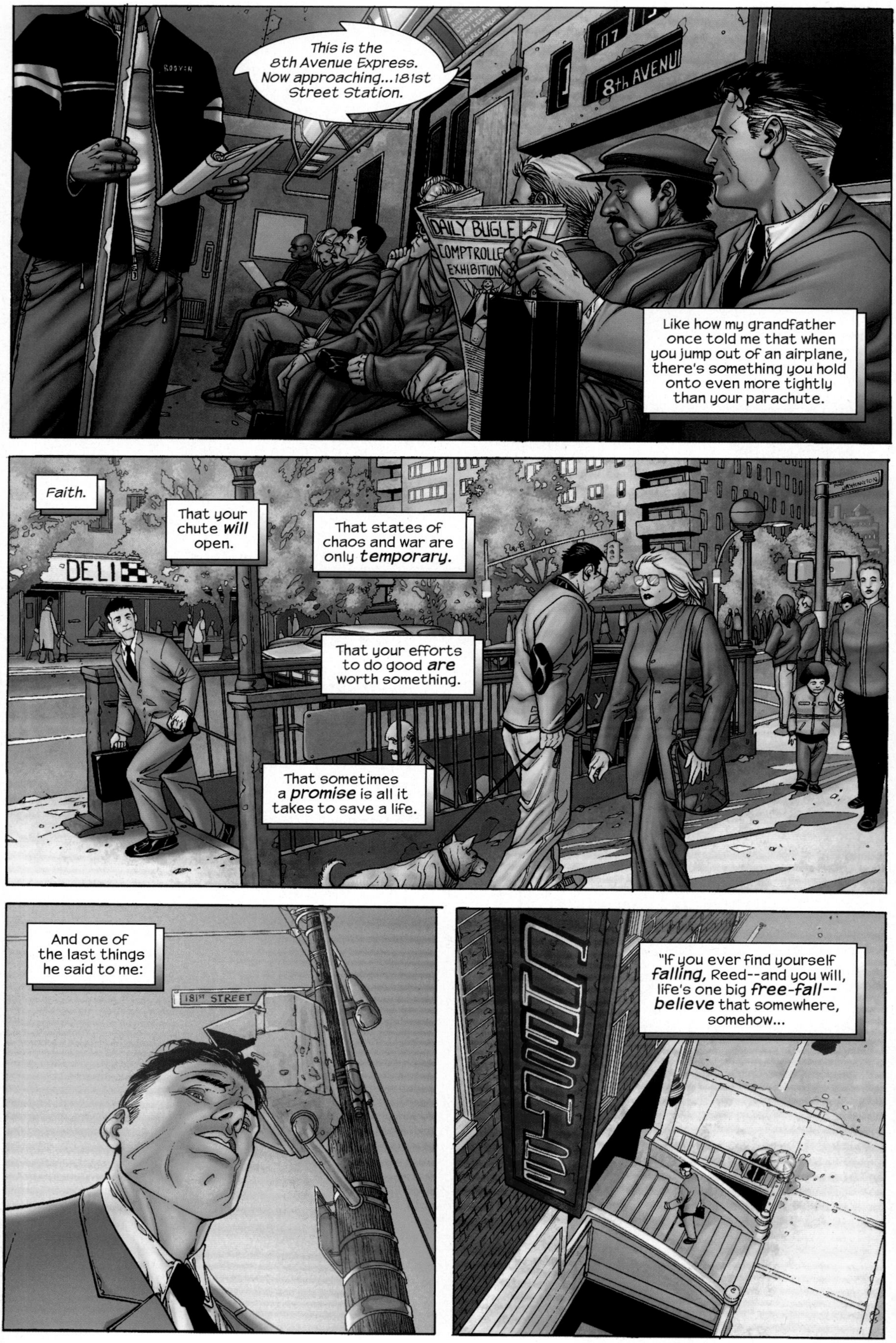
This is the 8th Avenue Express. Now approaching...181st Street Station.
8th AVENUE
DAILY BUGLE
COMPTROLLER
EXHIBITION
Like how my grandfather once told me that when you jump out of an airplane, there's something you hold onto even more tightly than your parachute.
Faith.
That your chute *will* open.
That states of chaos and war are only *temporary.*
DELI
That your efforts to do good *are* worth something.
That sometimes a *promise* is all it takes to save a life.
And one of the last things he said to me:
181st STREET
"If you ever find yourself *falling,* Reed--and you will, life's one big *free-fall--* *believe* that somewhere, somehow...

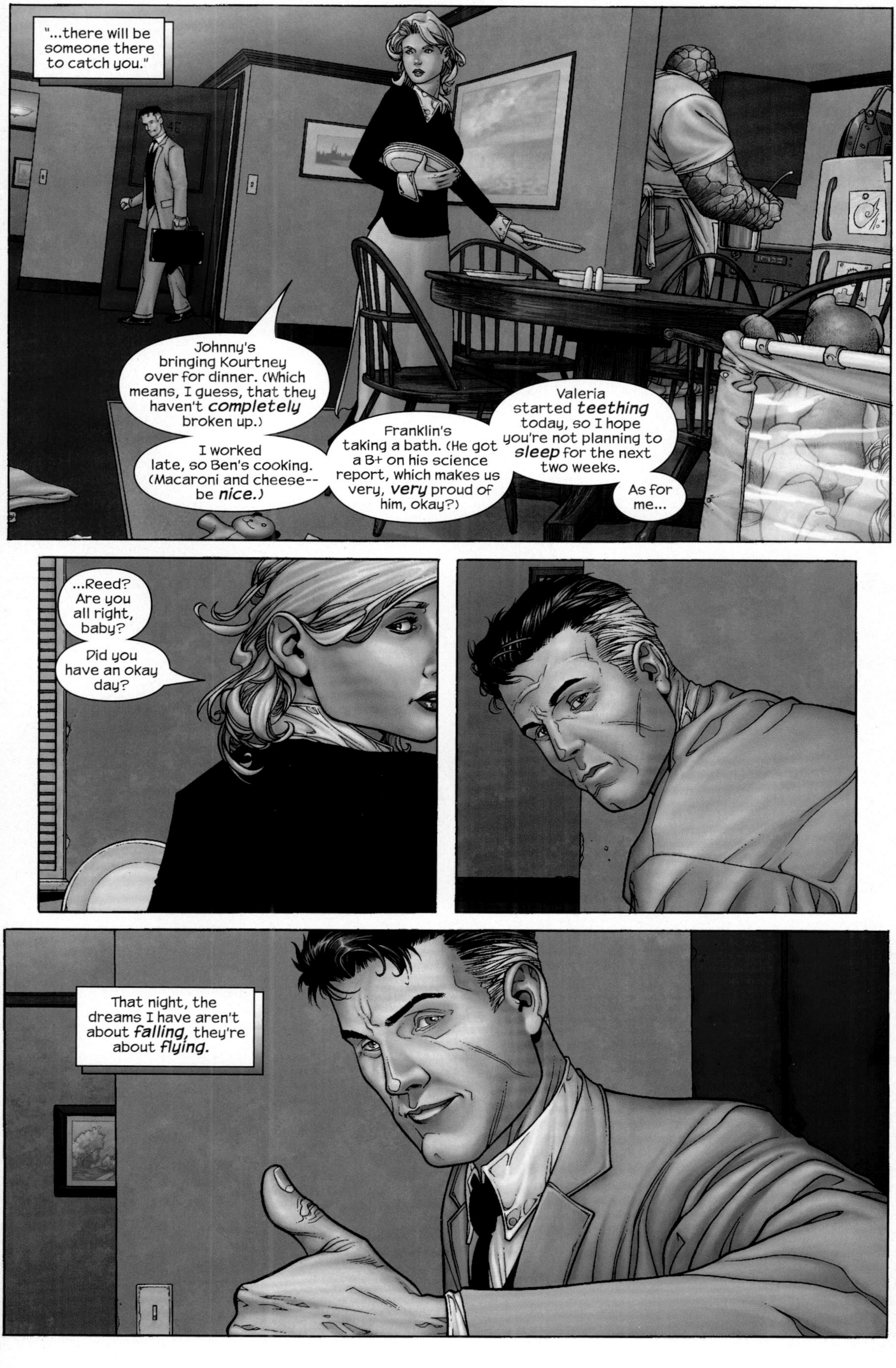
"...there will be someone there to catch you."
Johnny's bringing Kourtney over for dinner. (Which means, I guess, that they haven't *completely* broken up.)
I worked late, so Ben's cooking. (Macaroni and cheese-- be *nice.*)
Franklin's taking a bath. (He got a B+ on his science report, which makes us very, *very* proud of him, okay?)
Valeria started *teething* today, so I hope you're not planning to *sleep* for the next two weeks.
As for me...
...Reed? Are you all right, baby?
Did you have an okay day?
That night, the dreams I have aren't about *falling,* they're about *flying.*

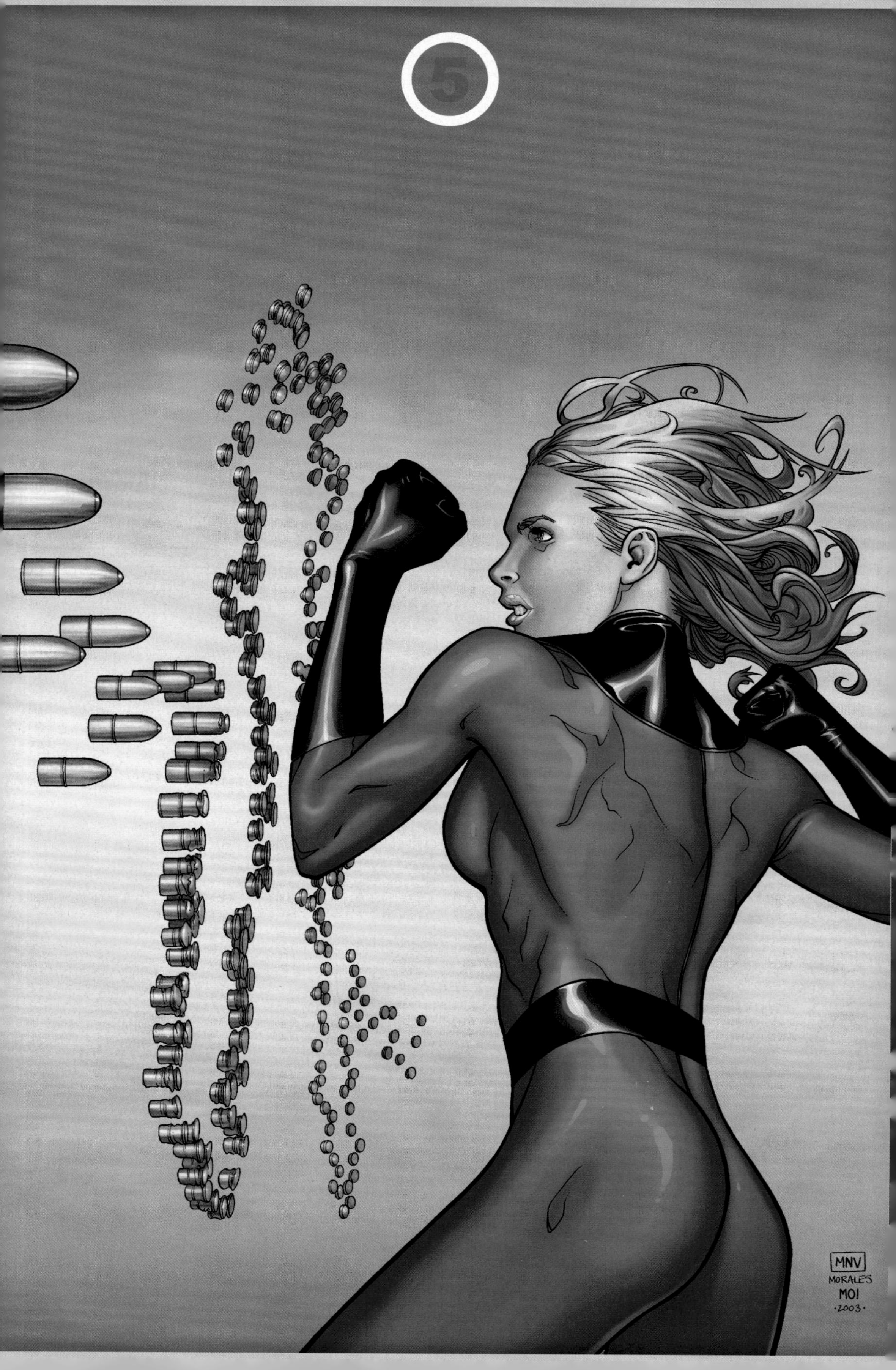

5
MNV
MORALES
MO!
·2003·

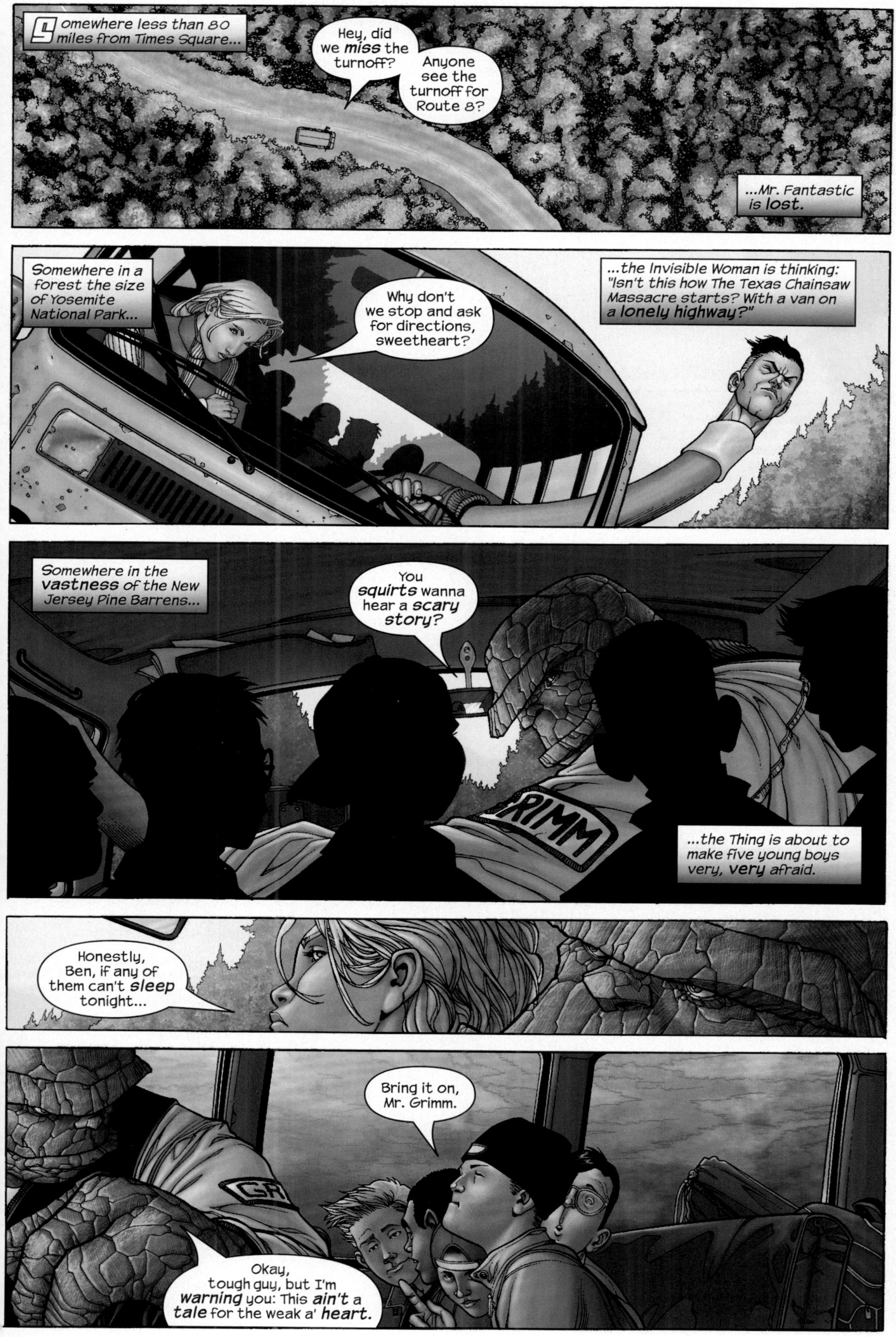
Somewhere less than 80 miles from Times Square...
Hey, did we miss the turnoff?
Anyone see the turnoff for Route 8?
...Mr. Fantastic is lost.
Somewhere in a forest the size of Yosemite National Park...
Why don't we stop and ask for directions, sweetheart?
...the Invisible Woman is thinking: "Isn't this how The Texas Chainsaw Massacre starts? With a van on a lonely highway?"
Somewhere in the vastness of the New Jersey Pine Barrens...
You squirts wanna hear a scary story?
GRIMM
...the Thing is about to make five young boys very, very afraid.
Honestly, Ben, if any of them can't sleep tonight...
Bring it on, Mr. Grimm.
Okay, tough guy, but I'm warning you: This ain't a tale for the weak a' heart.

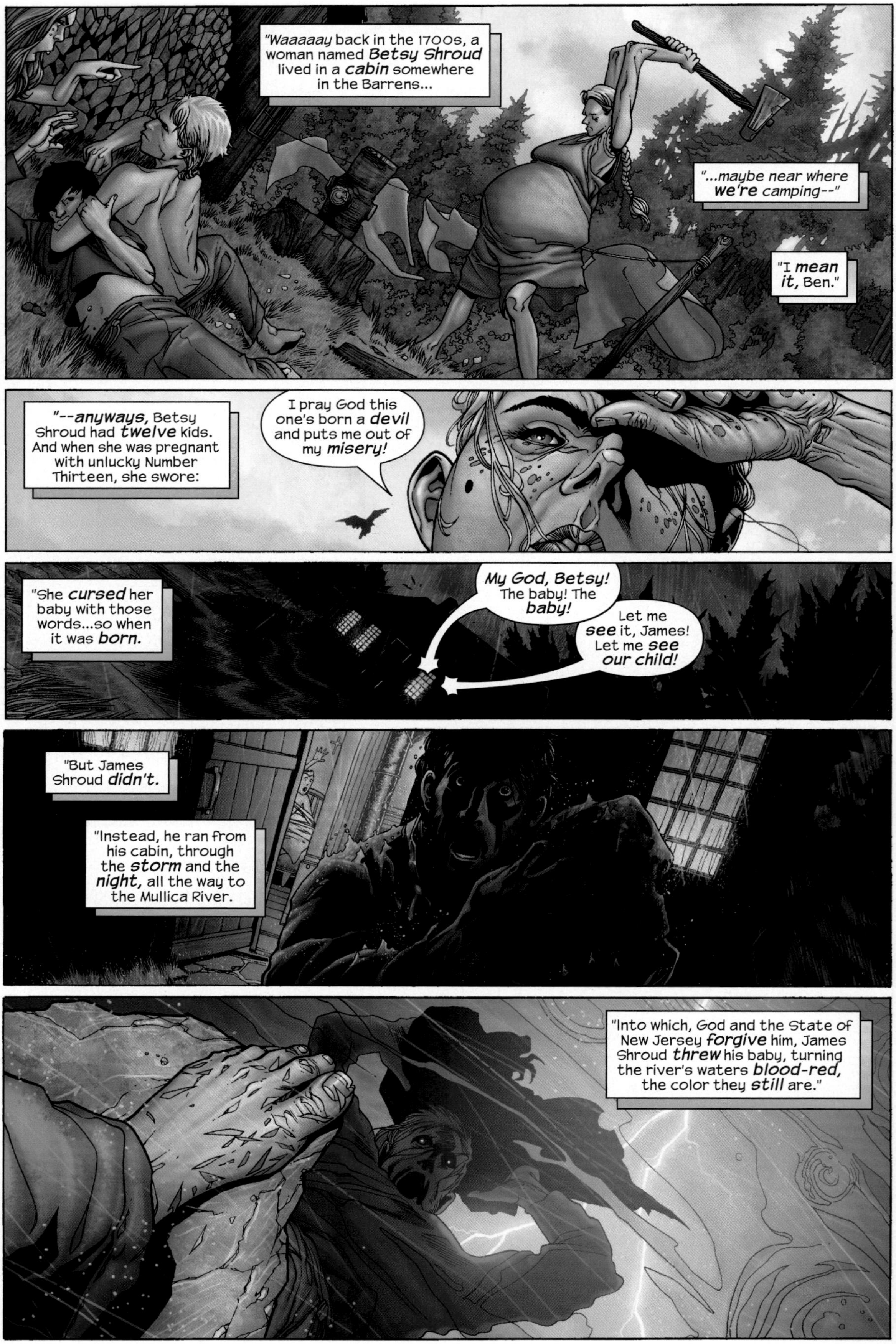
"Waaaaay back in the 1700s, a woman named Betsy Shroud lived in a cabin somewhere in the Barrens...
"...maybe near where we're camping--"
"I mean it, Ben."
"--anyways, Betsy Shroud had twelve kids. And when she was pregnant with unlucky Number Thirteen, she swore:
I pray God this one's born a devil and puts me out of my misery!
"She cursed her baby with those words...so when it was born.
My God, Betsy! The baby! The baby!
Let me see it, James! Let me see our child!
"But James Shroud didn't.
"Instead, he ran from his cabin, through the storm and the night, all the way to the Mullica River.
"Into which, God and the State of New Jersey forgive him, James Shroud threw his baby, turning the river's waters blood-red, the color they still are."

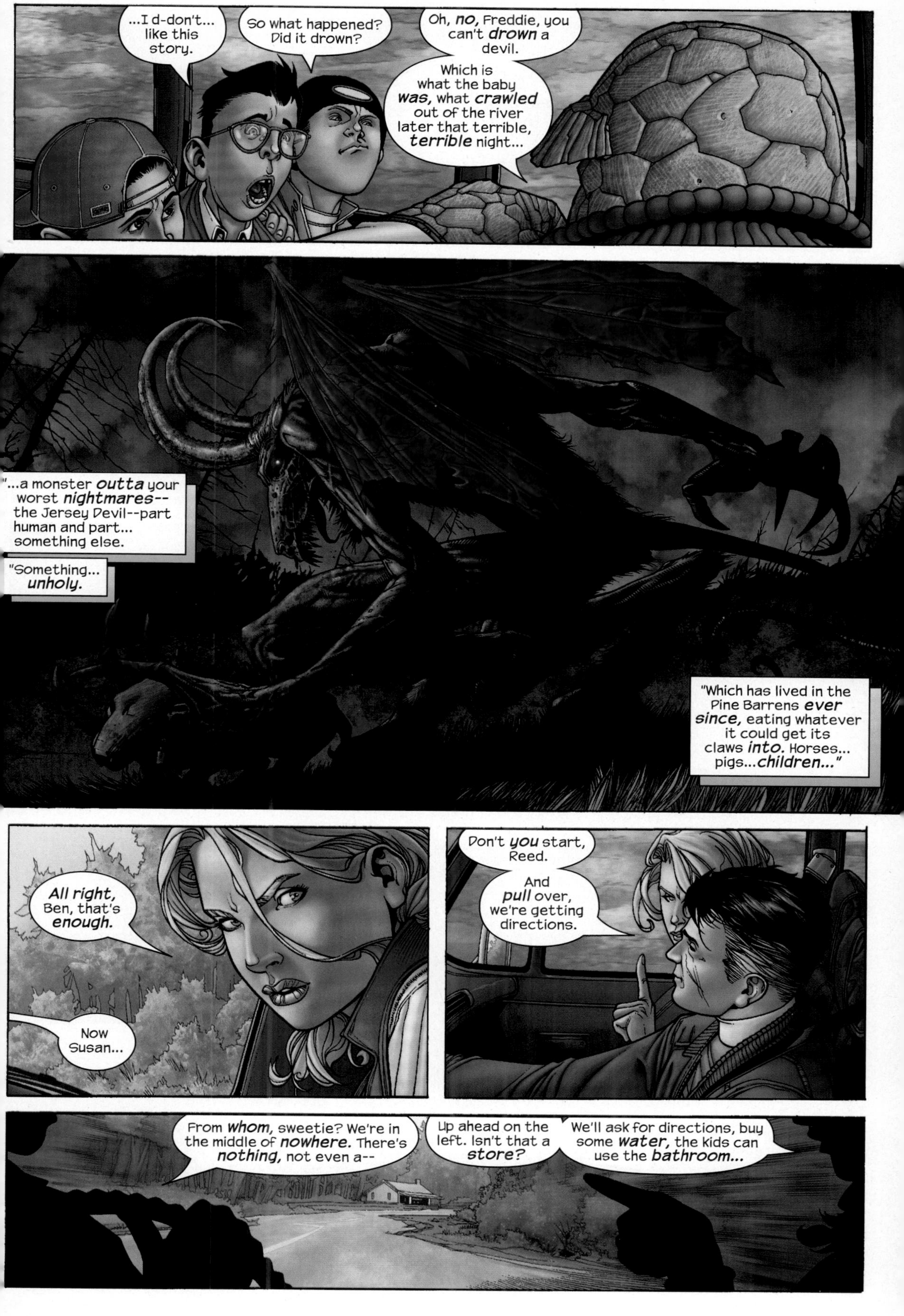
...I d-don't... like this story.
So what happened? Did it drown?
Oh, no, Freddie, you can't drown a devil.
Which is what the baby was, what crawled out of the river later that terrible, terrible night...
"...a monster outta your worst nightmares--the Jersey Devil--part human and part... something else.
"Something... unholy.
"Which has lived in the Pine Barrens ever since, eating whatever it could get its claws into. Horses... pigs...children..."
All right, Ben, that's enough.
Now Susan...
Don't you start, Reed.
And pull over, we're getting directions.
From whom, sweetie? We're in the middle of nowhere. There's nothing, not even a--
Up ahead on the left. Isn't that a store?
We'll ask for directions, buy some water, the kids can use the bathroom...

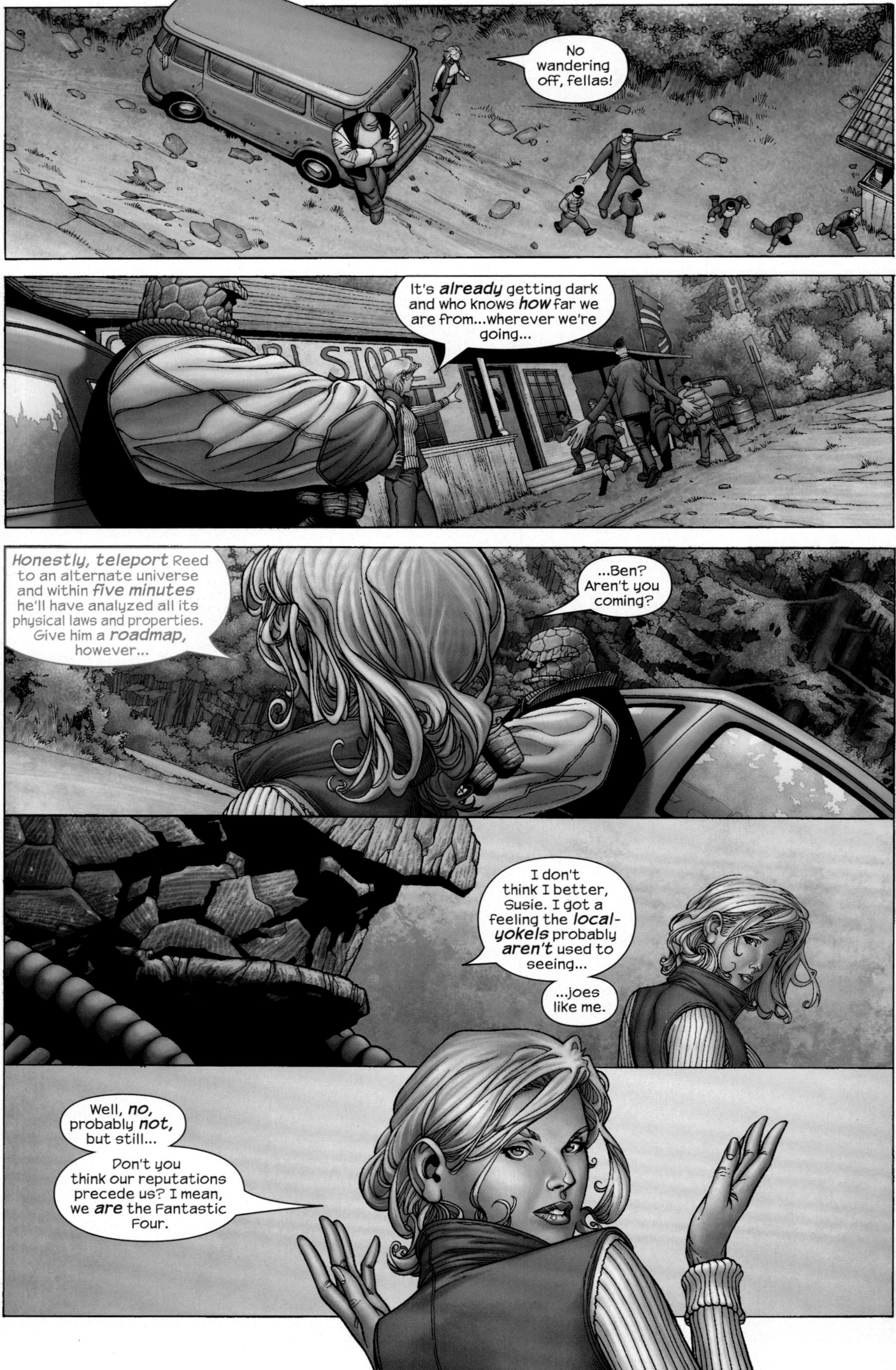
No wandering off, fellas!
It's already getting dark and who knows how far we are from...wherever we're going...
STORE
Honestly, teleport Reed to an alternate universe and within five minutes he'll have analyzed all its physical laws and properties. Give him a roadmap, however...
...Ben? Aren't you coming?
I don't think I better, Susie. I got a feeling the local-yokels probably aren't used to seeing...
...joes like me.
Well, no, probably not, but still...
Don't you think our reputations precede us? I mean, we are the Fantastic Four.

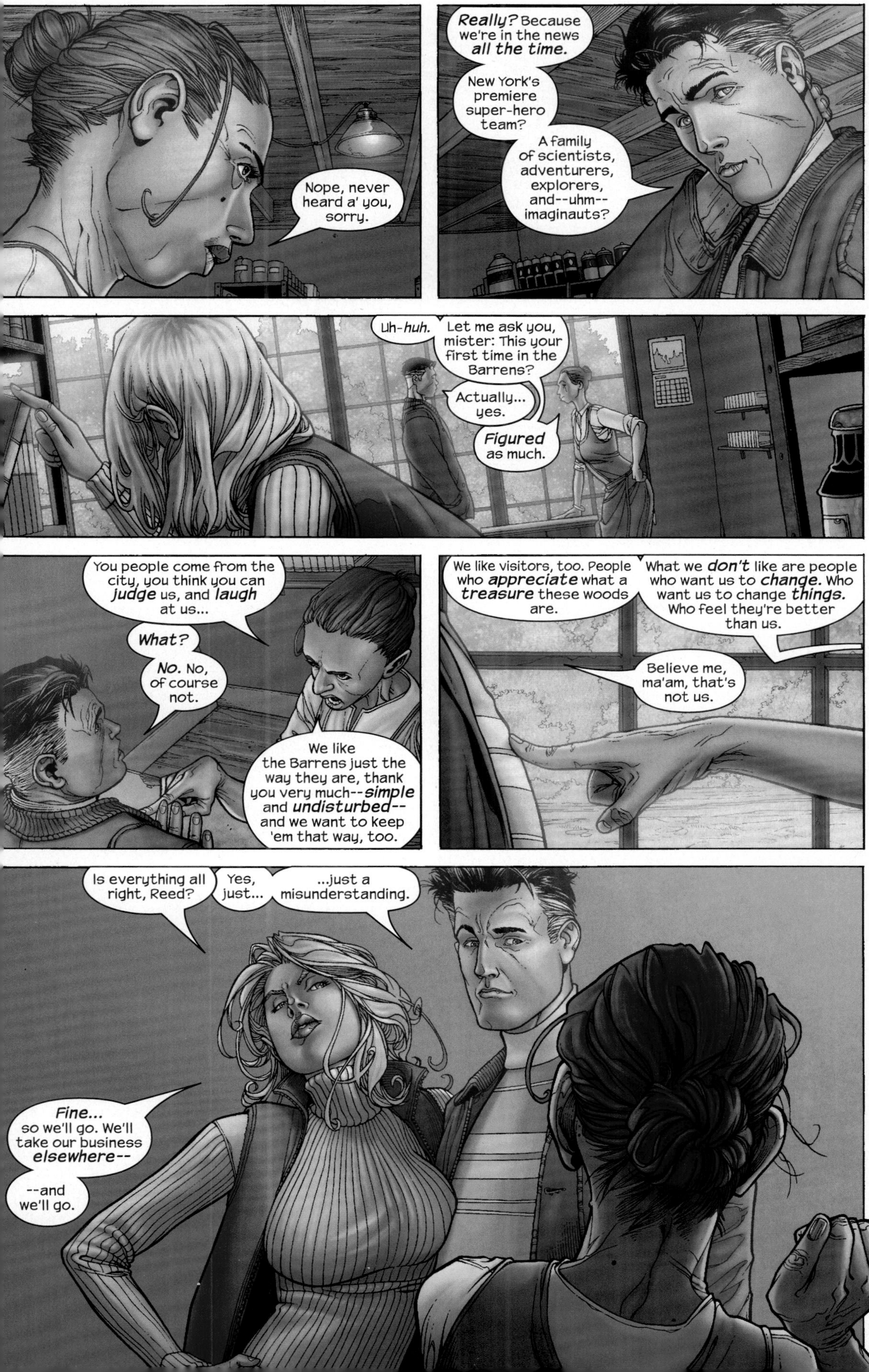
Nope, never heard a' you, sorry.
Really? Because we're in the news all the time.
New York's premiere super-hero team?
A family of scientists, adventurers, explorers, and--uhm--imaginauts?
Uh-huh.
Let me ask you, mister: This your first time in the Barrens?
Actually... yes.
Figured as much.
You people come from the city, you think you can judge us, and laugh at us...
What?
No. No, of course not.
We like the Barrens just the way they are, thank you very much--simple and undisturbed--and we want to keep 'em that way, too.
We like visitors, too. People who appreciate what a treasure these woods are.
What we don't like are people who want us to change. Who want us to change things. Who feel they're better than us.
Believe me, ma'am, that's not us.
Is everything all right, Reed?
Yes, just...
...just a misunderstanding.
Fine... so we'll go. We'll take our business elsewhere--
--and we'll go.

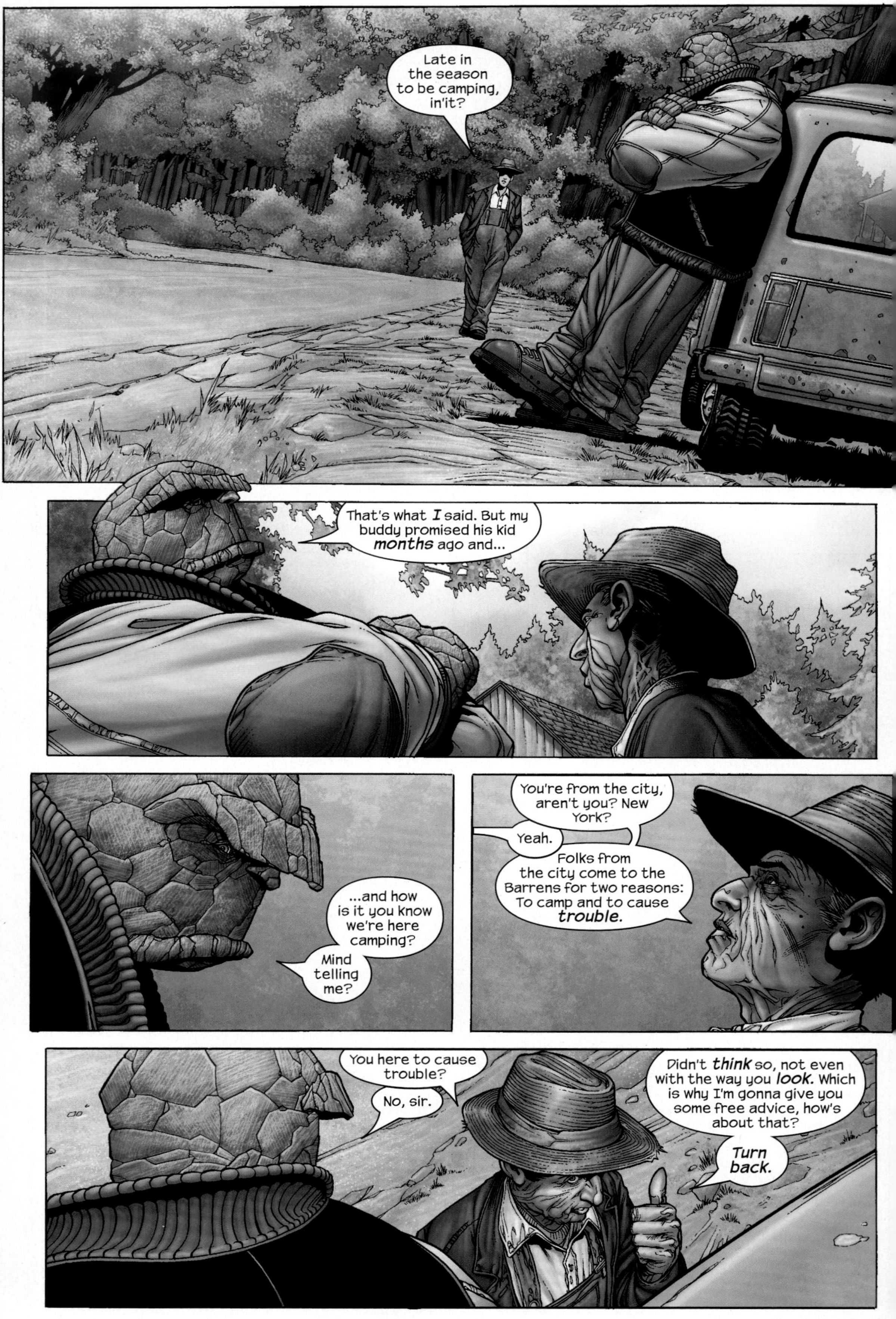
Late in the season to be camping, in'it?
That's what I said. But my buddy promised his kid months ago and...
...and how is it you know we're here camping?
Mind telling me?
You're from the city, aren't you? New York?
Yeah.
Folks from the city come to the Barrens for two reasons: To camp and to cause trouble.
You here to cause trouble?
No, sir.
Didn't think so, not even with the way you look. Which is why I'm gonna give you some free advice, how's about that?
Turn back.

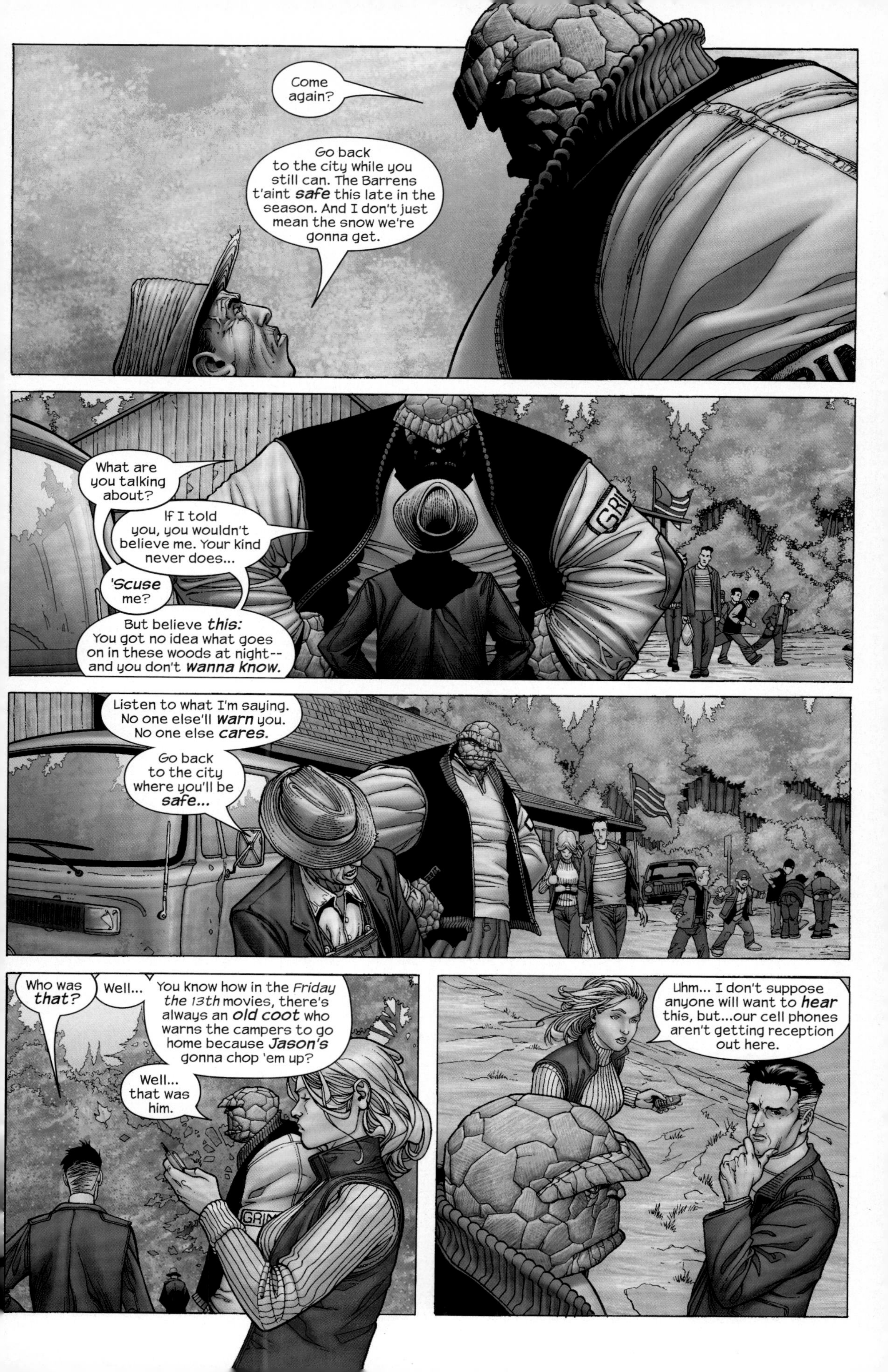

Come again?
Go back to the city while you still can. The Barrens t'aint *safe* this late in the season. And I don't just mean the snow we're gonna get.
What are you talking about?
If I told you, you wouldn't believe me. Your kind never does...
'Scuse me?
But believe *this:* You got no idea what goes on in these woods at night--and you don't *wanna know.*
Listen to what I'm saying. No one else'll *warn* you. No one else *cares.*
Go back to the city where you'll be *safe...*
Who was *that?*
Well...
You know how in the *Friday the 13th* movies, there's always an *old coot* who warns the campers to go home because *Jason's* gonna chop 'em up?
Well... that was him.
Uhm... I don't suppose anyone will want to *hear* this, but...our cell phones aren't getting reception out here.

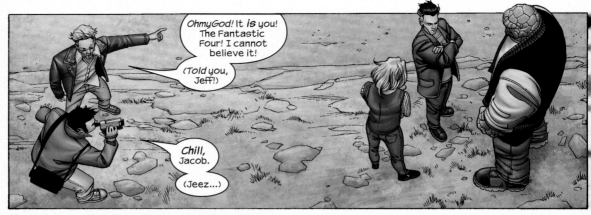

OhmyGod! It *is* you! The Fantastic Four! I cannot believe it!

(Told you, Jeff!)

Chill, Jacob.

(Jeez...)

Can we help you?

Oh, *no*, dudes, we're just--we're *huge* fans. We're here making a documentary. (We're *filmmakers*, you know? We went to *film school*?) About the Jersey Devil. (Well, the *legend* of the Jersey Devil. You know, kinda like *The Blair Witch Project*-- but *real*.)

What are you guys doing here? Tracking some super-villain? (Oh, man, are we in *danger*?)

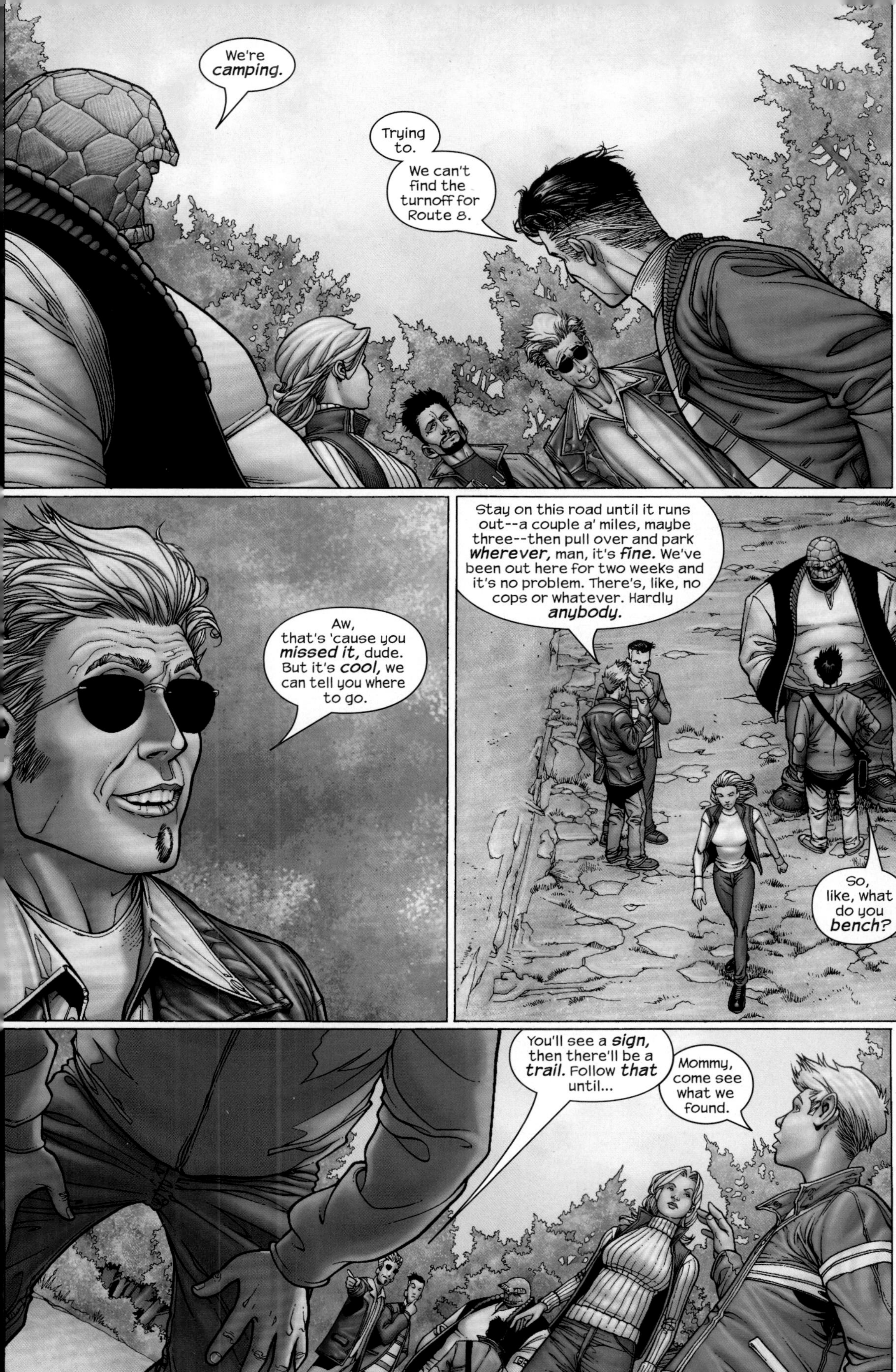
We're *camping.*
Trying to.
We can't find the turnoff for Route 8.
Aw, that's 'cause you *missed it,* dude. But it's *cool,* we can tell you where to go.
Stay on this road until it runs out--a couple a' miles, maybe three--then pull over and park *wherever,* man, it's *fine.* We've been out here for two weeks and it's no problem. There's, like, no cops or whatever. Hardly *anybody.*
So, like, what do you *bench?*
You'll see a *sign,* then there'll be a *trail.* Follow *that* until...
Mommy, come see what we found.

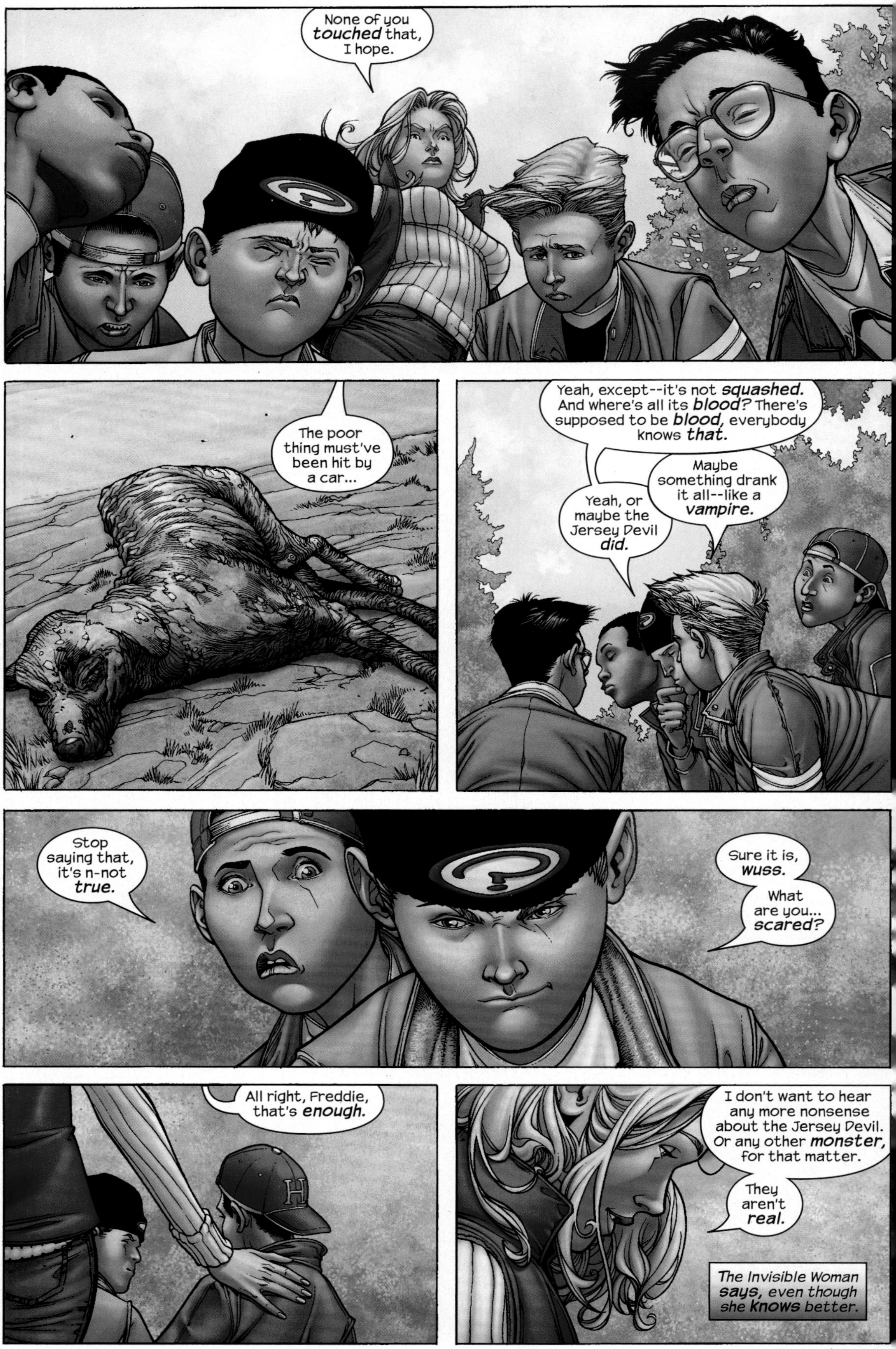
None of you touched that, I hope.
The poor thing must've been hit by a car...
Yeah, except--it's not squashed. And where's all its blood? There's supposed to be blood, everybody knows that.
Yeah, or maybe the Jersey Devil did.
Maybe something drank it all--like a vampire.
Stop saying that, it's n-not true.
Sure it is, wuss.
What are you... scared?
All right, Freddie, that's enough.
I don't want to hear any more nonsense about the Jersey Devil. Or any other monster, for that matter.
They aren't real.
The Invisible Woman says, even though she knows better.

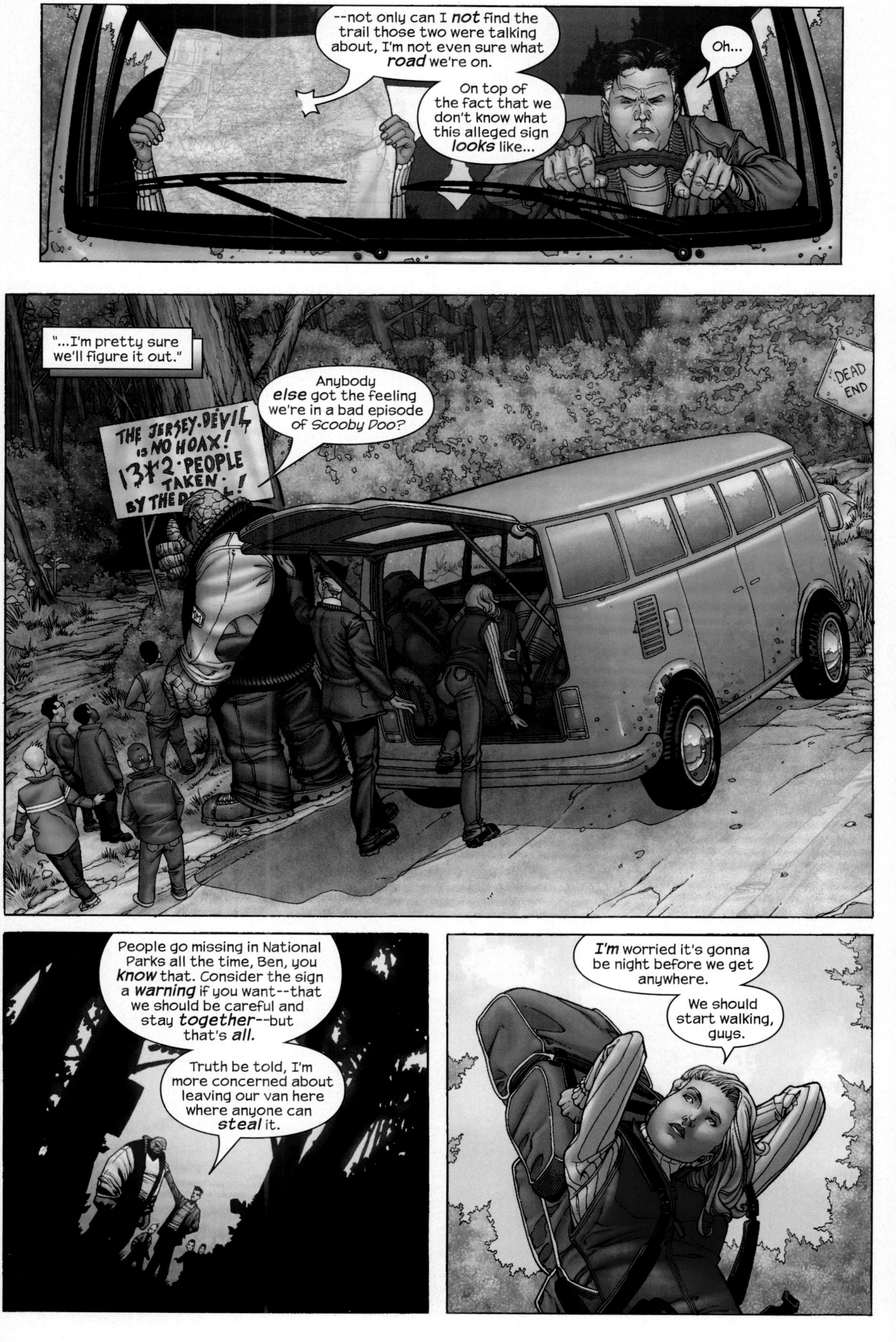
--not only can I *not* find the trail those two were talking about, I'm not even sure what *road* we're on.
On top of the fact that we don't know what this alleged sign *looks* like...
Oh...
"...I'm pretty sure we'll figure it out."
Anybody *else* got the feeling we're in a bad episode of *Scooby Doo*?
THE JERSEY DEVIL IS NO HOAX!
13 X 2 PEOPLE TAKEN
DEAD END
People go missing in National Parks all the time, Ben, you *know* that. Consider the sign a *warning* if you want--that we should be careful and stay *together*--but that's *all.*
Truth be told, I'm more concerned about leaving our van here where anyone can *steal* it.
I'm worried it's gonna be night before we get anywhere.
We should start walking, guys.

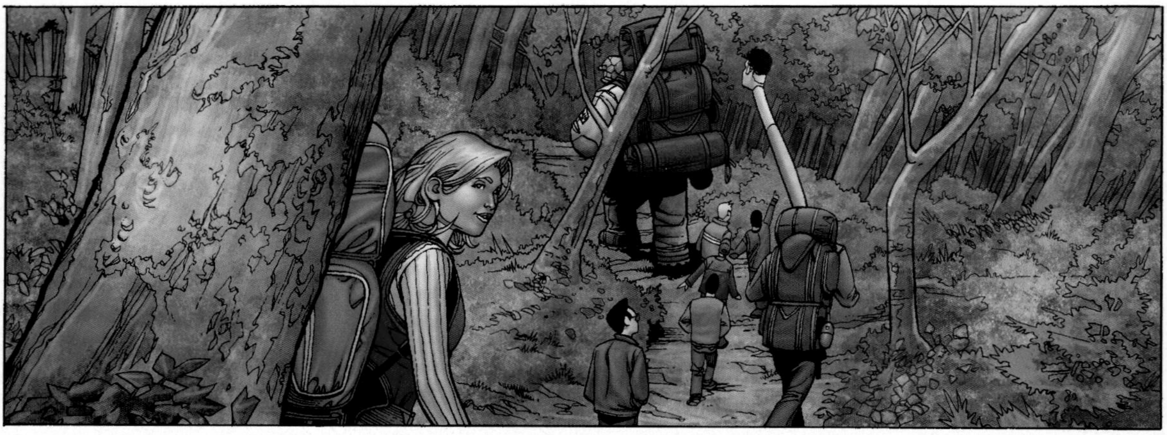

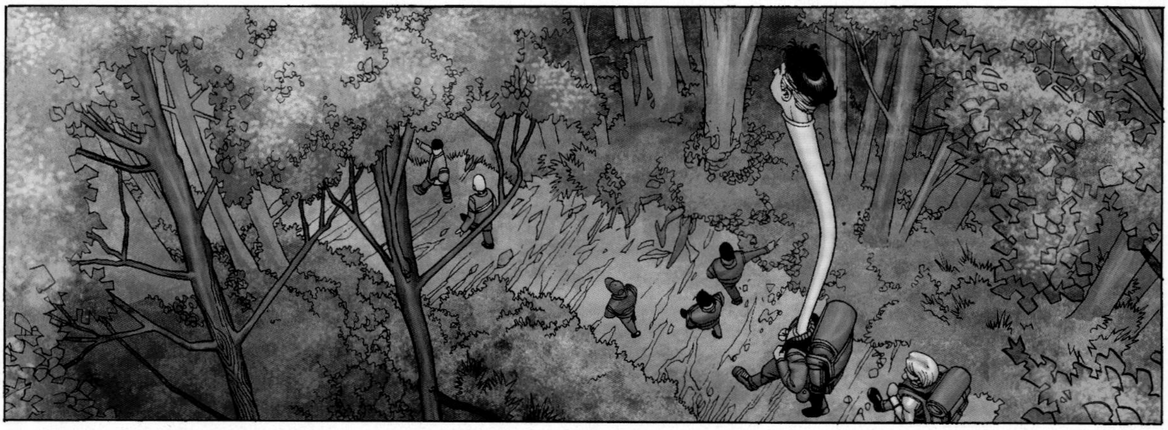

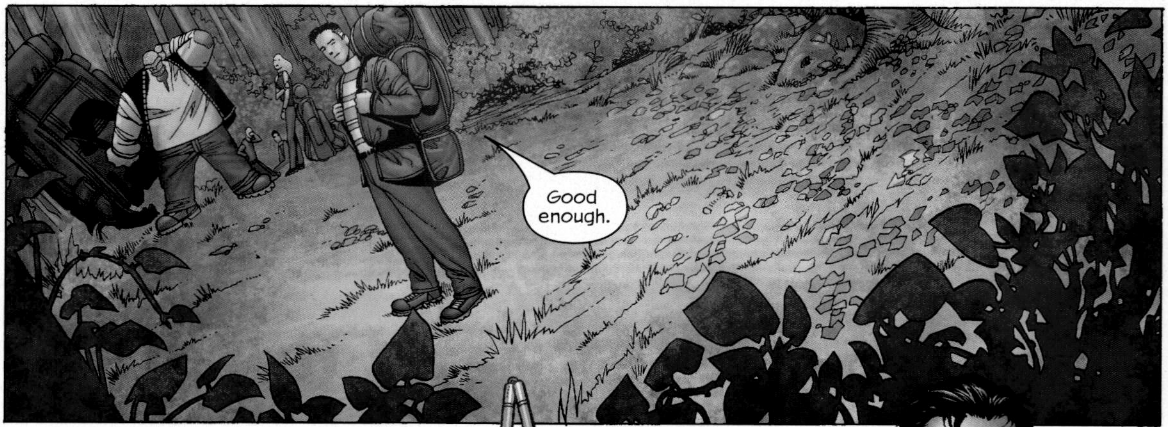
Good enough.

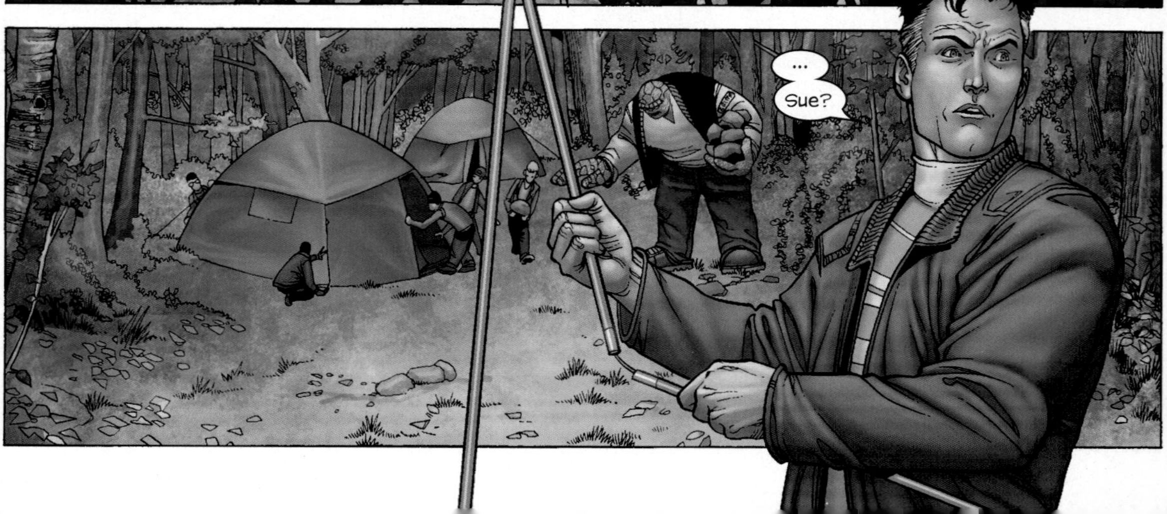
...
Sue?

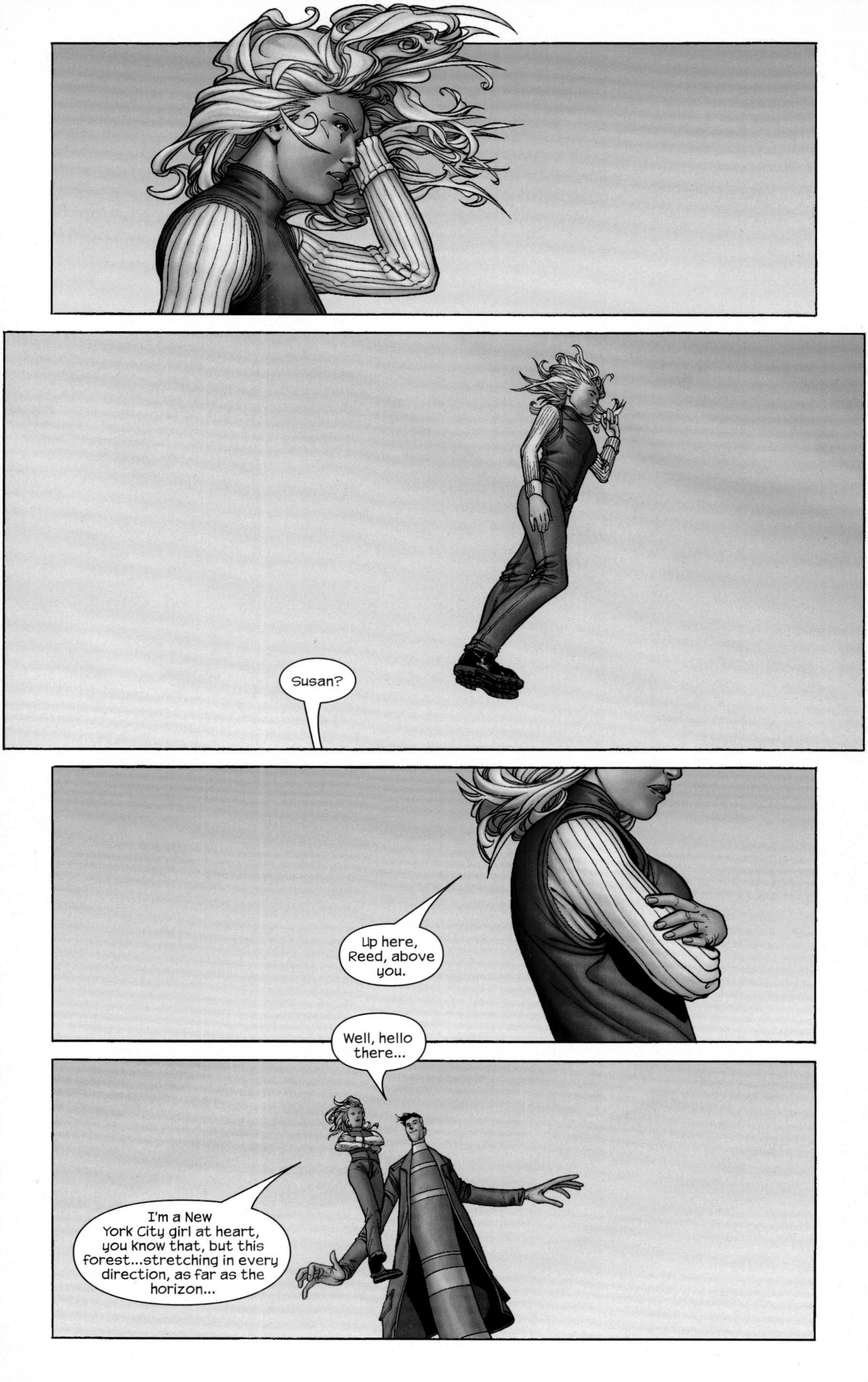
Susan?
Up here, Reed, above you.
Well, hello there...
I'm a New York City girl at heart, you know that, but this forest...stretching in every direction, as far as the horizon...

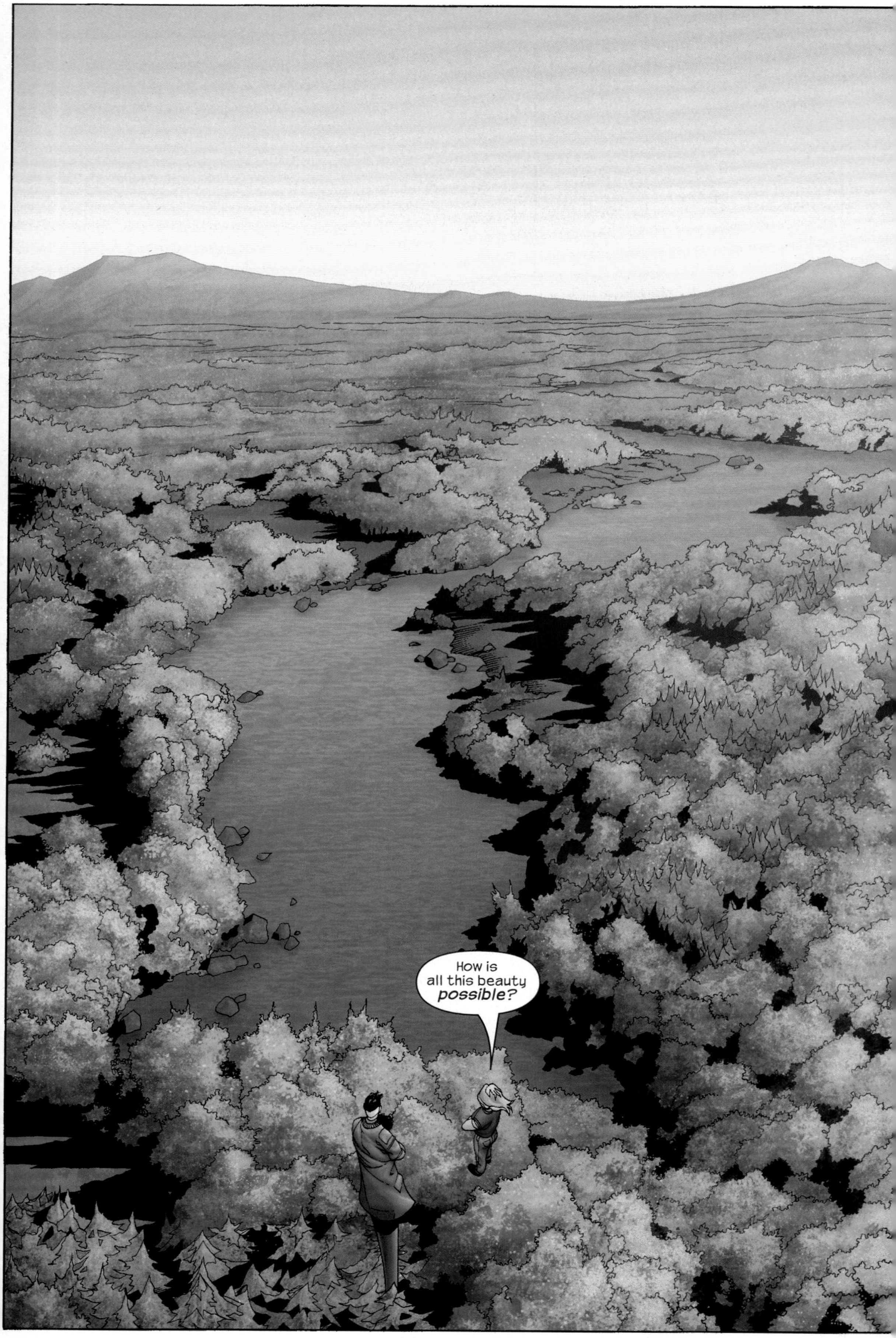
How is all this beauty possible?

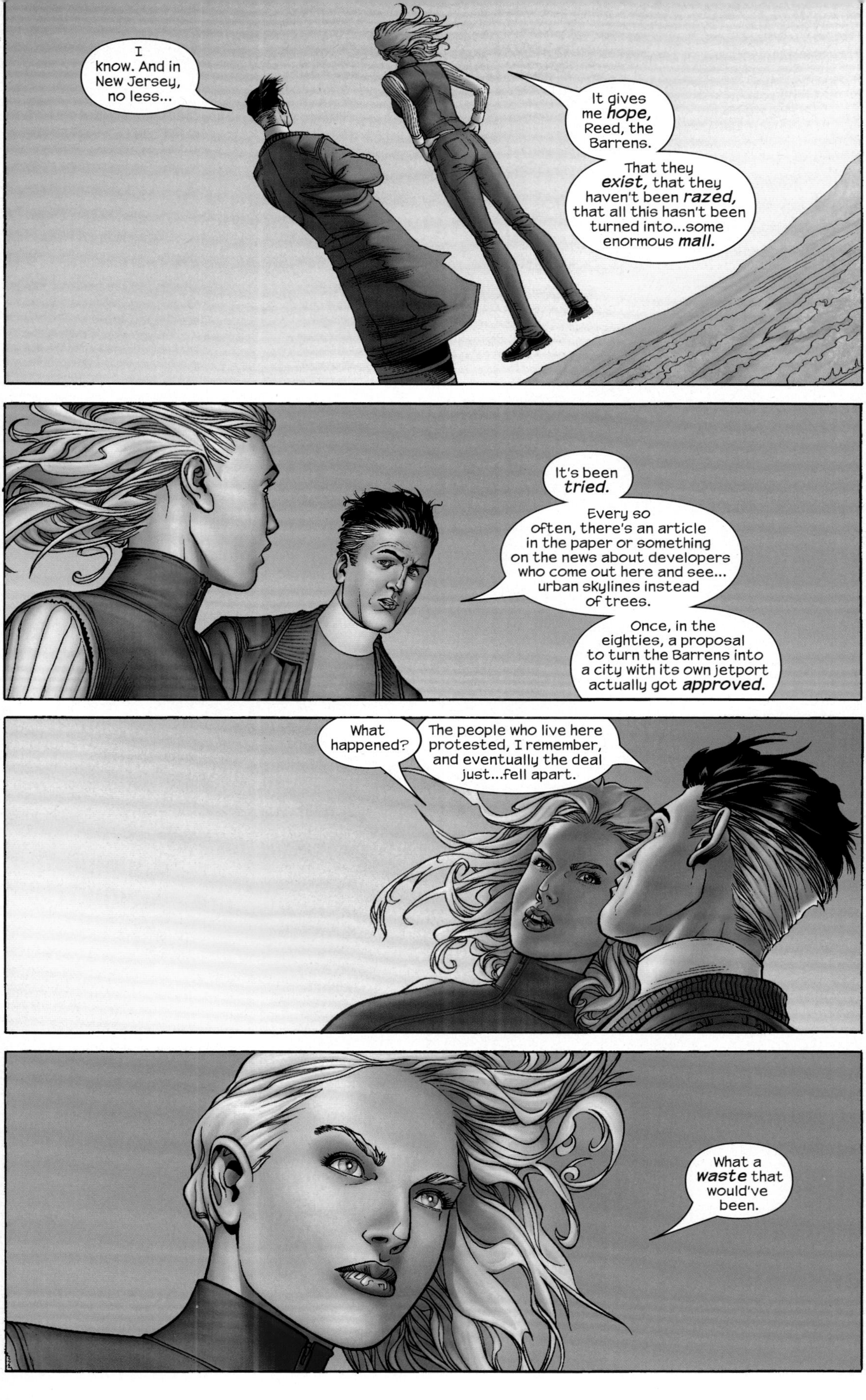

I know. And in New Jersey, no less...
It gives me *hope,* Reed, the Barrens.
That they *exist,* that they haven't been *razed,* that all this hasn't been turned into...some enormous *mall.*
It's been *tried.*
Every so often, there's an article in the paper or something on the news about developers who come out here and see... urban skylines instead of trees.
Once, in the eighties, a proposal to turn the Barrens into a city with its own jetport actually got *approved.*
What happened?
The people who live here protested, I remember, and eventually the deal just...fell apart.
What a *waste* that would've been.

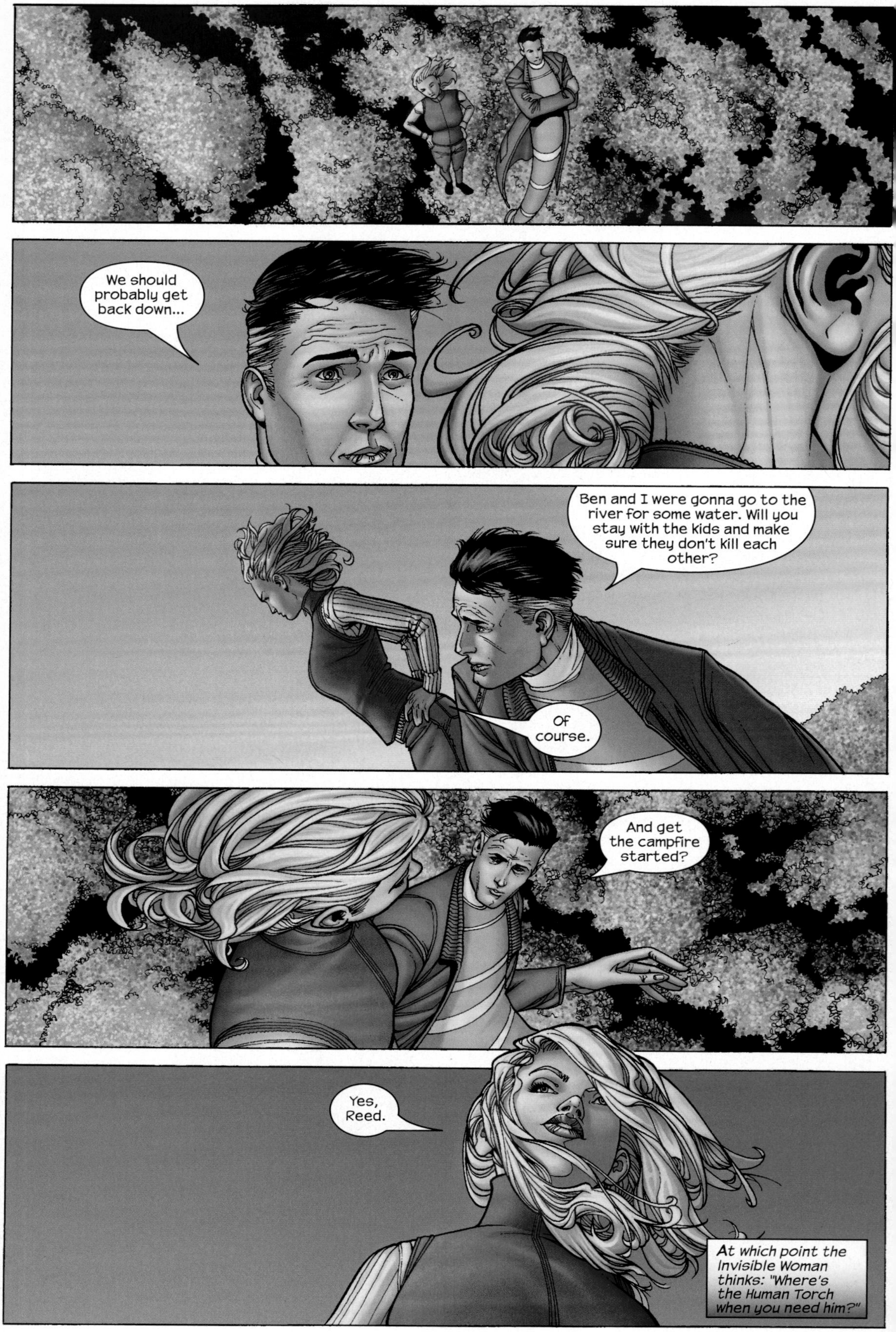
We should probably get back down...
Ben and I were gonna go to the river for some water. Will you stay with the kids and make sure they don't kill each other?
Of course.
And get the campfire started?
Yes, Reed.
At which point the Invisible Woman thinks: "Where's the Human Torch when you need him?"

--you're operating under a *serious* misapprehension, son. We're in the business of *putting out fires*, not *starting* them.

I realize that, Chief, but I...

...oh, *man*, this is hard...

...I've thought about it, and...

...that is...I *mean*...

You wanna be a fireman when you grow up?

Yes.

I've taken the written tests, I meet all the physical requirements, I'm mentally stable, I'm the right age, I'm healthy, I can *fly*...

(I know that's not a requirement, I just thought I would mention it.)

I can--

This isn't like getting a job at McDonald's, son.

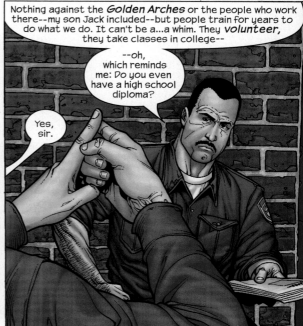

Nothing against the *Golden Arches* or the people who work there--my son Jack included--but people train for years to do what we do. It can't be a...a whim. They *volunteer*, they take classes in college--

--oh, which reminds me: Do you even have a high school diploma?

Yes, sir.

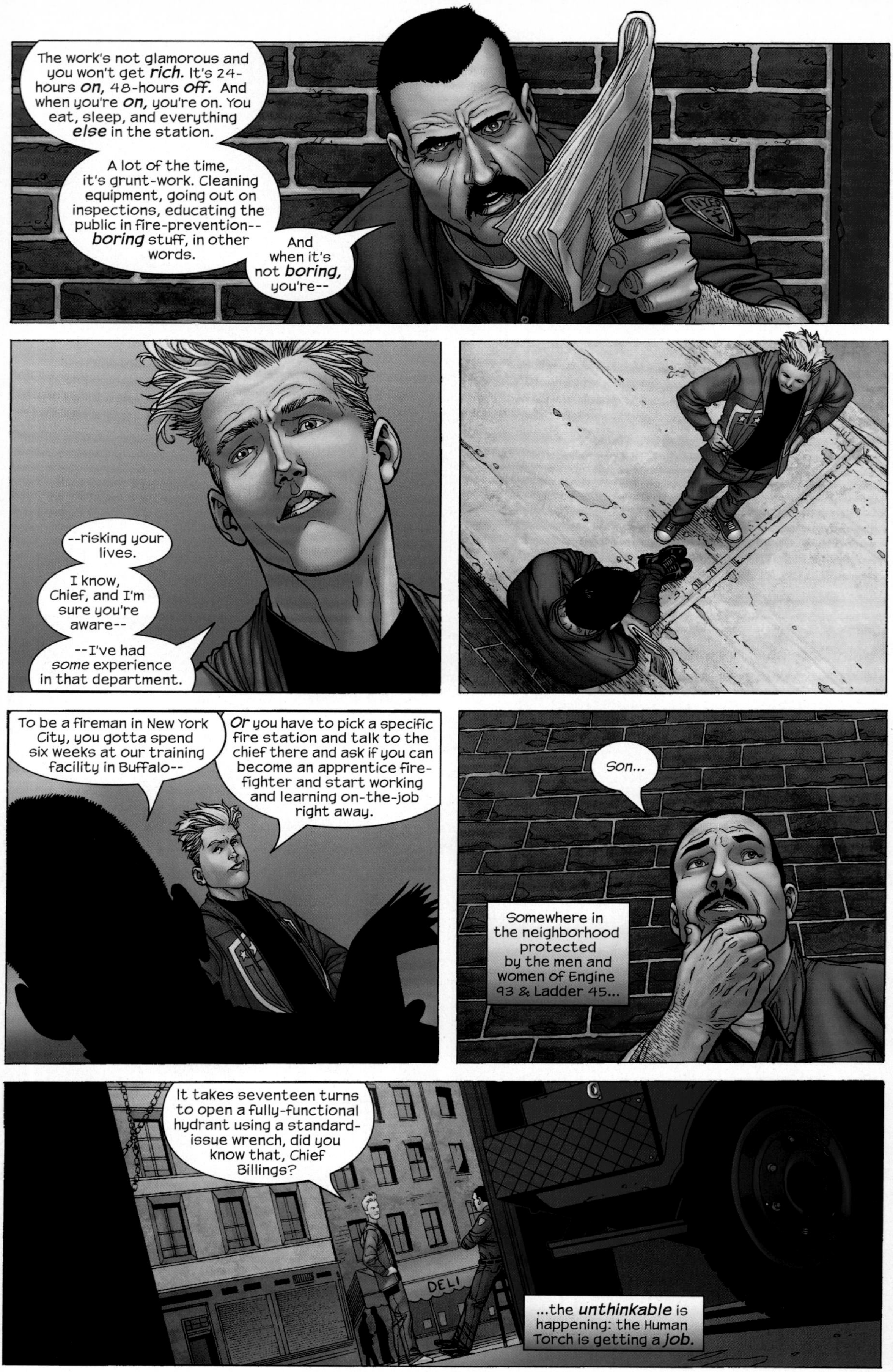

The work's not glamorous and you won't get *rich.* It's 24-hours *on,* 48-hours *off.* And when you're *on,* you're on. You eat, sleep, and everything *else* in the station.
A lot of the time, it's grunt-work. Cleaning equipment, going out on inspections, educating the public in fire-prevention-- *boring* stuff, in other words.
And when it's not *boring,* you're--
--risking your lives.
I know, Chief, and I'm sure you're aware--
--I've had *some* experience in that department.
To be a fireman in New York City, you gotta spend six weeks at our training facility in Buffalo--
Or you have to pick a specific fire station and talk to the chief there and ask if you can become an apprentice fire-fighter and start working and learning on-the-job right away.
Son...
Somewhere in the neighborhood protected by the men and women of Engine 93 & Ladder 45...
It takes seventeen turns to open a fully-functional hydrant using a standard-issue wrench, did you know that, Chief Billings?
DELI
...the *unthinkable* is happening: the Human Torch is getting a *job.*

You *sure* this is the way, Stretch?

From what I could tell when I was fifty feet up...

I *think* so.

Incidentally, Ben, the *real* reason the Mullica River looks blood-red?

It's the oak trees *lining* the river.

Their maroon sap soaks into the ground, into the water, making it *appear*...

...Ben?

What is it, Ben, the river?

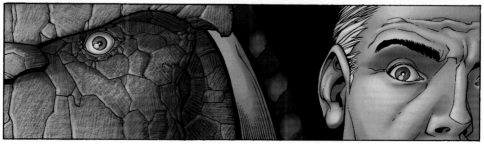

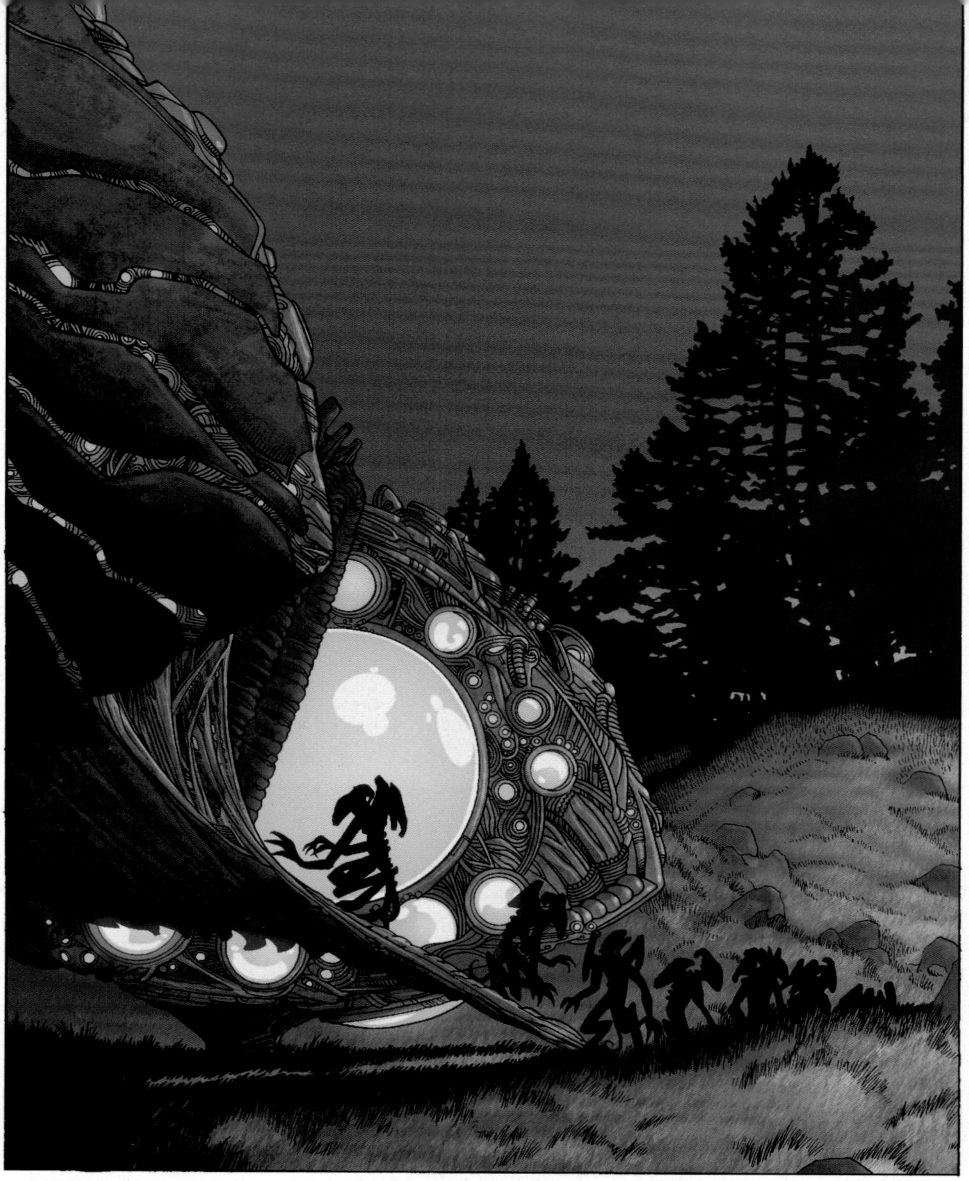

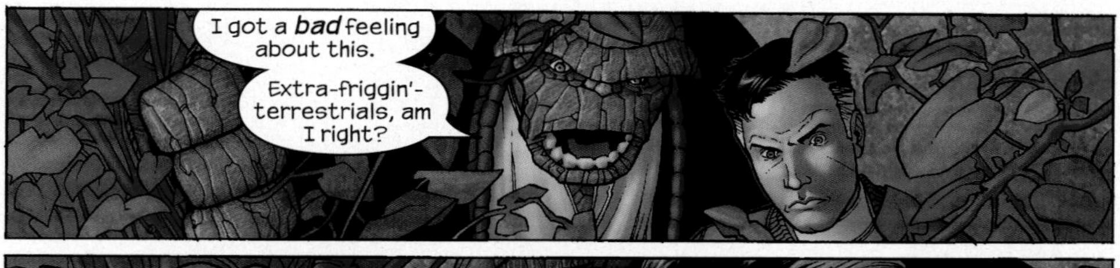
I got a bad feeling about this.
Extra-friggin'-terrestrials, am I right?

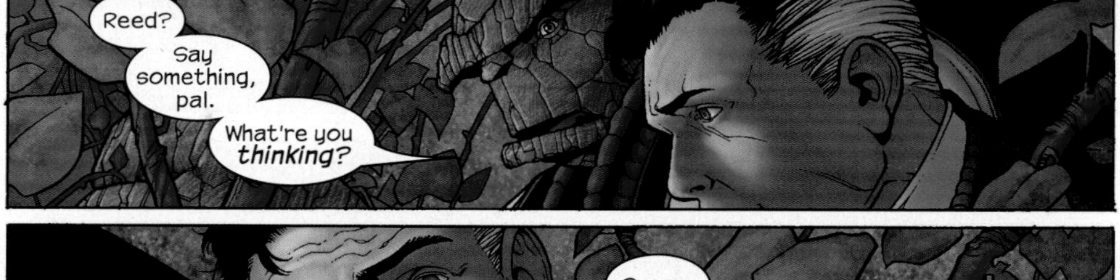
Reed?
Say something, pal.
What're you thinking?

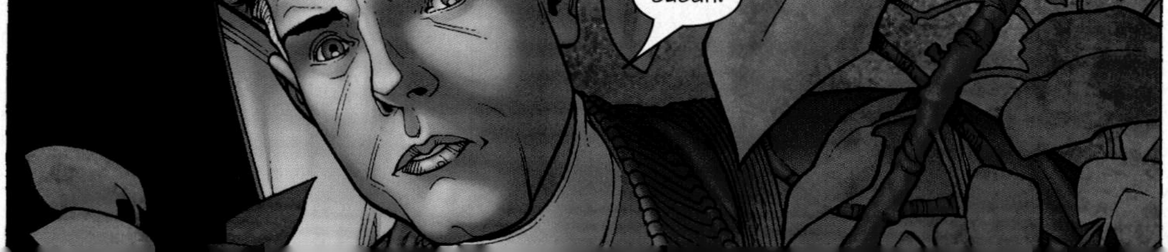
Susan.

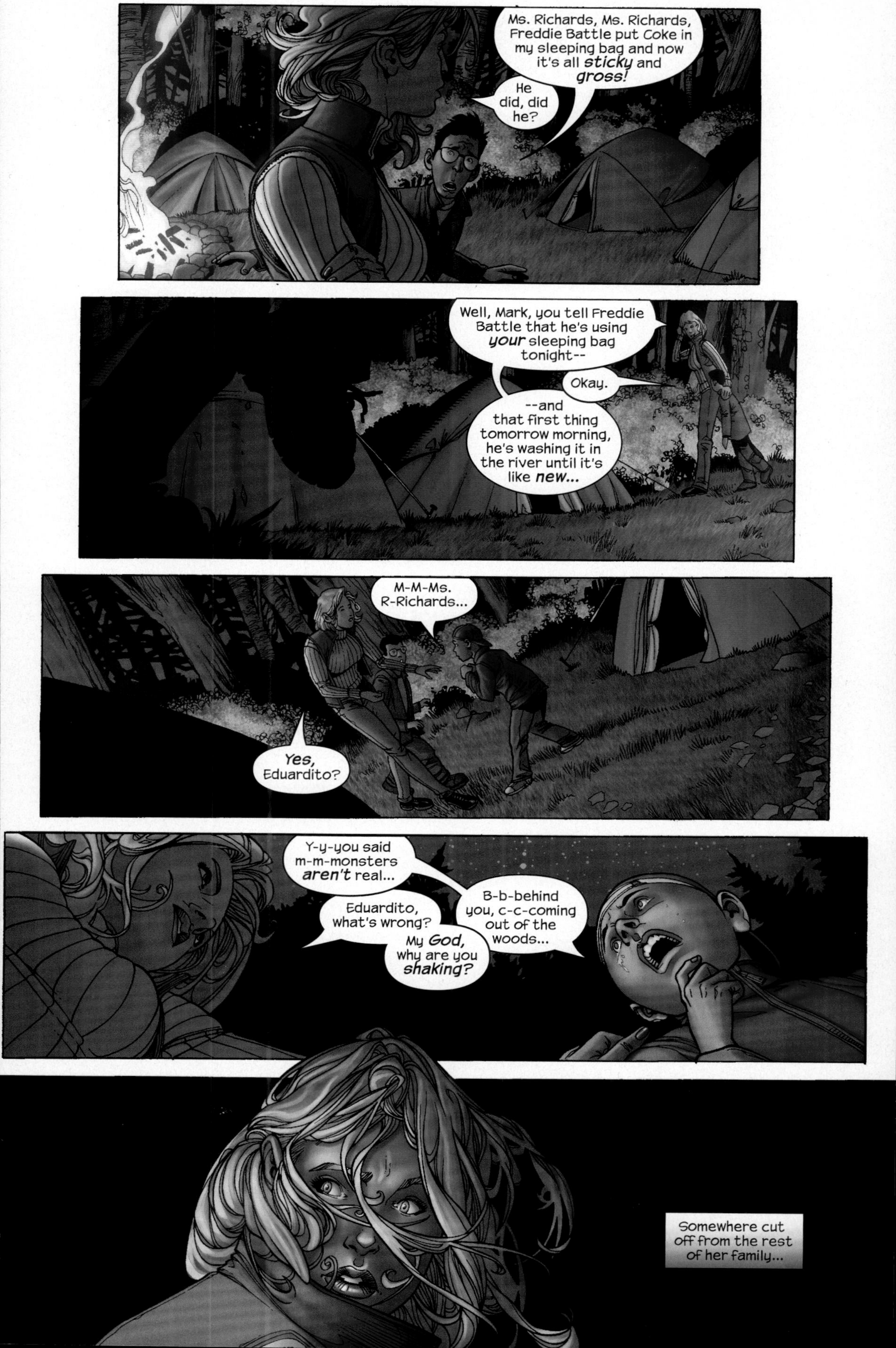
Ms. Richards, Ms. Richards, Freddie Battle put Coke in my sleeping bag and now it's all *sticky* and *gross!*
He did, did he?
Well, Mark, you tell Freddie Battle that he's using *your* sleeping bag tonight--
Okay.
--and that first thing tomorrow morning, he's washing it in the river until it's like *new...*
M-M-Ms. R-Richards...
Yes, Eduardito?
Y-y-you said m-m-monsters *aren't* real...
Eduardito, what's wrong?
My *God,* why are you *shaking?*
B-b-behind you, c-c-coming out of the woods...
Somewhere cut off from the rest of her family...

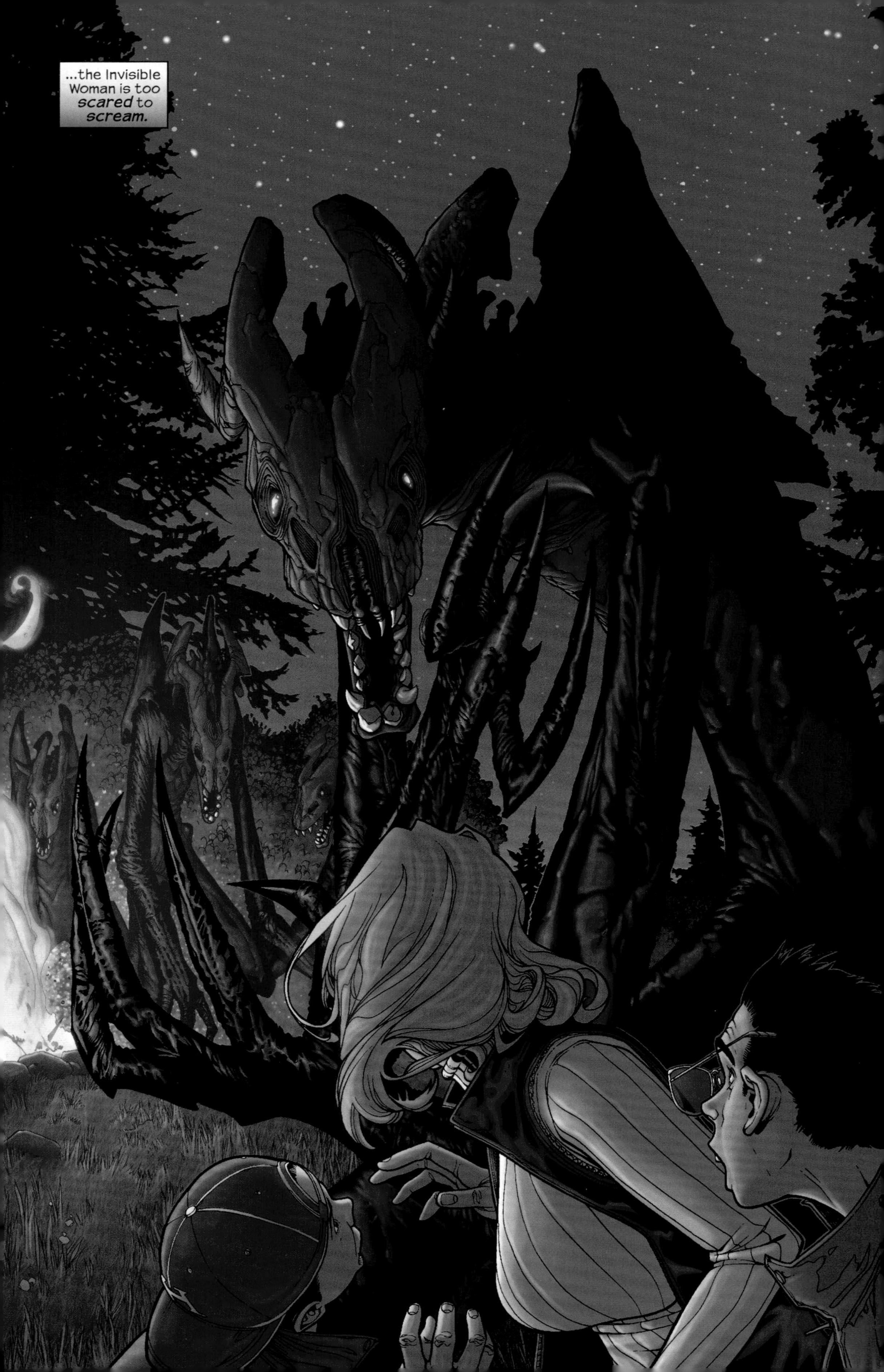
...the Invisible Woman is too *scared* to *scream.*

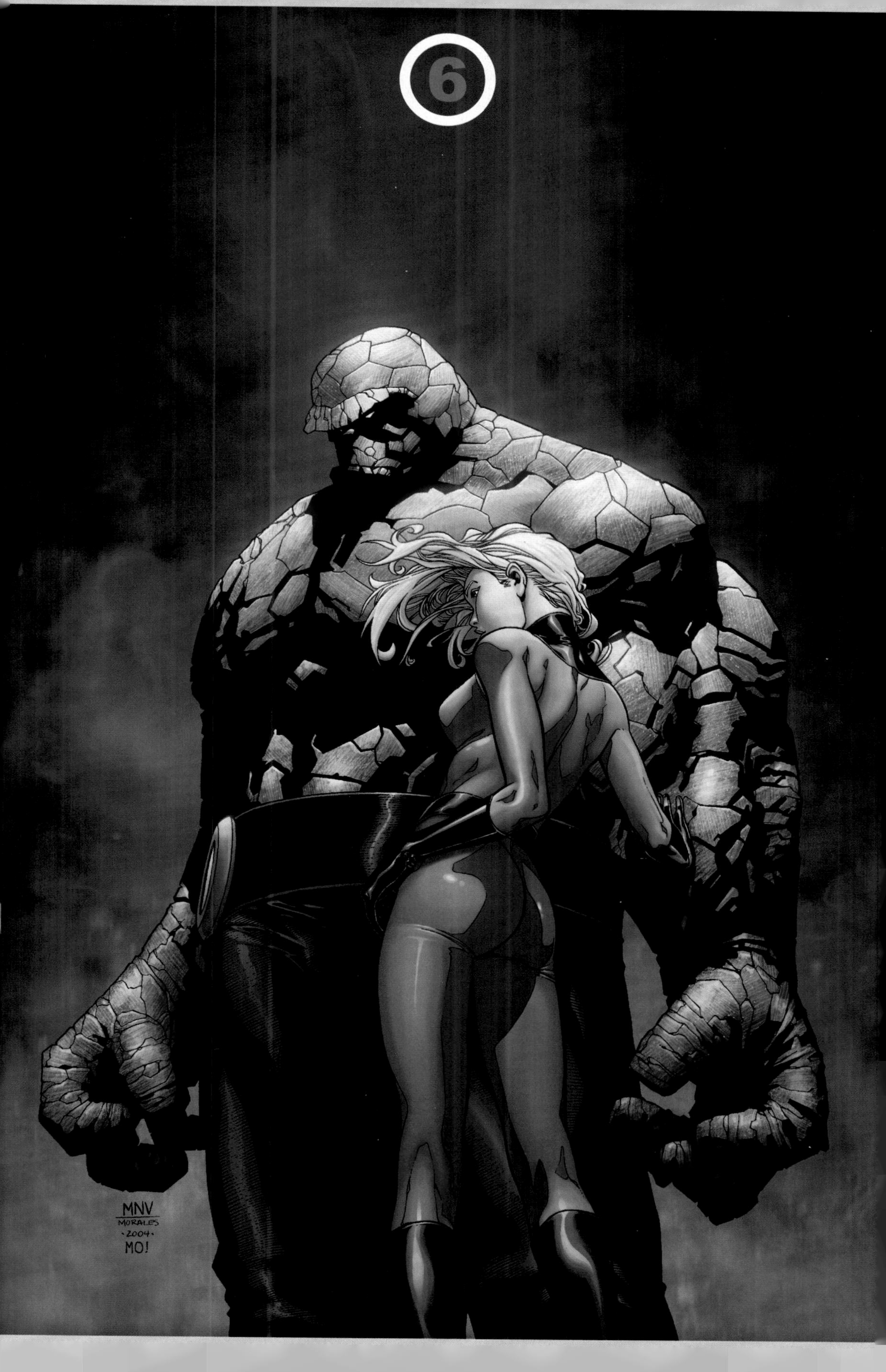
6
MNV
MORALES
·2004·
MO!

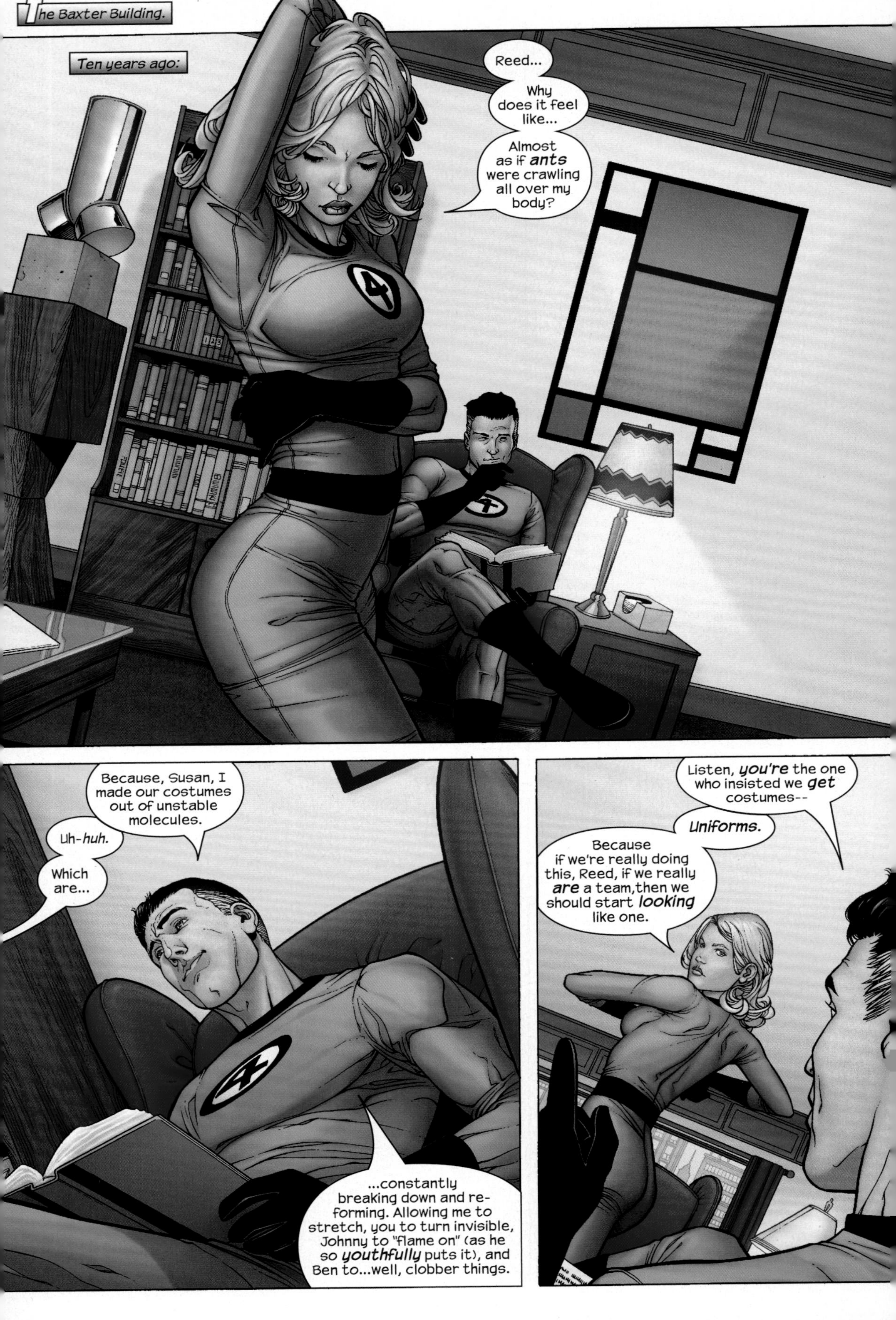
The Baxter Building.
Ten years ago:
Reed...
Why does it feel like...
Almost as if *ants* were crawling all over my body?
Because, Susan, I made our costumes out of unstable molecules.
Uh-*huh.*
Which are...
...constantly breaking down and re-forming. Allowing me to stretch, you to turn invisible, Johnny to "flame on" (as he so *youthfully* puts it), and Ben to...well, clobber things.
Listen, *you're* the one who insisted we *get* costumes--
Uniforms.
Because if we're really doing this, Reed, if we really *are* a team, then we should start *looking* like one.

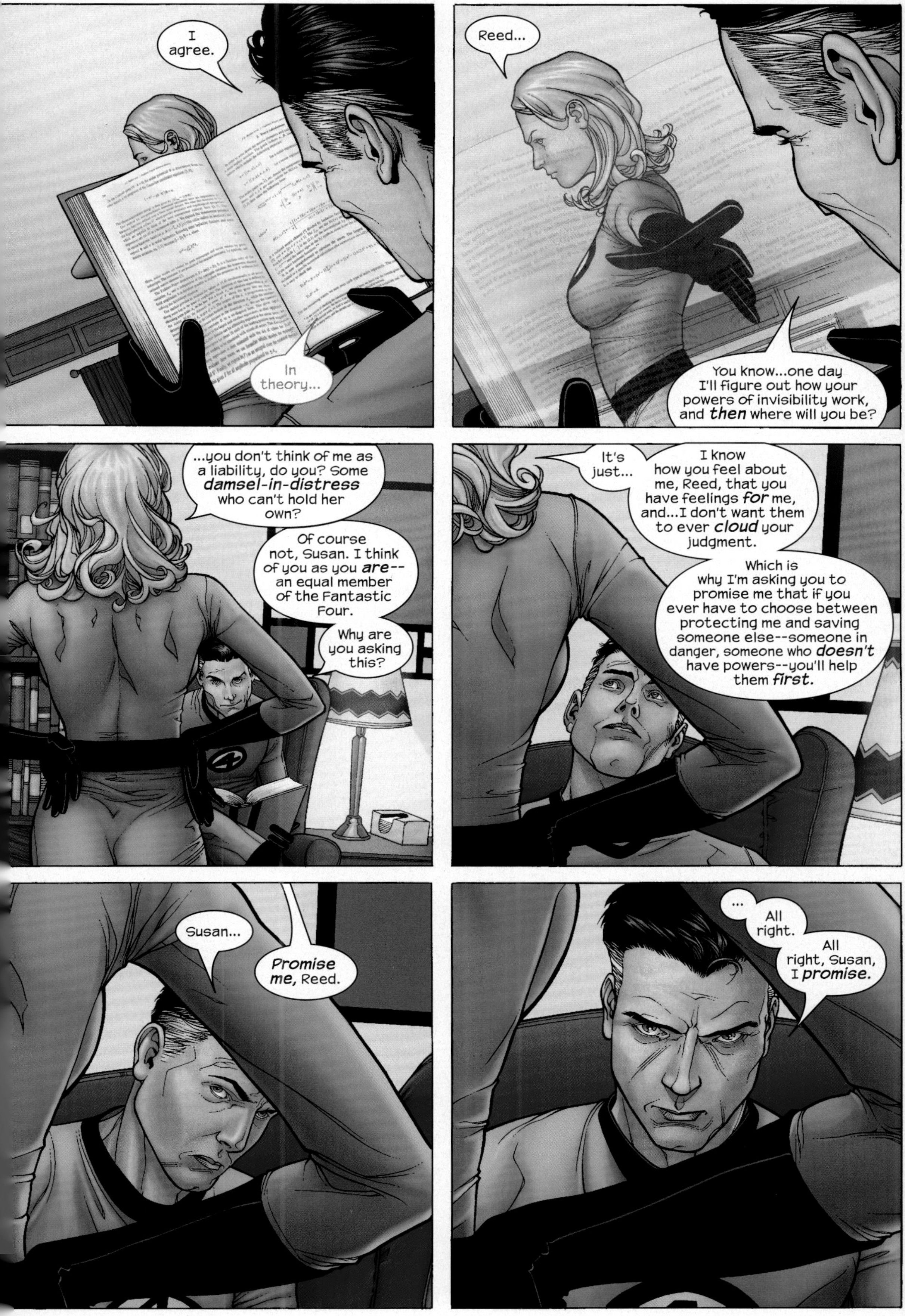
I agree.
In theory...
Reed...
You know...one day I'll figure out how your powers of invisibility work, and *then* where will you be?
...you don't think of me as a liability, do you? Some *damsel-in-distress* who can't hold her own?
Of course not, Susan. I think of you as you *are*--an equal member of the Fantastic Four.
Why are you asking this?
It's just...
I know how you feel about me, Reed, that you have feelings *for* me, and...I don't want them to ever *cloud* your judgment.
Which is why I'm asking you to promise me that if you ever have to choose between protecting me and saving someone else--someone in danger, someone who *doesn't* have powers--you'll help them *first.*
Susan...
Promise me, Reed.
...
All right.
All right, Susan, I *promise.*

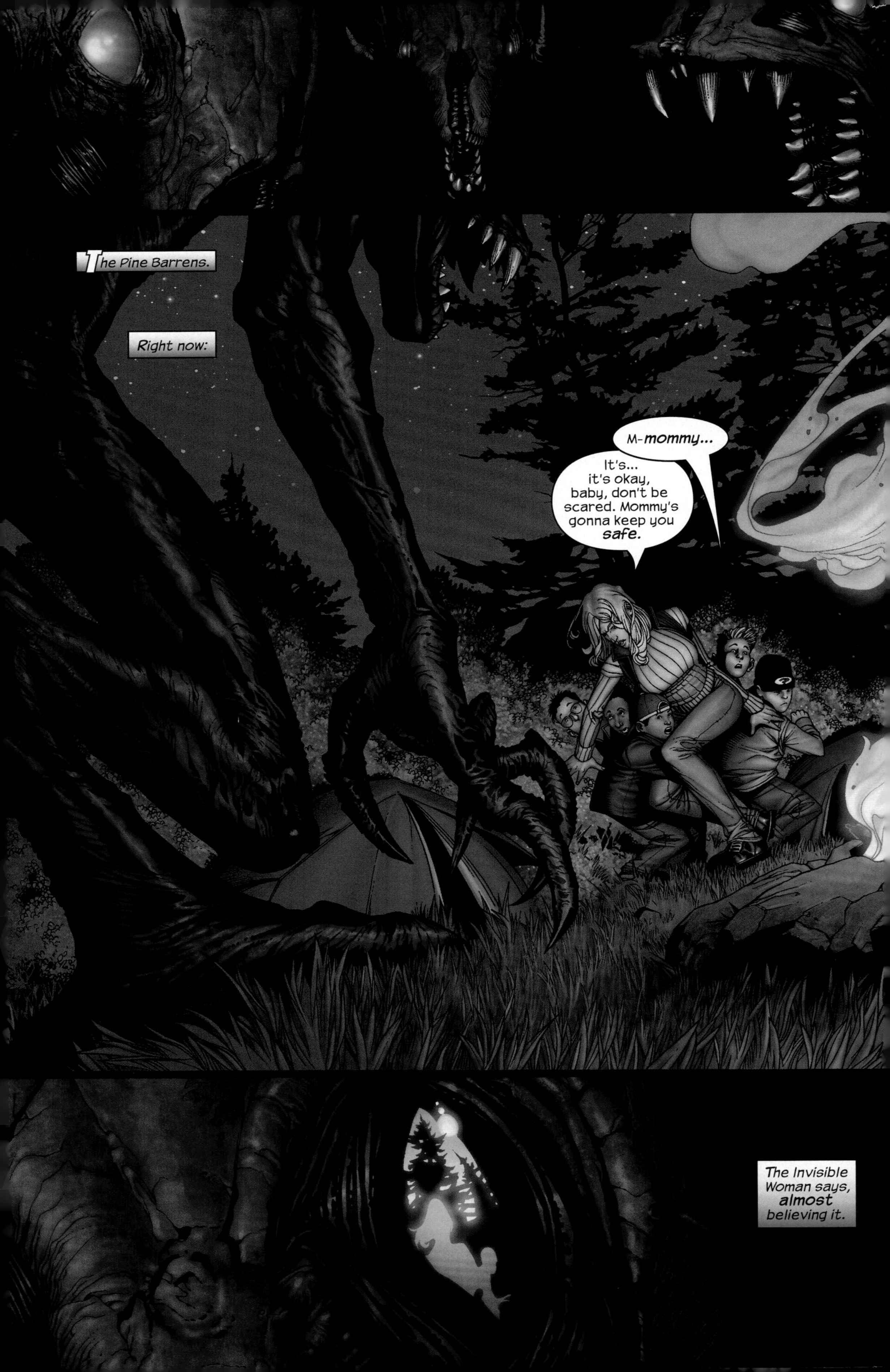
The Pine Barrens.
Right now:
M-mommy...
It's... it's okay, baby, don't be scared. Mommy's gonna keep you safe.
The Invisible Woman says, almost believing it.

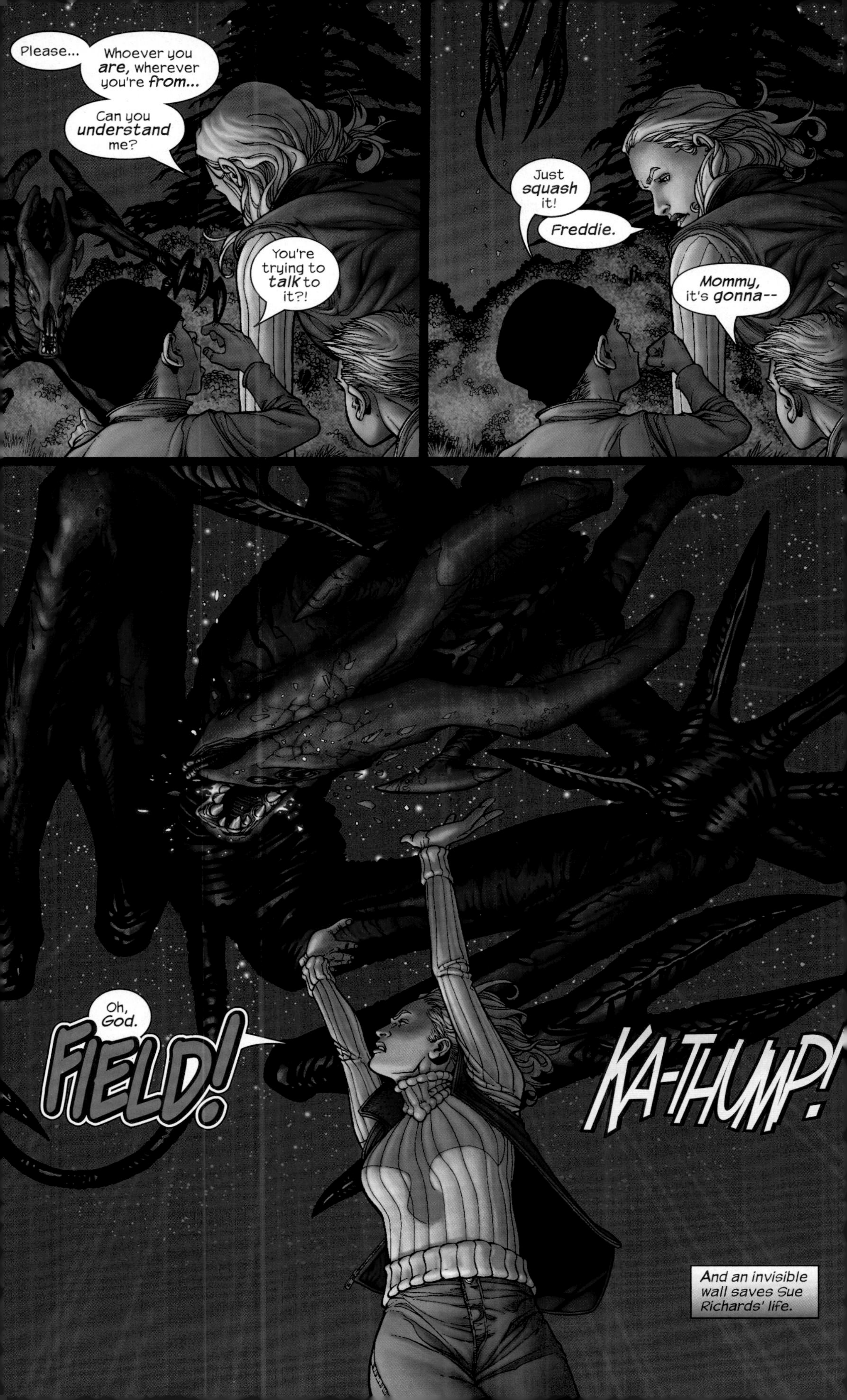
Please...
Whoever you *are*, wherever you're *from...*
Can you **understand** me?
You're trying to *talk* to it?!
Just **squash** it!
Freddie.
Mommy, it's *gonna--*
Oh, God.
FIELD!
KA-THUMP!
And an invisible wall saves Sue Richards' life.

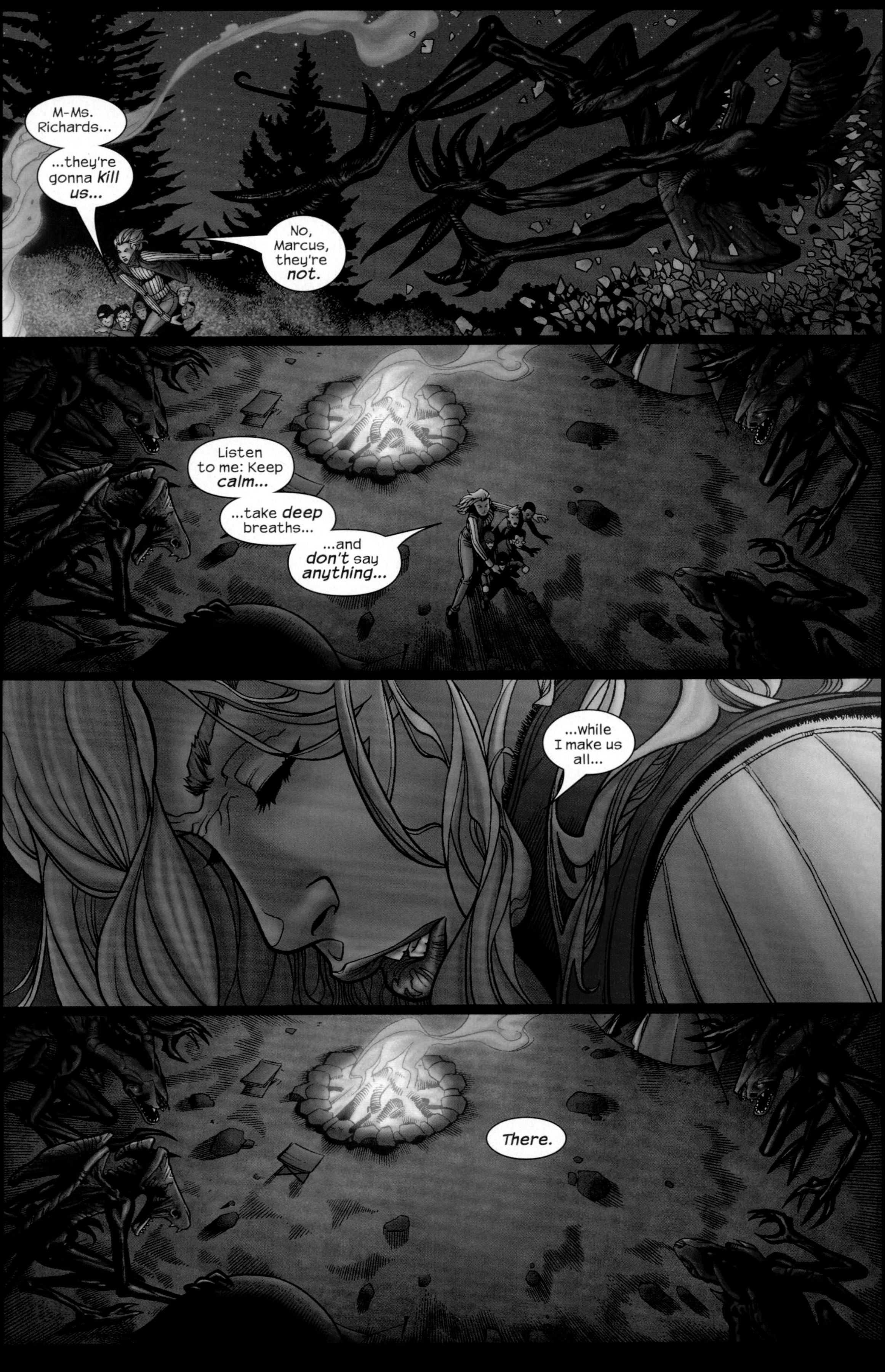
M-Ms. Richards...
...they're gonna kill us...
No, Marcus, they're not.
Listen to me: Keep calm...
...take deep breaths...
...and don't say anything...
...while I make us all...
There.

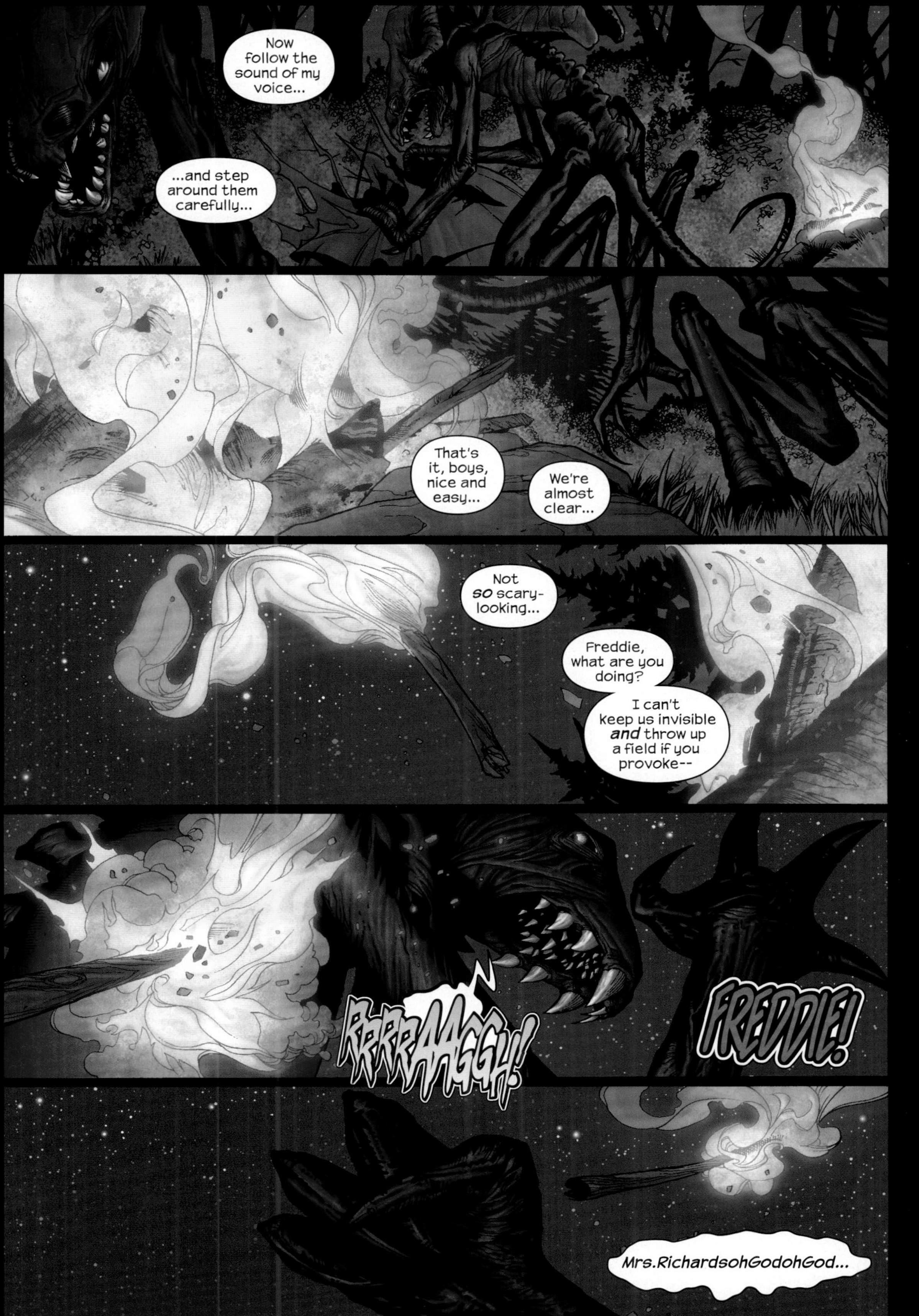
Now follow the sound of my voice...
...and step around them carefully...
That's it, boys, nice and easy...
We're almost clear...
Not SO scary-looking...
Freddie, what are you doing?
I can't keep us invisible and throw up a field if you provoke--
RRRRAAGGH!
FREDDIE!
Mrs.RichardsohGodohGod...

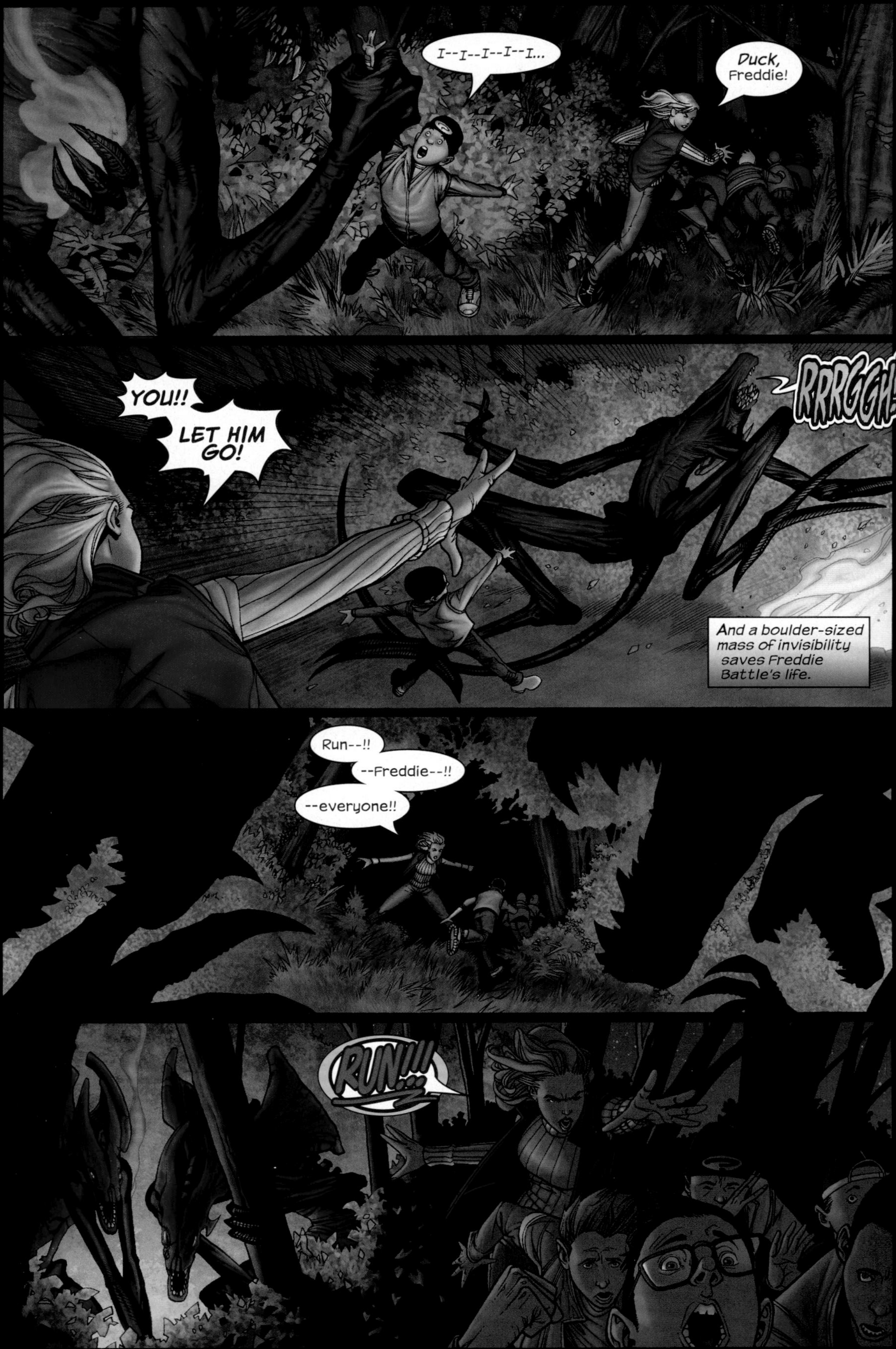
I--I--I--I--I...
Duck, Freddie!
YOU!!
LET HIM GO!
RRRGGH!
And a boulder-sized mass of invisibility saves Freddie Battle's life.
Run--!!
--Freddie--!!
--everyone!!
RUN!!!

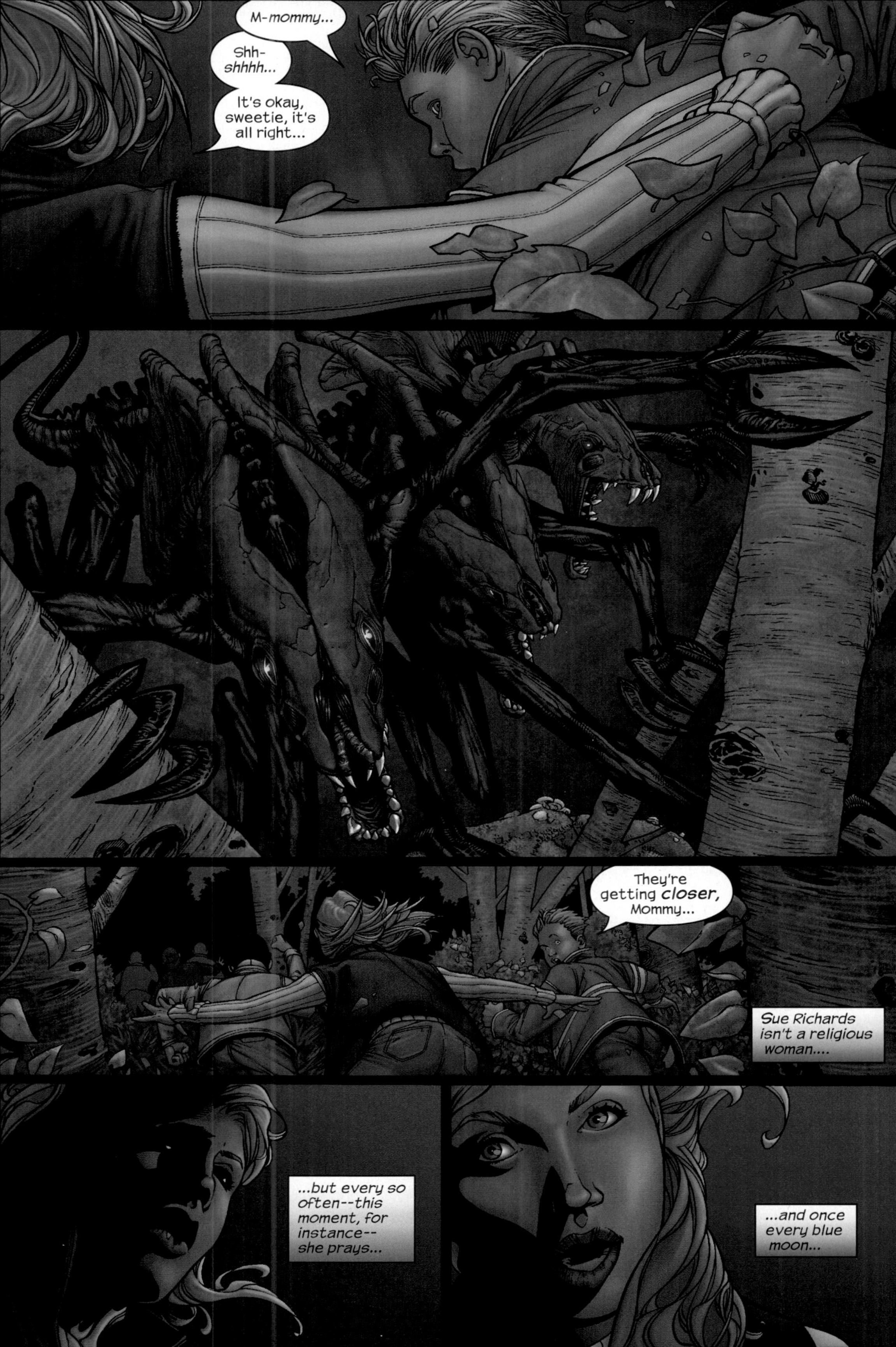

M-mommy...
Shh-shhhh...
It's okay, sweetie, it's all right...
They're getting closer, Mommy...
Sue Richards isn't a religious woman....
...but every so often--this moment, for instance--she prays...
...and once every blue moon...

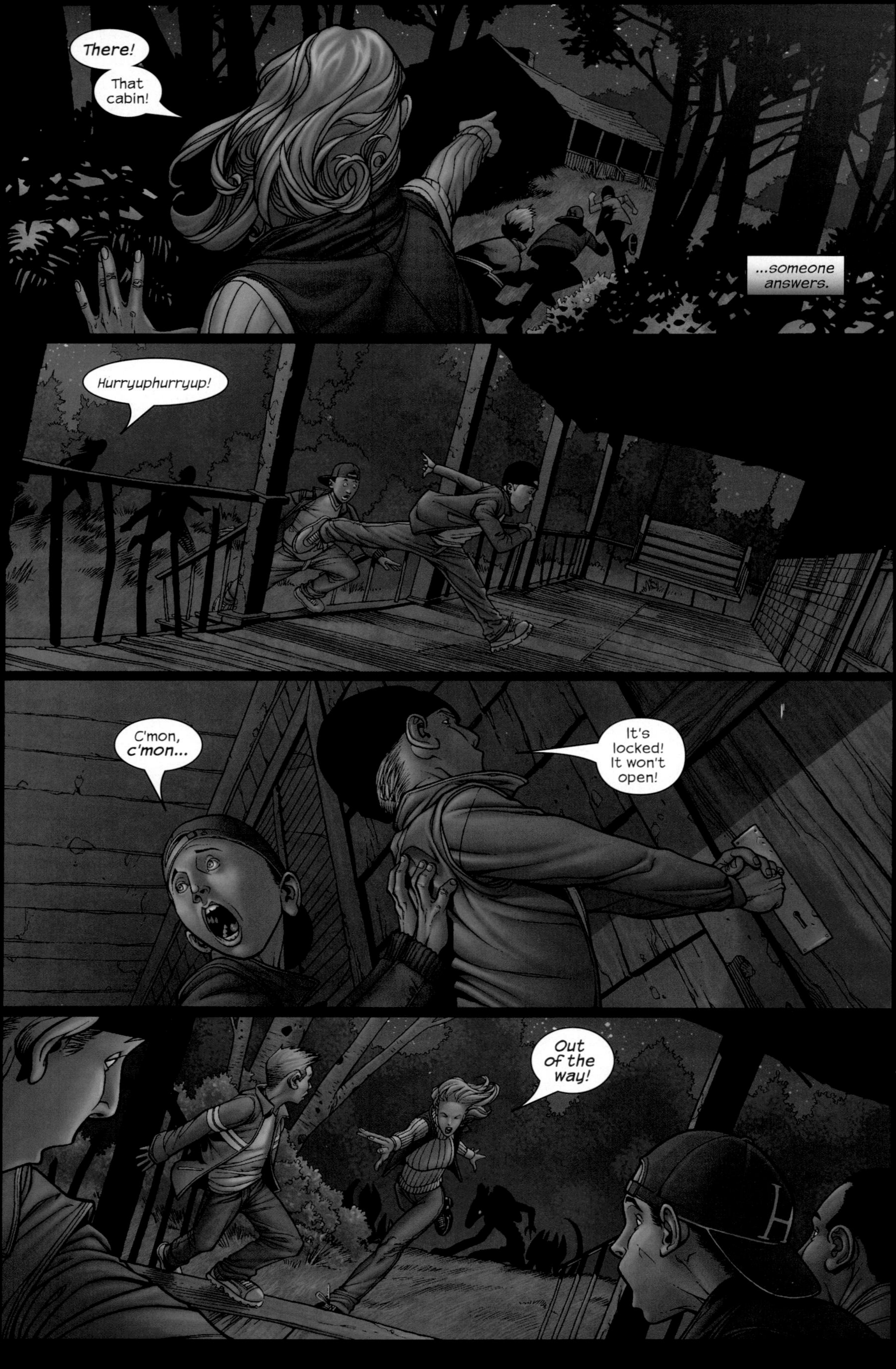
There!
That cabin!
...someone answers.
Hurryuphurryup!
C'mon, c'mon...
It's locked! It won't open!
Out of the way!

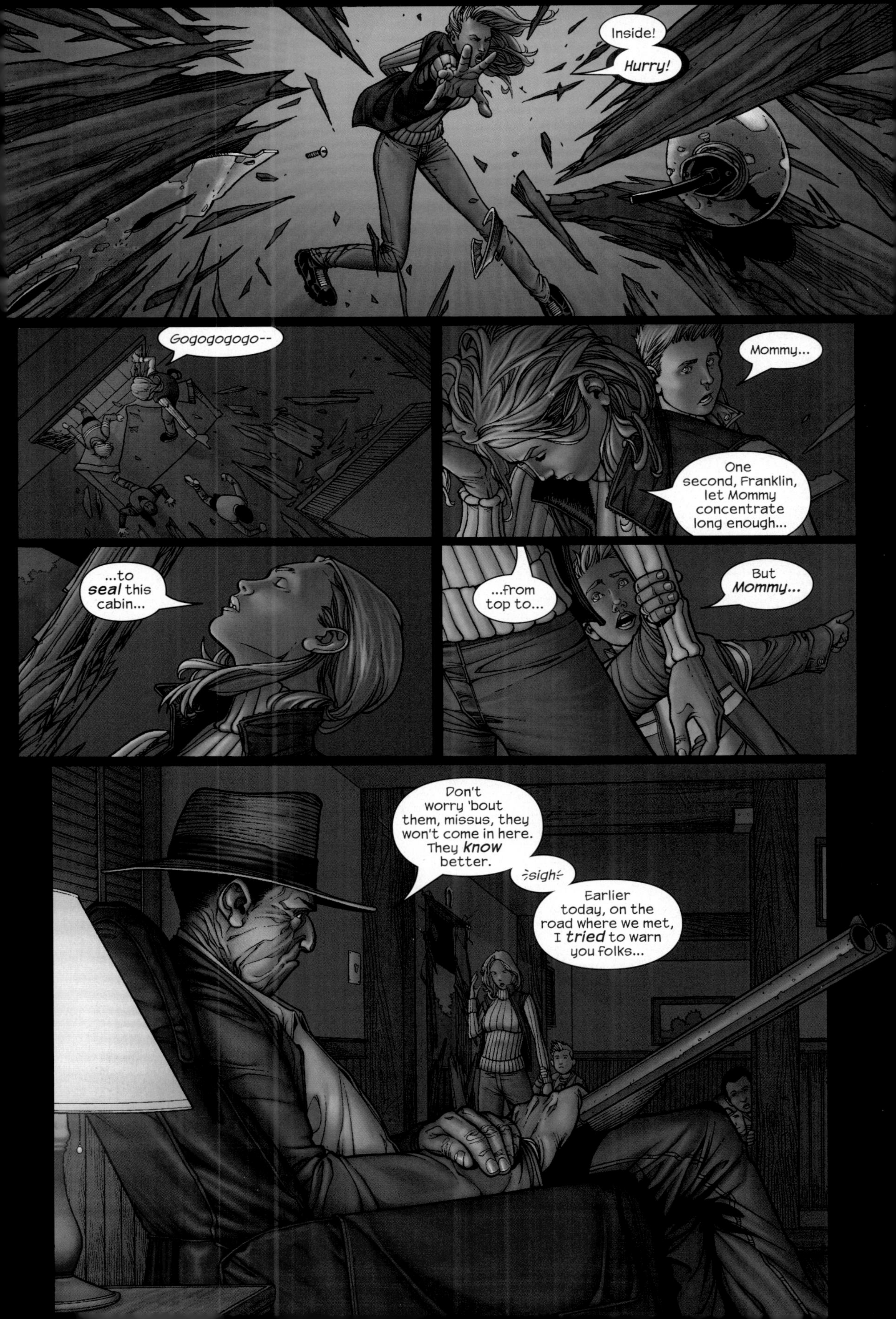
Inside!
Hurry!
Gogogogogo--
Mommy...
One second, Franklin, let Mommy concentrate long enough...
...to seal this cabin...
...from top to...
But Mommy...
Don't worry 'bout them, missus, they won't come in here. They know better.
sigh
Earlier today, on the road where we met, I tried to warn you folks...

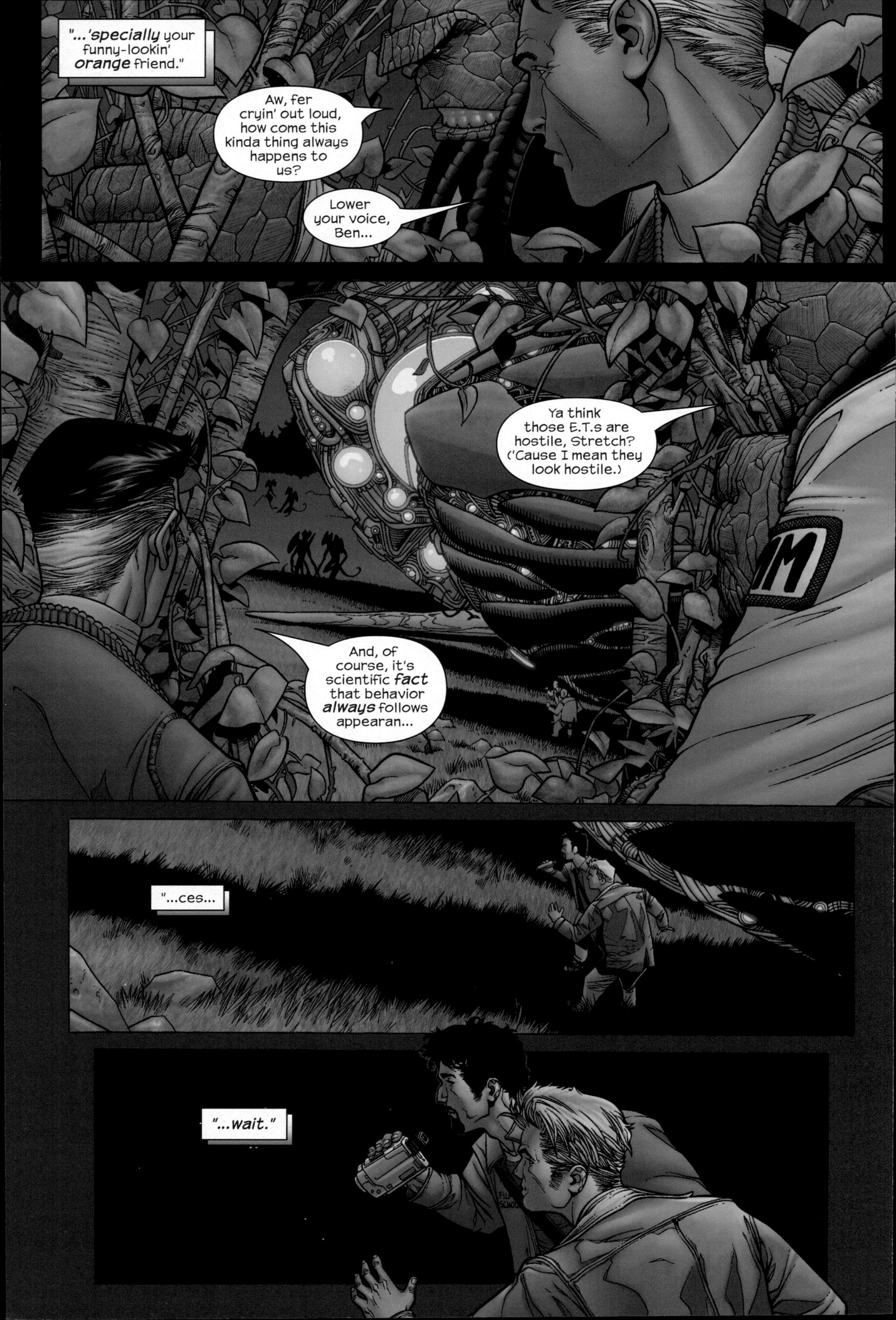
"...'specially your funny-lookin' orange friend."
Aw, fer cryin' out loud, how come this kinda thing always happens to us?
Lower your voice, Ben...
Ya think those E.T.s are hostile, Stretch? ('Cause I mean they look hostile.)
And, of course, it's scientific fact that behavior always follows appearan...
"...ces...
"...wait."

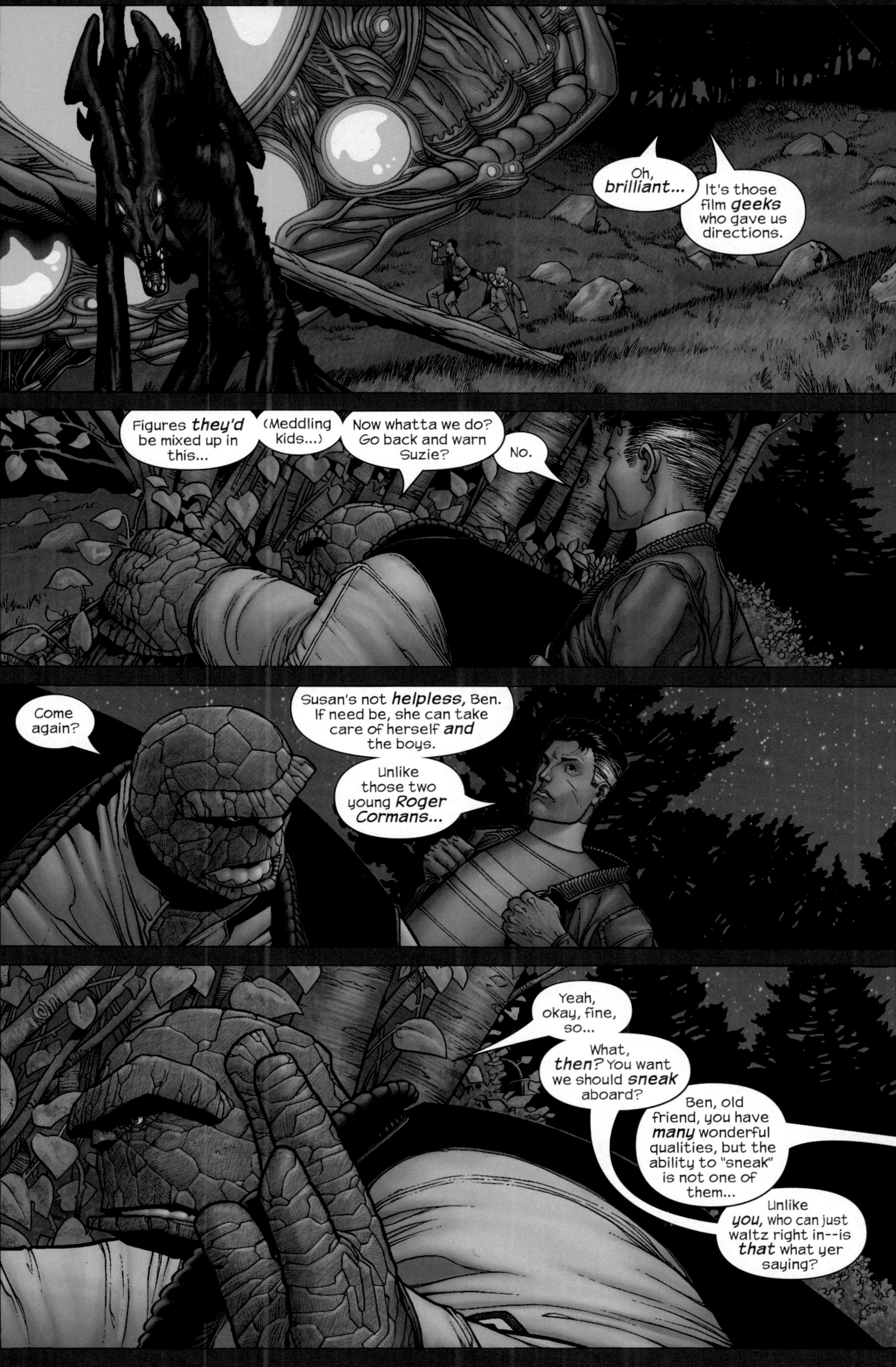
Oh, brilliant...
It's those film geeks who gave us directions.
Figures they'd be mixed up in this...
(Meddling kids...)
Now whatta we do? Go back and warn Suzie?
No.
Come again?
Susan's not helpless, Ben. If need be, she can take care of herself and the boys.
Unlike those two young Roger Cormans...
Yeah, okay, fine, so...
What, then? You want we should sneak aboard?
Ben, old friend, you have many wonderful qualities, but the ability to "sneak" is not one of them...
Unlike you, who can just waltz right in--is that what yer saying?

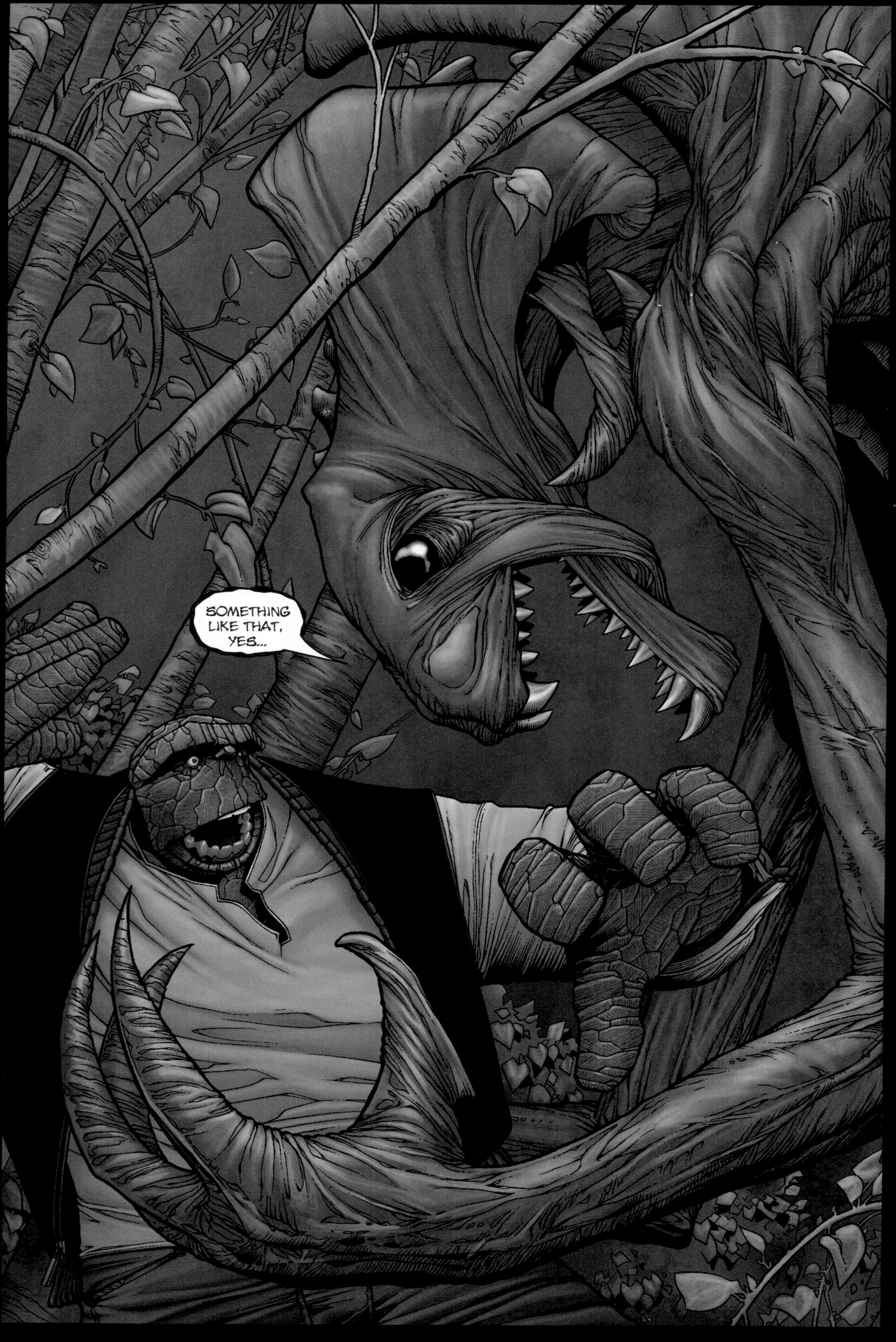
SOMETHING LIKE THAT, YES...

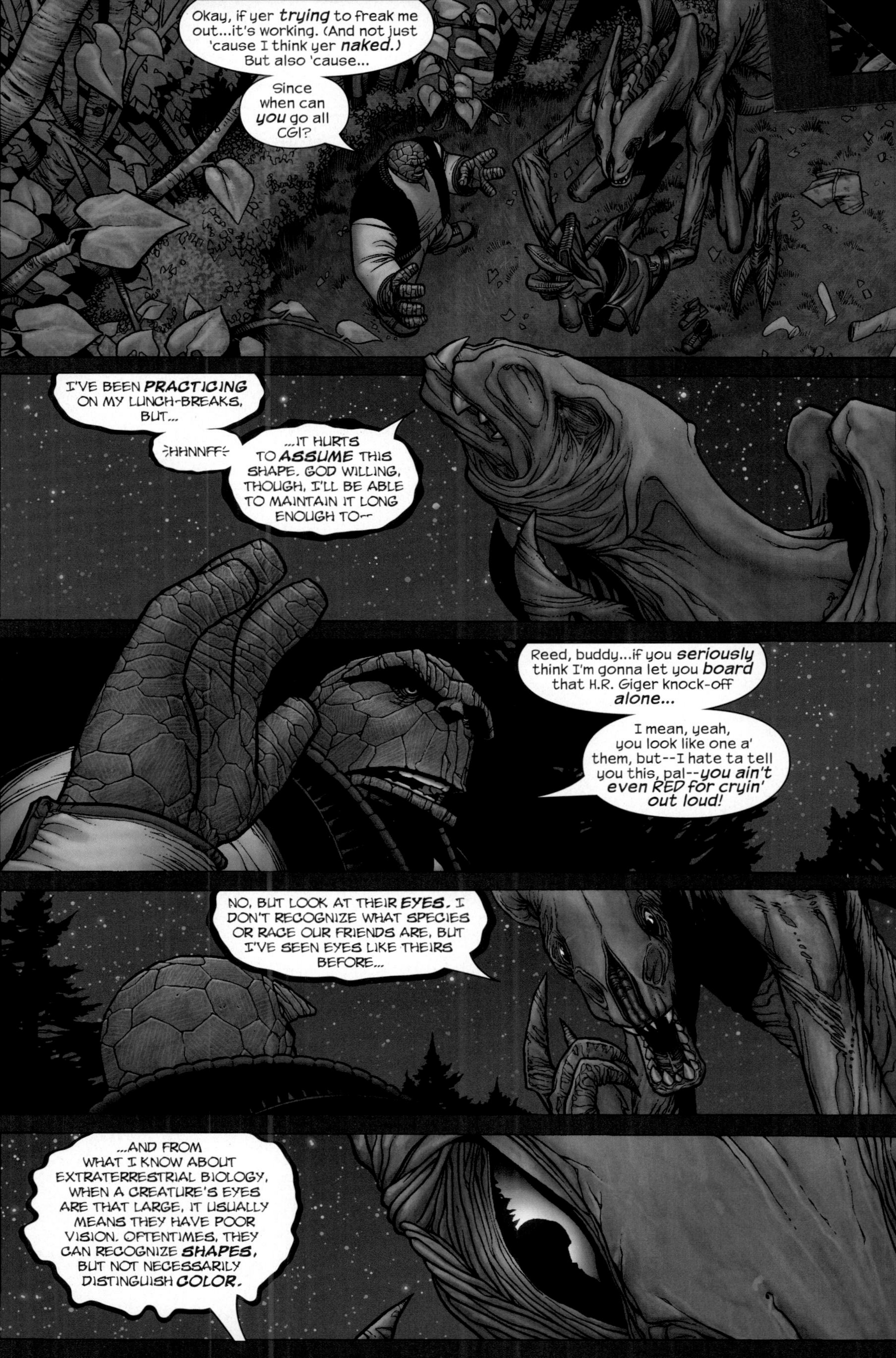
Okay, if yer trying to freak me out...it's working. (And not just 'cause I think yer naked.) But also 'cause...
Since when can you go all CGI?
I'VE BEEN PRACTICING ON MY LUNCH-BREAKS, BUT...
HHNNFF
...IT HURTS TO ASSUME THIS SHAPE. GOD WILLING, THOUGH, I'LL BE ABLE TO MAINTAIN IT LONG ENOUGH TO--
Reed, buddy...if you seriously think I'm gonna let you board that H.R. Giger knock-off alone...
I mean, yeah, you look like one a' them, but--I hate ta tell you this, pal--you ain't even RED for cryin' out loud!
NO, BUT LOOK AT THEIR EYES. I DON'T RECOGNIZE WHAT SPECIES OR RACE OUR FRIENDS ARE, BUT I'VE SEEN EYES LIKE THEIRS BEFORE...
...AND FROM WHAT I KNOW ABOUT EXTRATERRESTRIAL BIOLOGY, WHEN A CREATURE'S EYES ARE THAT LARGE, IT USUALLY MEANS THEY HAVE POOR VISION. OFTENTIMES, THEY CAN RECOGNIZE SHAPES, BUT NOT NECESSARILY DISTINGUISH COLOR.

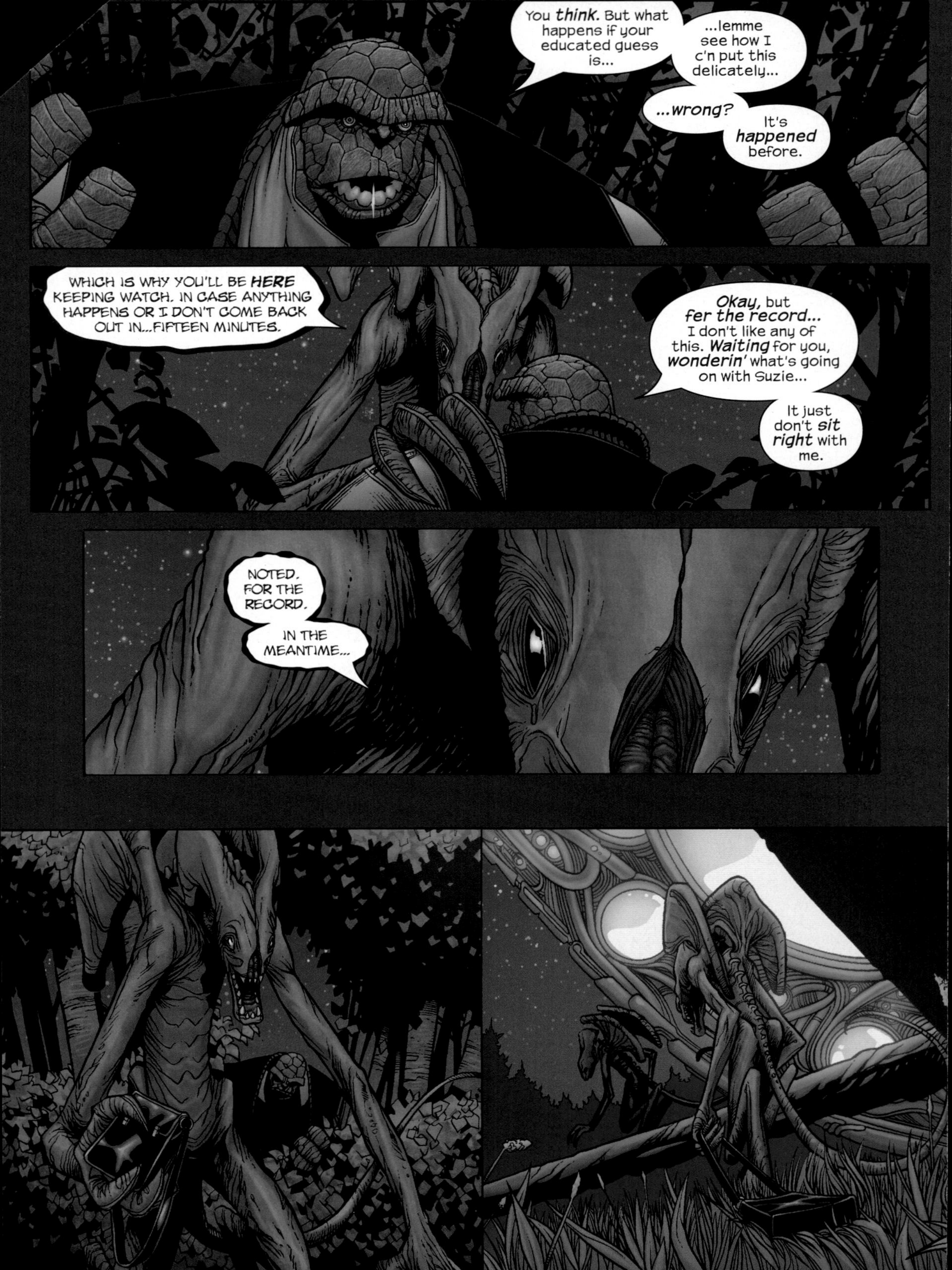
You think. But what happens if your educated guess is...
...lemme see how I c'n put this delicately...
...wrong?
It's happened before.
WHICH IS WHY YOU'LL BE HERE KEEPING WATCH. IN CASE ANYTHING HAPPENS OR I DON'T COME BACK OUT IN...FIFTEEN MINUTES.
Okay, but fer the record... I don't like any of this. Waiting for you, wonderin' what's going on with Suzie...
It just don't sit right with me.
NOTED. FOR THE RECORD.
IN THE MEANTIME...

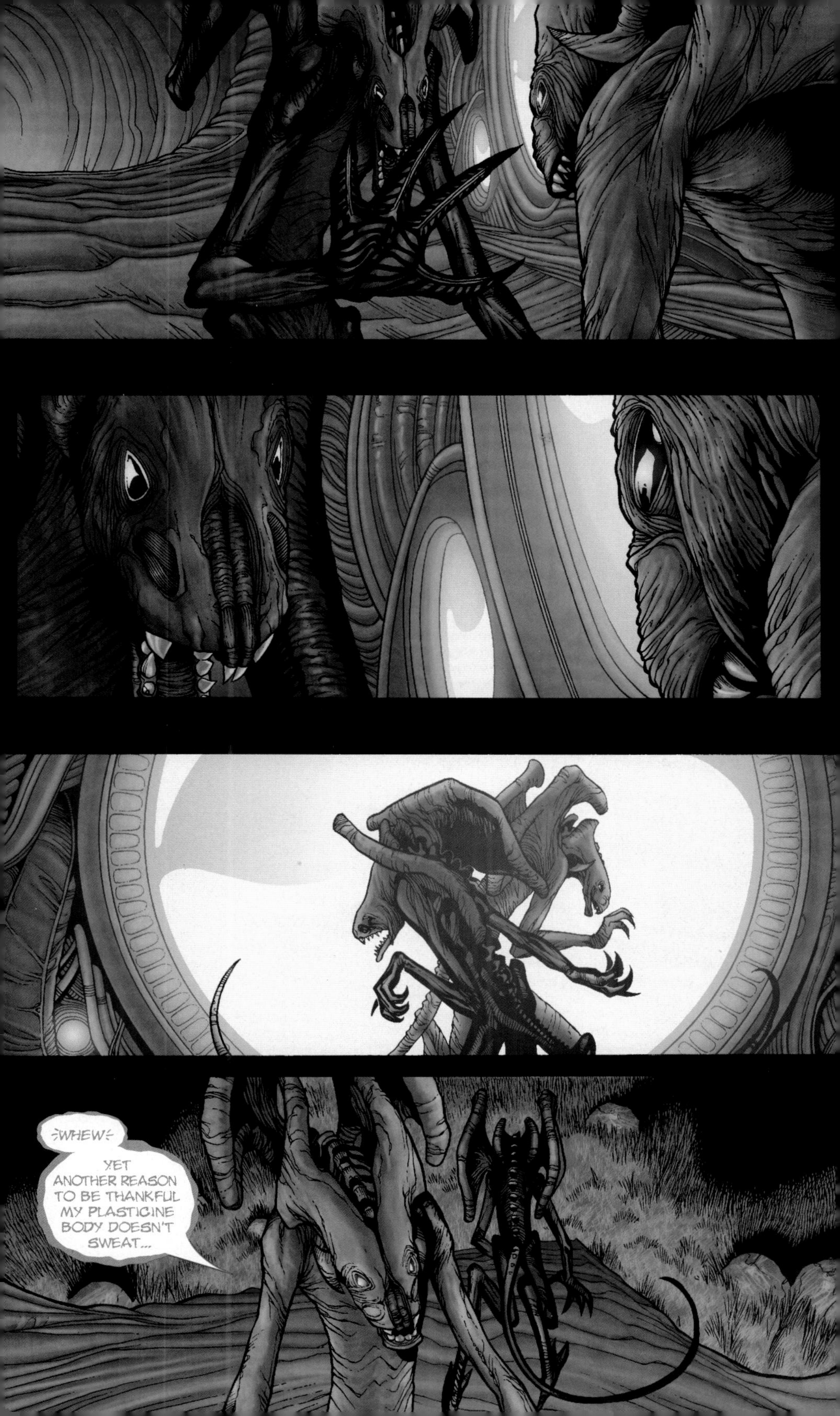
WHEW
YET ANOTHER REASON TO BE THANKFUL MY PLASTICINE BODY DOESN'T SWEAT...

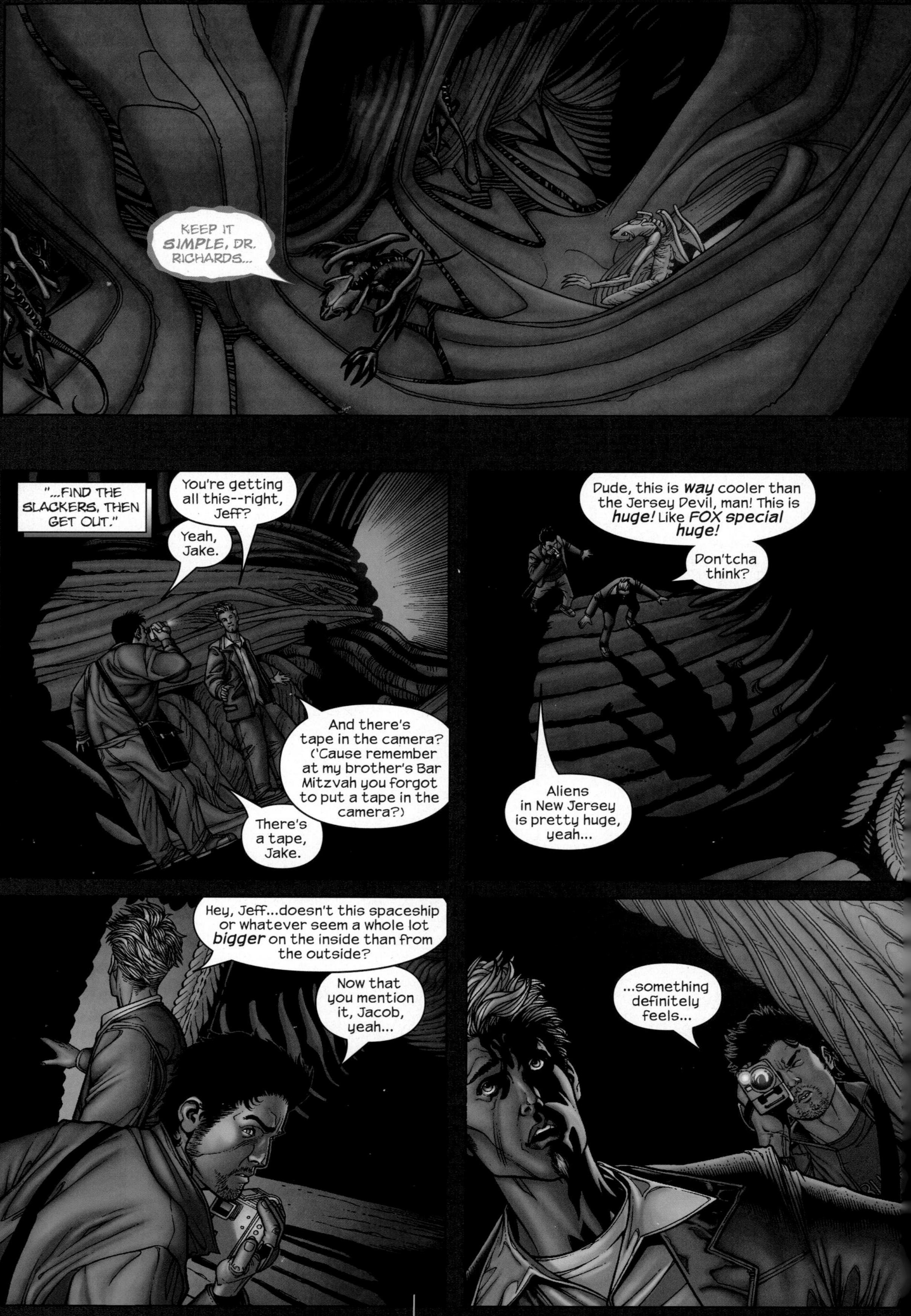
KEEP IT SIMPLE, DR. RICHARDS...
"...FIND THE SLACKERS, THEN GET OUT."
You're getting all this--right, Jeff?
Yeah, Jake.
And there's tape in the camera? ('Cause remember at my brother's Bar Mitzvah you forgot to put a tape in the camera?)
There's a tape, Jake.
Dude, this is way cooler than the Jersey Devil, man! This is huge! Like FOX special huge!
Don'tcha think?
Aliens in New Jersey is pretty huge, yeah...
Hey, Jeff...doesn't this spaceship or whatever seem a whole lot bigger on the inside than from the outside?
Now that you mention it, Jacob, yeah...
...something definitely feels...

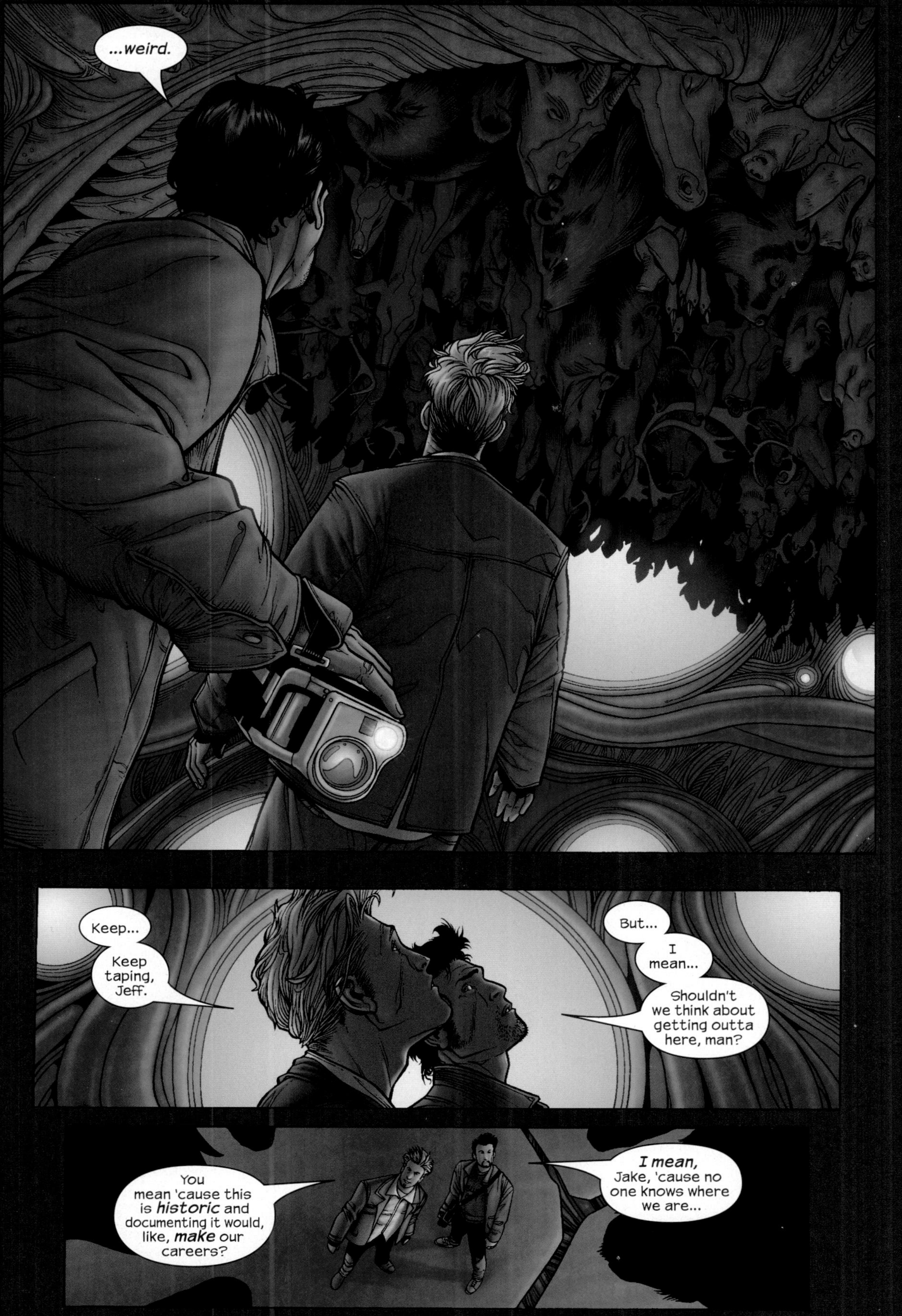
...weird.
Keep...
Keep taping, Jeff.
But...
I mean...
Shouldn't we think about getting outta here, man?
You mean 'cause this is *historic* and documenting it would, like, *make* our careers?
I mean, Jake, 'cause no one knows where we are...

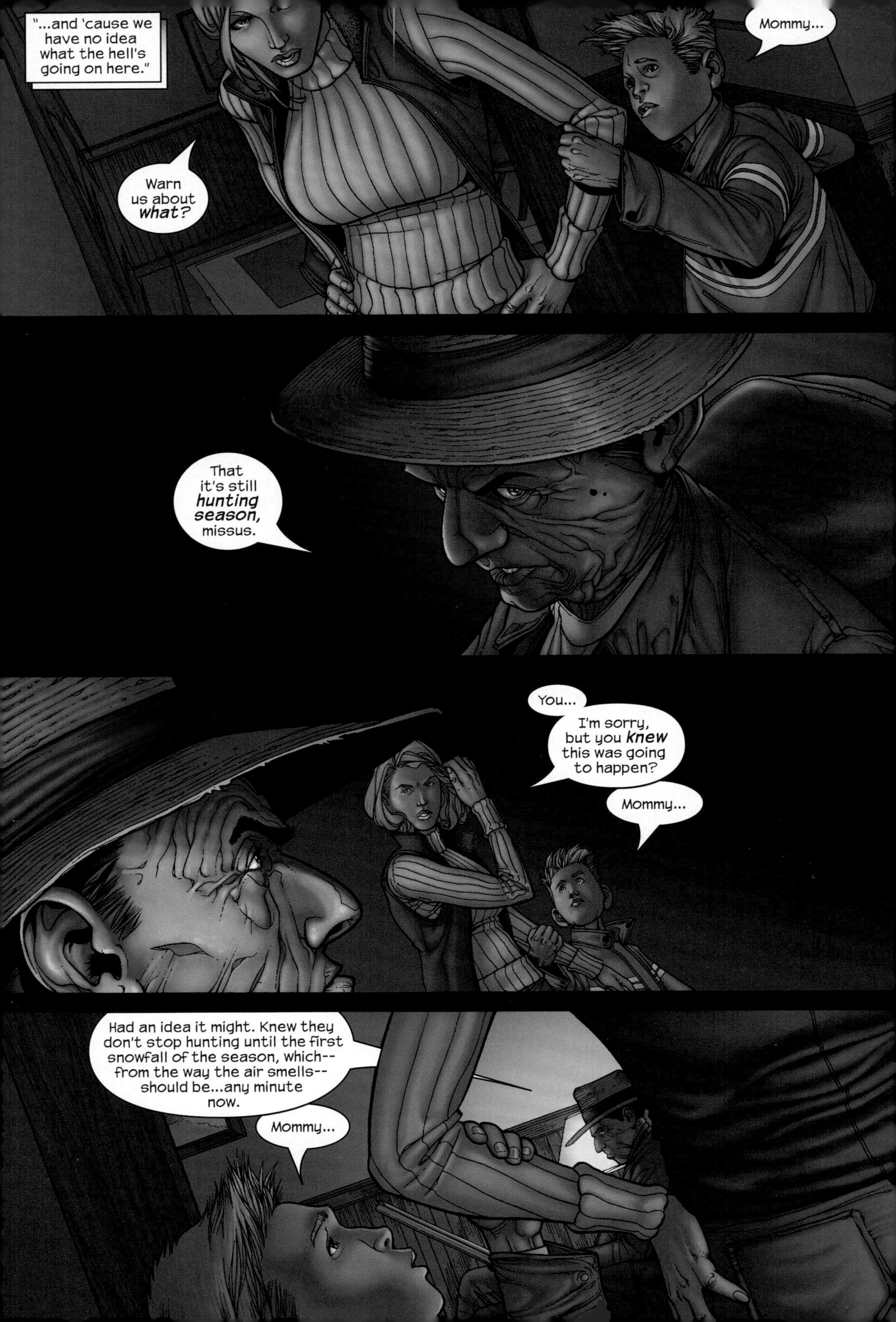
"...and 'cause we have no idea what the hell's going on here."
Mommy...
Warn us about *what?*
That it's still *hunting season,* missus.
You...
I'm sorry, but you *knew* this was going to happen?
Mommy...
Had an idea it might. Knew they don't stop hunting until the first snowfall of the season, which--from the way the air smells--should be...any minute now.
Mommy...

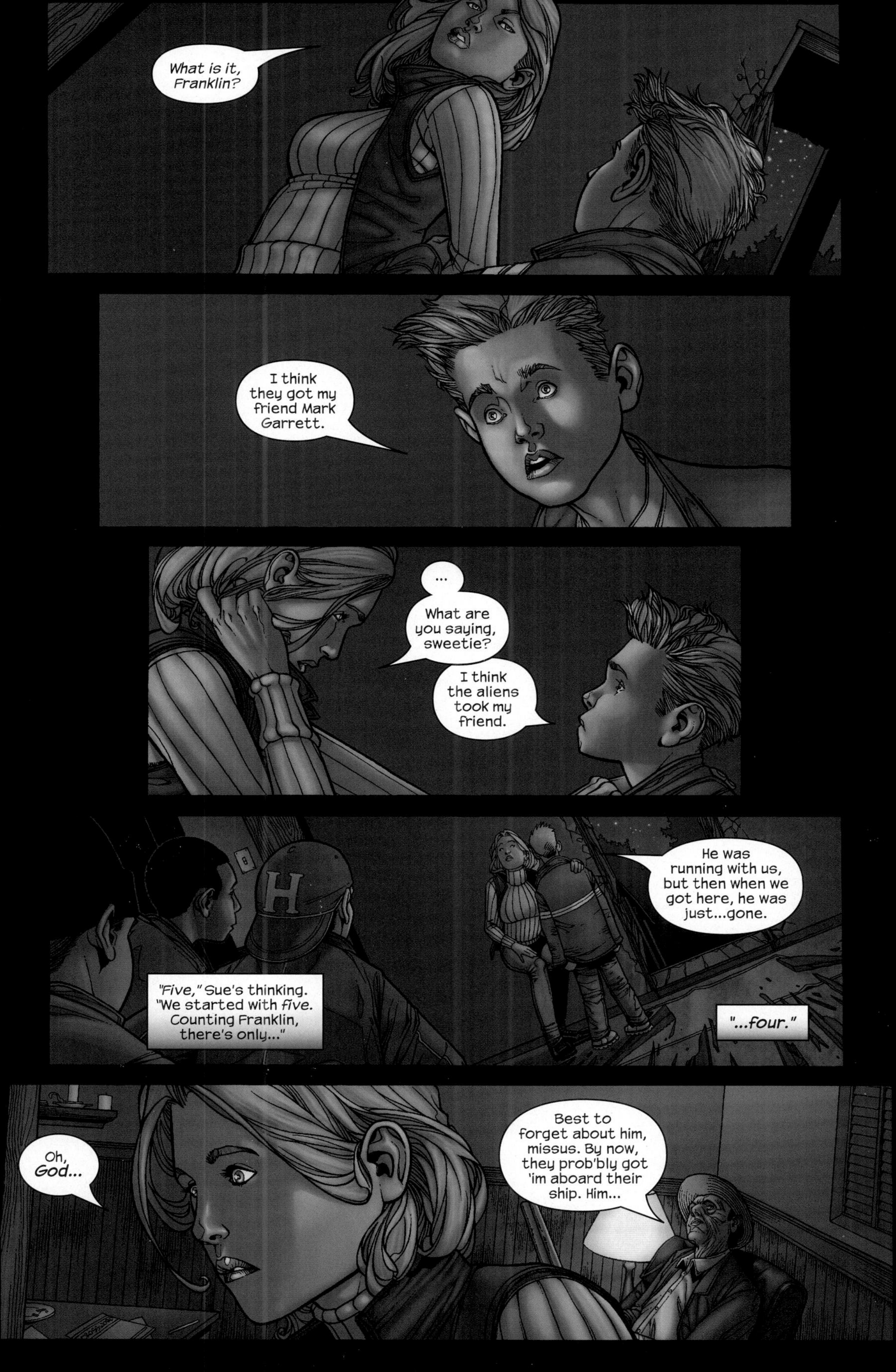

What is it, Franklin?
I think they got my friend Mark Garrett.
...
What are you saying, sweetie?
I think the aliens took my friend.
He was running with us, but then when we got here, he was just...gone.
"Five," Sue's thinking. "We started with five. Counting Franklin, there's only..."
"...four."
Oh, God...
Best to forget about him, missus. By now, they prob'bly got 'im aboard their ship. Him...

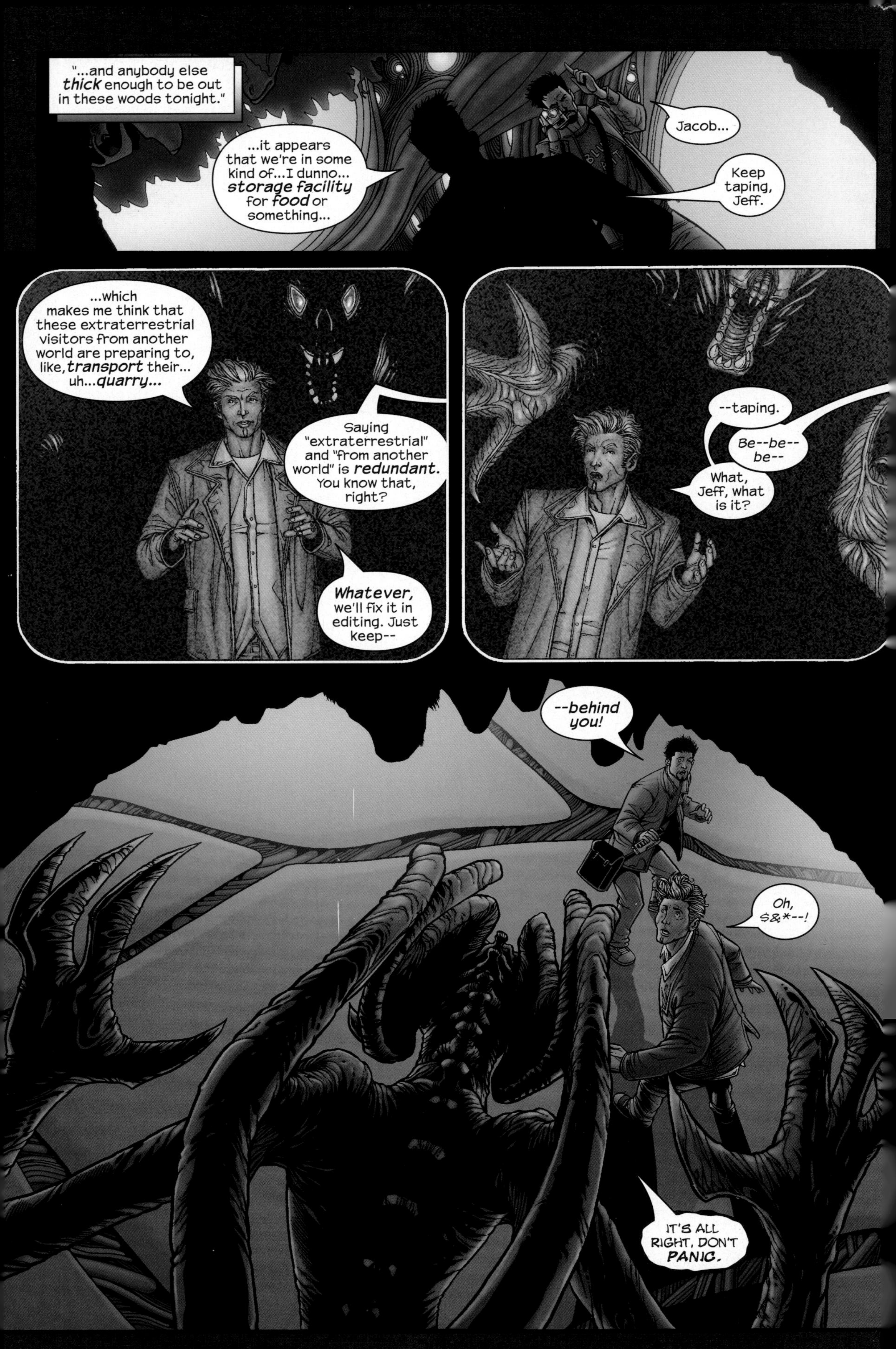
"...and anybody else thick enough to be out in these woods tonight."
...it appears that we're in some kind of...I dunno... storage facility for food or something...
Jacob...
Keep taping, Jeff.
...which makes me think that these extraterrestrial visitors from another world are preparing to, like, transport their... uh...quarry...
Saying "extraterrestrial" and "from another world" is redundant. You know that, right?
Whatever, we'll fix it in editing. Just keep--
--taping.
Be--be--be--
What, Jeff, what is it?
--behind you!
Oh, $&*--!
IT'S ALL RIGHT, DON'T PANIC.

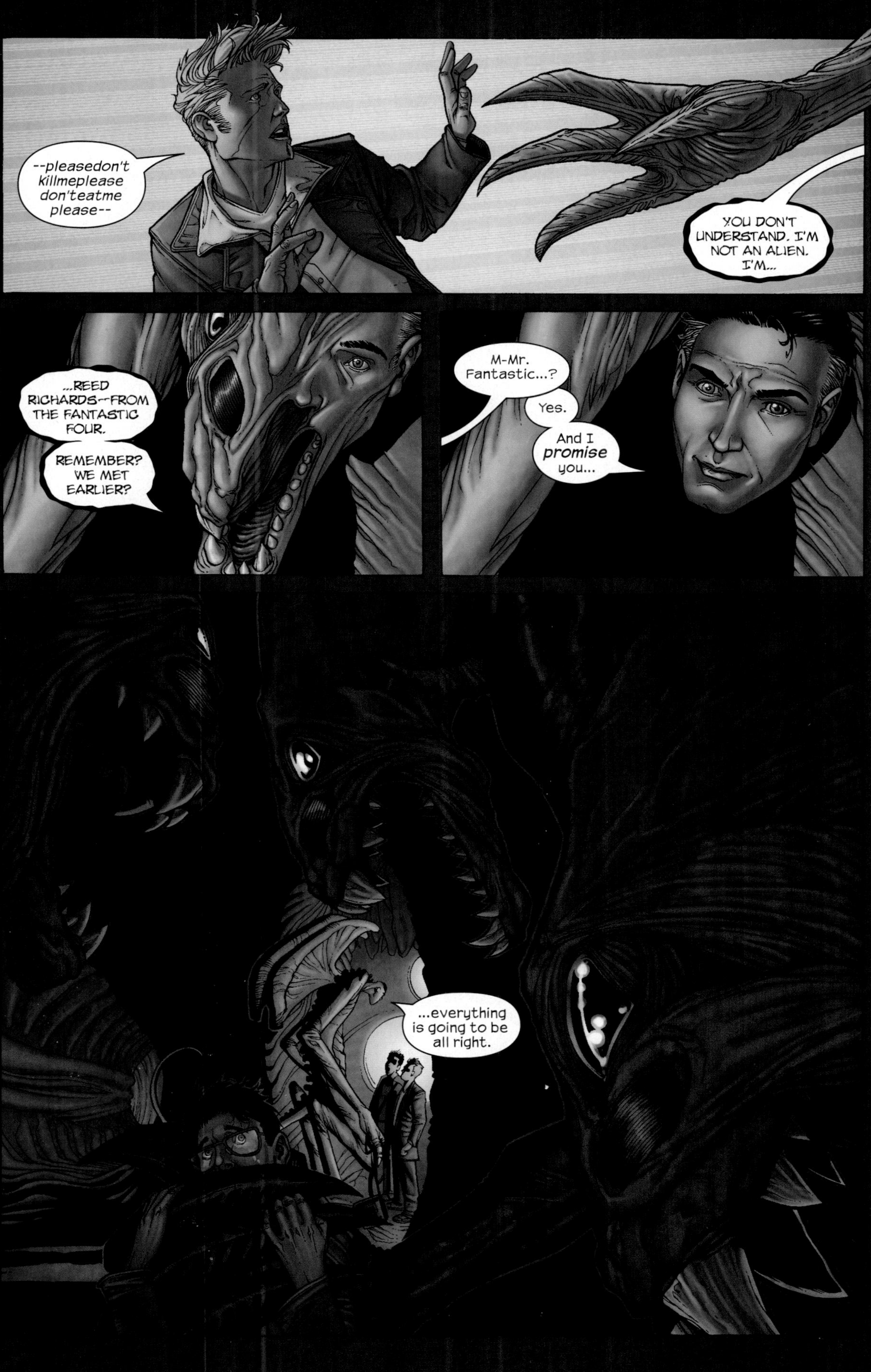
--pleasedon't killmeplease don'teatme please--
YOU DON'T UNDERSTAND. I'M NOT AN ALIEN. I'M...
...REED RICHARDS--FROM THE FANTASTIC FOUR.
REMEMBER? WE MET EARLIER?
M-Mr. Fantastic...?
Yes.
And I *promise* you...
...everything is going to be all right.

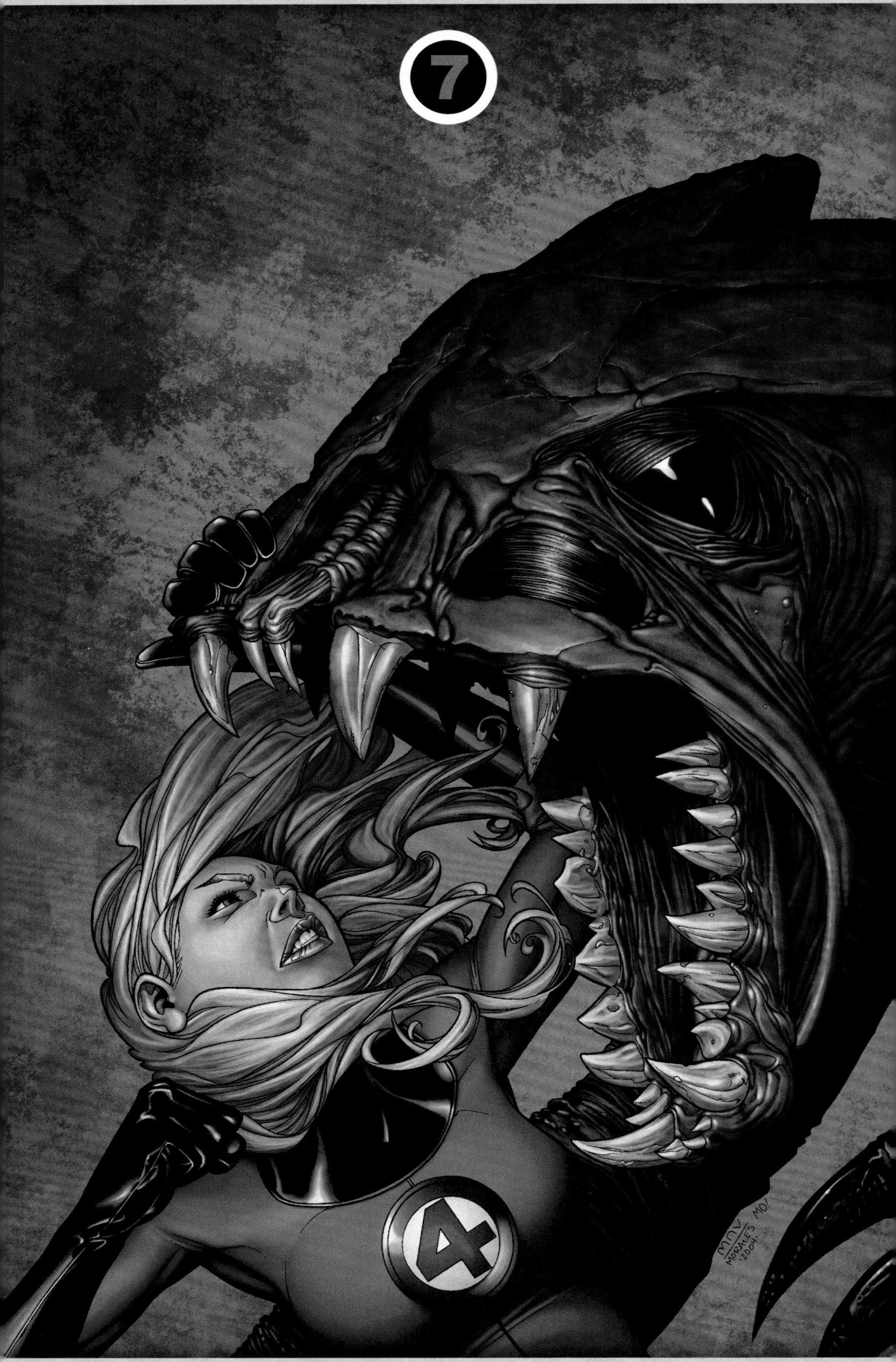
7

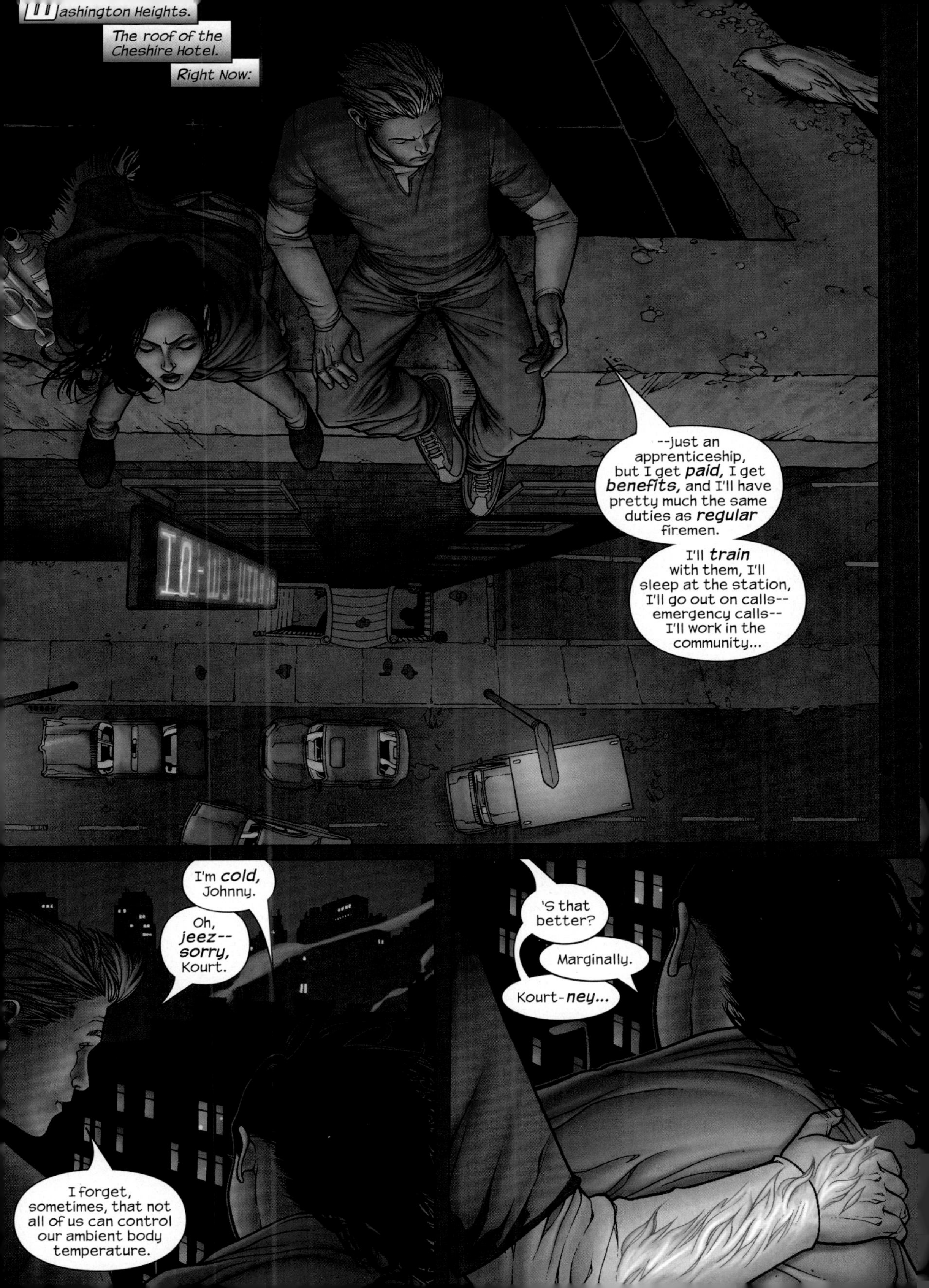
Washington Heights.
The roof of the Cheshire Hotel.
Right Now:
--just an apprenticeship, but I get paid, I get benefits, and I'll have pretty much the same duties as regular firemen.
I'll train with them, I'll sleep at the station, I'll go out on calls--emergency calls--I'll work in the community...
I'm cold, Johnny.
Oh, jeez--sorry, Kourt.
I forget, sometimes, that not all of us can control our ambient body temperature.
'S that better?
Marginally.
Kourt-ney...

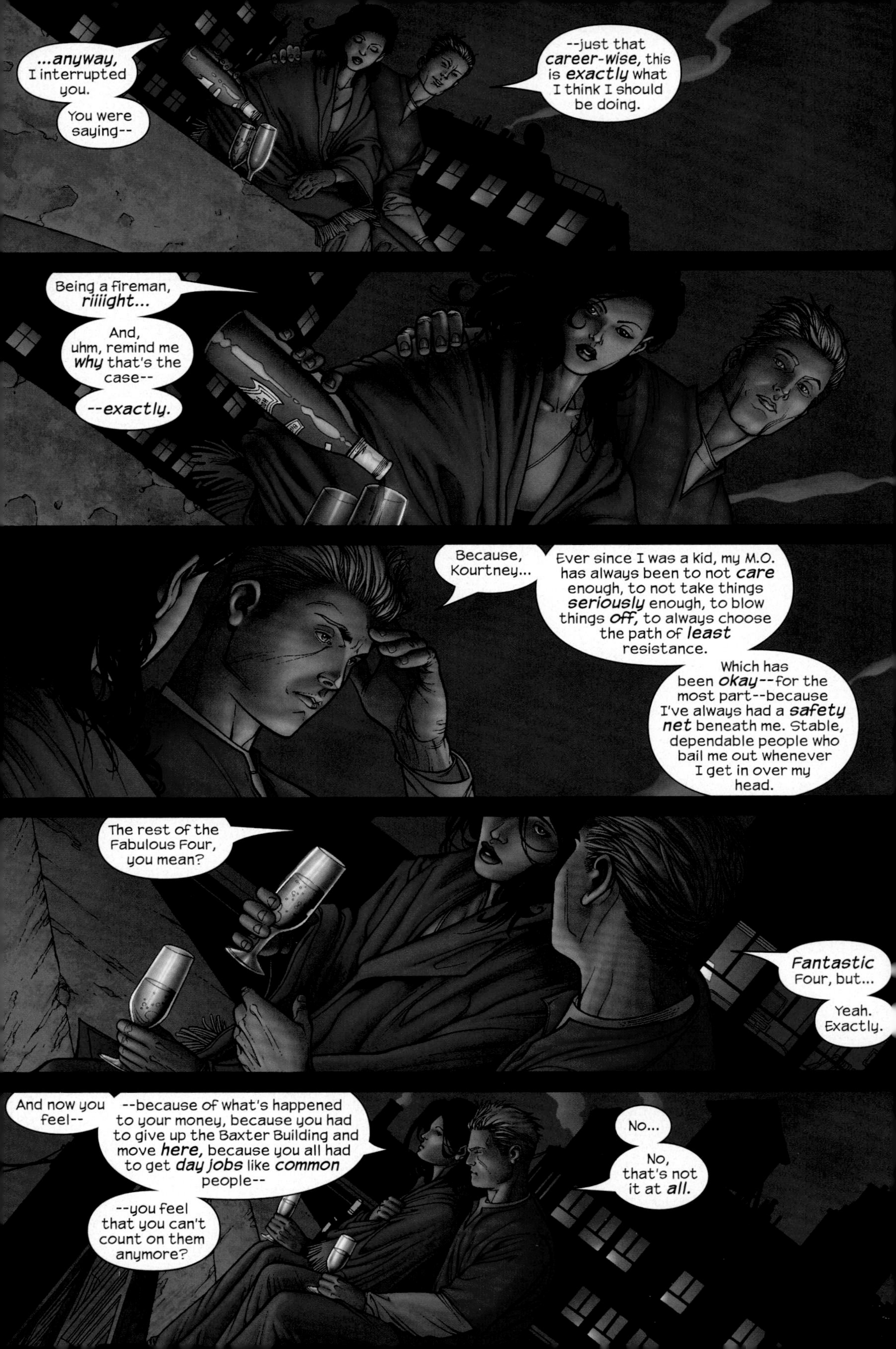

...anyway, I interrupted you.
You were saying--
--just that career-wise, this is exactly what I think I should be doing.
Being a fireman, riiiight...
And, uhm, remind me why that's the case--
--exactly.
Because, Kourtney...
Ever since I was a kid, my M.O. has always been to not care enough, to not take things seriously enough, to blow things off, to always choose the path of least resistance.
Which has been okay--for the most part--because I've always had a safety net beneath me. Stable, dependable people who bail me out whenever I get in over my head.
The rest of the Fabulous Four, you mean?
Fantastic Four, but...
Yeah. Exactly.
And now you feel--
--because of what's happened to your money, because you had to give up the Baxter Building and move here, because you all had to get day jobs like common people--
--you feel that you can't count on them anymore?
No...
No, that's not it at all.

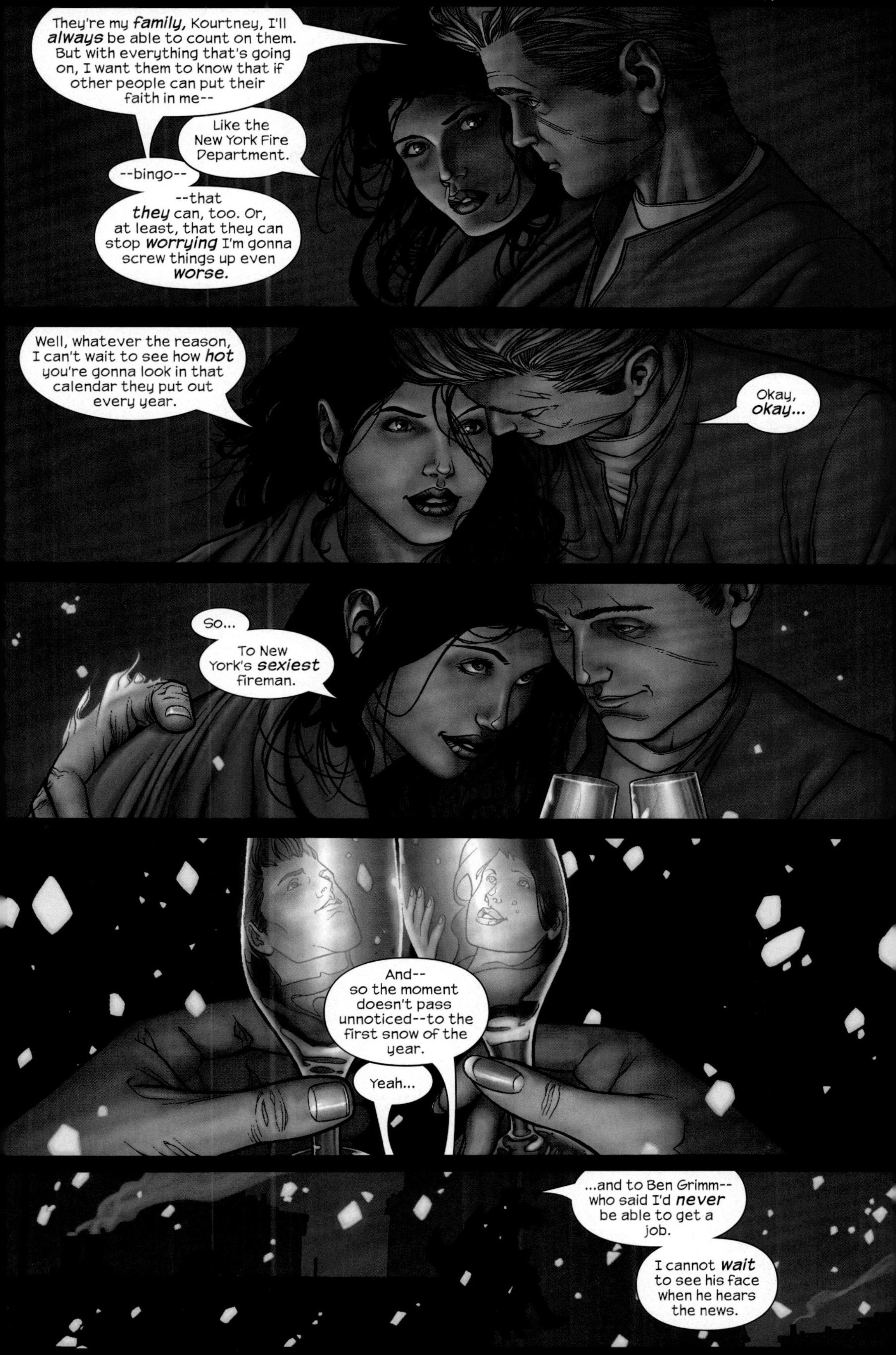
They're my family, Kourtney, I'll always be able to count on them. But with everything that's going on, I want them to know that if other people can put their faith in me--
Like the New York Fire Department.
--bingo--
--that they can, too. Or, at least, that they can stop worrying I'm gonna screw things up even worse.
Well, whatever the reason, I can't wait to see how hot you're gonna look in that calendar they put out every year.
Okay, okay...
So...
To New York's sexiest fireman.
And-- so the moment doesn't pass unnoticed--to the first snow of the year.
Yeah...
...and to Ben Grimm-- who said I'd never be able to get a job.
I cannot wait to see his face when he hears the news.

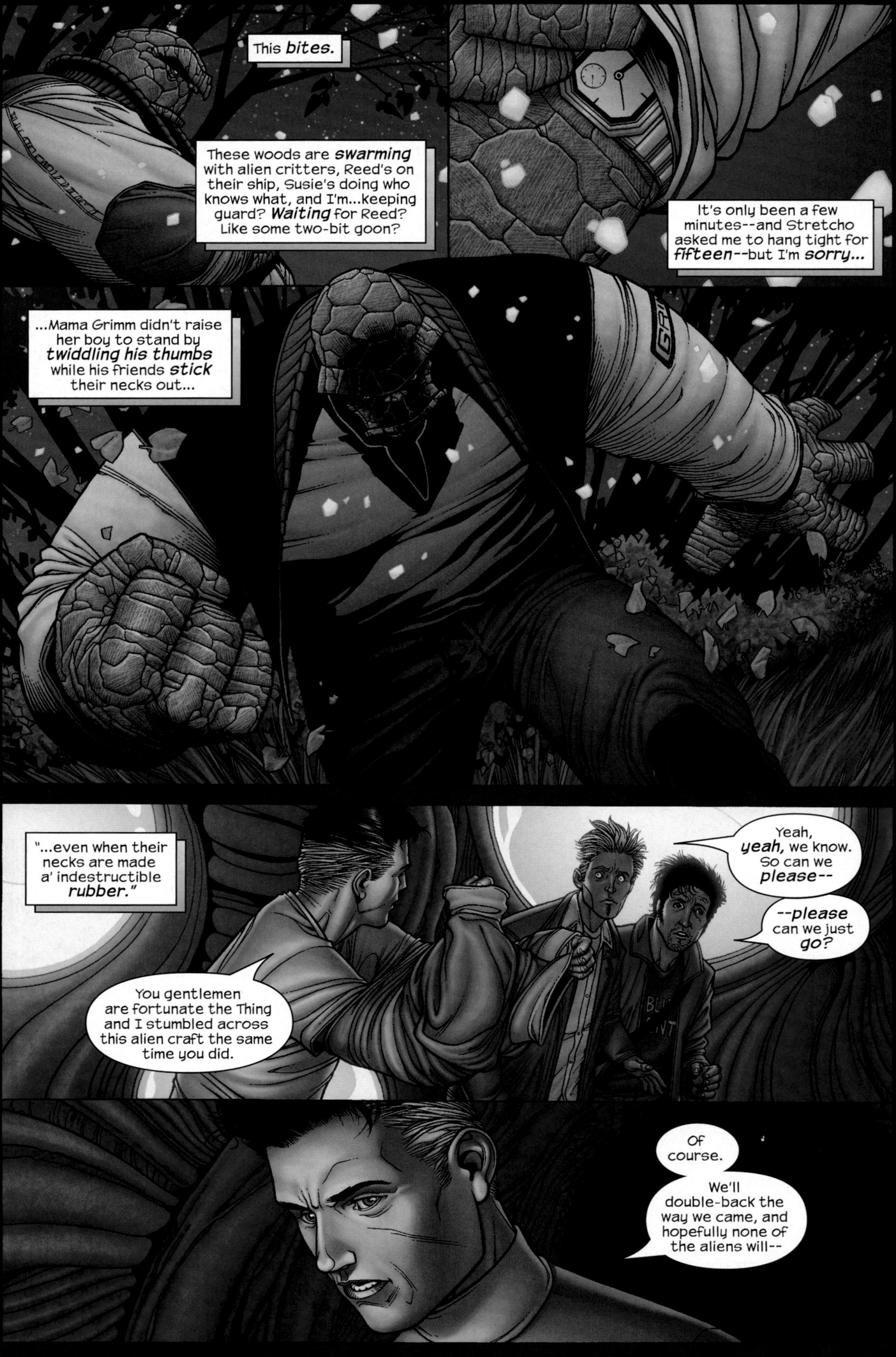
This bites.
These woods are swarming with alien critters, Reed's on their ship, Susie's doing who knows what, and I'm...keeping guard? Waiting for Reed? Like some two-bit goon?
It's only been a few minutes--and Stretcho asked me to hang tight for fifteen--but I'm sorry...
...Mama Grimm didn't raise her boy to stand by twiddling his thumbs while his friends stick their necks out...
"...even when their necks are made a' indestructible rubber."
Yeah, yeah, we know. So can we please--
--please can we just go?
You gentlemen are fortunate the Thing and I stumbled across this alien craft the same time you did.
Of course.
We'll double-back the way we came, and hopefully none of the aliens will--

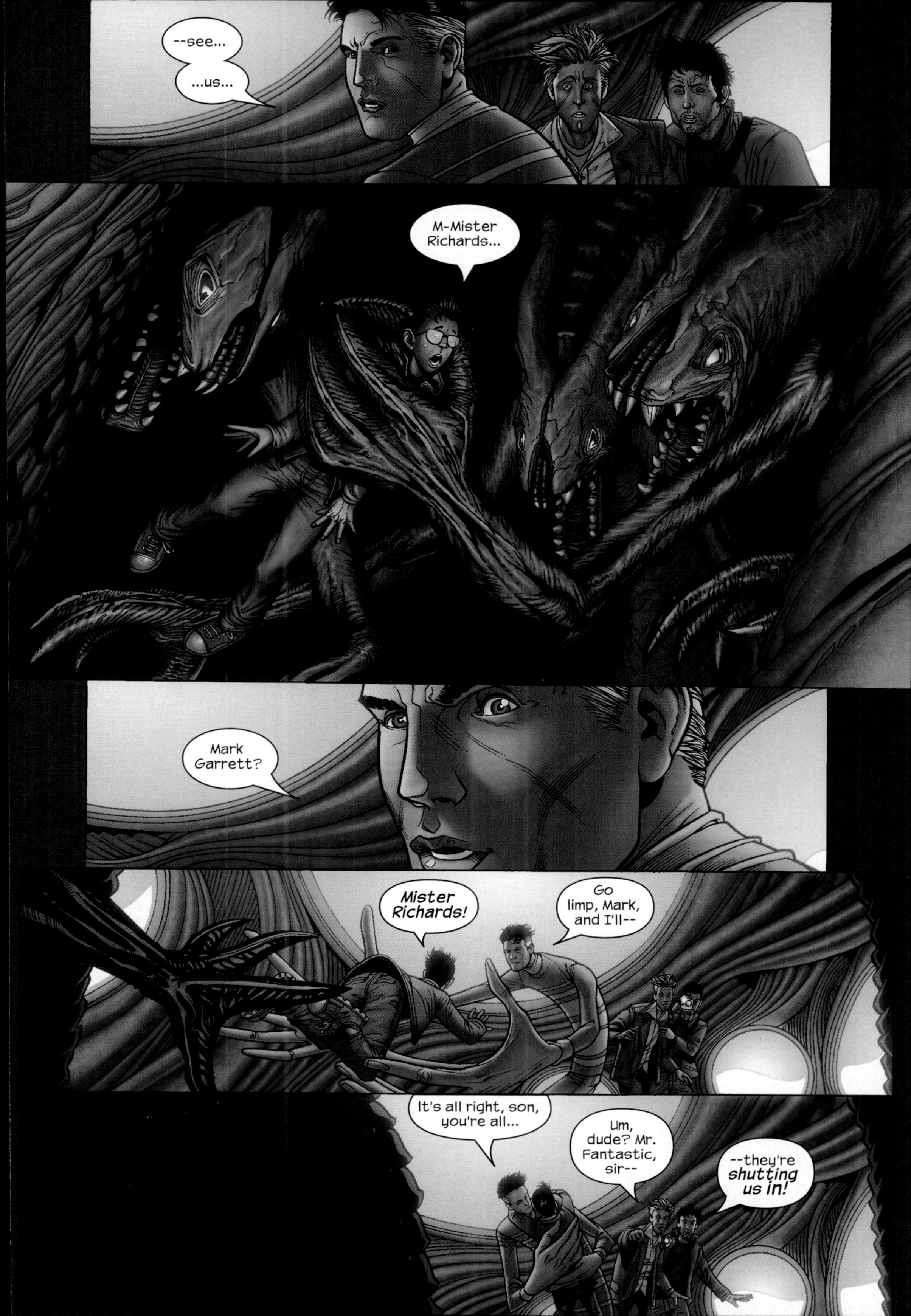
--see...
...us...
M-Mister Richards...
Mark Garrett?
Mister Richards!
Go limp, Mark, and I'll--
It's all right, son, you're all...
Um, dude? Mr. Fantastic, sir--
--they're shutting us in!

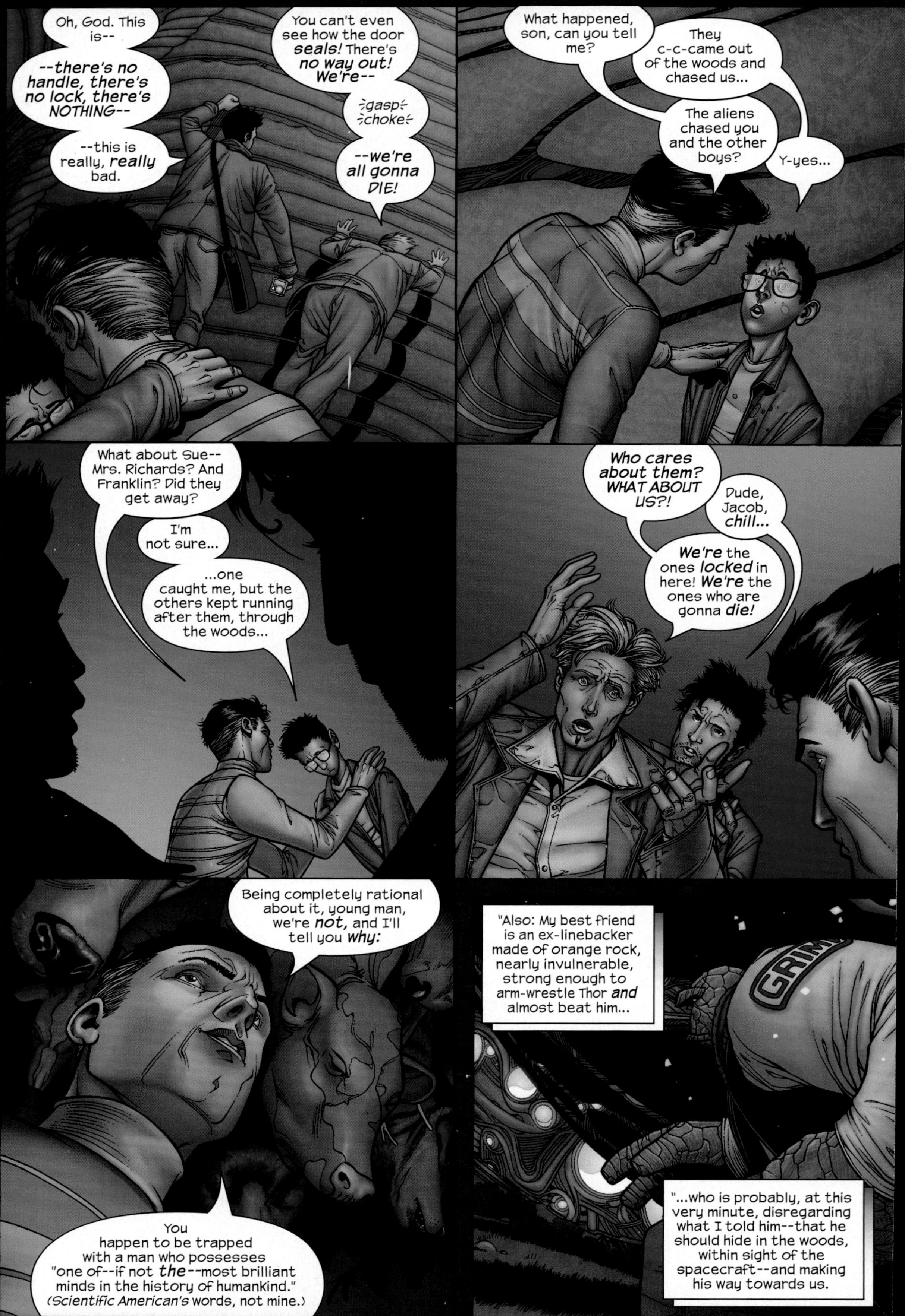
Oh, God. This is--
--there's no handle, there's no lock, there's NOTHING--
--this is really, really bad.
You can't even see how the door seals! There's no way out! We're--
gasp choke
--we're all gonna DIE!
What happened, son, can you tell me?
They c-c-came out of the woods and chased us...
The aliens chased you and the other boys?
Y-yes...
What about Sue--Mrs. Richards? And Franklin? Did they get away?
I'm not sure...
...one caught me, but the others kept running after them, through the woods...
Who cares about them? WHAT ABOUT US?!
Dude, Jacob, chill...
We're the ones locked in here! We're the ones who are gonna die!
Being completely rational about it, young man, we're not, and I'll tell you why:
You happen to be trapped with a man who possesses "one of--if not the--most brilliant minds in the history of humankind." (Scientific American's words, not mine.)
"Also: My best friend is an ex-linebacker made of orange rock, nearly invulnerable, strong enough to arm-wrestle Thor and almost beat him...
GRIM
"...who is probably, at this very minute, disregarding what I told him--that he should hide in the woods, within sight of the spacecraft--and making his way towards us.

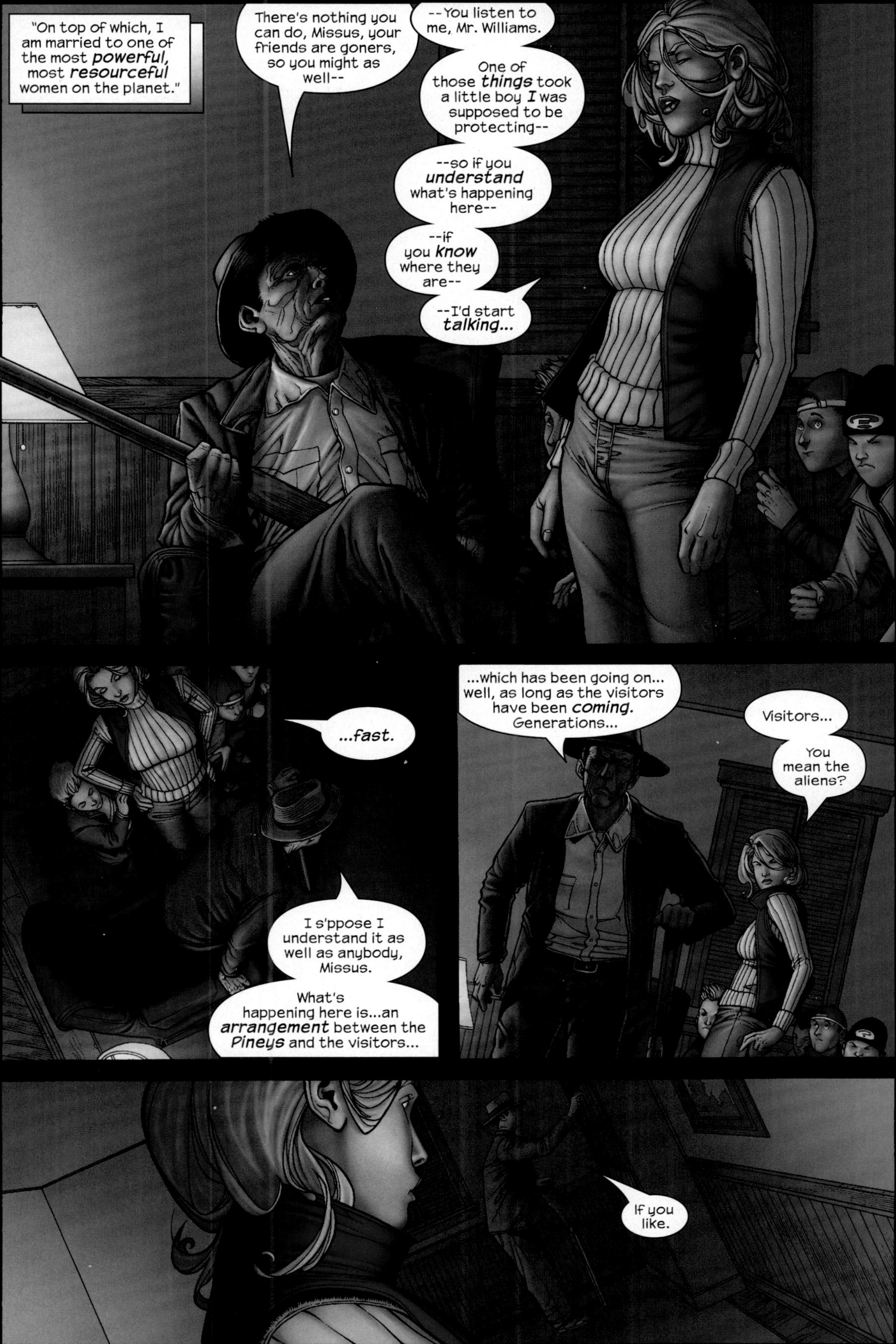
"On top of which, I am married to one of the most *powerful*, most *resourceful* women on the planet."
There's nothing you can do, Missus, your friends are goners, so you might as well--
--You listen to me, Mr. Williams.
One of those *things* took a little boy *I* was supposed to be protecting--
--so if you *understand* what's happening here--
--if you *know* where they are--
--I'd start *talking...*
...*fast.*
I s'ppose I understand it as well as anybody, Missus.
What's happening here is...an *arrangement* between the *Pineys* and the visitors...
...which has been going on... well, as long as the visitors have been *coming.* Generations...
Visitors...
You mean the aliens?
If you like.

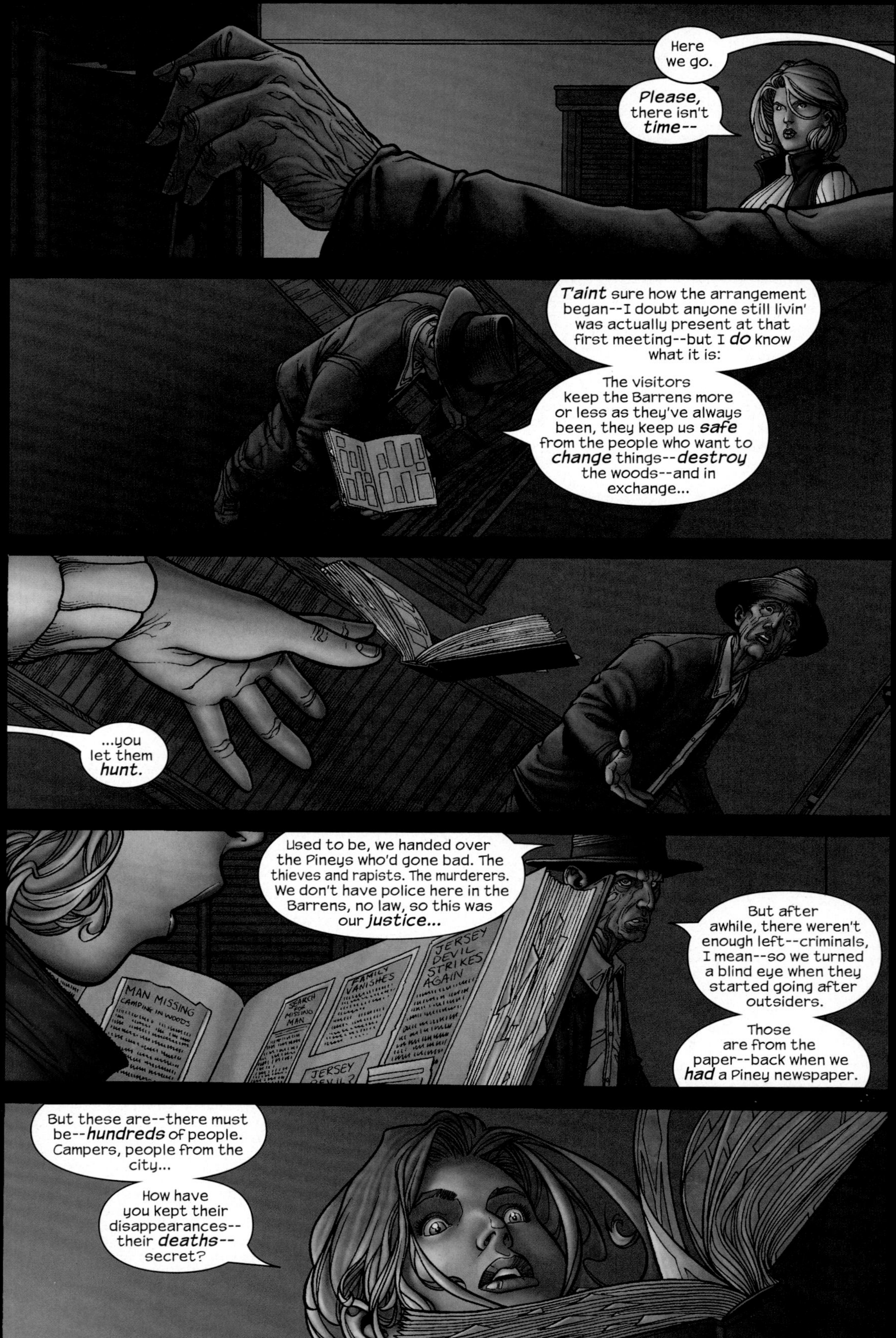
Here we go.
Please, there isn't *time*--
T'aint sure how the arrangement began--I doubt anyone still livin' was actually present at that first meeting--but I *do* know what it is:
The visitors keep the Barrens more or less as they've always been, they keep us *safe* from the people who want to *change* things--*destroy* the woods--and in exchange...
...you let them *hunt.*
Used to be, we handed over the Pineys who'd gone bad. The thieves and rapists. The murderers. We don't have police here in the Barrens, no law, so this was our *justice...*
MAN MISSING CAMPING IN WOODS
SEARCH FOR MISSING MAN
FAMILY VANISHES
JERSEY DEVIL STRIKES AGAIN
But after awhile, there weren't enough left--criminals, I mean--so we turned a blind eye when they started going after outsiders.
Those are from the paper--back when we *had* a Piney newspaper.
But these are--there must be--*hundreds* of people. Campers, people from the city...
How have you kept their disappearances--their *deaths*--secret?

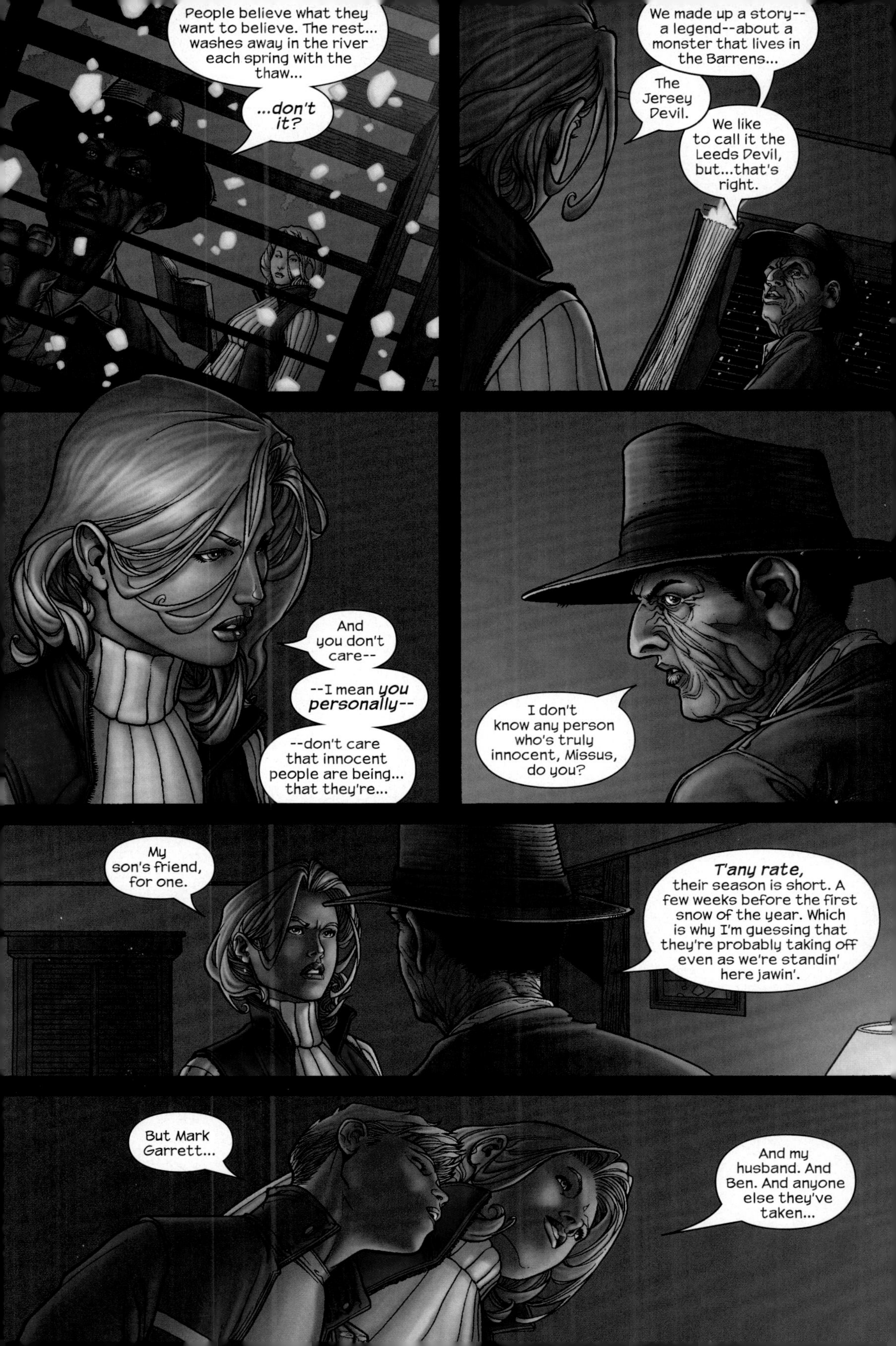

People believe what they want to believe. The rest... washes away in the river each spring with the thaw...
...don't it?
We made up a story-- a legend--about a monster that lives in the Barrens...
The Jersey Devil.
We like to call it the Leeds Devil, but...that's right.
And you don't care--
--I mean you personally--
--don't care that innocent people are being... that they're...
I don't know any person who's truly innocent, Missus, do you?
My son's friend, for one.
T'any rate, their season is short. A few weeks before the first snow of the year. Which is why I'm guessing that they're probably taking off even as we're standin' here jawin'.
But Mark Garrett...
And my husband. And Ben. And anyone else they've taken...

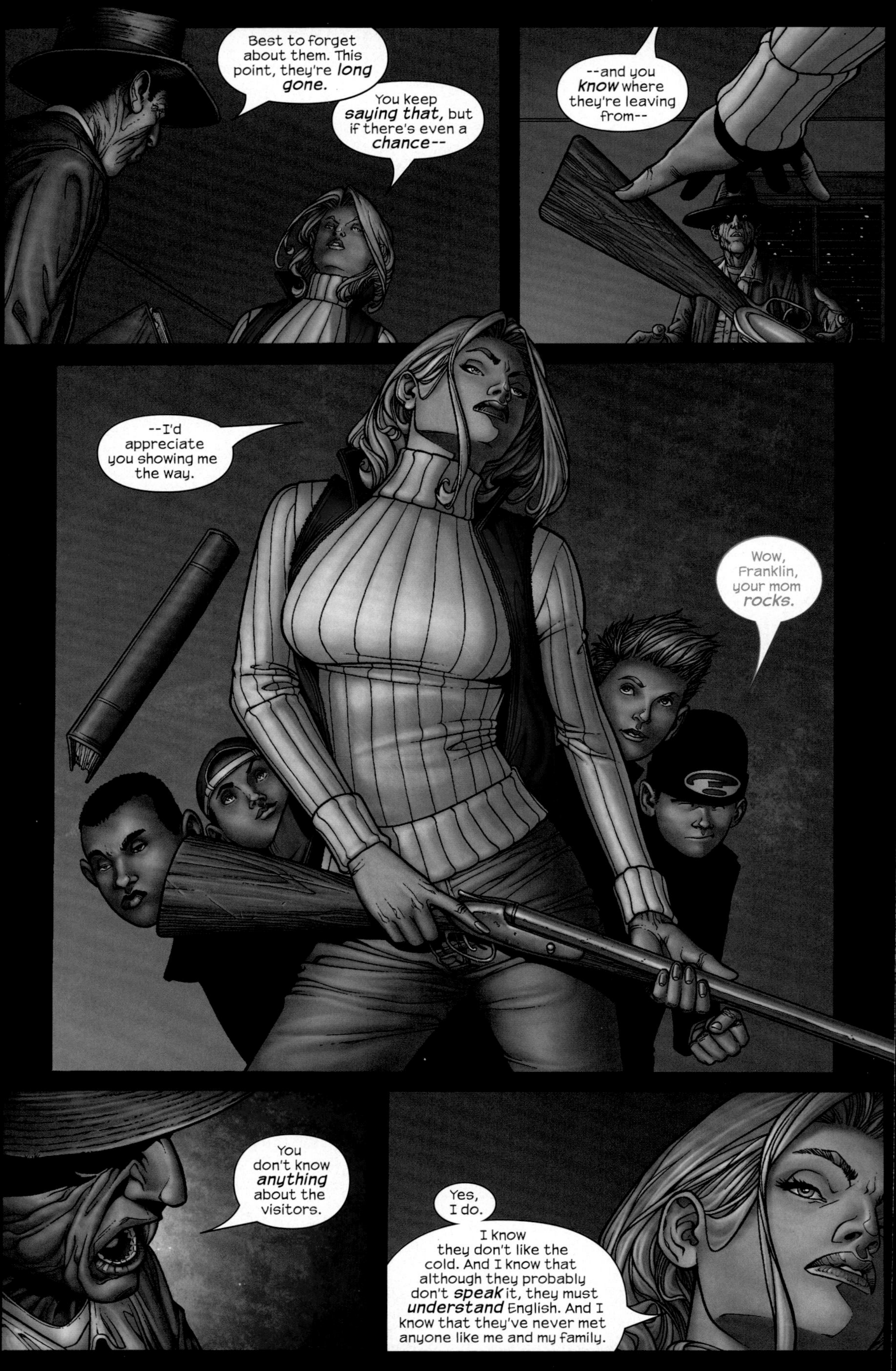
Best to forget about them. This point, they're *long gone.*
You keep *saying that,* but if there's even a *chance*--
--and you *know* where they're leaving from--
--I'd appreciate you showing me the way.
Wow, Franklin, your mom *rocks.*
You don't know *anything* about the visitors.
Yes, I do.
I know they don't like the cold. And I know that although they probably don't *speak* it, they must *understand* English. And I know that they've never met anyone like me and my family.

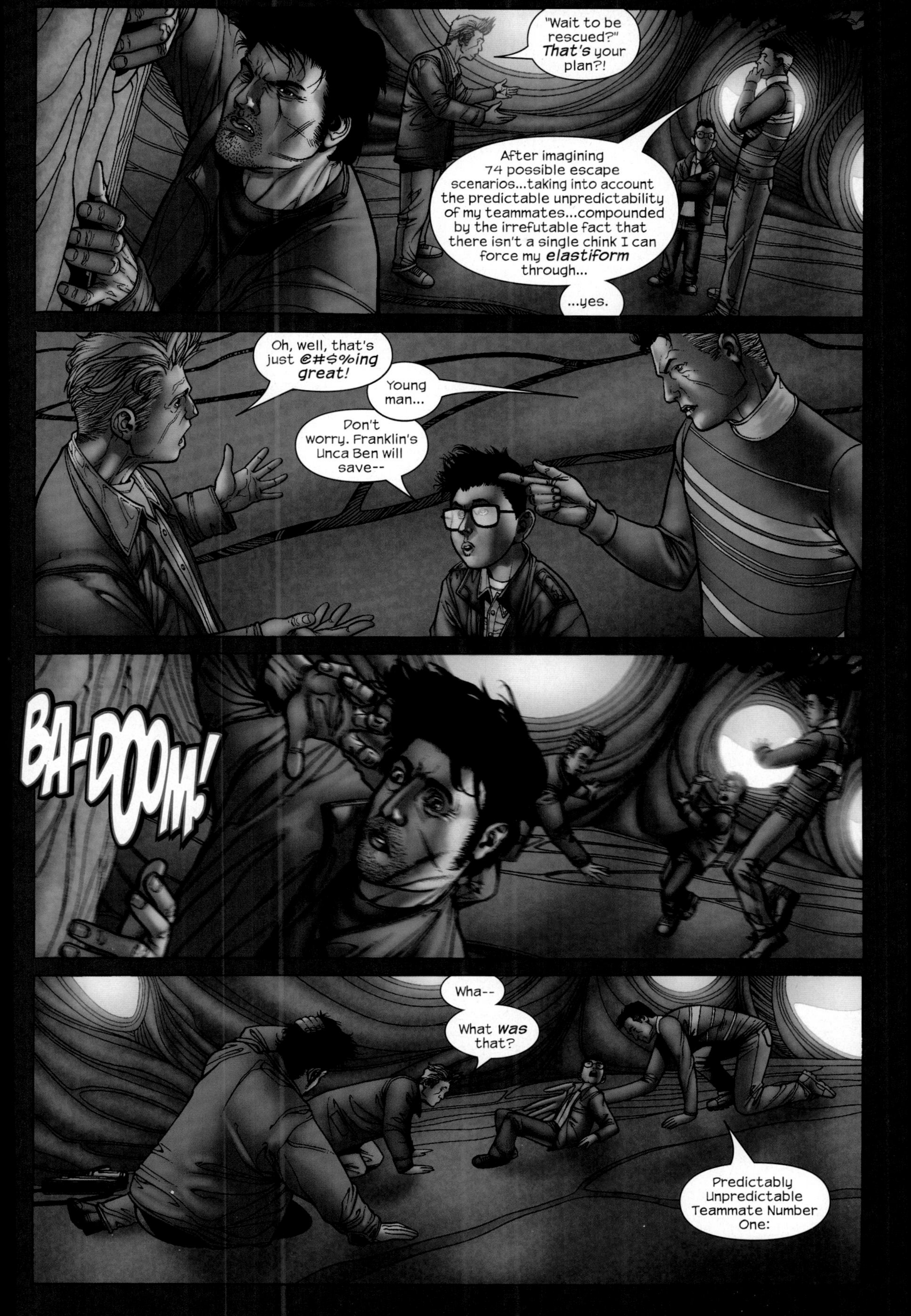
"Wait to be rescued?" That's your plan?!
After imagining 74 possible escape scenarios...taking into account the predictable unpredictability of my teammates...compounded by the irrefutable fact that there isn't a single chink I can force my elastiform through...
...yes.
Oh, well, that's just @#$%ing great!
Young man...
Don't worry. Franklin's Unca Ben will save--
BA-DOOM!
Wha--
What was that?
Predictably Unpredictable Teammate Number One:

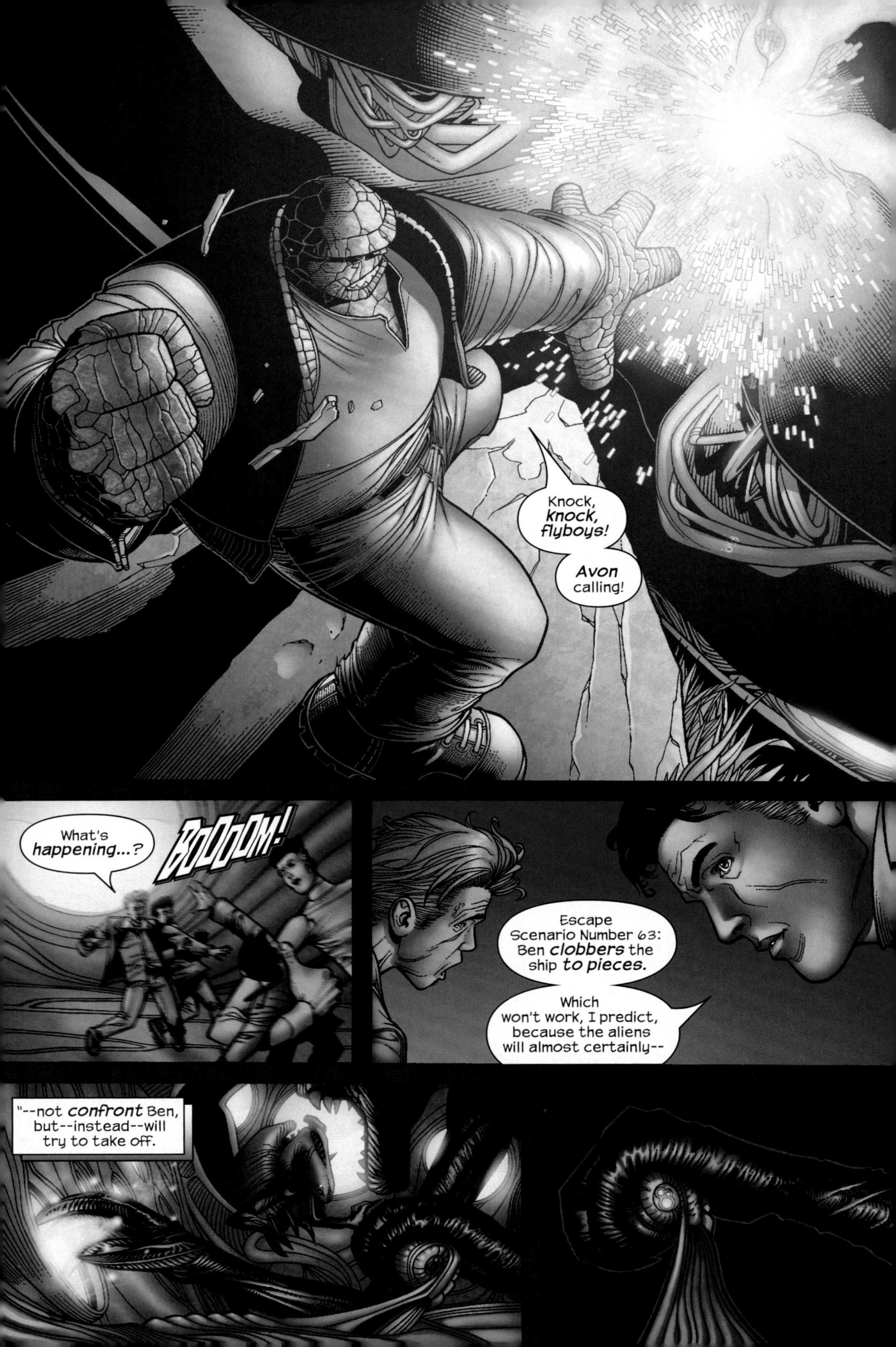

Knock, *knock, flyboys!*
Avon calling!
What's *happening...?*
BOOOOM!
Escape Scenario Number 63: Ben *clobbers* the ship *to pieces.*
Which won't work, I predict, because the aliens will almost certainly--
"--not *confront* Ben, but--instead--will try to take off.

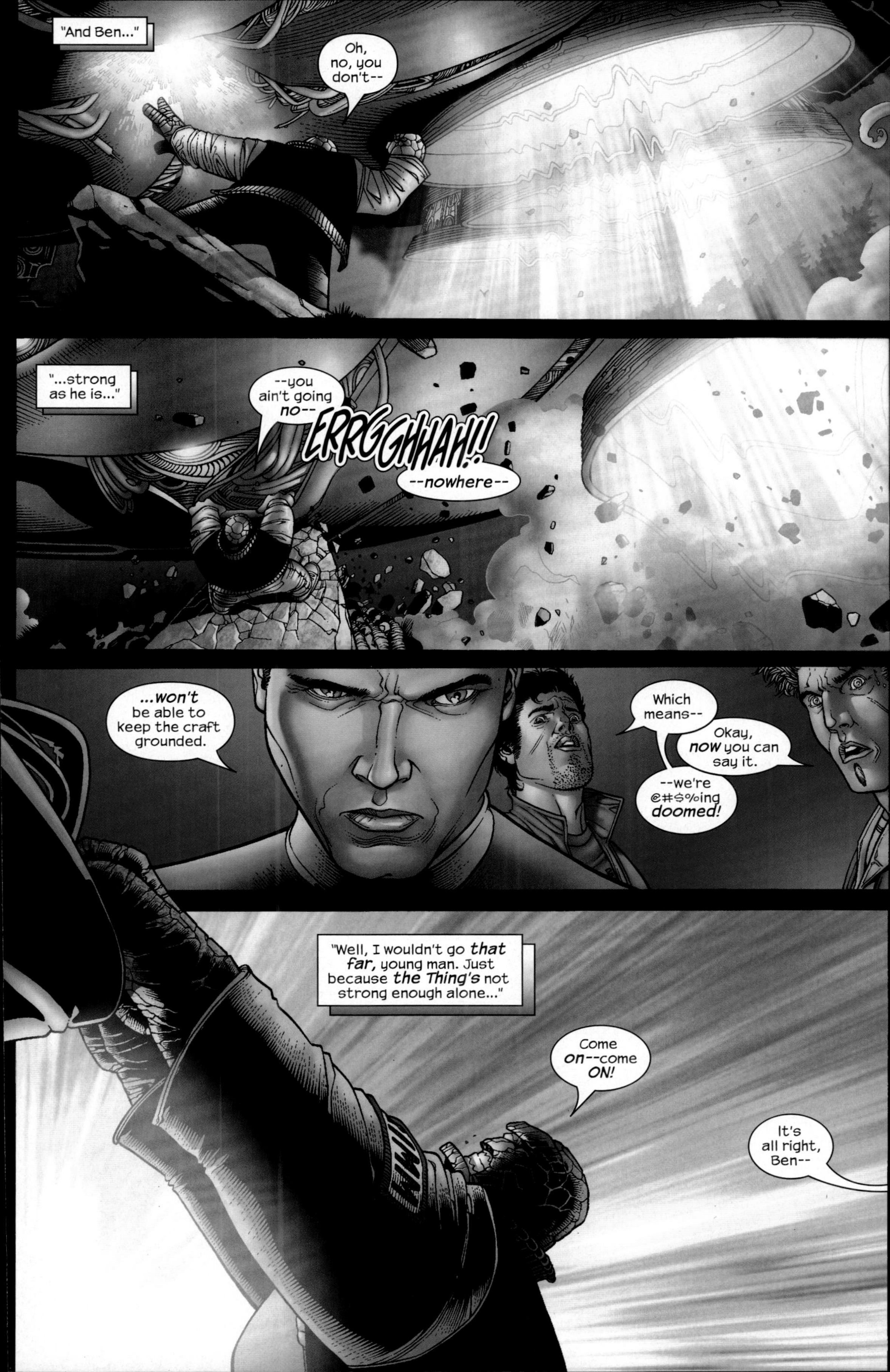
"And Ben..."
Oh, no, you don't--
"...strong as he is..."
--you ain't going no--
ERRGGHHAH!!!
--nowhere--
...won't be able to keep the craft grounded.
Which means--
Okay, now you can say it.
--we're @#$%ing doomed!
"Well, I wouldn't go that far, young man. Just because the Thing's not strong enough alone..."
Come on--come ON!
It's all right, Ben--

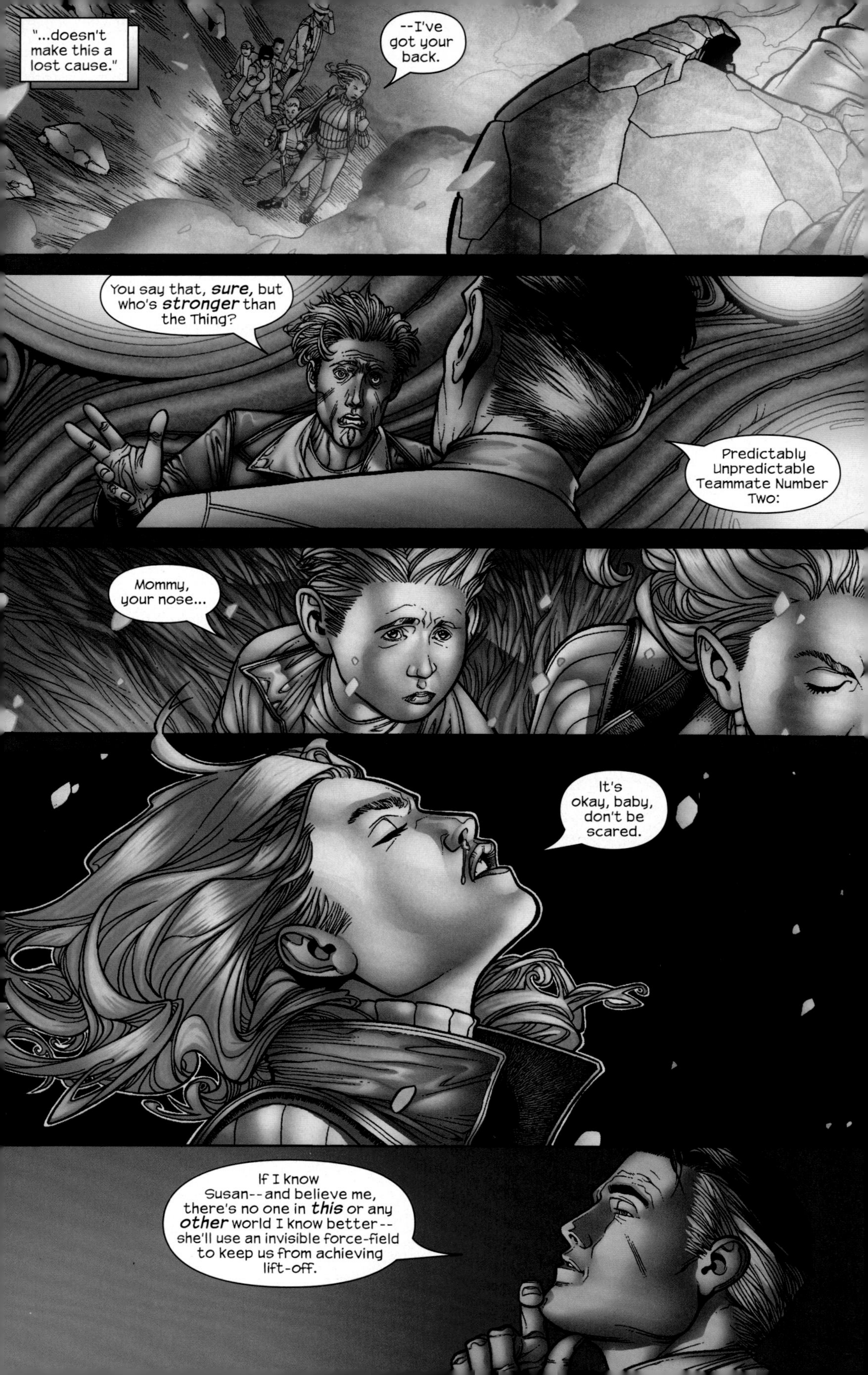
"...doesn't make this a lost cause."
--I've got your back.
You say that, *sure,* but who's *stronger* than the Thing?
Predictably Unpredictable Teammate Number Two:
Mommy, your nose...
It's okay, baby, don't be scared.
If I know Susan--and believe me, there's no one in *this* or any *other* world I know better--she'll use an invisible force-field to keep us from achieving lift-off.

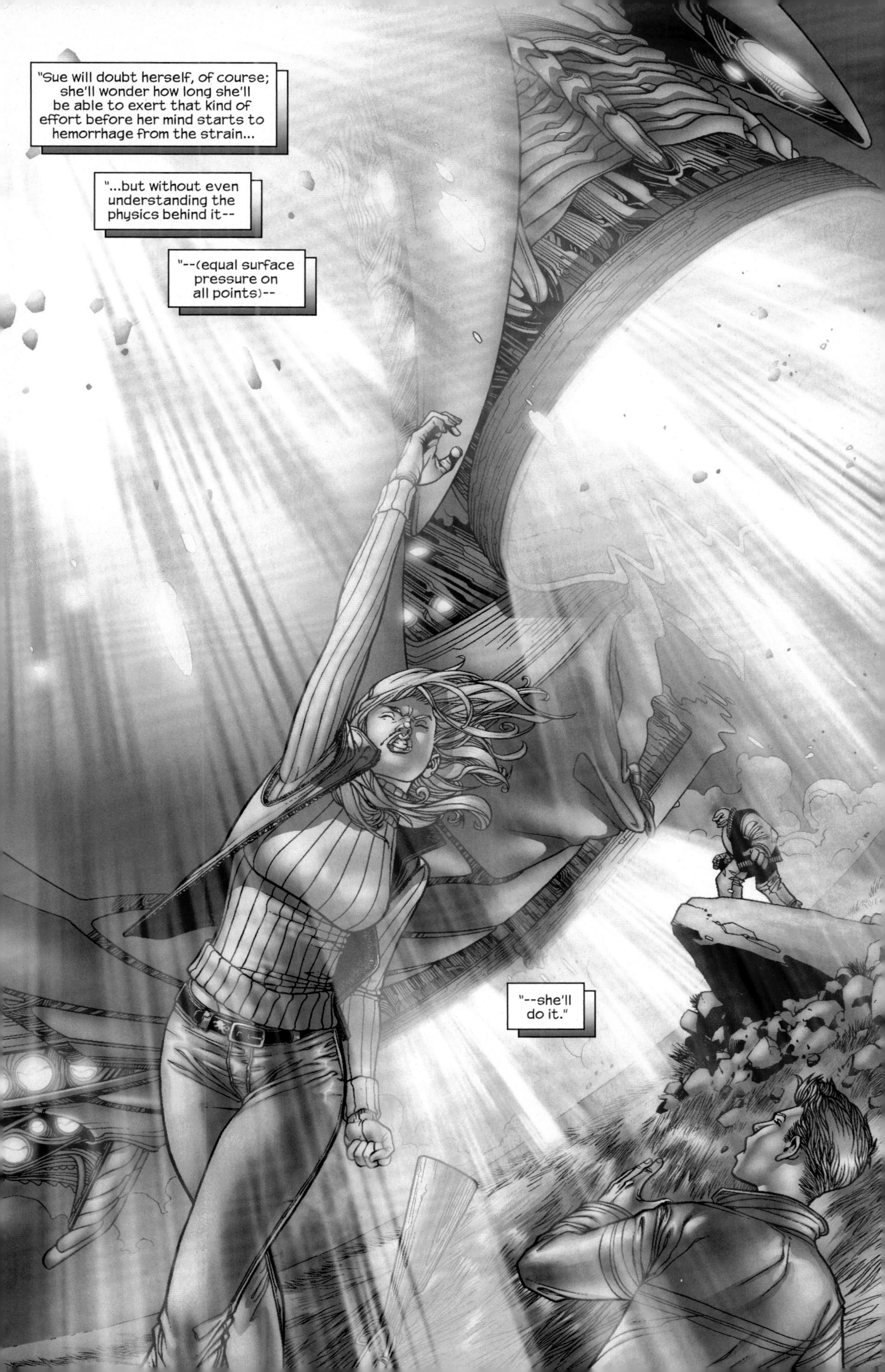
"Sue will doubt herself, of course; she'll wonder how long she'll be able to exert that kind of effort before her mind starts to hemorrhage from the strain...
"...but without even understanding the physics behind it--
"--(equal surface pressure on all points)--
"--she'll do it."

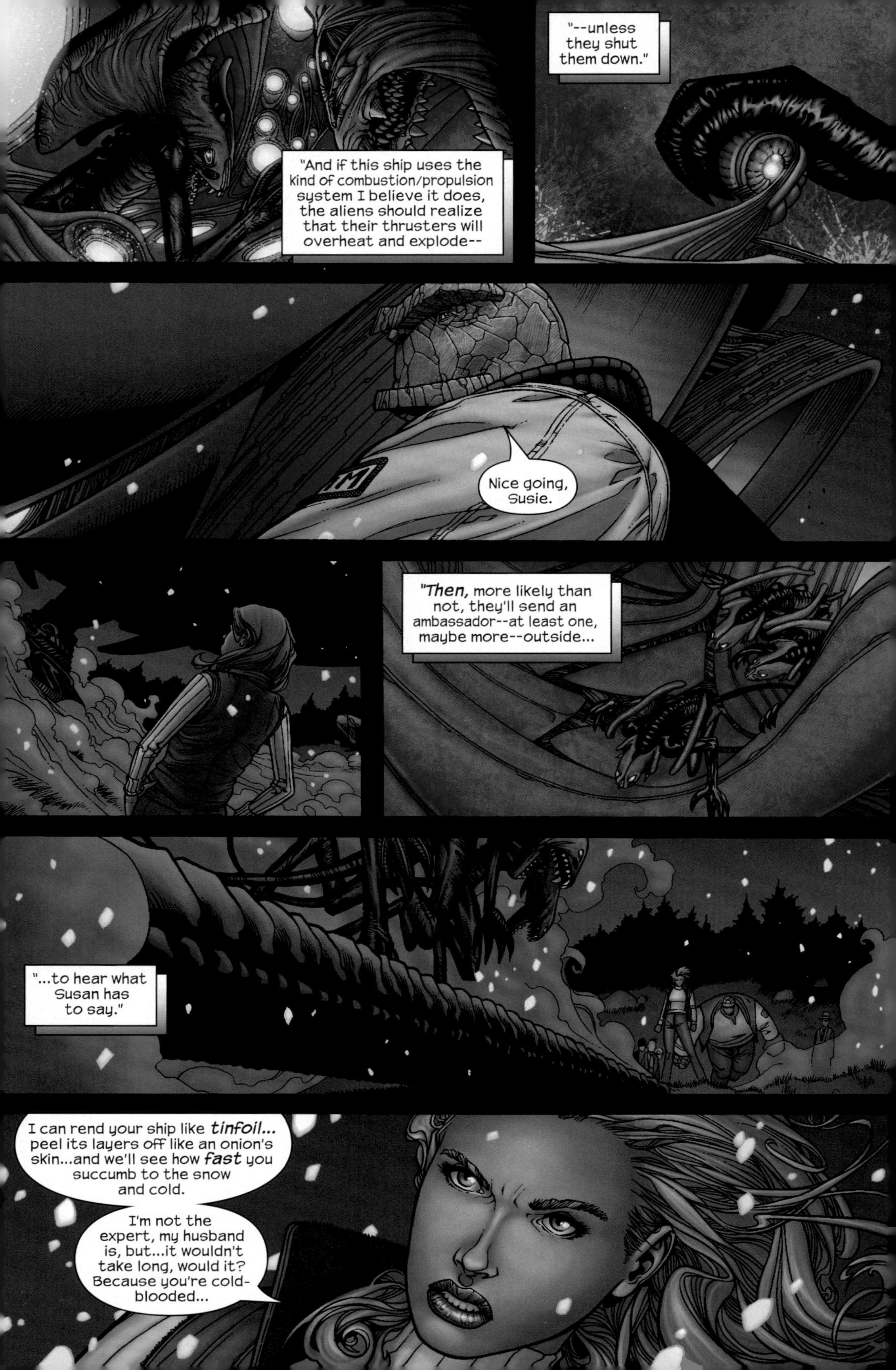
"And if this ship uses the kind of combustion/propulsion system I believe it does, the aliens should realize that their thrusters will overheat and explode--
"--unless they shut them down."
Nice going, Susie.
"Then, more likely than not, they'll send an ambassador--at least one, maybe more--outside...
"...to hear what Susan has to say."
I can rend your ship like tinfoil... peel its layers off like an onion's skin...and we'll see how fast you succumb to the snow and cold.
I'm not the expert, my husband is, but...it wouldn't take long, would it? Because you're cold-blooded...

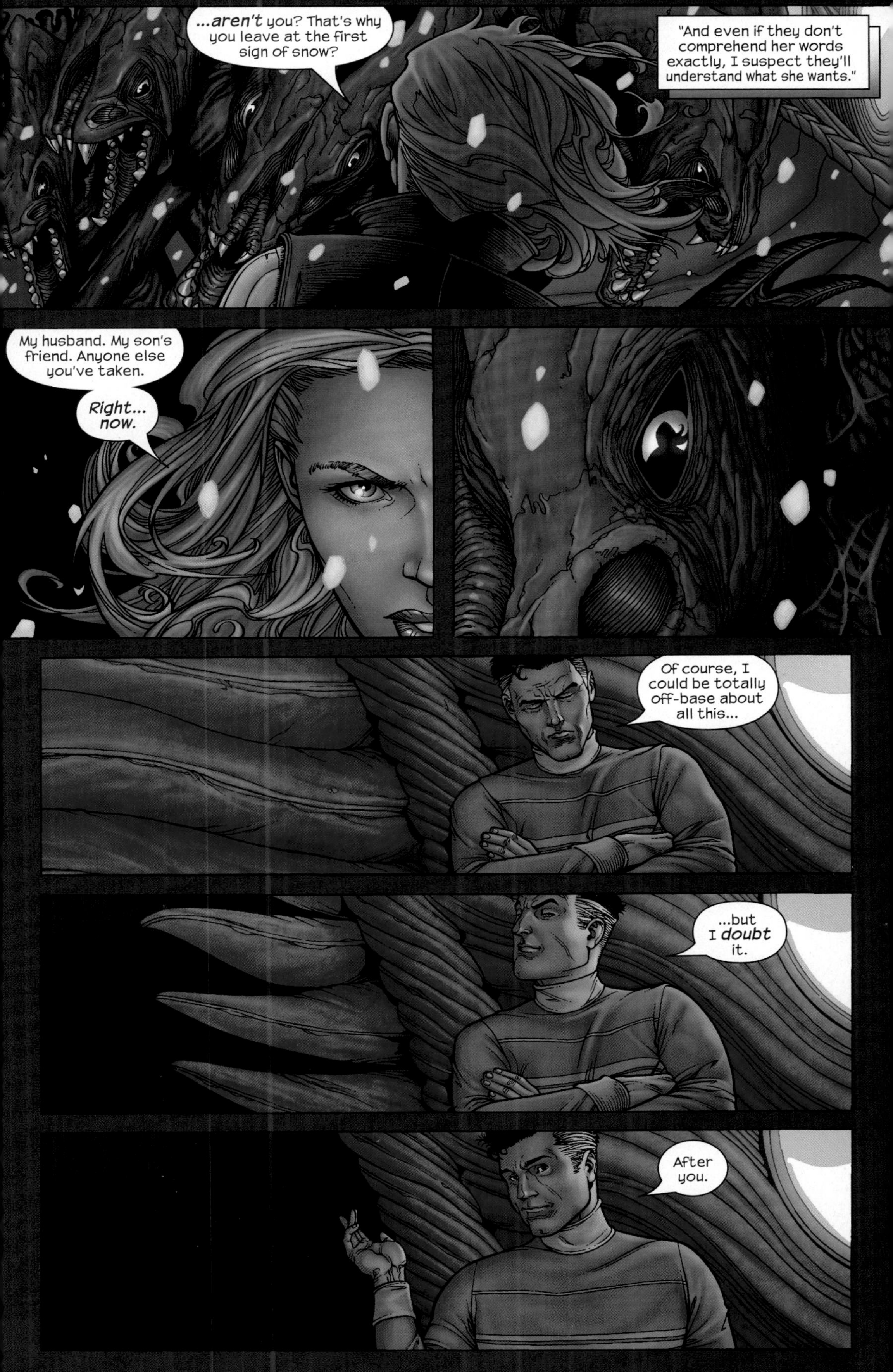
...*aren't* you? That's why you leave at the first sign of snow?
"And even if they don't comprehend her words exactly, I suspect they'll understand what she wants."
My husband. My son's friend. Anyone else you've taken.
Right... now.
Of course, I could be totally off-base about all this...
...but I *doubt* it.
After you.

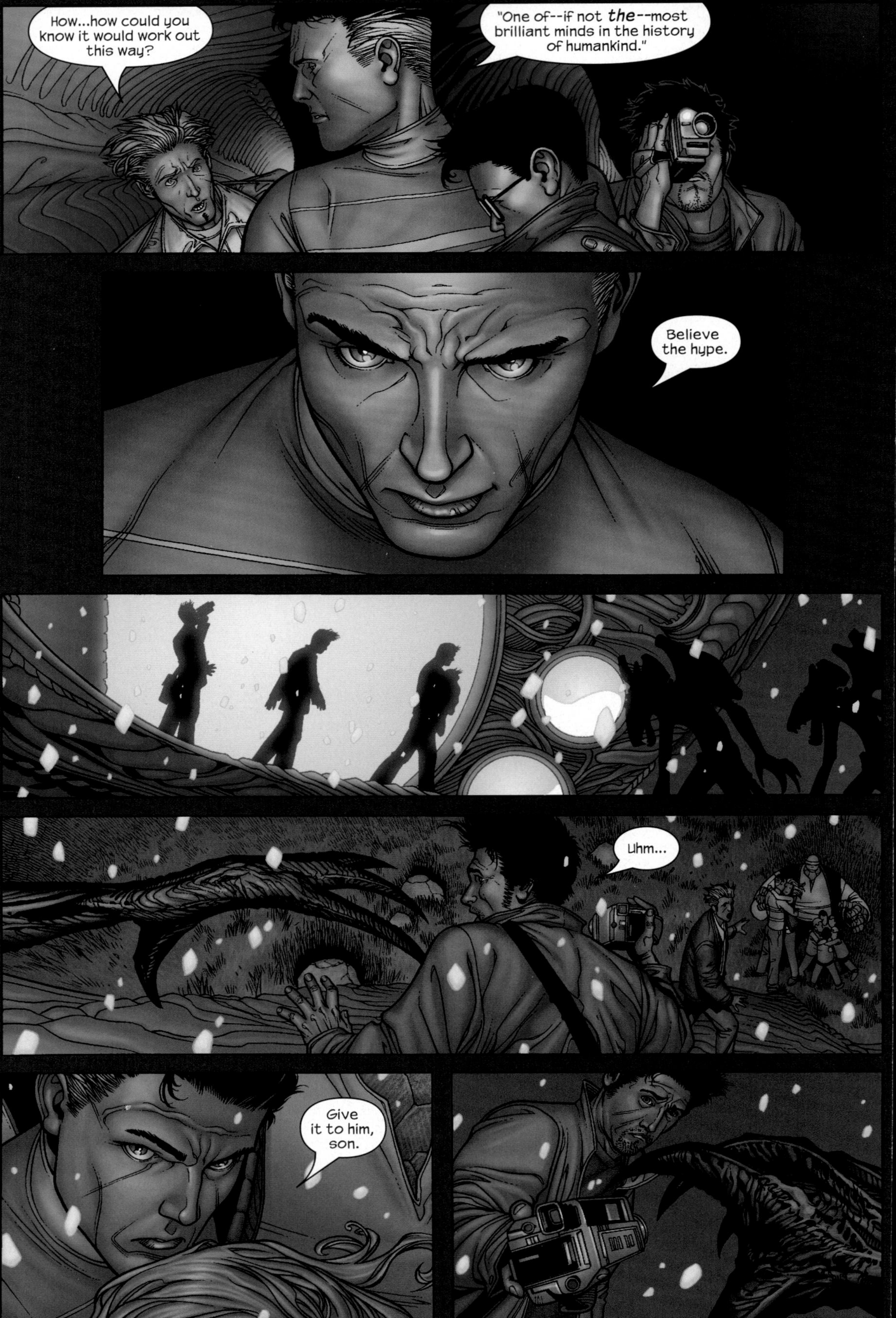
How...how could you know it would work out this way?
"One of--if not the--most brilliant minds in the history of humankind."
Believe the hype.
Uhm...
Give it to him, son.

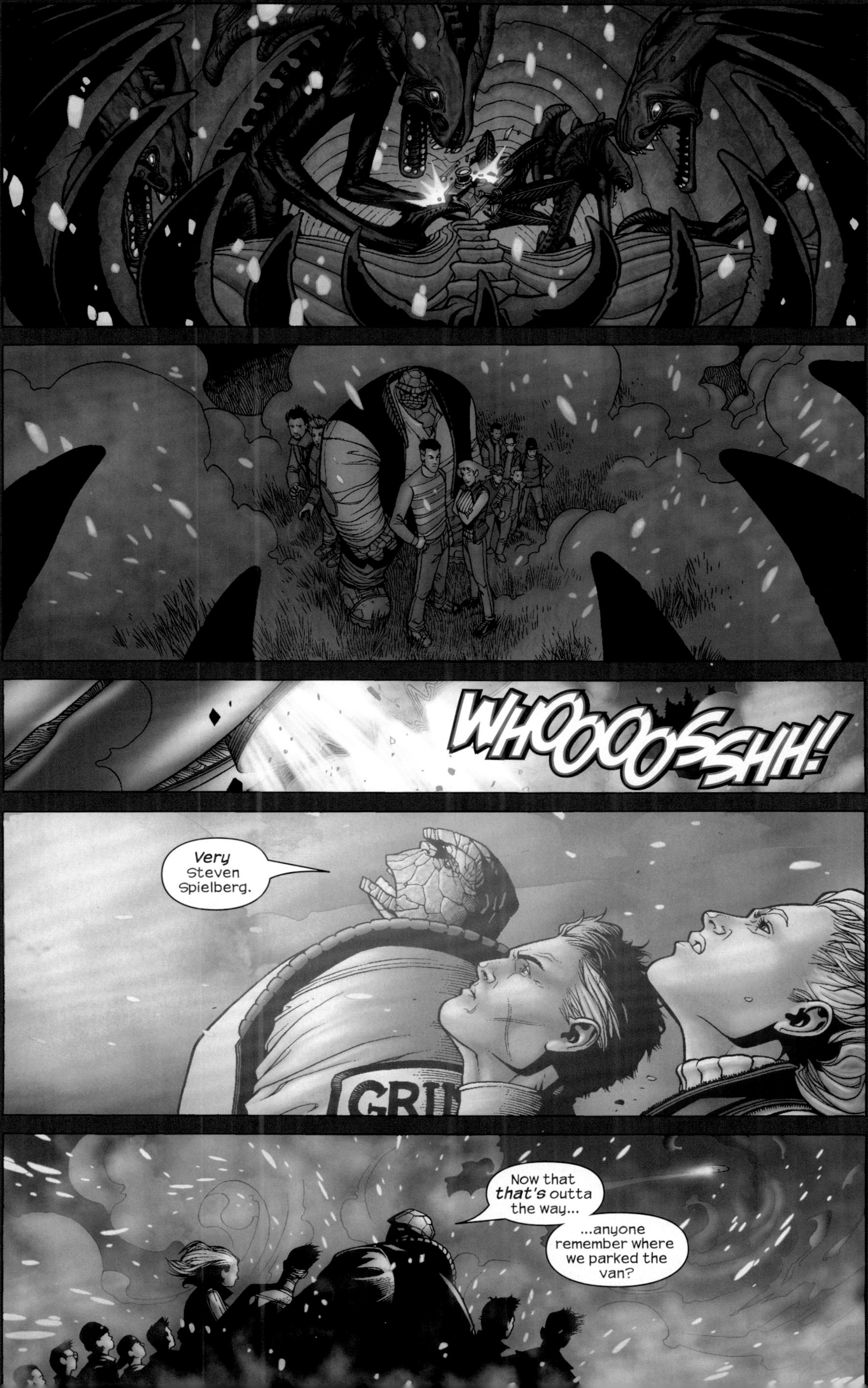
WHOOOOOSSHH!
Very Steven Spielberg.
Now that *that's* outta the way...
...anyone remember where we parked the van?
GRI

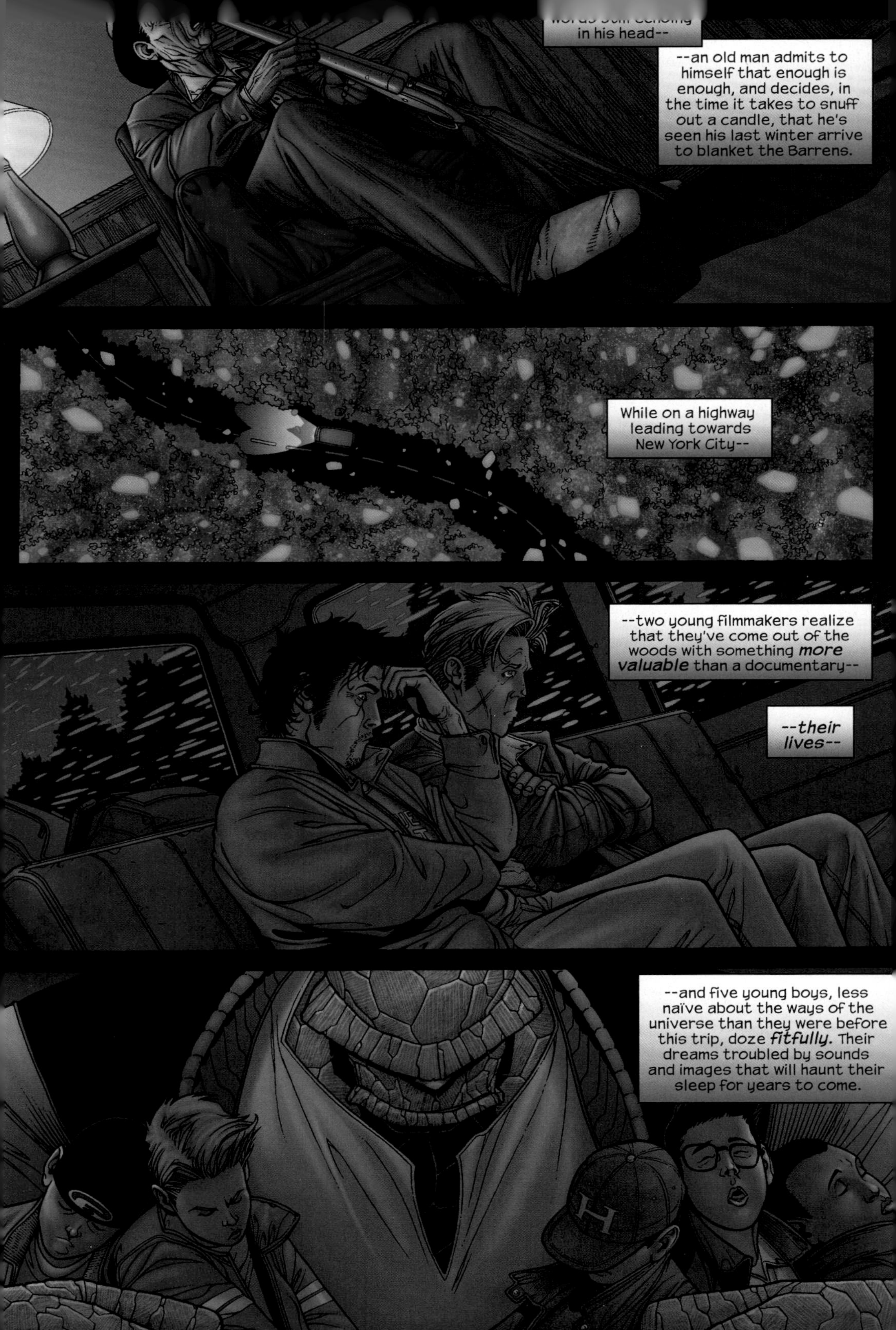
in his head--
--an old man admits to himself that enough is enough, and decides, in the time it takes to snuff out a candle, that he's seen his last winter arrive to blanket the Barrens.
While on a highway leading towards New York City--
--two young filmmakers realize that they've come out of the woods with something *more valuable* than a documentary--
--their lives--
--and five young boys, less naïve about the ways of the universe than they were before this trip, doze *fitfully.* Their dreams troubled by sounds and images that will haunt their sleep for years to come.

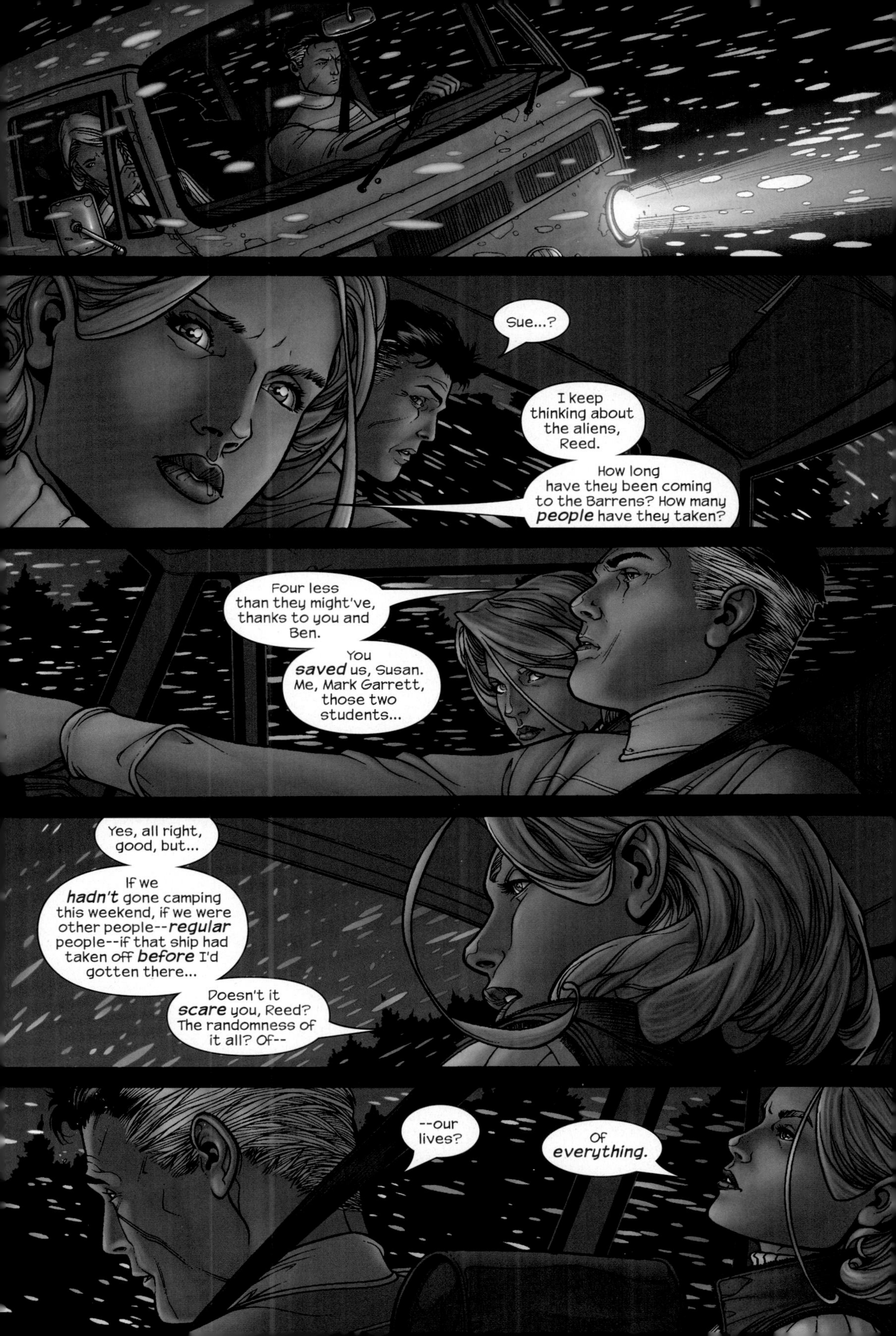
Sue...?
I keep thinking about the aliens, Reed.
How long have they been coming to the Barrens? How many people have they taken?
Four less than they might've, thanks to you and Ben.
You saved us, Susan. Me, Mark Garrett, those two students...
Yes, all right, good, but...
If we hadn't gone camping this weekend, if we were other people--regular people--if that ship had taken off before I'd gotten there...
Doesn't it scare you, Reed? The randomness of it all? Of--
--our lives?
Of everything.

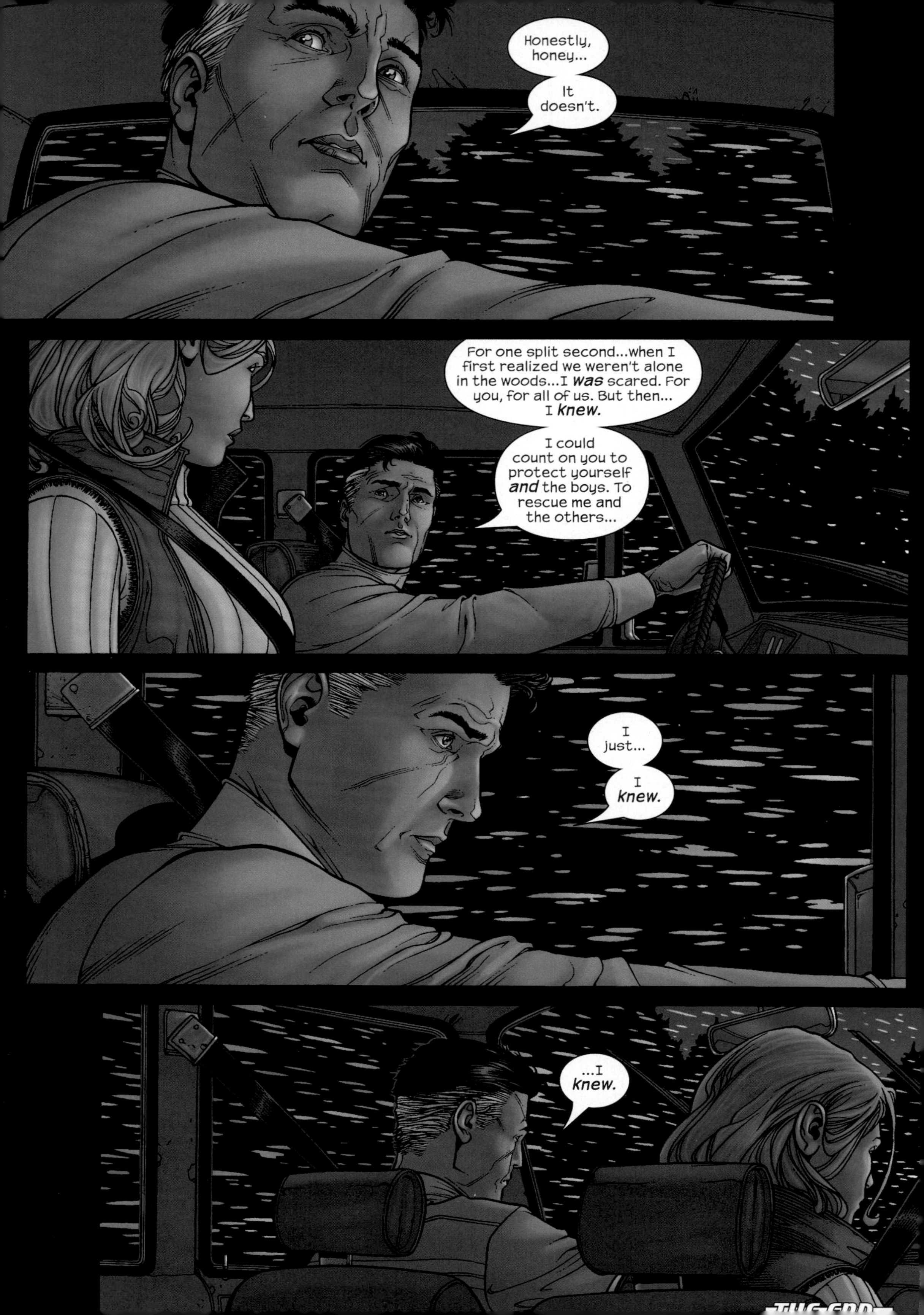

Honestly, honey...
It doesn't.
For one split second...when I first realized we weren't alone in the woods...I *was* scared. For you, for all of us. But then... I *knew.*
I could count on you to protect yourself *and* the boys. To rescue me and the others...
I just...
I *knew.*
...I *knew.*

Evolution of a page

Panel 1.

Reed in the shower, shampooing his hair. It's a hot shower, with lots of steam, because Reed's trying to wake up.

1. CAPTION: Two weeks before his twentieth birthday, my grandfather enlisted. During World War II, he served as a paratrooper with the 101st Airborne.

Panel 2.

Small panel—zooming into a close-up of Richard's face from Page One, Panel Four: John Richards is smiling, about to jump, giving us a thumbs-up.

2. CAPTION: He was a jumper.

Panel 3.

A wide, panoramic panel. A scene of war from the past. Plumes of smoke streak a ravaged, foggy sky. The air is filled—hauntingly, almost beautiful—with dozens of open parachutes, as paratroopers sail down through the air. On the ground (on the coastline), the chaos of battle.

3. CAPTION: On June 6, 1944, the young men of the 101st leaped into the fog-clotted skies over Normandy.

4. CAPTION: None of them were older than 22, and most of them died in the air.

5. CAPTION: My grandfather was lucky.

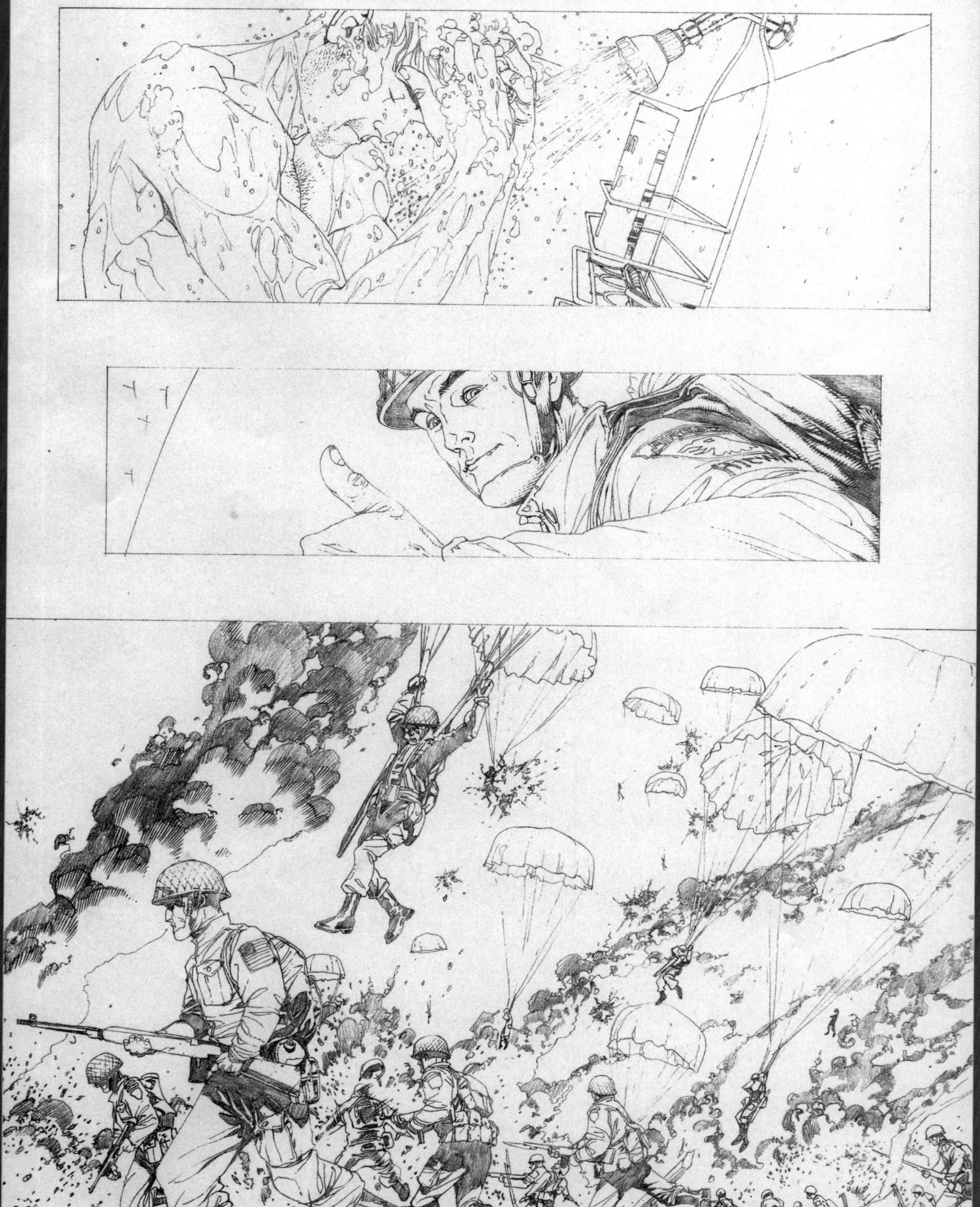

ISSUE #4, Page 4 **INKS**

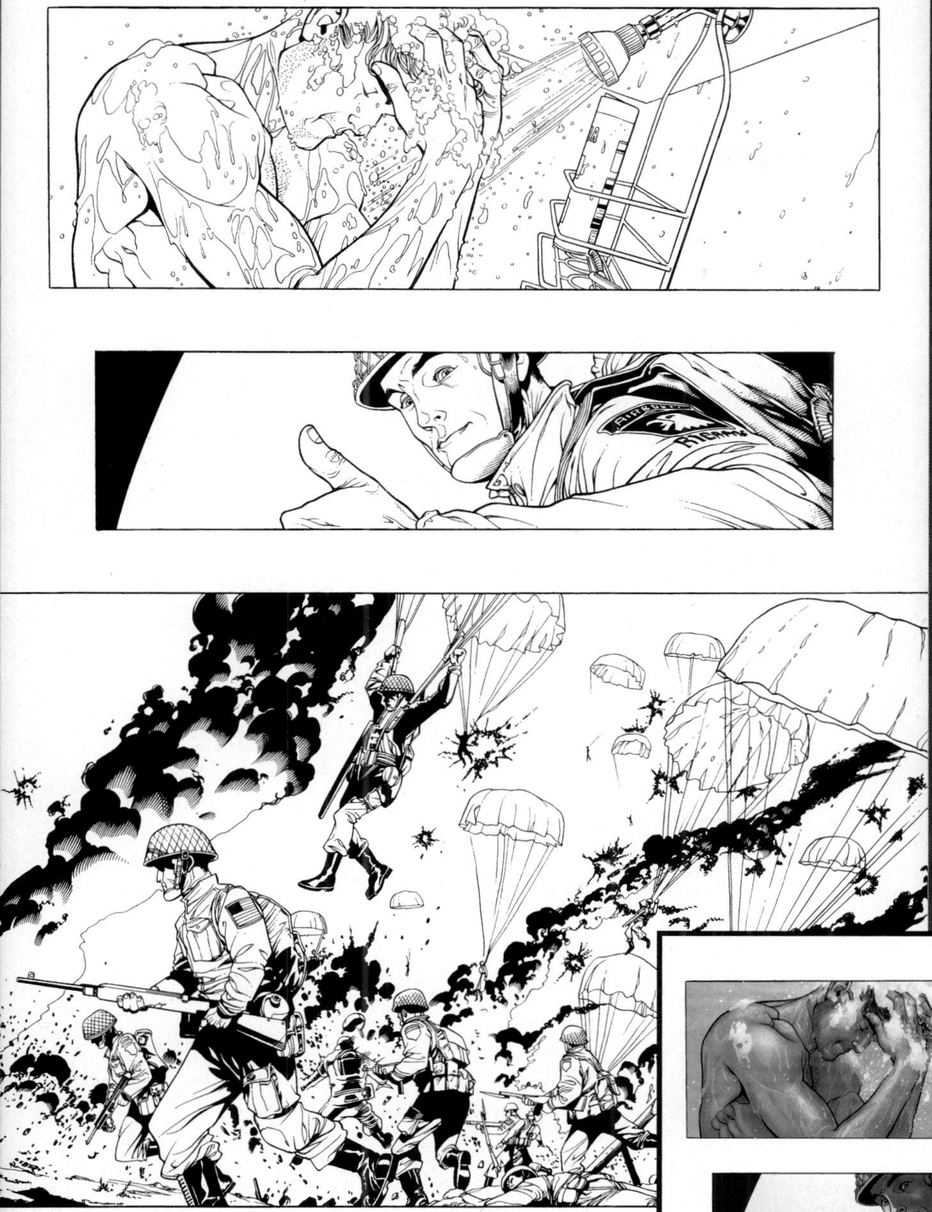

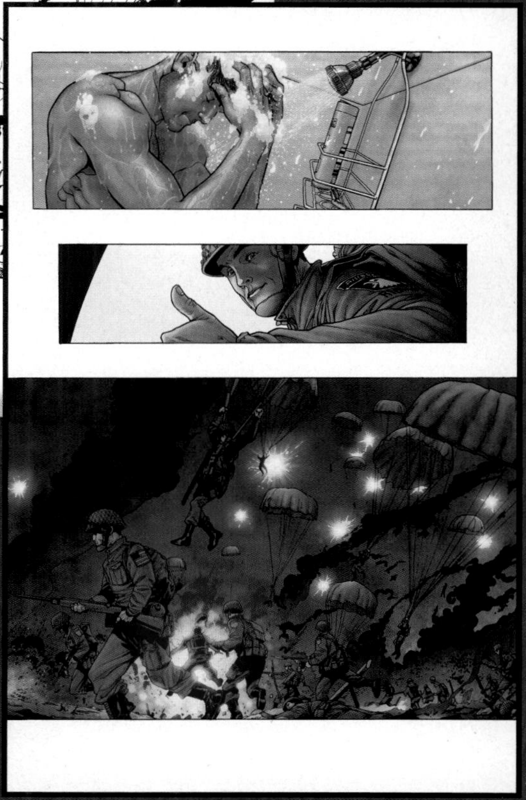

ISSUE #4, Page 4 **COLORS**

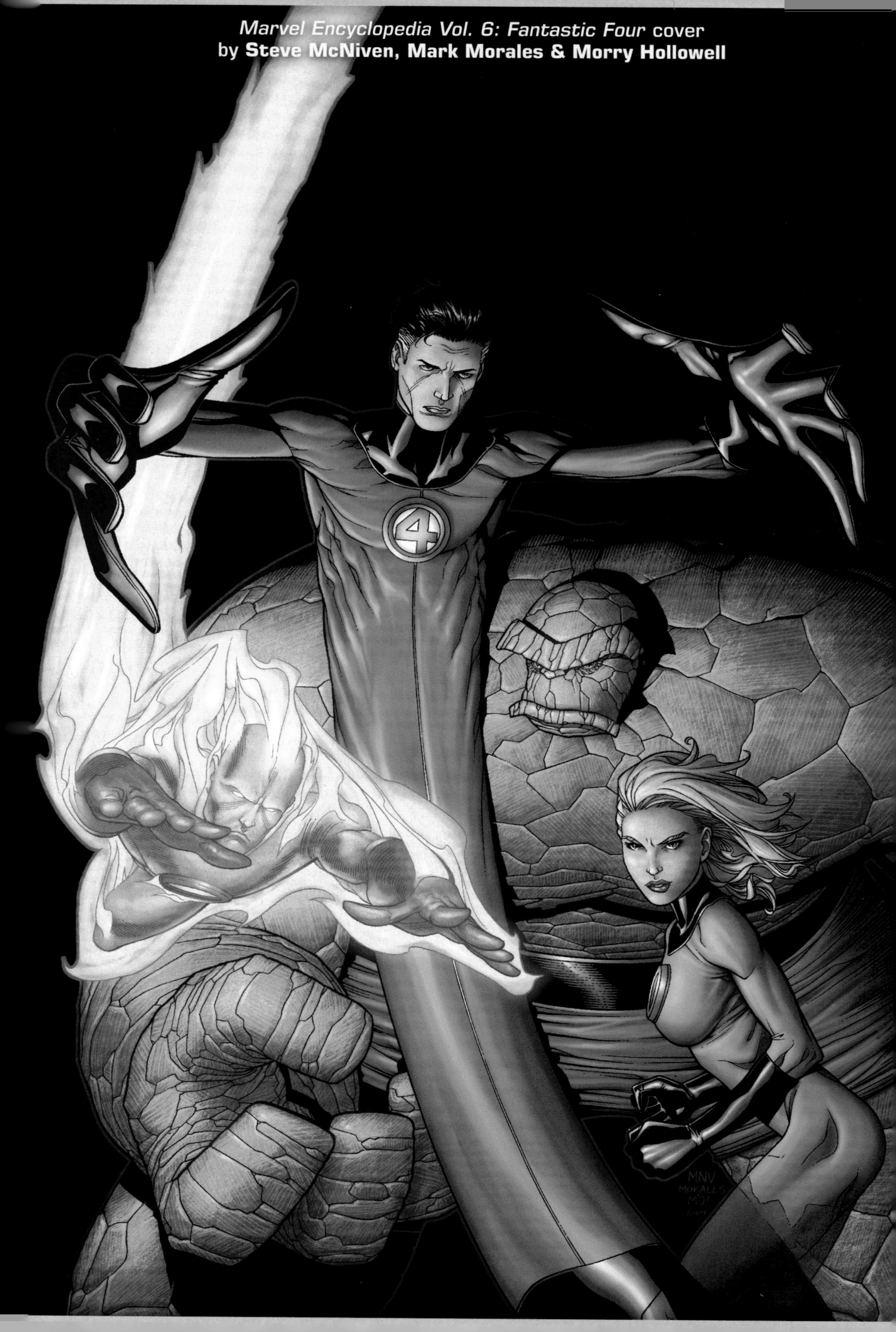

Marvel Encyclopedia Vol. 6: Fantastic Four cover
by **Steve McNiven, Mark Morales & Morry Hollowell**

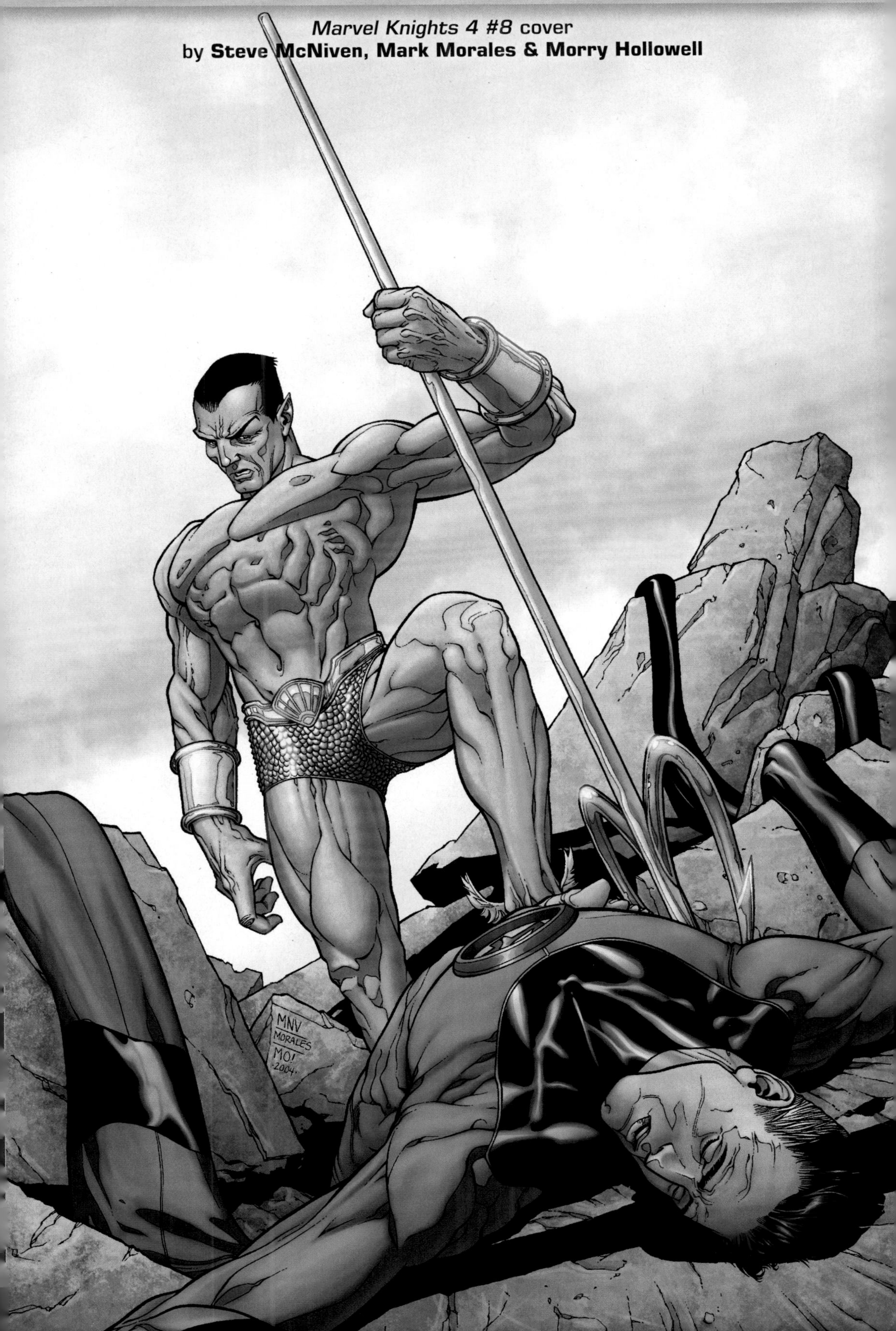
MNV
MORALES
MO!
2004

Marvel Knights 4 #8 cover
by **Steve McNiven, Mark Morales & Morry Hollowell**

Marvel Knights 4 #9 cover
by **Steve McNiven, Mark Morales & Morry Hollowell**

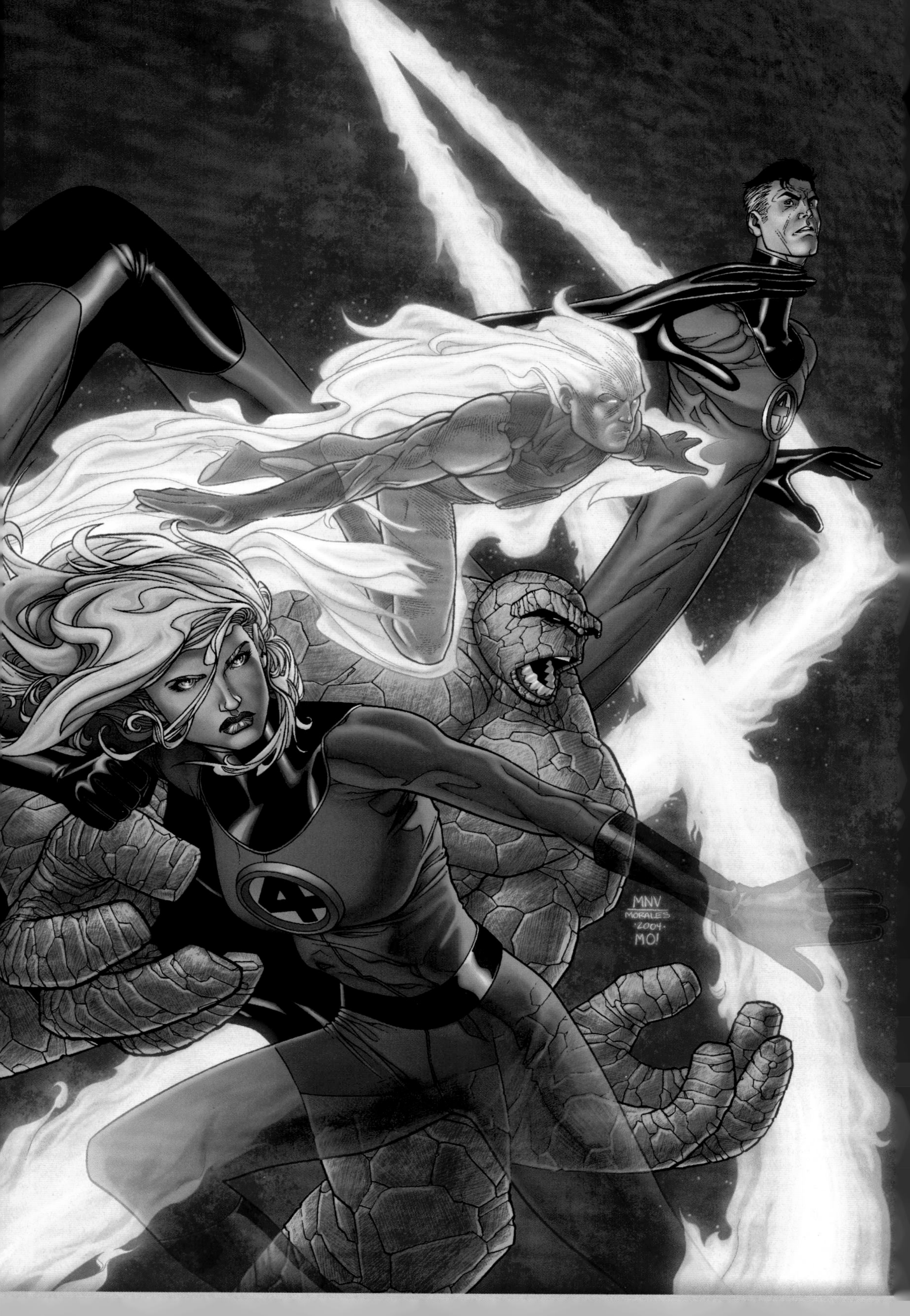
MNV
MORALES
·2004·
MO!

Marvel Knights 4 #10 cover
by **Steve McNiven, Mark Morales & Morry Hollowell**

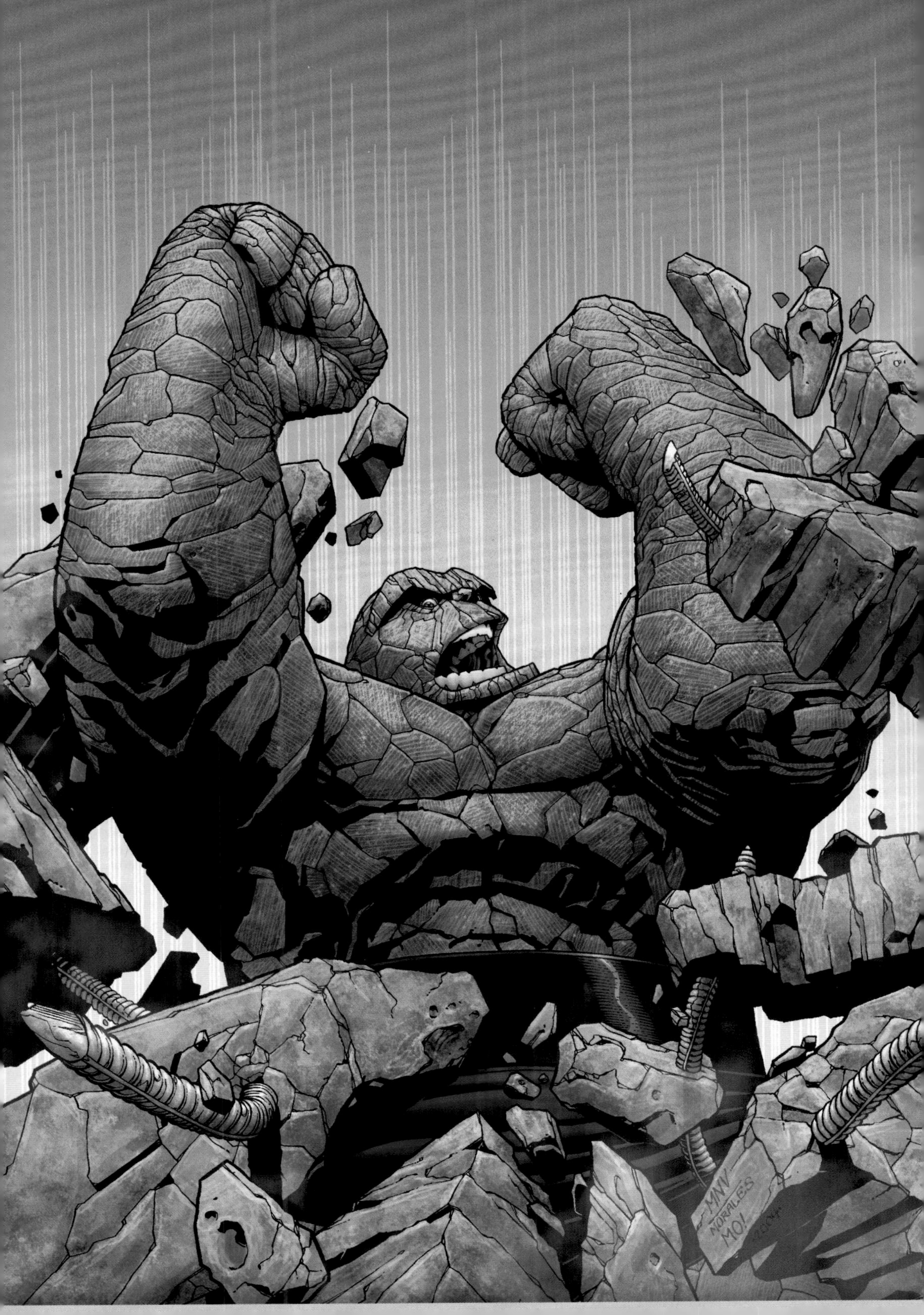
MNV
MORALES
MO!

Marvel Knights 4 #11 cover
by **Steve McNiven, Mark Morales & Morry Hollowell**

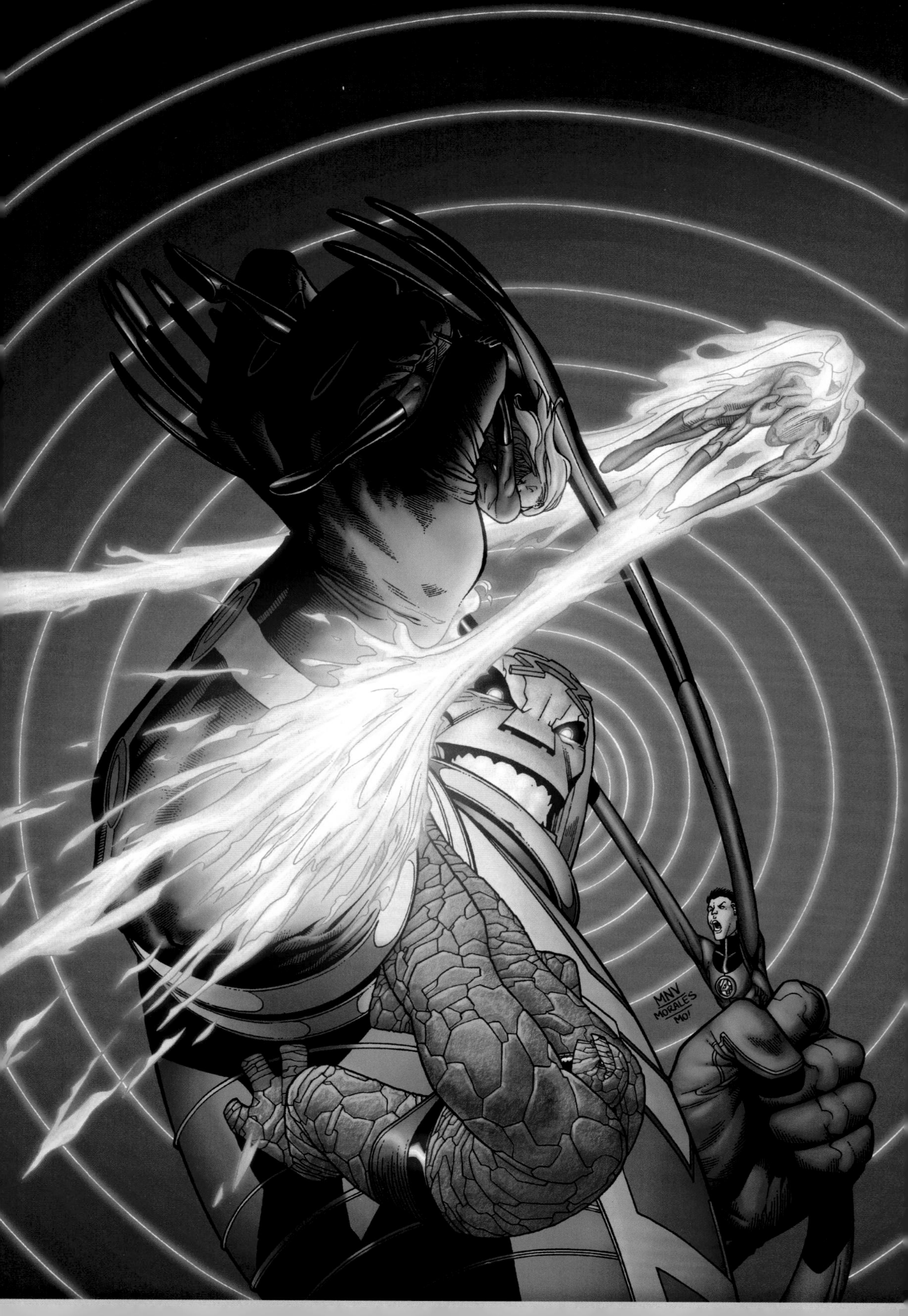
MNV
MORALES
MO!

Marvel Knights 4 #12 cover
by **Steve McNiven, Mark Morales & Morry Hollowell**

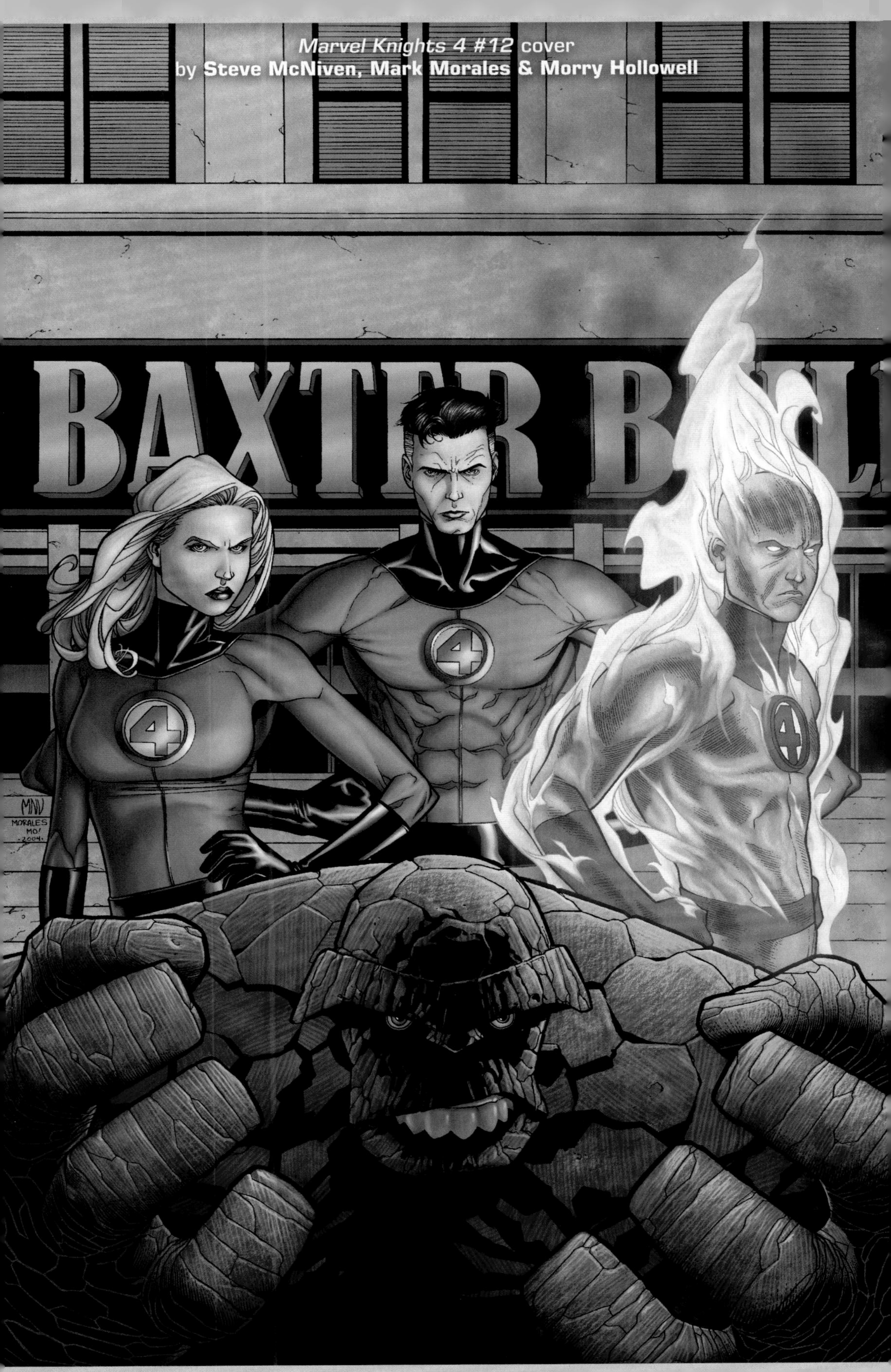
BAXTER BUIL
MNV
MORALES
MO!
2004.

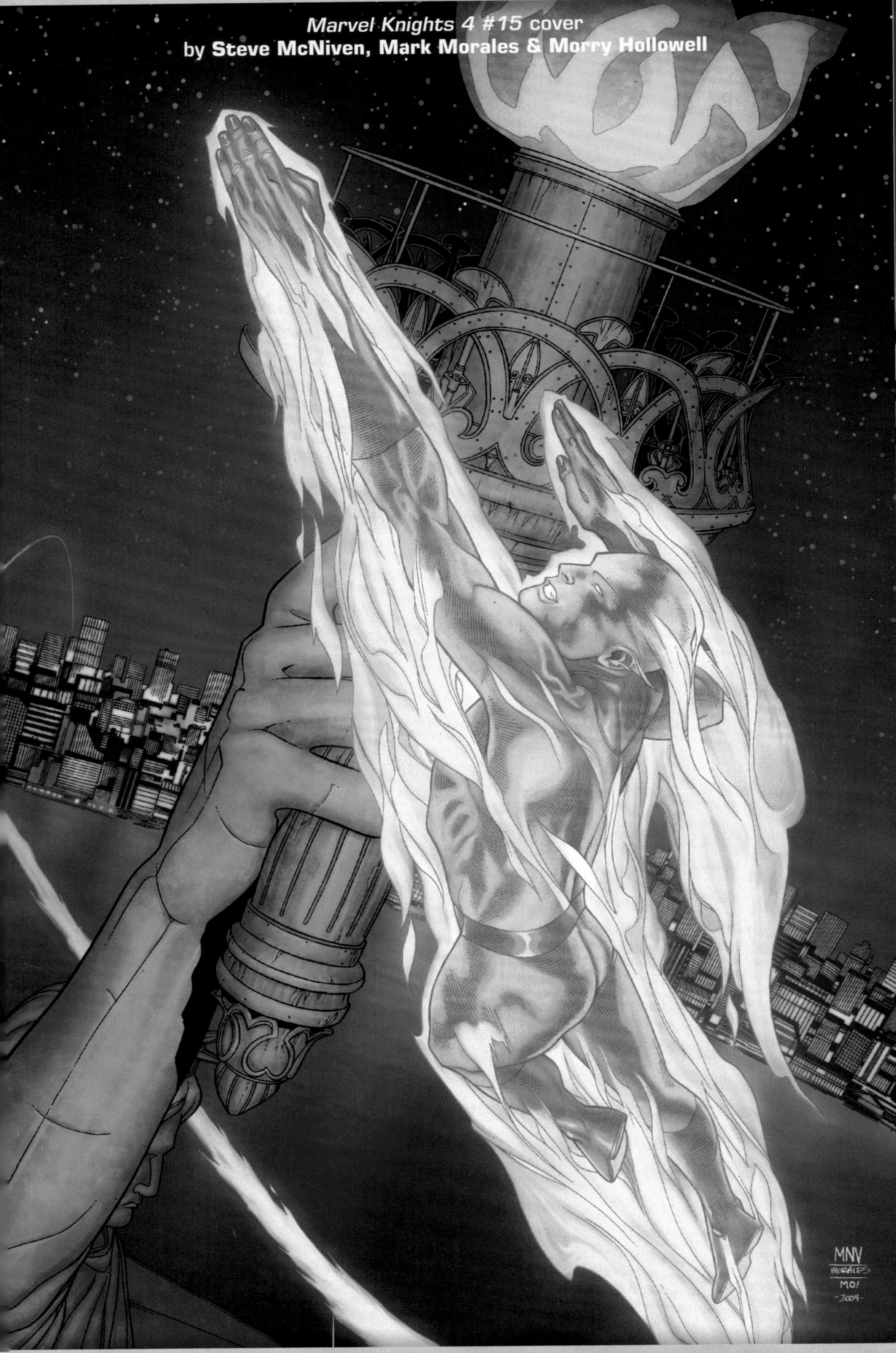
MNV
MORALES
MO!
-2004-

Marvel Knights 4 #15 cover
by **Steve McNiven, Mark Morales & Morry Hollowell**

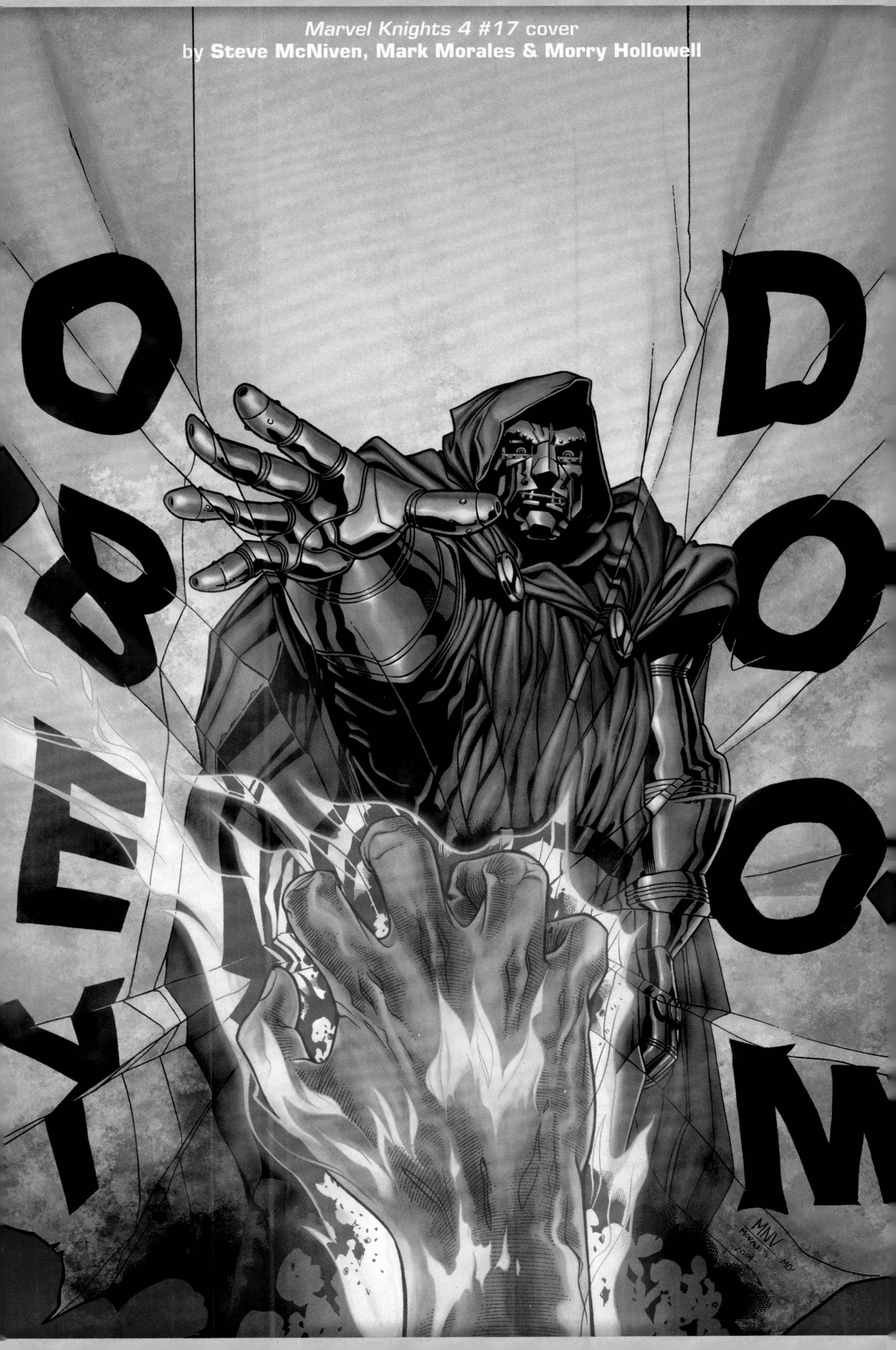
OBEY
DOOM

Marvel Knights 4 #17 cover
by **Steve McNiven, Mark Morales & Morry Hollowell**

Marvel Knights 4 #19 cover
by **Steve McNiven & Morry Hollowell**

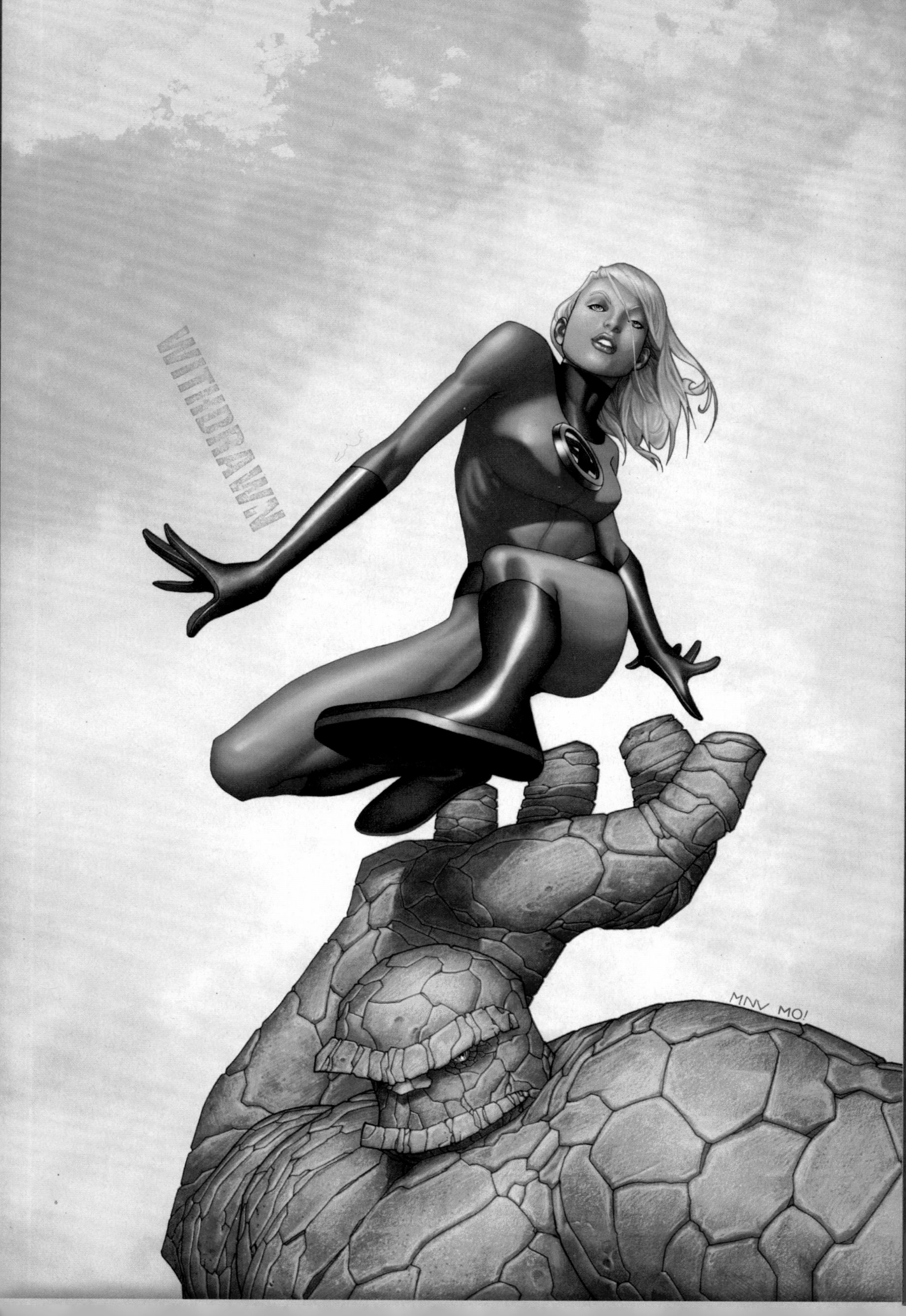
MNV MO!